Breaks in the Chain

Breaks in the Chain

What Immigrant Workers Can
Teach America about Democracy

Paul Apostolidis

 University of Minnesota Press | Minneapolis | London

Published by the University of Minnesota Press
111 Third Avenue South, Suite 290
Minneapolis, MN 55401-2520
http://www.upress.umn.edu

Library of Congress Cataloging-in-Publication Data

Apostolidis, Paul, 1965–
  Breaks in the chain : what immigrant workers can teach America about democracy / Paul Apostolidis.
      p. cm.
  Includes bibliographical references and index.
  ISBN 978-0-8166-6981-3 (hardcover : alk. paper)
  ISBN 978-0-8166-6982-0 (pbk. : alk. paper)
    1. United States—Emigration and immigration—Political aspects. 2. Foreign workers—United States—Attitudes. 3. Foreign workers—Political activity—United States. I. Title.
  JV6477.A66 2010
  323.3′29120973—dc22
                                                          2010013983

Printed in the United States of America on acid-free paper

The University of Minnesota is an equal-opportunity educator and employer.

17 16 15 14 13 12 11 10   10 9 8 7 6 5 4 3 2 1

This book is dedicated to the workers and organizers of Teamsters Local 556 and their families.

La lucha sigue

Contents

Acknowledgments

From its inception, this book has depended on the labors of many people. My thanks first go to the activists and organizers of Teamsters Local 556 for sharing with me their stories, their time, their hospitality, their friendship, and their political solidarity. I am especially grateful to Maria Martinez for making the agenda of interviews possible, for providing our vital first round of contacts, and for her inspiring model of leadership; to Tony Perlstein for planting the seed and for countless conversations over the picnic table or in the kitchen that were of inestimable value; and to Lorene Scheer and Melquíades Pereyra for trusting in this project and for their examples of creative commitment to justice.

This book benefited greatly from generous and astutely critical readings by Lisa Disch and Romand Coles, and I cannot thank them enough. Thanks are also due many others who read and offered comments on portions of the manuscript: Shampa Biswas, Aaron Bobrow-Strain, Katherine Gordy, Timothy Kaufman-Osborn, Kristy King, Bruce Magnusson, Gaurav Majumdar, Jeanne Morefield, Ella Myers, Paul Passavant, Jason Pribilsky, Nicole Simek, Matthew Voorhees, and Zahi Zalloua. Conference panels and colloquia where I presented versions of this work also helped me immeasurably, and I thank the following individuals for their engagement with the project in those contexts: Mark Anderson, Cristina Beltrán, Wendy Brown, Susan Buck-Morss, Samuel Chambers, Barbara Cruikshank, Jodi Dean, Steven Gerenscer, Judith Grant, Lisa Knauer, Jill Locke, Robyn Marasco, Timothy Pachirat, Anna Marie Smith, Holloway Sparks, Antonio Vásquez-Arroyo, Juliet Williams, Katie Young, and Karen Zivi. I am grateful to James Buckwalter-Arias for our many discussions about this project.

Many thanks to my editor, Pieter Martin, whose enthusiasm for and perceptive understanding of this project made working with him a true privilege and delight.

Paola Vizcaíno Suárez contributed mightily to this endeavor as my research assistant. I am grateful for her many efforts, above all for scheduling and conducting the interviews with me with dependability, compassion, and a remarkable ability to put our informants at ease; for transcribing multiple interviews with acute attention to detail; and for our invigorating conversations on rides back from Pasco where we shared and debated our interpretations of the stories we had just heard. My thanks also go to Sofia Mariona for transcribing a number of the interviews, to Luis Herrera for his participant-observation of Local 556 meetings, and to all the students who participated in our precedent-setting Fall 2002 community-based research project in partnership with Local 556.

Grants from Whitman College through the Perry and Abshire programs supported the participation of these research assistants. Thanks are due the politics department of Whitman College for its support of this research, and I am grateful for the support I received through the Judge and Mrs. Timothy A. Paul Chair of Political Science at Whitman College.

I thank Inés Arenas-Embarcadero for her diligent and thorough work reviewing my translations of the interviews.

This project benefited from pivotal conversations with these remarkable intellectuals and leaders: Steve Hecker, David Levin, Traven Leyshon, David Mark, Ramón Ramírez, David Rosenfeld, and Noah Seixas.

Finally, I thank Jeannie, Anna, and Niko for their tremendous love and support and for their companionship with me in the cause.

Acronyms

AMI	American Meat Institute
BCBP	Bureau of Customs and Border Protection
BLI	Bureau of Labor and Industries (Washington State)
BMI	Binational Migration Institute (University of Arizona)
CTD	cumulative trauma disorder
DHS	Department of Homeland Security
EOI	export-oriented industrialization
HRW	Human Rights Watch
IBP	Iowa Beef Processors Inc. (founded as Iowa Beef Packers; later IBP Inc.)
IBT	International Brotherhood of Teamsters
ICE	Immigration and Customs Enforcement
INS	Immigration and Naturalization Service
IRC	Interhemispheric Resource Center
IRCA	Immigration Reform and Control Act
ISI	import substitution industrialization
IWFR	Immigrant Workers Freedom Ride
MLP	Mujeres Luchadoras Progresistas (Progressive Women Activists)
MSD	musculoskeletal disorder
NAFTA	North American Free Trade Agreement
NIOSH	National Institute of Occupational Safety and Health
NLRA	National Labor Relations Act
NLRB	National Labor Relations Board
OLA	Organización de Lastimados Ayudando (Organization of Injured Workers Helping Others)
OSHA	Occupational Safety and Health Administration
PCUN	Piñeros y Campesinos Unidos del Noroeste (United Northwest Tree Planters and Farm Workers)

PERI   Political Economy Research Institute (University of
        Massachusetts)
PPD   personal protective device
PRI   Partido Revolucionario Institucional (Institutional
        Revolutionary Party of Mexico)
SEIU   Service Employees International Union
TDU   Teamsters for a Democratic Union
UFCW   United Food and Commercial Workers
UFW   United Farm Workers
USDA   U.S. Department of Agriculture
WVIP   Willamette Valley Immigration Project

Introduction:
Immigration, Power, and Politics in
America Today

IN THE FALL OF 2003, the United States Congress and
the Bush administration were getting serious about immigration control. Earlier that year, the Department of Homeland Security (DHS),
founded in the wake of the September 11, 2001, attacks, had assumed
full responsibility for border security. Flush with new funds from DHS's
rapidly increasing budgets, officials from the Bureau of Customs and
Border Protection (BCBP) were testifying on Capitol Hill to build
support for a vast expansion of military capacities and a major extension of fencing along the U.S.–Mexico border. A BCBP official justi-
fied these new steps to curb illegal immigration by invoking the newly
inaugurated war on terror, saying: "The priority mission of BCBP is to
prevent terrorists and terrorist weapons from entering the United
States. This extraordinarily important priority mission means improving security at our physical borders" (Garcia 2003). The Interhemispheric Resource Center (IRC), a progressive organization concerned
with immigrants' rights, saw such extravagant bombast as typifying the
agency's persistent blurring of the lines between terrorism and immigration. "Ranking migrants on the terrorist threat list has become
standard practice for BCBP," decried the IRC (Garcia 2003).

In an era when public authorities and private citizens' groups routinely voice suspicions that immigrants are the agents of death and
destruction in America, there is not much incentive for people to listen to what immigrants have to say about why they are here and what
their lives are like. There are also obvious reasons for those who have
migrated here from other countries to stay quiet about these things.
And so the debate about immigration control and reform proceeded
then, as it does today, largely through native-born Americans' statements *about* immigrants and proposals for what to do *to* and (less often)
for immigrants. Immigrants, in other words, were then and remain
the objects for discussion and analysis, the targets of apprehension

strategies, the dangerously inscrutable entities whose likely responses to carrot-or-stick incentives were the subject of predictive calculation and ceaseless debate. How many more miles in Arizona should the wall be lengthened to keep them out? How many more "detention facilities," as the prisons for undocumented immigrants are euphemistically known, are needed to keep them in but under lock and key? How steeply should they be fined if "we" grudgingly give them a chance to legalize? Should they be required to learn English as a condition of staying? When agents discover that they are in the country without legal documents, should they be saddled with civil violations or arrested and held on criminal charges? These are the questions that have held center stage as immigration issues have risen to recently unparalleled prominence in U.S. public discourse, as the 2008 presidential primary campaigns illustrated. They are noteworthy for the inert, passive position they assign to the people whose futures the pundits and policy-makers ruminate over and presume to govern.

This book responds to such silencing of immigrants in U.S. popular culture and policy debates by reintroducing their voices as workers, political activists, and narrators of power. It calls attention to what immigrants say about their experiences through a process of *political citation and engagement* that resists the rituals that keep things in order when immigrants do get the chance to appear and speak in U.S. public culture. Even in these moments, immigrants tend to be presented in ways that reinforce the claims of elite debates to superior rationality and legitimacy. Think of the last time you saw a story about illegal immigration via the U.S.–Mexico border on a television news program. If the news segment included an interview with an immigrant, you probably heard that person make remarks that invited you to attach a personal face and story to an otherwise abstract policy problem. Probably, it was something like "I just want to work and support my family" or "I don't know when I'll see my children again." Then the interlude for empathy predictably gave way to the pronouncements of experts who, from their detached, "objective," and therefore presumably trustworthy positions, cited the statistics and general arguments to which the merely "subjective" and particularistic points of view were supposed to defer.

But what if instead of hearing in an immigrant's life story the voice of "authentic" personal experience, so different from the ostensibly universal, rational languages of policy debate and public discussion, we were to approach that story as an articulation of more generally shared experiences, immigrant and nonimmigrant alike? What if we saw it as a way of putting a distinctive face not just on a single person but also on *social power?* What untapped political energies would this kind of encounter with immigrant narratives unleash? How might doing this bring into view the ways that immigrants are not just the passive objects of power but also, through their narrated actions of cross-border travel, productive work, and political organizing, people who help give power its characteristic contours in the United States and the western hemisphere today?

Something else was going on in the fall of 2003, in cities and small communities distant from the meeting rooms in Washington, D.C., where administration and congressional officials were mulling over proposals for deterring, interdicting, and incarcerating undocumented immigrants. A coalition of labor unions, religious organizations, and community groups had put together a bold strategy to arouse public concern about the unfair treatment of immigrant workers by employers and the state alike. Seeking to recharge the passions for social and racial justice that had infused the black civil rights movement of the 1950s and 1960s, organizers coordinated an Immigrant Workers Freedom Ride (IWFR). Busloads of immigrants and their allies departed from ten different cities across the country and ultimately converged at rallies and lobbying events in Washington, D.C., and New York City. Along the way, they held events to spark grassroots support for the participants' demands: providing legal status to immigrant workers; "clearing the path to citizenship and full political participation" by immigrants; reviving labor regulations to guarantee "the right to fair treatment on the job"; reforming immigration policies to "reunite families"; and ensuring strict enforcement of immigrants' civil liberties and civil rights (Immigrant Workers Freedom Ride 2003).

The IWFR organizers' main tactic was to publicize the personal narratives of the people on the buses. They sought to use these stories not only to elicit sympathy on a personal level for these individuals but also to teach "civics lessons" to all about the meaning of democracy, rights, class power, and racial justice. With the aid of this well-refined public relations strategy, the IWFR made a big splash in the national and regional media. I helped organize events in eastern Washington shortly after the Seattle and Portland riders got on their way; one event was a free community breakfast for riders and supporters at a Catholic church in the small city of Walla Walla. At the breakfast, and at a rally on the previous day coordinated by a politically engaged union made up mostly of Mexican immigrant food-processing workers, Teamsters Local 556 (about which much more is discussed in the pages ahead), individual riders took the microphone and told story after story of working themselves to exhaustion for poverty wages, long painful sep-arations from family members, and their undimmed hopes for some-thing better. Then a couple of the Seattle riders pulled out their gui-tars and led the crowds in singing a rousing ballad they had written on the bus: "Peregrinos de la libertad, por los campos y las calles van, vamos rumbo a la capital, defendiendo nuestra dignidad" (Freedom riders, going through the fields and streets, we're bound for the capi-tal, defending our dignity).

Five years later, however, with the failure of immigration reform in Congress and the fizzling of the massive immigrants' rights demonstra-tions that broke out in the spring of 2006, few members of the broader public remembered the bus rides or the travelers' tales. In the summer of 2008, I was interviewing some immigrant day laborers at a Seattle workers' center, and it turned out, coincidentally, that one of my in-formants had been a troubadour on that IWFR bus. Our conversation about his current work life halted as he groped for the lyrics, then softly sang the tune again. For both of us, there was something both heartening and forlorn about the moment—forlorn because the sto-ries this man and others had journeyed so far to spread, about immi-grants' struggles and demands for justice, had slipped out of the pub-lic airwaves, and pretty quickly, too. The presumptuous ambition that "illegal" immigrants had something important to teach Americans about democracy, hard work, and rights was apparently too much for the mainstream media and public to stomach.

This book begins from the premise that the repeated evacuation of politically challenging immigrant voices from public discourse must be resisted. Ordinary Americans have a great deal, indeed, to learn from immigrant workers about how to build a more robustly democratic society and how to combat the capitalist and state forces that relent-lessly thwart attempts to realize or even articulate radical democratic ideals. Soliciting the stories that immigrant workers tell about power lives and those of others, and recognizing and responding to the politically consequential dynamics of those narratives, thus becomes crucial to the democratic renewal of a society immersing itself ever-more perilously in the muck of imperialist war, obscene class inequalities, and an everyday social existence drenched all the more in fear the more incessantly we are told to idolize the fetish of "security."

The chapters ahead reveal a series of personal life stories that are at once typical and extraordinary. Their narrators are Mexican immigrant meatpackers who waged an exceptional campaign to democratize their union and their workplace in this country's most hazardous industry, after they, like millions of others in recent times, battled to survive in neoliberal Mexico, crossed the border clandestinely, and navigated the treacherous world of the undocumented. In 1999, at a cattle-slaughtering and beef-processing facility in eastern Washington State, these workers were among the roughly twelve hundred who pulled off the largest wildcat (illegal) strike among U.S. meatpackers in at least the last twenty-five years.[1] Instead of submitting mutely to the authority of Iowa Beef Processors Inc. (IBP), as the company expected of its supposedly docile immigrant employees, the workers stormed out of the gates, some with hooks and knives in hand, demanding "respect and dignity." Subsequently, the activists took over their local union, Teamsters Local 556, and transformed its internal structure: they changed the union's bylaws to shift power to the grassroots, held regular meetings in Spanish, worked hard to get disillusioned and injured workers to participate, and multiplied the number of officers elected by the rank and file. They agitated nationally for rank-and-file democracy within the International Brotherhood of Teamsters (IBT). They built coalitions with community, regional, and transnational supporters. They also launched two major lawsuits to address egregious health and safety hazards, which they won in the U.S. Supreme Court.

In 2001, Tyson Foods purchased IBP, thus becoming the world's largest producer of fresh beef, pork, *and* chicken commodities. Shortly thereafter, the company commenced an all-out push to bust the union. Although it eventually succumbed to the combined pressures of the corporation, the IBT (which sought to squelch Local 556's nettlesome agitation for Teamster democracy), and the Bush administration's National Labor Relations Board (NLRB), this movement of immigrant workers remarkably managed to sustain itself for about a decade. More particularly, the activists whose stories fill the pages of this book created a practical vision of how immigrant workers could help ignite democratic renewal in neoimperialist times. This vision offers important lessons to other immigrant workers and their allies. And the growth of that vision, amid the stench of the slaughterhouse and the sizzling heat of the eastern Washington State desert, is an experience that continues to inspire people in this region. (In February 2009, one of the activists showed up at a meeting I was attending in the town of Pasco, where the workers' movement had been based, that was held by a grassroots legislative advocacy organization for Latinos. When I remarked how glad I was to see him and that it was good to see he was involved with this recently formed group, he responded with a wry smile: "La lucha sigue" [The struggle continues]).

Health and safety issues were at the heart of the unrest at Tyson/IBP, and behind these problems, in turn, loomed one central factor: the shockingly high pace of the "chain," or the mechanical apparatus that moved meat between workstations at speeds that had dramatically driven up company profits—and job-related injuries. This book argues that to understand how these immigrant workers were able to disrupt the class and racial domination condensed in the slaughterhouse chain, and even to bring that chain to a grinding halt on that one portentous day in 1999, it is crucial to examine the links connecting their stories of work on the line and mobilization through the union to the ways they narrated their past experiences as people born in Mexico and illegal migrants across the border. At the same time, the *breaks* in the chain of narrated experience reveal much about the workers' contentions and complicities alike with these complex power relations. As I show in the pages ahead, the activists' life stories at once trace the contours of the formations of state and corporate power in which they were entangled and disclose their active participation as engineers, in part, of these very power structures, while precisely thereby gaining—and sometimes expressing in both story form and political practice—the capacity to transform the latter. As such, these narratives attest to the ability of immigrant workers more generally to reshape the terms of political life in America today.

Securing America against Immigrants: Coercion or Consent?

In view of the burgeoning array of institutional forces aimed at apprehending, monitoring, punishing, and banishing immigrants, some readers might view with skepticism my claim that immigrants not only *should* exercise more sway in U.S. political life but also *can* do so and, even now, already *are* shaping politics and society in this country in ways that mainstream public discourses ignore. These forces bear close scrutiny, as does the common perspective that they simply compel immigrants to occupy the social roles mapped out for them and show every sign of doing so for the foreseeable future. Antonio Gramsci's conception of "hegemony" stands at the center of this book's basic approach to power; and it is important right here at the outset to consider seriously whether it is appropriate to apply this concept to understand the situation regarding immigrants in the United States today. Gramsci uses the notion of hegemony to describe a generally shared understanding of how a society should organize itself and envision its progress toward common goals. This "national-popular collective will," as he calls it, both infuses key institutions and animates the emotional loyalties and everyday actions of ordinary people, but it does not do so automatically. Striving to cultivate such a collective spirit amid a large popular constituency is the essential task of any political force struggling for social leadership. This struggle, for Gramsci, advances through methods geared both toward applying coercion and eliciting consent. Drawing hard and fast distinctions between these two entities, however, is futile in practice; they are more like two poles marking the outer extremities of a force field where power always takes on characteristics of both types. Precisely because of this, to participate in a hegemonic formation is always, from a Gramscian perspective, *to help bring it into being, to perpetuate it, and to retain the capacity to transform it with others.* Hegemony, then, is a conception of power that differs notably from the more easily intuited notion of domination, which implies a one-dimensional relation in which a superior force rules over weaker entities, compelling them to do things against their will through means that the dominant exclusively possess.

Yet the fates of immigrants in America today often do seem determined by frank domination. The upward-spiraling militarization of the U.S.–Mexico border since the Reagan years, for instance, has driven increasingly more migrant traffic into the deadly zones of the southwest desert. In early 2007, the Binational Migration Institute (BMI) at the University of Arizona released new research showing "unambiguously" that U.S. Border Patrol policies during the 1990s comprised "the primary structural cause of death for thousands of unauthorized men, women, and children from Mexico, Central America, and South America"—between two thousand and three thousand people from 1995 through 2006. When the Border Patrol boosted its efforts to shut down illegal crossings in urban areas like Tijuana–San Diego, BMI argued, it created a lethal "funnel effect" that redirected migrants toward "Arizona's remote and notoriously inhospitable deserts and mountains" (Rubio-Goldsmith et al. 2007). As violence has escalated between U.S. border squads and smugglers, in turn, further hazards to the lives of undocumented crossers have arisen (Carl 2008). Then there are the perils that await those unfortunate individuals who end up in the burgeoning system of immigrant jails. Exactly how great the danger is can be hard to judge, because, as the *New York Times* reported in 2007, "no government body is charged with accounting for deaths in immigration detention, a patchwork of county jails, privately run prisons and federal facilities where more than 27,500 people who are not American citizens are held on any given day while the government decides whether to deport them."[2] However, data voluntarily released by the Immigration and Customs Enforcement (ICE) agency in mid-2007 showed that 62 immigrants had died while in "administrative custody" since 2004, "many more deaths than the 20 previously counted" (Bernstein 2007). From the mid-1990s through 2007, moreover, multiple reports have found that those languishing in these prisons receive inadequate health care, especially if they are children or pregnant women or have mental health needs; that they are subjected to excessive force by immigration officials during both arrest and detention; that they suffer physical and sexual abuse; and that they frequently are deprived of basic legal rights like access to counsel and knowing the charges against them.[3]

Unprecedented mass arrests at an Iowa meatpacking plant in May 2008, along with the constant stream of anti-immigrant vitriol from Lou Dobbs and other nativist commentators, have further blurred the lines between undocumented immigrants and criminals. Dobbs exaggerates the number of federal penitentiary inmates who are immigrants, the *New York Times* found, making it appear that immigrants pose a heightened threat of violence and lawlessness when in fact the crime rate among immigrants is lower than that for the native-born population (Leonhardt 2007). But the rebranding of unauthorized immigrants as criminal law-breakers went beyond rhetoric when federal immigration agents raided the Agriprocessors plant in Postville, Iowa, and arrested 389 men and women on *felony* charges (which became convictions for 297 of these people) (Hsu 2008). Subsequently, reported labor historian Peter Rachleff, "a legal procedure was cobbled together which placed the men in prison and the women under house arrest in electronic ankle bracelets for five months" (Rachleff 2008). The workers were mostly rural Guatemalans who were slated for deportation following these detention periods and who, investigations later revealed, had suffered a range of labor abuses for which Agriprocessors was eventually fined nearly $10 million by the state of Iowa (Associated Press 2008; Preston 2008a, 2008b, 2008c). Such criminalization of immigrants seemed shocking when the raid at Postville occurred, but by 2008, it was a matter of explicit federal policy under ICE's Operation Streamline initiative, which Homeland Security officials credited with driving down illegal immigration as measured by apprehensions in key areas of the border (Hsu 2008). In a further ironic twist to the growing lack of distinction between the way U.S. authorities treat immigrants and criminals, Colorado's Department of Corrections in early 2007 began contracting out low-security state prisoners to do the farm jobs for which growers could no longer find enough immigrant employees in the wake of federal crackdowns (Riccardi 2007).

The hardening of coercive forces directed at immigrants has occurred not only through such deployments of federal military, police, and carceral resources but also through state and local-level policy proposals as well as private citizens' activism. It operates, in other words, on all rungs of the American federalist structure of government and increasingly emanates from the state and civil society alike. A brief survey of anti-immigrant politics in various regions tells the story: the unanimous 2006 city council ordinance in a Dallas suburb that newly required landlords to verify the citizenship or immigration status of their tenants or face misdemeanor charges and a $500 fine; proposals in Texas and California state houses to deny birthright citizenship to undocumented immigrants' children; the bill proposed by Republican state legislators in Virginia in 2007 that would have made it unlawful for public colleges and universities to admit undocumented immigrants, even those who had attended public high schools and/or had arrived in the United States as young children; the 2006 bill passed by the Virginia House of Delegates barring state funding to charitable organizations that assisted the undocumented; a local measure in Prince William County, Virginia, creating a special police force to flush out undocumented immigrants and requiring local police to confirm the immigration status of all individuals arrested; and the 2007 and 2008 Washington State initiative campaigns to prohibit undocumented immigrants from obtaining drivers' licenses and public benefits.[4]

Far right citizens' groups, meanwhile, have been emboldened to issue calls to arms in what one member of the Yakima, Washington, nativist organization Grassroots On Fire termed "a life and death struggle to preserve the sovereignty of the United States of America" (Janovich 2007). Nourished by "anti-immigrant feelings," CNN reported in early 2007, the Ku Klux Klan had seen its membership jump by 63 percent during the several preceding years (CNN 2007). The leaders of Latino civic organizations, including the League of Latin American Citizens and the Mexican American Legal Defense and Education Fund, reported an upsurge in "anonymous threats of violence and death" in late 2008 (Fears 2008). And the day before the *Washington Post* publicized these menacing acts, a violent mob stabbed to death an Ecuadorian immigrant named Marcello Lucero in Patchogue, New York, after the attackers reportedly egged one another on by saying "Let's go find some Mexicans" (*New York Times* 2008).

One speaks of power in the mode of hegemony at the risk of sounding naïve, then, amid this increasingly desolate climate of repression and death where immigrants are concerned. At the same time, to see the current situation as the apotheosis of a police state, pure and simple, would be to overlook certain reemergent fissures in the class coalition that has propelled the intensification of anti-immigrant surveillance and repression. Major immigration reform nearly passed Congress in 2007 but ultimately joined a raft of alternative proposals in the legislative dustbin. These efforts have been fruitless largely because lawmakers, especially Republicans, have had to navigate the familiar minefield of tensions among vital constituencies: anti-immigrant populists versus business leaders needing cheap labor. Such conflicts have bedeviled would-be immigration reformers for decades, going back to the battles over the Rodino immigration reform proposals in the 1970s, the Bracero program in the 1950s, and even the debates over immigration policy in the 1920s (García y Griego 1996; Gutiérrez 1996; Reisler 1996). Caught in this bind after the compromise package was defeated, the Bush administration vacillated between, on the one hand, ramping up immigrant raids and jacking up immigration-processing fees to keep more immigrants out and, on the other hand, backing off when businesses (and unions) opposed more vigorous federal prosecution of employers who did not comply with new employee immigration status verification rules (McCombs 2007; Preston 2007a, 2007b). Administration officials also launched a "behind-the-scenes initiative" to ease farmworker visa restrictions in the midst of the 2007 farm labor shortage (Gaouette 2007). Also in 2007, the Texas Association of Business threw its ponderous and decisive weight behind efforts to push back a tidal wave of anti-immigrant state legislative action (Downes 2007).

Yet these thrusts and feints among state and business elites would seem to free up very little political terrain for immigrants to insert themselves into the struggle for hegemony. This is especially so given the long-term decline of the American labor movement, the erratic nature of its successes in attempting revitalization through the incorporation of immigrant workers, and the vanishing of judicial support for union rights.[5] When growers and food-processing companies blanch at Homeland Security initiatives to start following through on employer sanctions that have been on the books since 1986, and when they petition the administration and Congress to widen the valves modulating migrant workers' entry, they invariably do so on condition that these workers' labor rights remain largely unenforced. Provisions for the importation of temporary or "guest" workers, a stock characteristic of most recent immigration reform proposals, including those with the strongest bipartisan support, would likely repeat the history of the postwar Bracero program in exposing new migrants to anti-union pressures, paltry compensation, wage payment irregularities, and the discretionary determination of their working conditions by employers with little hope of legal redress (García y Griego 1996). With the Supreme Court's landmark 2002 decision in *Hoffman Plastic Compounds v. NLRB*, moreover, undocumented workers lost basic rights enshrined in U.S. law since the New Deal as well as in international labor law: they now can legally be fired for participating in union organizing.

Immigration and the U.S. National Imaginary

If something like hegemony operates in the current political environment, then it would appear more appropriate to look for it in the
media's and the state's cultivation among the mass public of a certain
sense of national identity built *around* conceptions and images of
immigrants and authorizing new government and corporate actions
toward immigrants but not significantly produced *by* immigrants, especially the most recent arrivals. In fact, some provocative and insightful academic work has recently illuminated such dynamics of nativist
American nationalism, explicating its main substantive features and
analyzing the ideological work it performs. Ali Behdad, for instance,
argues from a historical perspective that a conflicted mix of "hostility
and hospitality" toward immigrants has long nourished America's self-
conception as a nation: "Immigrants as others have a productive function in national culture, for they simultaneously shore up the mythical
view of the United States as the cradle of democracy and the view of
it as a threatened asylum. . . . Whether a corrupter of our principled
prosperity or the enabler of our democratic capitalism, the immigrant
is at once a critical supplement and a threatening other through whom
American identity is imagined and reproduced" (2005, 17). This fer-
mentation of the national culture by the yeast of ambivalence toward
immigrants, Behdad shows, not only has stamped American nationalism with a distinctly Janus-faced character but also has legitimated the
expansion of regulative capacities in the American state apparatus
(19–22).

Bonnie Honig (2001) draws attention to another crucial permuta-
tion of American narratives about immigrants: the tendency to see
those considered "foreigners" not only as vehicles for self-affirming expressions of American magnanimity, and also not just as assisting the
forward momentum of American progress, but additionally as perpetually *refounding* American political culture from the outside. Depicted
as a "supercitizen," the immigrant becomes "an agent of national reenchantment that might rescue the regime from corruption and return
it to its first principles" (74, 77). When the destructive side of capitalist growth manifests itself in abandoned rust-belt factories, vacated
neighborhoods, and fragmented families, Honig contends, along
comes the mythical immigrant to restore our faith in the bootstraps
mentality, the possibility of community renewal, and the endurance of

family ties. Nevertheless, for Honig just as for Behdad, such xenophilia always tows xenophobia along with it: our "national reenchantment" also depends on banding together against the (supposedly) greedy immigrants who steal American jobs, whose community "enclaves" prevent assimilation and nurture subversion, and whose antediluvian clan loyalties violate modern individualist sensibilities (73–106).

Why, then, do we see this rehearsal of historical mythmaking now, with a special stress on the negative poles of the immigrant figures that Behdad and Honig discern within the American popular imagination? One reason is that in the midst of the societal depredations wrought by neoliberalism, such as urban infrastructure decay, declining real incomes, soaring health costs, chaotic financial markets, cultural pressures mount for the fantasies of refounding that Honig analyzes— supercitizens to the rescue. At the same time, conservatives can avoid having to confront these problems head-on with new investments in social programs by restoking antipathy toward the welfare state through anti-immigrant nativism. Thus, for instance, the campaign for California's Proposition 187 in the early 1990s sought to retrench a wide range of health and social services by appealing to fears about overbreeding and overuse of hospital facilities by undocumented women from Mexico (Chavez 2008; Roberts 1996). Likewise, proponents of the federal welfare overhaul of 1996 built support for this epochal cancellation of New Deal–era rights, in part, by targeting immigrant women as abusers of the system. Anti-immigrant think tanks continue to churn out studies that blame immigrants, documented and undocumented alike, for rising poverty rates, health care costs, and tax burdens for public services (Preston 2007c). Jane Juffer (2006) suggests, furthermore, that the classically Reaganite antistatist discourse of private, civic voluntarism gets a new boost from the border vigilantism of the Minutemen. These soldiers understand their mustering of arms against undocumented crossers as an expression of freedom and citizenship. They not only multiply the hazards of the border for migrants but also fortify the ideological foundations of the new civil privatism. Overall, then, the neoliberal demand to reduce state social spending dovetails nicely with the right's efforts to restabilize its mass base among religious conservatives and militant rightists by counterposing the beleaguered, overtaxed and underserved "American family" to its dysfunctional immigrant foil.

At the same time, Behdad's analysis helps us see how inciting hatred and suspicion toward immigrants helps the American state gain the abilities it requires under neoliberalism to do *more*, not just less. David Harvey argues that a contradiction arises for the neoliberal state from its need to undertake authoritarian interventions to generate investment and accumulation opportunities, since this flies in the face of neoliberal celebrations of individual freedom. At the same time, the cultural cohesiveness and sense of common fate that might support such authoritarian measures erode as market competitiveness becomes the criterion for ever-more aspects of society and we witness "the commodification of everything" (2007, 79–80, 165). In this regard, too, it becomes functionally effective to scapegoat immigrants for the cognitive dissonances and sacrifices that neoliberalism imposes on ordinary citizens as a matter of daily life. The sense of order, stability, and purpose that nativist nationalism evokes helps to massage these contradictions of the neoliberal state. Neoliberal reformers need to promote a sense that the *public* interest is at stake in audacious efforts to enhance *private* business competitiveness in global and domestic markets, as the massive bailout of Wall Street in 2008 graphically illustrated (Harvey 2007, 85). Stirring up suspicions about "foreigners" provides one very convenient way to retool and refuel the patriotic feelings that facilitate such deployments of state resources.[6]

The United States' military interventionism abroad since 2003, along with its construction of a new penal apparatus for prisoners captured in the war on terror, also belong squarely within the roster of growing state activities that neonativism helps support. Antipathy toward immigrants helps consolidate a generalized, amorphous fear of the foreign that fuels at least grudging acquiescence to the massive, expensive, and unpopular military operations in Iraq and Afghanistan. Harvey characterizes such military imperialism as the main path the United States has adopted for reinforcing its global dominance as daunting economic competition from China and the European Union has mounted (2005, 74–86). In line with Behdad's theory of the link between immigration discourses and the expansion of state powers, moving anxieties about immigrants to the forefront of public debates also facilitates the unprecedented extension of state surveillance capacities in the purportedly besieged "homeland." It quells outrage, in addition, over the atrocities and human rights violations occurring in the liminally legal spaces of U.S. detention facilities at Guantánamo Bay, Abu Ghraib, and elsewhere. Of course, anti-immigrant discourses also help rationalize the buildup of military hardware and software in the U.S.–Mexico border region. This happens, as Peter Andreas (1998, 2000) argues, when the Border Patrol routinely invokes immigrant apprehension figures to justify further budgetary expansions for border security technologies and personnel by demonstrating that the stream of illegal immigration continues to flow. It also occurs in less obvious ways, such as through the peculiar twist in media reports about environmental degradation in the border region that blames this blight on the supposedly unhygienic bodies of Mexicans, thereby justifying policies to "contain" this human threat of "contamination" via stricter immigration controls (Hill 2006).

Immigrant Workers as Hegemony's Agents

All this amounts to a bleak and compelling case for a conception of neoliberal, nativist nationalism as a power formation forged through the consent of the American population and the bald coercion of immigrants, thus excluding the latter from the distinctive dynamics of hegemony. Yet as real and effective as the media discourses, legislative processes, administrative maneuvers, and military deployments just discussed are, they do not tell the whole story about the situation of immigrants in the United States today. More specifically, this narrative frame far too quickly dismisses the relevance of immigrants' actions when it tries to explain how this network of institutional forces has managed to reproduce and expand itself so persistently and where it might be vulnerable to change. For one thing, viewing immigrants as just pawns in the contest over hegemony between real players betrays a certain intellectual laziness in not taking the time to look more closely at these subjects of power. Such a perspective also colludes (inadvertently, one hopes) with historically rooted, racist assumptions about the supposed inability of subaltern groups, including Latin American immigrants, to govern themselves rationally or to exercise independent agency in the world around them (Reisler 1996; Rogin 1987). In addition, settling for this insightful but foreshortened critique of power in anti-immigrant America means ignoring or trivializing the multiple signs of immigrant mobilization, from the IWFR to the mass demonstrations of spring 2006, from recent outbursts of labor militancy vis-à-vis employers to the surge of Latino naturalization, registration, and voting that helped launch the Obama presidency.

One finds a very different approach to the question of immigrants' roles in social power formations in the writings of critical ethnographers who have examined the creation of subjectivities among such people with more microscopic care. In particular, such scholars take a crucial step that is very much in line with my own analysis: they pay attention to the means by which immigrants' conceptions of their own circumstances and corresponding practical actions *constitute fields of power.* Thus, for example, while Honig asks how the public's fantasies about immigrants achieving the "American dream" help prop up faltering national norms, Sarah J. Mahler (1995) shows how Salvadoran and South American immigrants in the New York suburbs live a self-generated semblance of that deceptive fantasy by inventing new patterns of relations to others and novel strategies for acquiring income. She does so by talking with them and "reading" their words and actions rather than exclusively attending to discourses that emanate from institutional realms like the law and the media. Mahler's analysis goes well beyond illuminating the personal idiosyncrasies of individuals' struggles to absorb and adjust to their inevitable disillusionment, this side of the border, though this is certainly part of what makes her contribution valuable. It also shows how immigrants organize new forms of social action for themselves, albeit not always in ways that make them content and often through processes that echo neoliberal refrains, like adopting a more "commodified" style of kin relationships and pursuing economic success through their ethnic niche. If neoliberalism continues its intrepid forward march in America today, one senses after reading Mahler, it is not only because of what the pundits say about immigrants but also by virtue of how immigrants themselves structure their spaces of work, habitation, and community. And if there is any hope of contesting the neoliberal juggernaut politically, surely the deep skepticism about upward class mobility that Mahler reveals among these folks whom "we" are so eager to applaud as supercitizens ought to be seen as a contradiction that presents a popular resource for such activism.[7]

Nicholas De Genova's masterful critique of a politicospatial configuration he calls "Mexican Chicago" likewise seeks to characterize how immigrants help create the systemic forms of power within which they live. Immigrants coax this new political-geographic terrain into being, for instance, when they tell stories that routinely connect events in the United States to events in Mexico, such that "the innumerable 'local' concerns of rural Mexico have a palpable presence in the everyday lives of migrant workers in Chicago" (De Genova 2005, 130). Such habits of narration, he argues, foster patterns of racial identification that interrupt "the racial order of the U.S." and "the presumably hermetically sealed containments of nation-state spaces" by constructing a transnational racial "conjunctural space" (96). This spatial entity generated partly by immigrants thereby also provides a specific "standpoint" for criticizing "U.S. nationalism and its imperial conceits," since within that location it becomes possible to think beyond the taken-for-granted racial differentiation between the United States and Latin America (96). On a more specific level, as De Genova shows, this political geography furnishes a perspective for understanding both the catalysts and limits to immigrant factory workers' attempts to organize against their employers, in particular the saturation of these struggles with discourses about Mexicans' racial distinctions from African Americans and white Americans alike.

Taking a dose of inspiration from authors like these, this book teases out the lines of affiliation and interference between immigrants' narrations of their experiences and broader arrangements of power characterizing the U.S. racial order and transnational capitalism in the Americas. Like Mahler, De Genova, and other critical ethnographers, I call attention to immigrants' active role in generating these conditions of power and sometimes destabilizing them as well. But my approach differs from theirs by staging an explicit, critical exchange between immigrants' life stories and extant theories of major power formations. In this respect, the reader will find an inquiry here that shares a kindred spirit with the writings of political and social theorists like Behdad, Harvey, and Honig. Certainly, a strategic benefit follows from knowing how amorphous entities like neoliberalism take concrete and directly consequential forms in specific locations like Mexican Chicago, or the commodified kinship networks of Salvadoran immigrants, or the "spaces of exception" in East and Southeast Asia that, for Aihwa Ong (2006), have been a signal, politicospatial component of neoliberalism's advance. In an important sense, the analysis in this book *is* a

study of power and politics in just such a delimited context, focusing as it does on an exceptional movement of Mexican immigrant
meatpackers who took on the world's leading producer of fresh beef,
chicken, and pork in the arid land of the inland northwest. Yet this is
also a study that, without apology, takes crafting general, critical social
theory seriously as an indispensable intellectual and political endeavor.
Hegemony for the leading formations of class and racial power may
indeed be won ultimately through culturally and spatially specific initiatives, but the lines of affiliation connecting these disparate projects
are no less potent for that fact, and they require a generous measure
of critical analysis.

Seeking theoretical guideposts to orient this ambitious approach,
I have found that Gramsci's theory offers crucial aid. It was precisely
the relations between tectonic movements of power on the broad social
level and micropolitical dynamics within communities that absorbed
Gramsci's attention. On the one hand, for Gramsci, writing a historically attuned and politically engaged critique of power meant paying
attention to the "effective needs" of distinct social and cultural groups
as well as to the quirky and syncretistic expressions of "common sense"
that developed through people's daily practices. It thus meant avoiding the temptation to superimpose abstractly preconceived notions
of a group's "real" interests upon it and to evaluate its politics mecha-
nistically in terms of adherence to or divergence from that template
of imputed, "true" concerns. Instead, analysts and activists needed to
observe how particular political forces succeeded or failed in making
the "effective reality" of that group resonate with its agenda through
"conscious, planned struggle" (Gramsci 1971, 166–68, 172). On the
other hand, this refocusing of Marxist theory on the local, the practical, and the ideological kept hold of the aspiration to conceptualize
the structural facets of power in society as a whole. The point, in
Gramsci's view, was to generate a dialectic such that intellectuals' political engagements with the common sense of ordinary people supplied
creative ferment for more abstract theory regarding the more generally pervasive dynamics of power, while theory contributed tangibly to
leadership development and political education in local spheres.

Critical theory today stands in need of the invigoration that would
come from recuperating a Gramscian regard for this method of theoretical inquiry. This is particularly so given certain dry patches amid

the stream of scholarship based on Foucault's theory that has irrigated the terrain of critical theory in recent years. As the immigrant workers' stories that I consider in this book graphically illustrate, Foucault's conceptual innovations in theorizing discipline and biopolitics continue to be highly fruitful for understanding the workings of power in late modern times. These ideas have made it possible to see how class, gender, racial, and sexual domination become interdependent and effective within historically specific orders of power that are distinguished by their operating methods, their entwining of ideology and institutional practices in discourse, and their productions of—rather than instrumental use by—political subjects. In a sense, Foucault radicalized the Gramscian insight that ordinary people become the agents of their own subjection through their everyday practices and conceptions of social truth. What has fallen by the wayside in most Foucauldian theory, however, is the concomitant (Gramscian) interest in exploring how, precisely for this reason, ordinary people could radically change society. Also, Foucault's figuration of the subject as constituted through discourse, or as an effect of power, has sometimes made it seem that little critical insight could be gained from trying to pass theory through the crucible of ordinary people's common sense, since it would appear more logical to study directly the institutions propagating discourse (e.g., the law, media routines, the writings of leading political intellectuals).[8] But approaching discourse analysis in this latter way both insulates theory from the critical leaven of common sense and perpetuates the ideological claim of culturally privileged intellectuals to speak unproblematically for and about subaltern groups.[9]

The reconstructive work I aim to do here with Foucault's theory involves not only critically reinvigorating these ideas through political contact with immigrant workers' common sense but also elaborating their connection to organized projects for contesting hegemony. Foucault, especially in his later writings, at least began the project of reconceptualizing how the individuals subjected by power could rework power's operations in novel and contrary ways through micrological techniques. Being receptive to this possibility precipitates a crucial starting place for the analysis ahead. Individuals *can* develop practices by which they deploy "counterpower," whether in the sense of the self's ethical regimens that Foucault envisioned or in terms of Gramsci's notion of performing "a criticism of 'common sense.'" I venture, however, into territory usually left unexplored by Foucauldian theorists by examining how disparate, individual acts of freedom-within-power congeal into *shared practices for narrating the social world* and thus help to constitute it and to expose it to *collective challenges.*[10] While biopolitical and disciplinary power formations often make immigrant workers the executors of their own subjection to racial and class domination, these individuals also create narrative currents that can swell into the tide of popular movements contesting these regimes at their very core. Considering how the micrological and the macrological may combine in large-scale transformations, and not just theorizations, of power is thus also a paramount interest of this book and an ambition I seek to recuperate from Gramsci for politically engaged intellectuals today.

Transnationalism, Labor, and the Long View of Immigrant Worker Activism

In this study, I am particularly interested in examining how immigrants' working lives provide a setting where critical conceptions of power and agency incubate. Americans today live in a time when the political right wing indiscriminately lobs the accusation of fomenting "class warfare" at even the most mild and paternalistic attempts to raise the issue of poverty.[11] Meanwhile, feminist, critical-race, and queer studies have come to comprise the vanguard for political theory in the academy, while theorists devote less energy to labor studies. In this political and intellectual climate, it is all too easy to dismiss the stirrings of immigrant workers' activism as hopeless and of little value either as an empirical reference point or as a regenerative solvent for critical theory. Yet scholars in Chicano/a and Latino/a studies have shown repeatedly that what happens in the working-class domains where Latin American immigrants and their descendents labor, live, and struggle is anything but marginal to the constitution and contestation of social power and hardly a matter of blind oppression. Consider, for example, the provocative studies by labor historians Vicki L. Ruiz (1987, 1998), Patricia Zavella (1987), and Miriam Ching Yoon Louie (2001) of how Chicana cannery workers in the 1930s and 1940s and Latina garment workers in the 1980s and 1990s, many of them immigrants, created new organizational forms, political networks, and public spaces for themselves as they fought against employer abuses and sexist treatment by male Chicano movement leaders. Or look to those accounts of how immigrant workers' union movements continue to arise all over the country and block, at least temporarily, the long and disheartening turn-back of New Deal labor rights by politically mobilized businesses and the ever-more pro-property courts (Delgado 1993; D. Fink 1998; L. Fink 2003; Milkman 2000). This book aims, in part, to fortify the attempts by such contemporary labor analysts to demonstrate that more fully appreciating immigrants' active contributions to hegemony, and to resistance against it, leads us directly into the slaughterhouses, frozen food plants, and orchards where immigrants work and, sometimes, rebel.

At the same time, the hegemonic dynamics of labor processes and union struggles, which Michael Burawoy (1990) has provocatively termed the "politics of production," need to be situated within that distinct set of encounters with and evasions of the border security and internal police apparatus that are crucial to the lives of immigrant workers. Better still, political analysts need to consider immigrants' stories of what their lives were like in their countries of origin before they ever set out for the north and the broader context such stories furnish for accounts of subsequent migration, labor, and political involvement. This book thus seeks to contribute, albeit in a modest way, to the fertile and growing field of research in transnational studies. Recent work in anthropology and other fields has challenged the traditional understanding of immigration as a linear process that leads a person (or a family, over the course of a couple generations) from identification with one national culture, through a period of reacculturation, toward eventual wholesale affiliation with the normative culture in the destination country. Migrants' cultural identities, financial networks, political activities, labor practices, and habits of geographic location and movement, scholars have shown, increasingly depart from this teleological schema (De Genova 2005; Glick Schiller 2001; Rouse 1992; Stephen 2007). Failing to appreciate this not only means missing what is actually going on in immigrants' lives but also leads one to overlook certain resources among immigrant communities for resisting the troubling implications of the myths about "Americanization" and the "melting pot": the reinscriptions of class, racial, and gender power that hierarchical ideologies regarding exclusive nationalities tend to enact.

The individuals whose stories make up the bulk of this book do not offer especially vivid illustrations of the emergent forms of transnationalism these other authors have discerned. Almost all of them gained legal U.S. residency through the landmark legislation passed by Congress and signed by Ronald Reagan in 1986, the Immigration Reform and Control Act (IRCA), which opened up new employment opportunities and unprecedented prospects of making their lives in the United States on a long-term basis. Abandoning a more economically tenuous existence as farmworkers and becoming meatpackers meant progressively loosening their ties to Mexico and investing more decisively in a future for themselves and their children in the United States. They traveled back and forth from Mexico less frequently, sent fewer cash remittances to friends and relatives (and often stopped sending them entirely), and became more interested in acquiring U.S. citizenship and learning English. And when they mobilized their rank-and-file workers' movement, they usually eschewed direct symbolism and rhetoric evoking the Mexican heritage that they shared with the vast majority of their fellow employees. Unlike the spring 2006 marches, their demonstrations and protests rarely featured Mexican flags waving or images held aloft of *la Virgen de Guadalupe*.[12]

Yet this book scarcely confirms conventional assumptions about "coming to America" as a willful rejection of one national framework and a happy assimilation to a new and better one. It is not that the immigrant workers we interviewed never spoke in terms redolent with the mythic accoutrements of the American dream. Sometimes they did, such as when Alejandro Méndez fiercely asserted his capacity for economic self-reliance or when Esperanza Soto insisted how she had gladly "sacrificed" herself for the sake of her children's upward mobility. However, by taking the long view of these individuals' stories of life in Mexico, travels across the border, travails in the "zone of illegality" within the United States before legalization, labor in the slaughterhouse, and activism in the union, one notices that what might initially look like a rehearsal of nostrums to the American dream actually departs from the script in manifold ways. According to U.S. fantasies about immigrant supercitizens, paragons of economic self-sufficiency are not supposed to become the ringleaders in illegal factory strikes. Similarly, while immigrants' self-sacrificial behavior is normally assumed to involve hard work and delayed gratification, even real material hardship, the protracted physical and psychological abuse that our informants endured at the beef plant is something altogether different.

I make no claim to advance very far the analysis of transnational modes of everyday life upon which a good deal of recent critical ethnography has focused—for instance, Lynn Stephen's (2007) studies of indigenous Oaxacans' "transborder lives," which span these migrants' communities in the northwestern United States and southern Mexico alike, or De Genova's mapping of Mexican Chicago. Such inquiries depend on a rigorous commitment to sustained participant observation and other methods of ethnography, whereas here the focus is on immigrant workers' retrospective life stories and their intersections with critical theory. Nevertheless, this book shows that even in the narratives of people who seem the most "settled," as immigrants who are staying rather than migrants who are coming and going, conceptions of self and world are transnational insofar as they incorporate within them certain views of power refracted through remembrances of their country of origin and their passages across the boundaries separating nation from nation. Nor do the stories of those who really have moved, for good, to the United States ever fully or even mostly confirm the ideological expectations of the assimilationist ideal. Rather, the *specificities* of these stories produce trajectories of hegemonic and counterhegemonic possibilities, alternately reinforcing or challenging the formations of state, capitalist, and racial power that collective wishes regarding "immigrant America" insulate from critique. I designate the people we interviewed as "immigrants" rather than "migrants" to emphasize that my analysis does not concern individuals who are more actively, materially, and self-consciously involved in everyday instantiations of transnational culture and thus indirectly to acknowledge the value of those different sorts of inquiries. Yet the transnational and counternationalist implications of these immigrant workers' narrative practices are plain to see in the pages ahead. This is a direct benefit of the expansive approach to these individuals' stories that we adopted by urging them to tell us their recollections of life in Mexico, of crossing the border without documents, and of living illegally in the United States, before going on to describe their working lives at the slaughterhouse and their exertions in the union.

Narrative Stages

Before considering our interviewees' stories about these various stages of their lives, which I do in chapters 2 through 5, I offer some initial reflections on what exactly a "narrative" is, how it might be construed as political, and how the interview situation set the stage for the emergence of political narratives. Behind these issues lies the larger question of how to understand the puzzling triangle of relations that links narrative, political action, and critical social theory. To begin to find answers, chapter 1, "Political Narratives, Common Sense, and Theories of Hegemony," returns to Gramsci's thought regarding the connection between hegemony and what he calls the common sense of people in subordinate social groups. For Gramsci, such people are not simply the passive dupes of dominant forces but rather actively produce their own subjection through their practical habits of understanding how power works and how they are situated vis-à-vis power—their common sense. Thus, any meaningful effort to *analyze* and *change* the structure of society has to address itself directly to these conceptions of self and world and ferment their mutation from within. I envision the process of telling and receiving narratives as a communication of common sense that catalyzes such moments of political engagement for the authors of social critique and ordinary working people alike. These encounters hold the potential both to make accounts of hegemony more critically reflective and to make strategies for opposing the powerful more effective.

Political theorist Lisa Disch provides the specific conception of narrative that brings this politicized understanding of the theory–narrative nexus into focus, as I discuss in chapter 1. Disch takes the vital step of reconceiving narratives as intellectual and political projects in their own right, interventions that order the world in certain ways rather than just the raw material for more "scientific" social criticism to use or ignore at will. Gramsci, too, urges politically involved theorists to appreciate this *generative* character of ordinary people's narratives when he writes that the "criticism of common sense" must "bas[e] itself initially, however, on common sense in order to demonstrate that 'everyone' is a philosopher and that it is not a question of introducing from scratch a scientific form of thought into everyone's individual life, but of renovating and making 'critical' an already existing activity"

(1971, 330–31). The critical sharpening of theory and the political intensification of narrative, then, do not come from the former objectifying and interpreting the latter in a one-way process, like a lab technician examining a slide under a microscope. Instead, they develop out of efforts to arrange strategic, reciprocally transformative alliances between these two intellectual–political undertakings, which do not differ fundamentally or in kind from each other.

Our interviews with the immigrant workers at Tyson/IBP staged precisely such political acts of narration. Thus, the analysis in chapter 1 effectively issues an invitation to these worker-narrators to join in the critical task of proposing and reformulating core elements in the conceptual armature of political theory, especially those of biopolitics and discipline stemming from Foucault as well as the notion of neoliberalism. At the same time, the first chapter reflects on how our diverse political commitments as community allies in the workers' cause added critical potential to this interchange between theoretical and life-historical narratives, ameliorating, though not eliminating, certain limitations in the reciprocity of this interaction. Readers who are eager to dive into the narrative material or who have little interest in these more theoretical questions can skip ahead to the second chapter. However, the matters treated in chapter 1 have every bit as much to do with practice as they do with theory in the sense that they address questions regarding the way interviews were conducted and how those interviews were situated within the context of concrete political struggles discussed in later chapters. (In addition, by explicating my core intention to engage theory's narratives with those that convey immigrant workers' common sense, this chapter explains why the portions of the book dealing with the slaughterhouse rely exclusively on workers' accounts and not on interviews with management, although the local plant managers' unwillingness to speak with me or to respond responsibly to my public statements about the findings also played a role in this regard.)[13]

Having spelled out my operative conception of the politics of narrative, I then take up my analysis of the material from the interviews. Chapter 2, "Hegemony in Hindsight: Immigrant Workers' Stories of Power in Mexico," begins this endeavor by considering our informants' stories of growing up in Mexico and deciding to travel to the United States. From the perspective I criticized earlier that preconceptualizes power as something exercised upon a passive immigrant mass, it would be easy to assume that the people who ended up picking apples in central Washington's orchards and later processing cattle at Tyson/ IBP were *driven out* of their homeland against their will as the forward march of neoliberalism in North America threw the Mexican economy into ever-deepening crisis. Yet what comes through most strongly in their accounts of these early years is that these individuals saw themselves as engaged in a genuine *struggle* to build satisfying and meaningful lives for themselves and their families, and not a hopeless struggle at that. Well acquainted with tough labor and some degree of impoverishment since early childhood, and accustomed to sacrificing their own educational progress when care for the family's welfare made that necessary (especially after a parent's death or departure), the immigrant workers we interviewed nonetheless laid stress on their personal fortitude and resiliency. They were the ones, they informed us, who estimated the economic costs and benefits of staying in Mexico or seeking opportunities north of the border, or who joined youthful pals in a daring and only half-serious adventure of crossing clandestinely, or who carefully mulled over their decisions about when it would be safe to bring their children across—or even, in one case, who took principled political stands that made leaving necessary to escape violent reprisals from greedy landowners.

My analysis makes plain the crucial variations in these accounts of the precipitants of immigration, more specifically the presence of three discernable patterns for claiming and asserting individuality through deliberations about leaving Mexico. Charting these various storylines, in turn, provokes a critical perspective on the concept of neoliberalism and the kinds of subjectivity that it requires and incites. Some recent theorists have modeled neoliberal subjectivity as a uniform type distinguished by the self's all-consuming, relentless effort to augment itself as a "portfolio" of personal assets, a pursuit that presupposes the enhancement of market-based value as the sole ethical criterion for all action. In place of this homogeneous subject form, the immigrant workers we interviewed displayed a plurality of neoliberal subjectivities that differed according to class and gender features. While one group of men laid the accent on the ways they had sought to actualize self-reliant masculinity through migration, responding pragmatically to worsening economic times in Mexico, another cohort among the men superimposed on this storyline an elegy about how they had seen their hopes for upward class mobility through higher education in Mexico dissolve with the onset of economic crisis. Meanwhile, women's accounts of the prehistory to emigration emphasized their realization of individual distinction, somewhat paradoxically, through decisions that were deeply conditioned by their husbands' actions, their own responsibilities to care for children and other family members, and their exposure to certain forms of mistreatment specific to women.

The upshot of this exploration, I argue in the second chapter, is the need to appreciate the *political contingencies* of immigrant workers' narratives about life and migration under nascent neoliberalism. These multiple and different ways of remembering Mexico, from a vantage point defined by intense political struggle through the union some or many years later, offered touchstones for their narrative constructions of other, later aspects of these workers' experiences. They helped generate the political variability of these other phases of the narratives—the tensions, for instance, between individualist and familial/mutualist visions of what belonging to the union meant as well as between an individualism oriented toward transforming future circumstances for oneself and an anxious, resentful egoism desirous of compensation for past harm from institutional authorities. By opening up such political contingencies, and particularly by imagining Mexico as a place where migrant workers could act with self-determining agency when faced with the hardships created by neoliberalism's advance, these narrative variations also contributed a low-level, germinally transnational quality to the workers' stories, because they established a narrative basis for further cultivating the workers' budding alliances with politically active groups outside the United States. At the same time, however, the consolidation of the three main narrative currents in a way that muted differences of culture and region within Mexico bespoke the common exposure of all these people to new, racially homogenizing forms of power directed at "Mexican immigrants" as a mass group and operating with particular intensity in the geographic, social, and political domains of the border region and the U.S. interior.

The next two chapters examine the workers' stories about their experiences of illegal immigration and labor in these realms. As chapter 3, "Stories of Fate and Agency in the Zone of Illegality," shows, two basic narrative tendencies structured our interviewees' accounts of navigating the zones of "illegality" while crossing the U.S.–Mexico border and then working within the United States prior to arranging their legal papers. On the one hand, these immigrant workers told us, to move and exist in this illegal domain was to experience a condition of utter helplessness and subjection to the whims of fate that made multiple indignities and mortal dangers loom before their eyes. It was to yearn for deliverance from some higher power—"God" or "luck," as they frequently put it—while lacking any practical ability to determine their fortunes for themselves. According to this aspect of the stories, power in this realm approached these people as an undifferentiated mass and exposed them collectively to terrifying risks of grave misfortune and even death. On the other hand, the people we interviewed also expressed, more subtly but still detectably, the desire to control their own destinies in the process of migrating north and living everyday life without legal documents. They conveyed a sense of satisfaction when they succeeded in doing so in small but significant ways. This alternative account of power relations allowed room for individuals to engage in struggle, whether it was to protest against abuses by human smugglers, to master the self's internal weaknesses, or to perform acts of self-concealment.

When these immigrant workers spoke about their experiences in the slaughterhouse, their stories expressed a similar ambivalence about how to conceptualize power and their own capacities in the face of power. These narratives of labor and injury in meatpacking, "the most dangerous job" in America, are the focus of chapter 4, "Labor, Injury, and Self-Preservation in the Slaughterhouse." Our interviews feature shocking accounts of abusive treatment from supervisors, understaffed workstations filled with untrained workers, superhigh chain speeds that made pain and injuries virtually inevitable for workers, and procedures for handling workers' health problems that seemed designed to humiliate workers and to intimidate them into either quitting or working despite injury. Even beyond the zone of illegality (since these individuals had all begun working at IBP after gaining legal status), our informants saw themselves as subjected to overwhelming forces that kept them in a constant state of crisis with little ability to forge their own destinies. Now and then, however, the workers found ways to make their labor a little less damaging to themselves. They described the work they learned to do not only on cattle carcasses but also on their own bodies and minds: applying skin creams to ward off infections, adopting habits of movement on the shop floor to avoid being lacerated by coworkers' knives, medicating themselves to dull the pain and boost their stamina, struggling internally to conquer their resulting addictions, and retaliating against abusive supervisors. In this competing current of the narrative, the workers thus asserted the capacity to meet their desires for a humane working life for themselves rather than the need to have management or the state do this for them.

Chapters 3 and 4 argue that these narrations about immigrant workers' experiences in the illegal zone and in the slaughterhouse have something crucial to say to political theorists who are interested in critically refining the Foucauldian concepts of biopolitics and discipline, reinvigorating their capacity to offer insight into power's key rubrics today. Discipline, for Foucault, employs intensive procedures of surveillance, evaluation, and training to generate socially adapted individuals with useful, reliable skills and habits of thought. By contrast, biopolitics directs itself toward mass populations rather than individual bodies and minds. It mobilizes the methods of statistical analysis as well as broadly construed public and industrial policies to regulate aggregate risks of death and disease and chances of life and psychophysical flourishing for these populations, which it differentiates according to a racial logic. It has become common to see both these modes of power as reinforcing each other and steadily acquiring more potency as modernity advances (Agamben 1998; Connolly 2002; Foucault 2003). Yet our interviews tell a different story about power: they speak of immigrant individuals to whom disciplinary power *refrains* from addressing itself, even while a multifaceted biopolitical regime governs this immigrant population from a plurality of institutional sites and with growing—deadly—intensity. Eschewing explicitly racial language, a *biopolitics by implication* nonetheless operates through a variety of discourses that apply to immigrant workers. For instance, the public and bipartisan consensus about "securing our borders" skews life chances and health along racial lines by making higher exposure to physical and emotional hazards a condition of finding adequate work or keeping families together for the immigrant population. Likewise, by relegating undocumented workers to jobs in the informal economy and consigning even legal immigrants to "the jobs that Americans cannot or will not do"—usually highly unsafe jobs like farmwork and meatpacking—the labor market produces racially differentiating physical and emotional effects. Other implicitly biopolitical discourses of this sort have to do with the food consumption lifestyles promoted by the beef industry and public policy on occupational safety and health, as I discuss in chapters 3 and 4.[14]

My analysis of the interviews traces the productive and deconstructive effects of immigrant workers' narratives with respect to these formations of power, thereby looking to these narrators to join in the task of critically theorizing contemporary biopolitics. When our informants depicted power in the illegal zone as herding them into frightful or humiliating situations where their evasion of harm depended simply on the vagaries of chance, they were describing what it felt like and what it meant to be governed by this racial order. Similarly, in telling us how the labor process forced them to endanger their bodies, how supervisors commanded their job performance with imperious authority, and how the company responded to their injuries with cold indifference or outright hostility, the workers once again bespoke the enactment of biopolitics by nonexplicit means. Not only that: this narrative current helped to reinforce the biopolitical regime by fostering habits of common sense premised on the idea that there really was no alternative to suffering in silence under the effects of such power. This habituation to power deepened the dynamic of racial homogenization and differentiation of Mexicans' life chances on a continental scale that our informants' shared remembrances of the neoliberal turn in Mexico suggested had begun even before their entry into the operative fields of U.S.-based biopolitical regimes of labor regulation and immigration control, despite their many varied backgrounds of region, class, and culture.

Yet at the same time, the other major narrative strand put a different face on power and, in so doing, partly contested its hegemonic status. As they described the modest "arts of hiding" and passing as legal U.S. Americans that they had used in their years as undocumented crossers and workers, our interviewees were characterizing an array of protective microtechniques of the body and psyche they had created for themselves through their own informal networks. Their accounts of talking back to supervisors or warding off injuries at work through practices of bodily posture, movement, self-medication, and moral self-control functioned in much the same manner. Of course, these narrations of self-regulative competencies helped acclimate them to the operations of biopolitics in a way that went beyond despairing fatalism: they made it possible for immigrant workers to see such conditions as tolerable insofar as they promised at least minor outposts of agency for immigrants within the zone of illegality and on the factory floor. Nevertheless, as we shall see, these aspects of the narratives generated friction against the more dour political implications of the dominant theme regarding workers' utter helplessness in the face of blind fate, which prompted more certain submission in the face of biopolitics. They also furnished a genealogical precedent for a narrative about collective uprising and political transformation that many of the workers invoked when they spoke of the union struggle.

In chapter 5, "¡Nosotros Somos la Unión! Immigrant Worker Organizing and the Disciplines of the Law," my consideration of the Tyson/IBP workers' multistage stories of their experiences culminates with a look at how they described their ventures into political activism to transform their working conditions and to democratize their union, Teamsters Local 556. In the interviews, we asked these individuals to tell us about how the rank-and-file movement originated at IBP in the 1990s, how the movement gathered strength through a combination of legal and administrative challenges and direct action–style protest, how events transpired during the massive illegal strike and the rank-and-file takeover of the union that occurred in 1999–2000, and how they understood the meaning and capabilities of the union in the era following its reform. The stories of workers who devoted themselves over the long haul to the cause of reform, I show, differ decisively from those told by the faction that began working against union leaders after the strike as well as from our interviews with nonaligned, politically disengaged workers. For the reformers, incursions against both the company and the union's "old guard" that relied on pursuing legal rights claims and securing state intervention operated symbiotically with workers' exertions to build a self-directed movement and to assert their desires and capacities to reorganize key, structural features of the labor process and the union alike. Their antagonists, however, offered accounts of the mobilization that underscored the workers' deficits in knowledge, resources, and power and, accordingly, their desperate need to have elites in positions of authority take remedial action on their behalf.

While chapters 3 and 4 reveal the muted quality of formal disciplinary training in these workers' encounters with the U.S. immigration control apparatus and the order of work at the slaughterhouse, in chapter 5 we see how the workers' stories of union activism reflected the disciplinary results of their entanglement with the law. In other words, it was when these immigrant workers sought to reinvent their contestations of power as more formally organized, self-consciously collective endeavors that they became newly implicated in a mutually reinforcing relation between biopolitics and discipline. Their stories about the movement made it clear that in this context they were avidly engaged with an intensive regime of disciplinary power that addressed itself to, and constituted, their specific desires and capacities as individuals: the legal and administrative apparatus governing workers' individual and group rights by establishing procedures for collective bargaining, grievances, lawsuits, and union elections. The normalizing effects of this situation could be heard especially distinctly in the counterreformers' shared tendency to view the enforcement of their legal rights *for them* by officials with the state, the union, and the company as the quintessence of their struggle and to see themselves as vulnerable, aggrieved victims who needed protection from and retribution against the perpetrators. These stories thus displayed precisely those effects that Wendy Brown (1995) dubs the "politics of *ressentiment*" and associates with a narrow focus on liberal-legalist activism. Moving beyond Brown, I show how this resentful disposition among the reformers' antagonists depended on and remobilized certain genealogical antecedents in the narratives about life in Mexico, the zones of illegality, and the work realm at Tyson/IBP. In particular, the counterreform discourse drew on the narrative current that lamented the immigrant worker's deprivation of opportunities for upward mobility in Mexico as well as this person's later, helpless suffering in the face of blind fate on the border and the cruel despotism of the company.

Still other genealogically precedent moments in our informants' narratives, however, helped the reformers sustain their own more radical practices and conceptions of what the workers' struggle meant, even as they encountered the same disciplinary forces of the law to which their opponents had so thoroughly acceded. In particular, the reformers' stories about the workers' movement generated a "criticism of common sense," as Gramsci would put it (1971, 330), that yielded a distinctive concern with *political education* by drawing upon the other major narrative strand in the accounts of the illegal zone and slaughterhouse work. This was the storyline that called attention to immigrant workers' abilities to develop informal techniques for presenting or caring for their bodies, confronting abuse and repression, and controlling their own emotions. As we shall see, this narrative current partly irrigated the workers' intellectual, emotional, and practical investments in legalist strategies as additional means of self-protection. But at the same time, it also prevented the workers from pinning all their hopes on these tactics alone. Instead, the dedicated reformers sought to integrate the project of teaching themselves to understand and employ their legal rights within a more encompassing agenda for cultivating a sense of *collective* responsibility, mobilizing *en masse,* and striving to change the work environment at Tyson. Precisely this narrative of political education gave them critical distance from the logic of resentment. Insofar as it also infused the workers' organized struggle as a group, moreover, and held forth the prospects of an expanding political coalition, it aimed a markedly more potent challenge at the mechanisms of racial biopolitics than their micrological techniques of self-care resistance could do on their own.

This challenge, however, was ultimately fleeting and unsuccessful in terms of creating lasting change either at the Tyson plant or for immigrant workers more generally. The final chapter thus looks back at the movement and the narratives of power that informed it, in search of lessons regarding what exactly it meant and what it implies for future mobilizations of immigrant workers and their allies. After offering a brief synopsis of how the union was destroyed in 2004–5 through collusions among the company, the counterreform contingent of workers, and the reformers' political foes at higher levels within the Teamsters international union (aided by a timely ruling from the NLRB), I explore the issue of whether the Local's entanglements with legalist actions like lawsuits and contract negotiations did, after all, embroil it within the self-defeating dynamic that Brown and other theorists have associated with such strategies. But what appears suspiciously like this self-undermining process, I argue, turns out to be a much more complex phenomenon when we give full due to the narrative politics that animated the workers' exertions. Key currents within their narratives and organizational practices, as the preceding chapters show, gestured toward the radical transformation of entrenched structures of capitalist, racist, and patriarchal power through the coordinated action of immigrant workers and their allies. These forward-looking elements suggest powerful affinities between the mobilization that occurred at Tyson/IBP and other more robustly institutionalized initiatives among Mexican immigrant workers in the United States, such as farmworker and tree planter organizing efforts in Oregon and the activism of another Teamsters union, Local 890, in California. Above all, these other exemplars of immigrant (or migrant) worker insurgencies have concretized and routinized connections between the struggle for immigrant/migrant justice and labor activism. My analysis in this book, in turn, elucidates the politically vital terrains of narration where stories about immigration, labor, and power can come together to propel immigrant workers' political enterprises in the most visionary directions.

Unseating the current regime of biopolitical and disciplinary power on which the steady advance of neoliberalism depends, however, requires a popular force much greater than any that immigrant workers alone or even broader migrant communities can muster. To be sure, the core emphasis of this book rests on the dynamism and political generativity of immigrants with respect to power in the present world. This perspective of immigrants, and my corresponding analysis of the power relations that enfold them as *hegemonically produced,* help clarify the shortcomings of alternative ways of conceptualizing contemporary biopolitics that recently have been en vogue among political theorists. As I discuss in the final chapter, this is markedly so with respect to Giorgio Agamben's dystopic rendering of late modern biopolitics as an operative mode of sovereign power that makes society increasingly approximate the management of "bare life" in a concentration camp. In light of the account of immigrant workers' politics that I offer here, biopolitics as conceived of by Agamben turns out to be a far less appealing framework for interpreting the situation of immigrants today than it might at first seem, even with the escalating counts of death, injury, and imprisonment of immigrant workers that I discussed earlier. But once we have a more adequate understanding of how biopolitics works, how discipline sometimes (but not always) complements it, and how these power mechanisms fortify the historically distinctive neoliberal project, then it is also readily apparent that to transform this society requires a broad counterhegemonic popular force.

My concluding reflections probe more deeply the internal contradictions according to which biopolitical power *adversely* affects large groups of nonimmigrant, racially privileged people in the United States and the western hemisphere today, making their conditions of living begin to resemble those of immigrants in certain ways even while categorically distinguishing the former's situation from that of the latter in the ways that chapters 2 through 5 establish. The narratives of the remarkable immigrant worker-activists from Teamsters Local 556 point to the biopolitical methods and discourses that foster these contrary moments in the hegemonic framework. For the abstract possibility of extensive, cross-racial, counterhegemonic alliances to become concrete, it would be of no little value if those who are privileged enough neither to be doing the dirty jobs of these immigrants nor to have had to travel vast distances to get them would attend carefully to the stories that unfold in the pages ahead. Giving them such politically catalyzing attention, on the one hand, would mean pondering the specific differences of these immigrant workers' racialized experiences and constructions of the world from more generally respected forms of common sense. On the other hand, it would mean recognizing in these narrators individuals who may bear unsuspected resemblances to more socially advantaged groups in the increasing circumscriptions of their freedom and comprises of their bodily well-being as well as in their too often unnoticed capacities to shape power in contemporary society.

1. Political Narratives, Common Sense, and Theories of Hegemony

WHAT ASSUMPTIONS do people bring with them when they confront the personal life stories of immigrant workers? It would be understandable if one main expectation were that these narratives "tell it like it is"—that they provide an authentic, firsthand account of what it was *really* like to struggle to keep one's family afloat in Mexico in the late twentieth century as the national economy deteriorated; to make it across the U.S.–Mexico border without documents and without being robbed by *coyotes*, shot by vigilantes, stricken with acute dehydration, or arrested by the Border Patrol; to work day after day in one of the country's largest beef-processing plants, enduring constant pain and regular abuse by supervisors; and to attempt to make things better at work by breathing new life into a decaying but still functional local union organization. Latina feminists and critical race theorists frequently urge the importance of listening to the *testimonios* (life stories) of immigrants and their descendents as a way of countering the tendency of abstract theories to suppress concrete particularities of their experiences (Delgado 1998; Latina Feminist Group 2001; Moraga and Anzaldúa 2002). Media reports on undocumented immigrants popularize this message, in turn, when they depart from their routine characterizations of these immigrants as "living in the shadows," "silently" flowing into the country and working at their jobs. When the media let undocumented immigrants speak for themselves, this rhetorical backdrop gives their comments the aura of truths that have been suppressed and are now suddenly being brought to light.

I once witnessed a media-based rendering of immigrant narratives as the pure expression of experience, in dualistic contrast to commentaries about immigration by nonimmigrants, when I participated in the recording of a public television town hall meeting on immigration. The session was held in 2006 in the city of Yakima in central Washington State, where a robust—and angry—chapter of the Minutemen had organized along with a splinter group called Grassroots On Fire. Local Latino residents and sympathizers had responded by mounting a campaign of opposition to these groups' xenophobic accusations against immigrants.[1] The panel of expert commentators included a member of Grassroots On Fire, an apple farmer, an official from the governor's office, a representative from a social services center for Latinas, the Mexican consulate general, and an immigrant rights attorney. Shortly after the taping began, I noticed a young woman with several small children making her way into some seats close to the center aisle where microphones had been set up for questions from the audience. Their presence seemed curious because there were no other children there, and a few times the mother had to quiet her children when they made noise in the middle of one of a speaker's remarks. About two-thirds of the way through the recording, however, it became clear that the program's directors had planned her presence there because the host turned to her, handed her the microphone, and invited her to stand up and tell her story to the panelists and the audience.

This invitation was extended immediately after the town hall discussion had paused for the showing of video footage with the counterposed personal narratives of "Maria," identified on the screen as an "illegal immigrant" and shown only in silhouette in a box on the left side of the frame, and a woman named Eloisa who was a naturalized U.S. citizen from Mexico, shown in full color in another box on the right.[2] In the video, Eliosa explains how she came to the United States illegally when she was sixteen years old and pregnant, wanting her child to "have a future." Maria echoes that she crossed the border clandestinely from Mexico seeking "a better life for me and my family." Both the shadowing of Maria's body as she speaks and her heartfelt exhortation to fellow undocumented immigrants to seek legalization so they can obtain higher education and begin careers—"don't lose the passion"—generate the impression that she is exposing the plain reality of the life of an undocumented mother (KCTS 2006). But this sense comes through even more starkly when the program reverts to the live format. With "Blanca," the mother from the audience, standing beside him, the host says to her: "You can relate to that person that was in the shadows," to which Blanca responds:

My family has been split apart. . . . I have been here since 1991. . . . I have never been to Mexico. I've always been here in the Yakima Valley. It's hard for

me to even think about going over there because I have my children, I have
three of them, the oldest is five and he is just starting his school. They're doing
really great, you know, right here. I have a lot of experience because my aunt
has just told me a lot about her going back to Mexico. She just got deported
about a year ago, and she is over there. Her children are not learning—it's not
the same education here as over there. (KCTS 2006)

Notice how Blanca explicitly invokes her personal experience as part
of a family living constantly under the threat of fragmentation because
of deportation—an imminent threat because she herself now faces
deportation proceedings, as the host quickly clarifies. Blanca's tears
and the startling sense that right before our eyes, in living color, a real
person is stepping out of the shadows have the unmistakable impact
of certifying Blanca's story as authentic, the simple truth about what it
is like to live in the United States under the conditions she and Maria
and the millions of people like them face.

Blanca's narrative seems intended to lend a halo of obvious common sense to the more detached, objective-sounding remarks that
quickly follow from the expert figures of authority—but this does
not quite pan out, and the faltering of the program's bid to construct
a complementarity between these two forms of rhetoric tells us something significant about the politics of narrative. The first comment
comes from the immigration attorney, who attests that the tragedy
Blanca imminently faces is a "common situation" and that the laws need
to be changed. Then the superintendent of the Yakima Public Schools
weighs in, affirming that he can "show data that we can educate [un-
documented immigrants'] kids as well as anybody" (KCTS 2006). Liberal supporters of immigrants' rights, of course, might like to see
Blanca's testimony as imbuing these professionals' statements with the
irresistible force of living truth. But Blanca's narrative yields no readily apparent epiphanies for the speaker from Grassroots On Fire or her
supporters, who have packed the audience. They have stories of their
own, it turns out, of being shoved to the back of the line for social services behind greedy, grasping immigrants or of being quite capable of
arranging the necessary documents for foreign-born spouses to immigrate legally. Eventually, the program wraps up with the host's game
but highly dubious claim that the meeting has initiated some good
conversations and public deliberation about this touchy and difficult
issue. The immigration supporters' comments have been periodically

punctuated by booing and heckling from the Grassroots On Fire group, belying this pretension. In addition, the host is tacitly conceding that even the supposedly plain manifestations of real experience through the personal narratives of immigrants, at the climax of the taping, have failed to elicit any conclusive, broadly shared decision about how to solve the problems related to immigration or even about what those problems are.

What those stories have produced, instead, is a binary division between two modes of speaking: narrative and objective commentary. This dualism ironically undermines the power of narrative to spark critical changes in people's conceptions about immigrants and ideas about immigration policy. Precisely by juxtaposing abstract legal and social-scientific claims with storytelling as concrete truths spoken from the heart—but truths that are multiple and that change according to the individual's particular perspective—the program reaffirms the superiority of the more objectivist forms of speech because they seem more inclusive, more capable of transcending the limitations of self-interest and personal experience. At the same time, the whole minuet between personal life story and objective commentary fosters a certain cynicism about the latter: the debates among the experts can never come to terms with the authentic reality of personal experience, and will probably never be resolved either, but this is the best we can do; and at least the stories give us a glimpse, fleeting and forlorn though it may be, of what we are bound to miss.

In preparation for my presentation and analysis of the stories of immigrant workers in the chapters ahead, this chapter ponders how it might be possible to engage these narratives without romanticizing them as the expressions of authentic experience and thereby setting off the dualizing dynamic that detracts from their ability to reshape politics and social critique. Is there another way to understand what these stories are and how they function so that they may shed light on the ways immigrants participate in the construction and contestation of social power in contemporary America? The discussion in this chapter operates mainly in the registers of political and literary theory in finding an affirmative answer to this question. Yet it also proceeds from this very concrete concern about how personal life stories can transform the ways leaders and ordinary people understand the workings of power in society today, a problem that the town hall meeting in

Yakima vividly illustrates. It also moves ultimately from the realm of theory to the practical aspects of the interview situations in which the immigrant workers from Mexico whose stories fill the pages of this book told my research assistants and me about their lives.

I begin this search for an alternative, more politically and theoretically fructuous conception of narrative by returning to the writings of the Italian political theorist and Marxist leader Antonio Gramsci. I examine Gramsci's thought regarding what he calls the "common sense" of ordinary people in oppressed social groups, which for him must play a crucial role in developing both a genuinely critical account of social power relations and an effective political strategy for changing these arrangements of power. Gramsci employs the concept of hegemony to describe his distinctive characterization of fundamental power dynamics in modern liberal-capitalist societies. This conception of power emphasizes that political leadership, through the construction of passionately held national identities and the welding of people's concrete needs to programs of action asserted as in the national interest, is vital to the exercise of domination by a ruling class. Hegemony puts the accent on the "consent" that ordinary working people express to the group that commands the uses and ownership of the bulk of society's private property as well as to the agencies of the state. For Gramsci, the working and middle classes provide such consent not only in the views they hold about political ideals like justice and rights but also through their everyday cultural activities in which conceptions about social power and personal agency take on tangible form. Because ordinary people are not simply the passive victims or dupes of dominant forces but actively produce their own subordination, Gramsci reasons, any meaningful effort to analyze and change the structure of society has to address itself directly to their commonsense, practical conceptions of self and world and ferment its mutation from within.

The project of connecting the common sense that personal life stories communicate both with the critique of social power (as hegemony) and with political action lies at the very core of Gramsci's thought. It is therefore advantageous to begin with Gramsci in our present attempt to clarify how we understand what immigrant workers' narratives are and what they do, the better to gain indications from them about how immigrants might organize politically today without reinforcing established patterns of hegemony. The next section thus probes Gramsci's argument that "intellectuals," or individuals who take on the twin tasks of leading political organizations and critically analyzing hegemony, can develop genuine insights into social power relations only in the midst of political struggles that bring them into routine contact with the mass participants in their political initiatives. For Gramsci, being politically engaged in this way means that a regular and invigorating contact exists between ordinary people's common sense and the theories and strategies that intellectuals devise. I propose, in turn, that we envision the processes of telling and receiving narratives as the communication of common sense that catalyzes those moments of political engagement for the authors of social critique and ordinary people alike, making their accounts of hegemony more critically reflective and their strategies for opposing the powerful more effective.

When it comes to defining precisely what this sort of contact between intellectuals and the rank and file of a movement entails, however, a well-known tension emerges in Gramsci's thought. Gramsci at times writes as though he envisions a reciprocal process of mutual transformation and political animation between leaders and ordinary people who are carrying out critical activity of their own. In other passages, however, he favors antidemocratic binary distinctions between intellectuals and those he calls "the simple," with the former providing the elements of mind, spontaneity, and creativity and the latter furnishing the subordinate components of body, unreflective enthusiasm, and regimented obedience. When articulating their common sense, the simple just voice their experiences; then the intellectuals interpret those experiences for them and everyone else and formulate programs of action accordingly, just as the expert panelists did in response to the *testimonios* of Blanca and Maria.

Rather than adjudicating the dispute over how best to interpret Gramsci,[3] I theorize more fully the radically democratic fork in Gramsci's thought by focusing on narrative as a significant form of common sense and by turning to a recent theoretical argument that calls into question the preconception that narratives convey unmediated, authentic—and in itself politically inert—experience. Instead, suggests political theorist Lisa Disch (2003), the narratives of oppressed people should be viewed as political discourses that *generate constructions* of both events in the world and the narrator, making them seem real rather than simply reflecting a reality they already possess. This understanding of storytelling as a creative and political act, or as having what Disch (following Hayden White) calls effects of "narrativity," resonates profoundly with the more democratic vein of Gramsci's thought regarding common sense. Both stress the ways these forms of expression actively call into being certain identities and conceptions of the world. Narrative heightens the critical purchase of theory and the strategic acumen of political activism, then, when intellectuals approach these stories as creative intellectual and political projects with which strategic alliances can be formed. Such alliances exert transformative effects on intellectuals and ordinary people alike.

If stories do not reveal the naked truth about the experiences of the oppressed, however, then how can those attempting to make critical refinements in their theories about power and resistance be sure that exposing their critiques to stories' effects of narrativity will, in fact, change those theories in progressive ways rather than reinforcing their gaps and misconceptions? The talent for storytelling is in no sense the exclusive property of those whose oppressions have escaped appreciation. I address this problem by drawing from Wendy Brown an argument that the *genealogical* qualities of narrative lend it the potential for critically sharpening existing theoretical accounts of hegemonic power relations. Narrative functions genealogically when it brings to the surface desires and attributes of the narrator that expose the irregular, nonteleological, temporally extended processes by which particular elements of personal experience have come into being. As Brown points out, genealogically precedent moments within these processes can encode "memories of desire" that conflict with the normative identities ordained by the hegemonic order. Such moments therefore represent opportunities for reconstituting both identity and the understanding of power that grounds a certain conception of the self (1995, 75).

In short, this chapter explains why it makes sense to consult the personal life stories of immigrants when politically engaged intellectuals seek to increase the critical purchase of extant theories regarding the workings of power in late modern times, theories for which the concepts of biopolitics, discipline, and neoliberalism are crucial, as we shall see in the chapters to follow. The chapter at hand sets the compass for the analysis of interviews to follow, showing the importance of posing two central queries in response to the stories these immigrant workers tell. First, what common conceptions of power and of the narrator's position in relation to power do the stories generate? Where is it possible to identify shared narrative currents among our interviews with immigrant meatpackers, and what theories of power do these narrative streams suggest? Second, how do narrative frames about specific institutional and life-historical contexts (e.g., about crossing the U.S.–Mexico border or about working in the slaughterhouse) rely on genealogical links to storytelling patterns about other such episodes? Where, in particular, is it possible to discern counterintuitive and tension-laden affiliations between those desires that fortify neoliberal, biopolitical, and disciplinary power formations and others that destabilize them?

Finally, I offer a brief discussion at the end of this chapter detailing the questions and procedures for the program of interviews I conducted with immigrant workers in compiling the material for this book. I argue that narrative analysis *politicizes* the search for an adequate theoretical account of how power works and how to resist it, that it involves social critique in a form of political engagement capable of making it more self-reflective. I then discuss in more conventional terms the political aspects of our interview program. In particular, I explain how we performed these interviews in the context of an open alliance with these workers, as community supporters in their struggle to expand democracy in their union and in our geographic region as well as to address harsh working conditions at Tyson. And I argue for seeing this embroilment in the workers' struggles as a virtue rather than a fault with respect to the analysis that follows, through enhancing the overall investment in political engagement of this intellectual exercise—and thereby inciting all that much more the critically intensifying effects for this analysis that, in various but complementary ways, Gramsci, Disch, and Brown all suggest are essential for politically astute theory.

Gramsci on Intellectuals and Common Sense

Antonio Gramsci was an innovative and imaginative theorist of political, class, and cultural power who also worked as a dedicated leader in the Italian Left in the years before his political commitments landed him in prison. Many of Gramsci's writings prior to his imprisonment in 1926 deal directly with matters of political strategy for the Italian

Communist Party and introduce ideas about hegemony and counter-hegemonic struggle that he would later develop in the *Prison Notebooks*. In his life's work, Gramsci strove to illustrate a core principle of his approach to the critique of hegemony: that genuinely critical theory can only germinate in an atmosphere of dedicated political struggle.

Gramsci's theory of hegemony not only provides an account of how power operates in society but also advances an epistemological argument about how it is possible to gain a critical, and self-critical, understanding of social power relations. Gramsci proposes the concept of hegemony to counter what he calls Marxist "economism." The economistic outlook holds that structural changes in the sphere of economic production are the exclusive motor forces of history and will autonomously and inevitably yield working-class revolution. By contrast, Gramsci argues that political leadership and organization play a vital role in constituting the relation of forces among class groups. Economistic Marxists fail to appreciate these dynamics of power; in addition, they prevent themselves from gaining a critical awareness of what they do not understand by believing their theories to be true without testing them in the context of live political struggle (Gramsci 1971, 166). For Gramsci, only theory that directly confronts the complexity of lived experience and the practical linkages between prevailing ideologies and the needs and desires motivating ordinary people's actions in everyday life, making itself felt in history, can be assured of its own critical potency (166). Political initiatives relying on theory that lets these tasks slide have no realistic chance of gaining traction with a popular base. In turn, the ability of a particular account of social power relations to inspire mass action furnishes an indispensable metric of theory's success in having identified the salient particularities of everyday life and properly conceptualized their function in the schema of hegemony. Political action becomes a vital source of self-reflectivity for a critique of hegemony just as such critique becomes crucial to transformative politics.

Gramsci assigns the weighty task of fostering this mutually invigorating connection between theory and political engagement to "intellectuals," defined in his strict sense as leaders who strive both to elaborate a philosophically "specialized" conception of hegemony and to "organize . . . masses of men" to strengthen or oppose this power formation (5, 334). A movement succeeds in recognizing the tides of history and bringing its collective will to bear on events in the world, he argues, to the degree that there exists "a dialectic between the intellectuals and the masses" (334). The interesting and thus far irresolvable question in reading Gramsci concerns the precise character of this dialectic, both the substance of the relation itself and the composition of the two terms engaged in it. Sometimes, Gramsci seems to view intellectuals along vanguardist lines borrowed from Lenin. He writes, for instance, that when a movement is characterized by "democratic centralism," there is "a continual adaptation of the organisation to the real movement, a matching of thrusts from below with orders from above, a continuous insertion of elements thrown up from the depths of the rank and file into the solid framework of the leadership apparatus which ensures continuity and the regular accumulation of experience" (188–89). Here, the relation between the leaders and the led is clearly one of command and obedience. Orders descend "from above" and must be obeyed. Instead of systematically developing their own critical and leadership capacities, the masses seem capable of only reflexlike, spasmodic acts.

When Gramsci writes about common sense, in turn, he at times reinforces and elaborates this dualism between the intellectuals, who perform autonomous, politically active, philosophically creative work, and the simple, who seem to lack the capacity for this sort of labor. He asks rhetorically:

> Is it better to take part in a conception of the world mechanically imposed by the external environment, i.e. by one of the many social groups in which everyone is automatically involved from the moment of his entry into the conscious world (and this can be one's village or province; it can have its origins in the parish and the "intellectual activity" of the local priest or aging patriarch whose wisdom is law, or in the little old woman who has inherited the lore of the witches or the minor intellectual soured by his own stupidity and inability to act)? Or, on the other hand, is it better to work out consciously and critically one's own conception of the world and thus, in connection with the labours of one's own brain, choose one's sphere of activity, take an active part in the creation of the history of the world, be one's own guide, refusing to accept passively and supinely from outside the moulding of one's personality? (323–24)

Here the dualism between common sense and critical consciousness is extreme and fully elaborated: where the first is in the thrall of heteronomous power, the second is autonomous; where the first is mechanical, the second is living and spontaneous; where the former is passively receptive to the ideas and prejudices of others, the latter is active both philosophically and politically; where common sense merely perpetuates stagnant givens, critical consciousness creates a new world. Gramsci then furrows the division between common sense and critical consciousness even more deeply by diametrically opposing the internal manifoldness and confusion of common sense with the uniformity and cohesiveness of critical historical thinking:

When one's conception of the world is not critical and coherent but disjointed and episodic, one belongs simultaneously to a multiplicity of mass human groups. The personality is strangely composite: it contains Stone Age elements and principles of a more advanced science, prejudices from all past phases of history at the local level and intuitions of a future philosophy which will be that of a human race united the world over. To criticize one's own conception of the world means therefore to make it a coherent unity and to raise it to the level reached by the most advanced thought in the world. . . . The starting-point of critical elaboration is the consciousness of what one really is, and is "knowing thyself" as a product of the historical process to date which has deposited in you an infinity of traces, without leaving an inventory. (324)

Gramsci thus emphasizes that world-transforming action is only possible when human collectivities achieve a substantial degree of internal coherence in identity, purpose, and logistical coordination. The critical cohesiveness of thought that enables generative political action, however, comes exclusively from intellectuals and is their gift to "the simple." To be sure, the cadre of intellectuals only succeeds if "it never forgets to remain in contact with the 'simple' and indeed finds in this contact the source of the problems it sets out to study and resolve" (330). Yet the exercise of critically reflective social analysis is a function reserved entirely for intellectuals, who presumably have no politically relevant experiences of their own that require "critical elaboration" through agencies that they themselves do not already possess. Instead, the simple and their experiences become objects for intellectuals to study—at close proximity, to be sure, but through a form of contact that lacks both a sense of universal agency and a dimension of reciprocity.[4]

Countering this tendency to see common sense as something that must be rejected and replaced with something wholly unlike it, however, is another current in Gramsci's theory that understands common sense as the *constitutive basis* of critical social analysis and transformative political action. Even in the passage quoted previously on the need for a "coherent unity" of thought, we see leanings in this direction as Gramsci writes of the effort "to criticize one's own conception of the world" in a way that is developmental rather than dependent on some sort of external revelation. He gestures toward a practice of self-examination that begins by sensing the orphan "traces" of history in oneself as well as one's "intuitions" of a radically different future and building out from there toward a new awareness of self and society (324). Gramsci makes this alternative view of common sense even more explicit in a subsequent passage, arguing:

A philosophy of praxis . . . must be a criticism of "common sense," *basing itself initially, however, on common sense* in order to demonstrate that "everyone" is a philosopher and that it is not a question of introducing from scratch a scientific form of thought into everyone's individual life, but of *renovating and making "critical" an already existing activity.* (330–31; emphasis added)

This take on common sense is necessarily more open to a form of mobilization that abstains from placing too high a premium on the fantasy of total movement coherence. More importantly, Gramsci identifies ordinary movement participants as the primary agents of their own philosophical and political development, through cultivating the cultural practices they already perform for themselves. The scare quotes Gramsci places around the term critical also suggest that he wants to avoid any hard and fast distinction between critical and non-critical, or precritical, activity. In a passage where Gramsci invokes the notion of "a dialectic between the intellectuals and the masses," he confirms this sense of the generative and critical agency of ordinary movement participants, writing: "The intellectual stratum develops both quantitatively and qualitatively, but every leap forward towards a new breadth and complexity of the intellectual stratum is tied to an analogous movement on the part of the mass of the 'simple,' who raise themselves to higher levels of culture and at the same time extend their circle of influence towards the stratum of specialized intellectuals, producing individuals and groups of greater or less importance" (334–35). In other words, Gramsci suggests that the structure of a successful counterhegemonic movement must contain a momentum toward *internal democratization,* notwithstanding the indispensable function of leaders and the necessity of some division of theoretical and practical labor.

How, then, might it be possible to formulate more precisely this understanding of common sense as not essentially different in kind from social critique? The goal, that is, is to flesh out this notion of common sense as possessing a creative, dynamic quality of its own, and also an internal coherence and integrality, that makes it capable of critically invigorating theory rather than merely serving as theory's instrument or working material. Gramsci does not provide much assistance in this regard. The tension between his alternate visions of the "dialectic between the intellectuals and the masses" persists unresolved in the *Prison Notebooks,* and his comments on common sense as a constitutive basis for hegemony critique remain sporadic and gestural. However, more recent debates about the politics of narrative enable an extension of the more radical democratic conception of common sense that Gramsci tentatively proffers. Specifically, I have in mind discussions about the relation of storytelling by oppressed persons to theoretical critiques of structural domination, especially patriarchy and racism.

On Narrativity: Resisting the Temptation to Romanticize
the Voice of the Oppressed

If the chief task of intellectuals is to ensure a continuous line of contact between the social and political theory that orients a popular movement and the lived experiences of the movement's mass following, then one way to think about narrative would be as a crucial form in which such lived experiences are rendered available for contemplation. As Disch argues, a prominent current of thought in feminist studies and critical race theory makes exactly this claim about the political import of narrative: that storytelling allows the voice of the oppressed, in its concrete specificity and immediacy, to gain a hearing. Usually, Disch observes, theorists counterpose this ability of narrative to express situated particularity against analysis or argument that bases itself on "the Archimedean fiction of disembodied objectivism" (2003, 256). For Iris Marion Young, for example, storytelling is a mode of communication by which socially and culturally marginalized groups can make known to others the thoughts, values, and life circumstances that elude expression through the "operative premises and frameworks" of dominant conceptions of the world. Young argues that the reigning

systems of analysis and judgment are themselves grounded in historically specific cultural and social contexts, which their pretensions of
universalism disavow but from which women, racial minorities, and
working-class people traditionally have been excluded. People in these
subordinate social groups therefore lack training in the cultural skills
necessary to characterize social problems and to advocate solutions in
what would be recognized as reasonable terms. Young writes: "Storytelling is often an important bridge in such cases between the mute
experience of being wronged and political arguments about justice"
(2000, 72). In the face of norms defining legitimate, public-spirited
communication as dispassionate, disembodied, logical argumentation,
narrative validates emotion, evokes a keen sense of physicality, and
eschews universal humanist appeals in favor of underscoring the particularity of experience.

    While Young focuses on the critical impact storytelling can have
on conversations geared toward the resolution of ethical political questions, her approach can be easily adapted to the question that is paramount for Gramsci: how to vouchsafe the critical purchase of social
analysis and political strategy. In terms of the practices that make a
movement both democratic and historically efficacious, perhaps the
dialectic between the intellectuals and the masses should be construed
as a dialectic between theory and popular narrative. If it is the job of
intellectuals to analyze hegemony scientifically and to envision and
actively create a popular front that is seamless in its unity and coherence, then attending to the stories circulating among ordinary people
as common sense may give intellectuals moments of essential contact
with those aspects of lived experience to which their counterhegemonic
program fails to respond. Narrative, viewed in the terms that Young,
Richard Delgado, Martha Nussbaum, and other theorists supply, "models a way of making knowledge that does not pretend to be abstract and
impartial but discloses itself to be situated and context-specific" (Disch
2003, 257). Narrative expressions of common sense, it seems, could
provide a vital corrective to the abstracting and universalizing momentum of intellectuals' labor and to intellectuals' efforts to legitimate their
critique of hegemony by claiming for it a rational ground that is not
conditioned by the power relations the critique calls into question.

    The problem with this elaboration of Gramsci's dialectic of democ-
racy-in-movement, however, as Disch suggests, is that it presupposes a

binary opposition between theory and narrative that ultimately may exacerbate antidemocratic tendencies rather than alleviate them. Disch discerns the prevalence of "two themes" in the feminist and critical race literatures on the political value of narrative, both of which she holds up to critical scrutiny: "First is the assertion that narrative displays its critical force in opposition against abstraction in its various guises—argumentation, theory, positivism. Second is the conviction that voice makes narrative qualitatively different from and critical of abstract discursive modes" (260). This cascading series of dualisms—"narrative and theory, story and argument, voice and dogma"—actually buys into the modern opposition between "reason and rhetoric" that has so deeply disempowered feminism and other subordinate discourses (260, 261). If theorists privilege the former terms in these pairs as uniquely expressing concrete particularity, then they fail to subject the normativity of the latter terms to radical criticism because they reaffirm the sense of absolute difference between these two sets of terms. Such thinking also unintentionally reinforces the ideological pretension of argumentative and objectivistic texts to transcend their culturally and historically situated locations: "Far from challenging such hegemonic discourses as law and science, this opposition shores up the basic disjuncture between fact and fiction on which those discourses rest" (262). Translated into the Gramscian language with which I have been working, this way of understanding the relation between narrative and theory recapitulates precisely that hierarchical notion of the dialectic between theory and common sense that Gramsci sometimes favors. Narrative, as the unalloyed manifestation of the subaltern's lived experience, becomes a kind of primary datum available for critical contemplation and political utilization by intellectuals, among whom the narrators themselves are not counted.

Disch, however, proposes an alternative understanding of the narrative–theory nexus that contains fertile affinities with the more radically democratic tack in Gramsci's thought. Drawing on the literary criticism of Ross Chambers and Hayden White, Disch urges theorists to consider "the effects that a text produces when it 'feigns to make the world speak itself and speak itself as a story'" (263), or, in White's terms, when that text "narrativizes" (1987, 2). Storytelling, for these critics, *produces* a dualism between the narrator and the ostensibly real events being narrated. It thus imparts to those events the sheen of

genuine experience and authorizes the narrator's voice as the naturally appropriate agency for making those events known. In doing so,
it satisfies what Disch describes as our "desire that reality be storied,
that it have a point" (264). In short, rather than allowing lived experience to surface in its concrete immediacy, for Disch, narratives "lend
immediacy" to the events they represent in a manner akin to the way
self-proclaimed rational, critical texts operate (264).

This notion of an isomorphism between narrative and theory
pulls in two directions. On the one hand, it helps to solidify a vision of
the critical and creative energies of common sense by suggesting how
to see the contact between theory and common sense as a moment
of critically invigorating political engagement based on a mutualist,
democratic understanding of this connection. The relation between
leaders, who develop a specialized critique of hegemony and a corresponding political strategy, and ordinary movement participants,
whose common sense takes the form of stories, is no dialectic between
opposites utterly unlike each other. Rather, there is a constant mutual
negotiation between agencies that stay distinct, though not wholly different, because both are involved in producing a world at a distance so
that it can be known and acted upon. Counterhegemonic politics can
arise when these parallel, reciprocally affecting productive activities
make this democratic negotiation deliberately self-reflective, finding
the energy and motivation for such reflection in the process of collaboration. On the other hand, the White-inspired recognition that stories
are not just told but narrativized means that just like the critical theory
of intellectuals, the common sense articulated by the oppressed often
reiterates established frames of meaning that are complicit with domination because both sorts of narratives emerge in a historical, political
context shaped by the extant hegemonic formation. For instance, think
of how Blanca's comments about U.S. schools evoked the ideological
trope about "America" as an enlightened land of opportunity in contrast to cultures elsewhere in the Americas that presumably do not
value educating the young.

This last point leaves us with another problem to solve: how does a
politics of narrative engagement distinguish between those effects of
narrativity that will spur the critical reformulation of theory and those
that will merely reiterate hegemonic conceptions of power and subjectivity? While no definitive answer exists in the abstract, or apart from

the concrete circumstances of theory's involvement in specific political struggles, further theoretical reflections can at least bring to light
certain devices for sensitizing intellectual involvements with common
sense to counterhegemonic possibilities. The notion of genealogy helps
orient our inquiry in this direction. In particular, it offers an additional tool for exposing to critical reflection, via engagement with subaltern narratives, the theoretical constructs that chiefly concern me
in the analysis of immigrant workers and hegemony in the chapters
ahead: the Foucauldian concepts of biopolitics and discipline.

Genealogy and Narrative's Critical Impact on Theory

Any personal life story is inevitably a tale about desires that animate a
certain casting of identity. As I show in the next few chapters, immigrant workers' invocations of personal desires also carry with them
distinctive ways of characterizing the landscapes of power where desire
arises as well as the sorts of agency that the self can (or cannot) exercise to act on desire from within that terrain. This means that the shifts
and continuities of *desire* that impart a determinate texture to a narrative can offer clues about how the accompanying narration of *power*
accords with or diverges from currently esteemed models of power in
intellectual circles. To explore narrative material in search of such contingencies of desire, I propose, is to approach these stories genealogically and thereby to enable politically engaged theory to augment its
ability to reformulate conceptions of power critically.

I take inspiration for this methodological move from a brief passage about genealogy in Wendy Brown's *States of Injury* (1995) that has
heuristic value for theorizing the politics of narrative even though
Brown seems to intend it more as a provocative coda to her fully elaborated critique of the "politics of *ressentiment.*" For Brown, such politics comprises the prevailing trope of identity formation in current
times; and this politics proceeds from, reflects, and reinforces historically particular forms of state and capitalist power. According to this
logic of identity, the individual embraces the status of being "injured"
as fundamental to his or her existence while also "fixing" the identity
of the perpetrator of harm in a similar fashion (27). For Brown, the
person as a "subject" in the philosophical sense (i.e., having certain
deeply set and apparently innate approaches to knowing truth and

to making moral judgments) actually comes into being through the actions taken in accordance with this identity centered on woundedness. Turning to the state as a supposedly neutral source of revenge, compensation, and protection, the subject not only solidifies its own resentful identity but also reproduces the power of both the state and the social forces (e.g., capitalism, racism, patriarchy) that produced the injury in the first place (27). Yet Brown contends that the formation of these "wounded attachments" can be destabilized through genealogical interventions:

> What if we were to rehabilitate the memory of desire within identificatory processes, the moment of desire—either "to have" or "to be"—prior to its wounding? . . . This project might involve not only learning to speak but to *read* "I am" this way: as potentially in motion, as temporal, as not-I, as deconstructable according to a genealogy of want rather than as fixed interests or experiences. The subject understood as an effect of an (ongoing) genealogy of desire, including the social processes constitutive of, fulfilling, or frustrating desire, is in this way revealed as neither sovereign nor conclusive even as it is affirmed as an "I." In short, if framed in a political language, this deconstruction could be that which reopens a desire for futurity where Nietzsche saw it foreclosed by the logics of rancor and *ressentiment.* (75)

For Brown, to recollect desires antecedent to those that have been disciplined to conform to the politics of *ressentiment* is to open the possibility of refiguring one's identity, in part by gaining a new awareness, perhaps even a new sense experience, of the perpetually contingent quality of identifications.[5] As well, reconceiving of the subject as resulting from "an (ongoing) genealogy of desire" brings to light the motivational and world-forming power associated with "social processes" that differ from the dominant ones entwined with the hegemonic logic of identity, thus exposing new prospects for political and social change.

While Brown does not specify further what this process of genealogy might look like in practice or how to negotiate the inevitable differences among potential participants' roles and capacities, the politicized, narrative interface between common sense and theory is one useful way to envision such an endeavor. Given that identity is continually "in motion" and entangles the "not-I" with the "I," the act of telling a personal life story most likely allows complexities and disjunctions in the trajectories of the narrator's desire and therefore also in the narrator's visions of the power that calls subjects into being, to surface. Narrative necessarily presents the formation of a subject in temporally extended terms and also may involve characterizations of identity across multiple spatial locations. The immigrant workers we interviewed, for example, told stories stretching between Mexico and the United States and bridging the years of childhood and adulthood, just as Blanca connected her imperiled situation as an undocumented adult to her innocent childhood migration and speculated about how her present difficult circumstances in Washington State could lead to an uncertain future south of the border. But even as narrative forges a chain that links spatially and temporally diverse moments in a unified conception of a desirous personality and its power environment, it also can enact discernible breaks in that chain, supplying alternative and even inconsistent renderings of identity and society.

To see both the storytellers and their interlocutors as *collaborative genealogists* in the labor of constructing narratives-in-dialogue about power and agency that are deliberately open to their own variable permutations is to heighten the chances that these narratives will have critical force with respect to hegemony. Again, narrating a life does not necessarily produce such force: as Brown argues, a certain rubric for remembering desire, based in a contingent social process, may well reinforce a given schema of power. Mindful of this possibility, for instance, she criticizes feminist consciousness raising as a "confessional" practice that intensifies disciplinary power of the sort that Foucault analyzes in *The History of Sexuality, Volume I* (1990, 41–42). In this case, the disciplinary effect comes from privileging an incident of violation as the axially defining event of one's life that makes other events and experiences intelligible. For the teller and her partners in critical political conversation to probe that same story genealogically, however, could release from within it unruly notions of the self and the world capable of sharpening the critique of patriarchy and recomposing the narrator's identity in new ways that evince a keener desire for "futurity." While Brown raises such genealogical work as a constructive possibility, in my analysis of immigrant workers' narratives, I move a step further toward carrying it out, albeit in provisional and incomplete fashion. I not only employ concepts borrowed from Foucault to gain critical leverage on our interviewees' conceptions of self and world—I also expose the notions of biopolitics and discipline to the reinvigorating solvent of immigrant workers' common sense, relying on an alertness to the genealogical slips, variances, and ties among spatially and temporally distant narrative episodes to help distillate this solvent.

These thoughts about Brown and genealogy begin to bring the specific, communicative, and situational context of our interviews into focus and suggest the need to scrutinize these conversational dynamics more carefully and critically. Before doing so, however, I want to address two additional issues of theory that concern the wider political context for performing the genealogical task of narrative engagement that I have sketched and, more specifically, that help answer the question of what conditions or processes *motivate* this work. Brown provocatively notes that when desire is represented "in a political language," subjects acquire the motivation to investigate and activate their forgotten or suppressed desires genealogically (1995, 75). Her own use of the passive voice here is somewhat obfuscating, however: it is unclear how a desire gets translated into a political idiom and also what characteristics make a particular form of language political.[6] Gramsci's thought enables a helpful clarification of Brown, indicating that it is possible to bring the genealogical moments within narrative to the fore through explicit activities of political organizing. This would require intellectuals in a popular movement to develop a political idiom in mutually critical engagement with the stories of ordinary participants in that collective undertaking. Thus, we need to take Brown's somewhat undeveloped but instructive comments on genealogy and political action a step or two further to account for how to initiate the project of activating the fugitive memories of desire harbored within narratives.

Transposing Brown's evocative notion of genealogies of desire to a more self-consciously intersubjective key also suggests one further modification to this idea. If the context for the articulation of a remembered desire is at least informally *interpersonal*, and certainly if it is *collective* in the stronger sense of being systematically organized, then working genealogically means something more than ferreting out prior memories of desire in a single individual's life story. In addition, memories of desire can flow from one person to another in a commonly shared pool containing various narrative streams. Thus, an individual could come to acquire a "political language" for expressing a distinctive conception of power and identity that borrows from a common culture of remembered desire to which others have contributed, including others who reject that particular political idiom in favor of another. Precisely such a crossbreeding dynamic characterized the political narratives of the immigrant meatpackers in this study, as the discussion in chapter 5 demonstrates.

Power and Narrative in the Interview Situation

To what extent and in what ways, then, did the techniques of interviewing and interpretation employed in this study make good on the promises of collaborative genealogy that I have outlined? In practical terms, the meeting between critical theory and common sense that informs this book took place through the interviews that my research assistant (a Whitman College undergraduate from Mexico named Paola Vizcaíno Suárez) and I carried out with the immigrant workers at Tyson's Pasco beef-processing plant as well as in the subsequent process of writing and interpretation. That this book is a monograph, written by myself in English and in an academic style of prose, and thus very unlikely to be read by the workers, means that there is a tenacious gravitational force pulling this study in precisely that inegalitarian direction that I have criticized throughout this chapter. Moreover, the interview situation was, of course, fraught with the educational, linguistic, racial, and other cultural polarities that distinguished us from those with whom we were speaking. Given these magnetic conditions, how can this study hope to avoid recapitulating the dynamic of authority's assertion shared by the town hall meeting on immigration, the vanguardist passages in Gramsci, and the dominant tendencies in feminist and critical race narrative studies that Disch questions—the analytical bent that ends up anointing the interpreter to say what the stories mean after the person being interviewed "spontaneously" narrates them?

While I aim to acknowledge the serious flaws in this regard that my research process entailed and the need to continue even now to counteract them, I also want to make clear the steps I took to give the interviews and the analysis, to the greatest extent possible, the character of a reciprocally critical construction of political (i.e., world-generating) narratives and alliances. In designing an approach to interviewing the Tyson/Iowa Beef Processors (IBP) workers, I sought to solicit stories that would accomplish several things. In part, I wanted these interviews to furnish a rich and specific body of material conveying what it meant to the individual to grow up in Mexico, to cross the border illegally, to work and live subsequently in the United States, and to engage in political struggles with fellow immigrant workers. I hoped that each conversation, most importantly, would shed light both on the ways the individual construed the operations of power governing her or his actions, thoughts, and desires and on the sense of self that she or he developed in that context. To that end, Paola and I asked open-ended questions about specific experiences and encounters that left maximum latitude for the interviewee to articulate the characteristics of power and the contours of self-identity on his or her own terms. Thus, the conversations we conducted with these immigrant workers took the form of loosely structured interviews rather than regimented question-and-answer sessions. Of course, I developed a formal list of questions to give the interviews a general common direction, but these were broad queries meant to elicit people's anecdotes and free associations. They needed to be flexible enough to allow us to follow the momentum of the conversation into topics, events, and issues that we could not have anticipated before speaking with the individual we were interviewing. We also discussed the questions with union leaders before beginning the interview program, thus including them in the research design process.

We began these discussions by encouraging the workers to tell us their stories about their early years growing up in Mexico and their families of origin and about the events that precipitated their decisions to come to the United States. Then, we inquired about what it had been like to cross the U.S.–Mexico border, which they almost all had done illegally, and then to live and work in the United States for a certain period of time without legal documents. After this, we turned to their experiences on the cattle disassembly line at Tyson/IBP and, more often than not, in the infirmary and on various "light duty" jobs for the injured; and we asked them to put these experiences in the context of the other kinds of work they had done while living in Mexico and in the United States, which for the majority included significant stretches of farm labor. Finally, we invited our informants to tell us their stories about the union: about how, if at all, they had participated in the union and in the early, grassroots rank-and-file movement; about what they considered to be the union's successes and failures; about the kinds of leadership they saw in the people who headed the organization; and about the forms of collaboration between the union and others in the community they thought would help bring about progress at the plant.

The narratives these immigrant workers provided during the interviews, which ranged from one-and-a-half to two-and-a-half hours for each person, were inevitably highly partial accounts. Obviously, major portions of each person's life did not find their way into the conversation, whether because of the limited time we had together, because of the way we posed the questions, or because we simply did not know the individual intimately. Still, on our hour-long rides back to Walla Walla from interview sessions in Pasco, my assistant and I were continually astonished at the depth and vividness of the accounts we had heard. While we often sensed the repetition of common themes, every person's story was distinctive and moving in its own way. We never came close to tiring of the interviews, even after conducting full sessions with thirty people.

Why, then, were the workers on the whole so generous with their time and so dilatory and candid about their experiences, even those that were traumatic, humiliating, infuriating, or tragic? Largely this occurred because we approached them neither with the impartial pose of reporters seeking "their side of the story" in the conflict with the company nor with the objectivistic attitude of a social scientist interested only in getting "the facts" about the lives of immigrant worker–activists. Instead, we presented ourselves from the very start as allies who intended our work to contribute to the strength and vitality of the workers' cause. When we initially met with each individual on a different day before the interview (to get acquainted, to schedule the interview, and to talk about the main purposes of our inquiry), we stressed that aside from collecting material for my book and my assistant's senior thesis, we were doing this work so that the union's leaders and the surrounding community could learn more about rank-and-file members' lives and concerns. Having become accustomed to seeing us regularly at union health and safety workshops and other meetings, and having eaten tacos and marched with my family and me at union social events and community mobilizations, the workers signaled that they saw us as part of their endeavor even though we did not share their experiences of labor at the slaughterhouse and organizing with fellow workers. We gained an even deeper level of trust in the fall of 2002 when many of the people we interviewed along with other workers met repeatedly with the undergraduate students enrolled in a seminar I taught at Whitman. This course involved a community-based research project with Local 556 that produced additional, valuable interview material that contributes to the analysis in chapter 4. At the final meeting for this project, after a group of some twenty-five workers had discussed the research findings with these students in a public school cafeteria, the workers expressed their appreciation for our partnership by leading everyone in one of their classic rituals of solidarity. A few people clapping their hands slowly and rhythmically, in a steady beat, gradually became more people clapping faster and faster until the din filled the whole room and our cheers echoed off the concrete walls.

Even though I did not become active in the workers' movement until several years after the 1999 strike, my participation in the movement from late 2001 until the union's termination in early 2005 thus was constant and multifaceted, and it was something to which I felt strongly, personally dedicated, as my memory of that rousing applause still reminds me. During that time, I was involved in a range of activities with the union, some of which specifically incorporated the interviews into the context of the movement. For instance, my research assistant and I made copies of all the recordings and began a rudimentary oral history archive for the union. We routinely met with the union's officers and organizers to describe what we were learning in the interviews. In cooperation with other supporters in Walla Walla, I also founded a local nonprofit organization called Safe Work/Safe Food that brought together activists from various community groups to coordinate public education about the hazards meat consumers and producers alike faced from the industry's manufacturing practices, and I found myself frequently referring to the workers' accounts of their struggles as we built our base. Conducting the interviews also gave me an entrée into assorted other activities with the union in the years that followed. I traveled with Local 556 activists to a national meeting of Teamsters for a Democratic Union in Detroit to hold workshops about organizing immigrant workers and building community support for rank-and-file labor initiatives. I taught two other undergraduate courses that yielded additional community-based research in partnership with Local 556. I worked with the union to host the travelers on the 2003 Immigrant Worker Freedom Ride when the buses drove into Pasco and Walla Walla. Students and Safe Work/Safe Food activists sponsored a massively attended public lecture by Eric Schlosser in the thick of the union's campaign to fight off a decertification drive in 2004–5. And I was in the cold, foggy parking lot outside the plant at 5:00 in the morning on the day of the final decertification election, having driven the forty miles to Pasco from Walla Walla with the Catholic priest whom the workers had asked to come and pray with them; and I later shared in the dejection about the outcome.

Naturally, since leadership in the workers' movement was contested, my personal involvements in the movement led to different kinds of relations with the two main groups of activists, both of which are well represented among our interviewees. As one might expect, the immigrant workers who energetically supported the leaders of the reform movement in the union and at Tyson were more than happy to participate in the interviews and to talk about their experiences at great length (not uncommonly inviting us to stay for a meal), because they recognized that our efforts would contribute directly to their cause. These same activists also turned out en masse and recruited their friends and coworkers to come to the basement of the central Catholic church in Pasco one afternoon in October 2002, where they met with the students in my seminar and supplied an additional set of twenty-two interviews about their troubles with job-related injuries and health problems as well as the treatments and job changes they had gone through as a result. These activists were the people with whom Paola and I genuinely became friends, not only through the interviews but also because we saw them repeatedly at the union workshops, meetings, rallies, fundraisers, and marches that we attended and observed and in which we actively participated by giving updates on our research and on the growth of the allied community group.

At the same time, the activists in the smaller oppositional faction recognized that the success of *their* project could be aided by persuading us that the rank-and-file movement had gotten off track and that *they* represented the hope for genuine "reform" through a more bureaucratically savvy unionism and a less confrontational posture toward the company. When we first met with this group at one of their joint meetings, we had the distinct sense that these activists had prepared for our presence at the meeting. The dubiously naïve tone of the workers' comments, along with the way some kids outside the house seemed to have been on the lookout for our car and darted inside as we parked, indicated that things had been planned somewhat in advance. The conversation tended to go like this: first, a worker would express his or her frustration over having failed to get the union's official representatives to respond to a certain job-related problem. Then Diego Ortega, who had convened the event in his living room, would illuminate how the problem could be easily solved if only the union's officers would take a seemingly obvious, sensible course of action, usually contacting a state agency or filling out a form. It was an intriguing performance, and when it was our turn to speak, our request that the attendees give us their phone numbers and agree to be interviewed was definitely part of the act. Our presence probably helped make Ortega look more legitimate to the workers in attendance, and we were uncomfortably aware of this. At the same time, these workers all knew very well that we had been collaborating with their opponents in the union's leading activist corps. Precisely because they understood that we were implicated politically in the trajectory of the movement, they were keenly interested in winning over our support for their project or at least interrupting our cooperation with the group running the Local. In turn, although we were frankly uneasy about playing into Ortega's gambit through our attendance at the meeting, we also made the political-intellectual calculation that learning more about the concerns and experiences animating these opponents of rank-and-file reform through the interviews would ultimately be more beneficial to the union's genuinely devoted activists, not to mention that it would substantially enrich and diversify the content of our research. We were not disappointed in either respect.

In short, my own political engagement in the workers' struggles was explicitly part of the premise of all these conversations, as was that of my assistant. By intentionally seeking to operate within the thicket of contestation in which our interviews were implicated, we acquired the kind of material we were seeking: records of immigrant workers' stories *as told to us* within an electrified political context where we were trying to be critically self-conscious agents in alliance with the worker-activists. In turn, because we were so thoroughly implicated in the workers' cause on so many levels—practical-logistical, intellectual-strategic, and moral-emotional—a common context of political mobilization and struggle existed among us that enhanced the *genealogical* potential of our inquiry. In the first place, our personal involvement in the struggle probably made the workers more readily permit diverse and even discordant effects of narrativity to arise within the stories they told us. With some assurance about our commitment to the cause, they could speak without being tied to a single script but rather in a way that allowed the various and sometimes competing discourses of their movement come to the surface, discourses examined in detail in the chapters ahead. And on my side, gaining an extensive familiarity with the distinctive feel, sounds, declarations of principle, and repeated moments of contention within the political environment created by the movement gave me an added basis for recognizing what I referred to earlier as "the genealogical slips, variances, and ties among spatially and temporally distant narrative episodes."

The advocates of "objectivity" in social science no doubt would argue that the trouble with such an approach is that by making our political endeavors and affiliations known, we likely steered our informants' comments in certain directions; and they would have a point. By presenting ourselves as allies of the workers in their struggle to make the union function most capably in the interests of justice, we created an incentive for the workers to say things that they thought would intensify or attract our support for their movement or faction (e.g., excessively emphasizing unfair treatment by the company or trash-talking the union's officers). Likewise, we might have thereby discouraged them from mentioning views that would have diminished our enthusiasm for their cause (e.g., criticisms of their own leaders). A more objectivistic approach, however, in no sense would have been free of its own dynamics of power. It simply would have communicated to the workers that their comments were meant for a different audience, with connections to political projects that had little if anything to do with their own aspirations. The workers probably would have surmised that we were only planning to report their stories to a vaguely curious, mostly white, privileged audience that understood little about their struggles and cared about them in only a passing sense. Having assumed an inherent skepticism on the part of this audience about the union's endeavor, based on their ample experiences of racial misunderstanding and class marginalization, if anything the workers would have felt more pressure to leave out details that conveyed the complexities and inconsistencies of their experiences. In other words, to present our inquiry as free of both values and political interest likely would have implied to the workers that the political involvements of our project lay mainly in a privileged realm where such discourse is normative, where cultural training in these norms of communication is a condition of entry (as Young reminds us), and thus where no one really expects them to participate as active subjects (although their objectified stories periodically become topics of fascination for the elites who feel at home in this political sphere). By avoiding this particular political construction of our interaction, we hoped to elicit records of immigrant workers' common sense that were more variegated and less formulaic than a purportedly neutral approach would have yielded.

To say that our explicit avowal of the political context for these conversations encouraged more openness and richness of detail in the workers' remarks, finally, is not to claim that we thereby gained transparent access to these individuals' common sense. Different forms of substance, allusion, and rhetoric would have characterized these immigrants' stories about themselves in interactive contexts differing from our interview situation. The stories we heard were not, in particular, the stories, jokes, criticisms, arguments, gossip, or truisms these immigrant workers would have shared among themselves in their everyday lives and in our absence. James Scott's influential ethnographic work on the discourses of oppressed people draws attention to the political significance of these forms of communication. For Scott, routine patterns of discursive exchange that he terms "public transcripts" emerge in "the open interaction between subordinates and those who dominate" (1990, 2). Regarding such contexts of communication, Scott writes:

> The dominant never control the stage absolutely, but their wishes normally prevail. In the short run, it is in the interest of the subordinate to produce a more or less credible performance, speaking the lines and making the gestures he knows are expected of him. The result is that the public transcript is—barring a crisis—systematically skewed in the direction of the libretto, the discourse, represented by the dominant. In ideological terms the public transcript will typically, by its accommodationist tone, provide convincing evidence for the hegemony of dominant values, for the hegemony of dominant discourse. (4)

Subordinate people, however, have alternative means of expressing themselves when they are not confronted directly with those who dominate them. Scott thus introduces the notion of the "hidden transcript," which refers to "discourse that takes place 'offstage,' beyond direct observation by powerholders. The hidden transcript is thus derivative in the sense that it consists of those offstage speeches, gestures, and practices that confirm, contradict, or inflect what appears in the public transcript" (4–5). The "normally taciturn and deferential black cook" who mutely "look[s] on, powerless to intervene" while her master beats her daughter, for example, can cry out to the white governess—after the master has left the room—that Judgment Day will come and "white folks" will be "shot down like de wolves" and devoured by "buzzards" (5).

Our conversations with these immigrant workers were not public transcripts in Scott's precise sense. A more exact analogy to Scott's conception of the public transcript would be an exchange between a worker and one of Tyson's company managers, who directly dominated the workers by extracting surplus value from their work, setting production speeds with no regard for their physical limitations, intimidating them on the shop floor, and thwarting their efforts to act on their legal rights. My research assistant and I did not have such a relation of domination to the workers. However, we held social privileges that clearly marked our experiences as distinct from theirs and gave us unequal power in the conversations. We could speak English, even though we conducted the interviews in Spanish, while most of the workers spoke only Spanish along with some broken English. Paola had grown up in a fairly well-off, middle-class family in the city of Toluca, Mexico, and had been recruited as a tennis player to the liberal arts college where I teach, while the workers had been brought up either in small farming villages or in urban families scraping to get by through small businesses or wage labor. We were both highly educated and affiliated with an expensive private college well beyond the means of meatpacking factory workers. By contrast, few of the workers had finished more than sixth-grade schooling, virtually none had any education past high school, and if they had ambitions of college for their children, they thought in terms of community colleges and perhaps state universities. Finally, and most immediately, we were the ones setting up the interviews, posing the questions, and operating the recording equipment (although they chose the physical location, usually either the individual's home or a room at the public library). Thus, even though the workers possessed a degree of power because they knew they had something we wanted—their stories—these procedural aspects of the interview situation gave expression to the power differential that separated us, hierarchically, from the people with whom we spoke.

Because of these complex and intertwined differences of power, we did not and could not record the workers' hidden transcripts, the stories they could comfortably tell one another about power in the factory, in the union, on border crossings, and on U.S. territory in general—we sought and obtained different *kinds* of stories. This means that we lack a perspective here on certain vital forms of resistance and interpretations of these immigrants' struggles that developed within spheres of their everyday lives, which included only fellow workers and others in their personal networks of family, kin, and acquaintances and which they neither intended nor attempted to communicate to us. Clearly, we ought not to minimize the import of these processes for the critique and contestation of hegemony—the crucial significance of these hidden transcripts for understanding, in Gramsci's terms, the "already existing activity" that immigrant workers are "renovating and making critical" by and for themselves (1971, 330–31). The analysis at hand thus suggests the need for a complementary approach in a different academic project based in research of the sort employed by Scott and other critical ethnographers, including some like Lynn Stephen and Nicholas De Genova whose insightful work on Mexican immigrants I discuss elsewhere in this book. Nevertheless, what this study does uniquely capture are *political narratives* that were composed in an activist context and that, understood as such, contain special potential for critically renovating political theory and activist strategies. These concerns tend to be less urgent for ethnographers, whose texts, as I read them, evince a paramount aim to represent as adequately as possible the genuine experiences of the people and cultures they study, even given (or precisely through) the self-consciously critical interrogations that politically astute ethnographers like Stephen and De Genova conduct regarding their own subject positions and the situationally constructed character of ethnographic narratives.[7]

This intellectual, methodological difference notwithstanding, I find an affinity with authors like these in our efforts to reflect on the politics of our research processes and our shared sense that doing this sort of research involves us in a common enterprise with the people and movements we are researching. Responsible scholarship, in such a context, must involve a practical ethic of reciprocity. While I endeavored to show such reciprocity through my activism with the union and, more specifically, through extracting positive benefits for the movement from the interview program, the obligation of mutuality extends into the process of interview interpretation and also into the phase of communicating publicly about the analysis. Moreover, such an ethic proceeds directly from the notion of collaborative genealogy I have discussed, which involves putting narratives of theory and common sense, and their narrators, in live dialogue with one another. In light of this value, the scholarly exercise of writing a monograph such as *Breaks in the Chain* should be seen as just one (very one-sided) part of a more extended analytical process, a prelude to more collaborative endeavors to come.

The production of this book, in other words, highlights the need for more of a joint effort—among workers, their families, activists, organizers, political allies, and myself—to rethink what power means in the lives of immigrant workers on the basis of what these individuals said in the interviews. When Lynn Stephen reflects thoughtfully and critically on what it means to do "collaborative activist" research, she emphasizes: "Conducting collaborative activist research in situations where there are high levels of conflict requires intense scrutiny about the impact of research on those who participate" (2007, 324). In particular, she contends, analysts need to think carefully about how to generate "different types of 'products' from the collaborative research" because different products yield varying consequences for people who are variously positioned with respect to "a particular set of political forces" (324). Partly, this is a matter of protecting people from potentially adverse consequences of research, for instance, by taking precautions to insulate workers who criticize Tyson in this book from possible retribution by the company (even as those same criticisms work to my advantage by making the book compelling to my academic peers and other readers). But it is also a question of designing products in ways that reflect critical attention to the qualities and relations of labor involved in their creation and that end up having practical utility for all the participants. Hence, the publication of this book is partly intended to spur renewed conversations within the community of former activists in Pasco and elsewhere about what the struggle at Tyson/IBP meant, how best to envision forms of power that they confronted and exerted, how their experiences of immigration informed their labor activism, and what the lessons of the struggle ultimately are for future mobilizations of immigrant workers. These discussions are one product of the overall research endeavor, as will be any further writings or other communications that emerge out of such gatherings.

Having undertaken these critical reflections on the multiple political dimensions of our interviews, let us now turn to the narratives themselves. While reading the chapters ahead, bear in mind, above all, that these stories were proffered strategically to people with reciprocally beneficial political projects, notwithstanding our different positions of power. Thematizing this politically saturated quality of the narrative texts, and also carrying forward the work of analysis into more participatory contexts beyond the pages of this book, sets in motion a counterforce to the structurally inescapable problems of power involved in gathering and interpreting the interview material for this particular product of collaborative activist research. More positively, doing these things also enables a potent, if idiosyncratic, means of critically reimagining neoliberalism, biopolitics, and discipline in an era marked by mass immigration and politically defined, in part, through the agencies of immigrant workers.

2. Hegemony in Hindsight: Immigrant Workers' Stories of Power in Mexico

Understanding the Struggle

In December 2002, in Walla Walla, Washington State, my research assistant and I interviewed Maria Martinez about her experiences leading the movement of Mexican immigrant meatpackers at Tyson/IBP. By that time, the workers had achieved some of their greatest successes and institutionalized their rank-and-file upsurge in the union. Those who demanded *respeto y dignidad* (respect and dignity) had waged a major strike and then had taken control of Local 556, democratizing its internal structure in terms of both electoral processes and day-to-day efforts to spark broad and deep member participation. They also had altered the culture of the factory: more injured workers were standing up for themselves and for each other when the company withheld proper medical services or tried to fire them; and new contract language requiring that the company respect the dignity of the workers offered a potential legal basis for workers to assert some control over the primary structural contributor to their severe risks of injury—the speed of the line. Not surprisingly, Martinez and the main leadership cadre had gone on to win a convincing reelection victory in 2002 over an upstart pseudoreformist opposition. Thin in numbers but vocal in its suspicious resentments, this band of former strike activists and injured workers had made little headway with its ill-founded insinuations that Martinez was using her office for personal gain and that the union had lagged in producing tangible results.

Yet despite these developments, and even though her slate had thumped the dissident faction by a margin of nearly 50 percent, Martinez was obviously worried as she talked with us. The younger contingent at Tyson, she sensed, especially those born in the United States, did not have the same knowledge of or loyalty to the union's cause that the older immigrant workers had:

The younger kids that were born and raised here . . . they're trying to get a better position, right? Not caring about nobody else . . . [mimicking these workers] "Look what the company gave me, a better position." They don't understand the struggle. . . . They didn't know what it was to work in the fields. . . . The hardest thing they've ever had to go through was work there [at Tyson], so they're trying . . . to better themselves.[1]

"They don't understand the struggle." What exactly was the struggle to which Martinez refers? Clearly it had something important to do with the hardships of farm labor that most of the stalwart activists, including Martinez herself, had faced prior to signing on with IBP. But to speak about "working in the fields," we learned in our interviews with Martinez and her comrades, was also to invoke a more wide-ranging set of personal events and collective experiences beyond farm labor as such. It meant, in part, work under conditions of physical exposure to extreme heat, cold, and other kinds of inclement weather as well as to the chemicals farmers sprayed on their crops; work that was irregular and lacked contractual health or retirement benefits; and off-work hours spent cooped up "like chickens," as one activist put it,[2] in the cramped and dirty quarters of farmworker shacks. It also meant enduring perilous, clandestine journeys across an increasingly militarized U.S.–Mexico border and then living with continual anxiety over being discovered within zones of illegality in the U.S. interior, as we shall see in the next chapter. In addition, "to work in the fields" and to engage in "the struggle" that extended to the factory floor at Tyson/IBP was to have a past in Mexico that, in a sense, one had left behind but that one also brought along into everyday life in the present.

My interest in this chapter lies with this last element of the struggle: the persistence of a past in Mexico within these immigrant workers' organized opposition to transnational capital through the narratives they constructed, in the United States, about their experiences abroad and their motivations for leaving. Children born during the postwar Mexican economic expansion under the stewardship of a socially interventionist state, yet who came of age as economic crises broke out and the epochal turn to neoliberalism commenced, these individuals offered recollections during the interviews of the relations of power they had encountered in Mexico through the mid-1980s. Yet here we are dealing with narratives from a political context beyond the storytellers' places of origin in Mexico, both temporally and geographically:

the site of communication with my assistant and me during the immi-grant worker mobilization at the slaughterhouse, after most of them had lived in the United States for many years. As I discussed in chapter 1, we conducted these interviews to find out how workers' conceptions of power in a broad array of sociopolitical contexts—from cities and villages in Mexico to the hills near the border, and from the factory floor to federal courtrooms—shaped both their particular struggle at Tyson/IBP and more general dynamics of hegemony in neoliberal cul-ture. The main question to ask in relation to these interviews, there-fore, is not the one that seems most obvious: What do these stories tell us about how power operated in Mexico in the 1960s through the 1980s when most of these people were growing up and making their decisions to leave? Instead, I raise an alternative and more politically attuned question: What possibilities for contesting power in the present emerge from these people's patterns of remembering life in Mexico prior to their departures? Here, remembering is understood to be an active process of constructing a world of the past rather than a more or less faithful record of "actual" events. As narrators and political agents in a later historical moment, following their own re-embedding into the productive apparatus of regional capitalism after a tortuous migratory process, what did their stories imply about how neoliberal-ism functions *today,* what transnational qualities it has, and how immi-grant workers help to construct and/or challenge it?[3]

Neoliberalism is a contested term. Many social scientists treat neo-liberalism as a set of major, interrelated changes in the actions of nation-states, corporations, and supranational bodies with regard to the distribution of capital and the regulation of labor, initiated after the global dissipation of the postwar accumulation boom and acceler-ating through the 1990s and up to the present. From the perspective of Mexico and other Latin American countries, in addition, the neoliberal turn marks a new era in the history of subordination to U.S. economic and military imperialism in which mounting immigration rates play an important role. At the same time, some critical social theorists such as Wendy Brown (2005) and Aihwa Ong (2006) envision neoliberal-ism not just as a complex of policy reforms, institutional innovations, and social-structural adaptations but also as a new mode for generating novel types of subjects suited to emergent modes of capitalist accumu-lation and state power. As well, Ong sees it as a historically distinctive array of techniques for creating such power through the administration of mass populations. For Ong and Brown alike, neoliberalism thus does not simply reorganize relations of primacy and subjection among previously existing actors such as private business and the regulatory state, Mexicans and U.S. Americans, nation-states and international organizations like the International Monetary Fund, or workers and corporations. More than this, neoliberalism actually *reconstitutes* the very identities, capabilities, desires, and modes of actions of these various agents and thus brings entirely new entities into being.

Both standard empirical accounts of neoliberalism's advance and critical theoretical conceptions of neoliberal "technologies of governance," however, require the political leavening that comes from attending to the "common sense" of ordinary actors who are affected by— and help create—these historical circumstances. I premise this chapter on the Gramscian view, developed in chapter 1, that critical theory "must be a criticism of 'common sense,' basing itself, initially, however, on common sense in order to demonstrate that 'everyone' is a philosopher and that it is not a question of introducing from scratch a scientific form of thought into everyone's individual life, but of renovating and making 'critical' an already existing activity" (Gramsci 1971, 330–31). Gramsci defines common sense as those conceptions of the self and world that encode practically efficacious notions of how power works and contain at least an anticipatory sense of how to contest it (323–24, 330–31). For the scholar-activist, writing a historically specific and politically consequential critique of power thus means dialectically engaging, in a reciprocally critical fashion, with ordinary people's common sense, which in its own philosophical, political, and world-generating character does not essentially differ in form from "theory." Thus, I explore what the narratives produced by the activists of Local 556 suggested about how best to theorize what neoliberalism *is,* how to *challenge* it politically, and what kinds of *subjectivities* immigrant workers design for themselves within struggles over neoliberal hegemony.

Our informants' stories of their earliest days in Mexico composed a fairly coherent vision of the sociohistorical setting that predated neoliberal changes but eventually would prove hospitable for their implantation. Virtually all our informants spoke of childhood years spent laboring, sometimes from a very young age, to help their families meet onerous economic needs. Work invariably took precedence over school, which dimmed the prospects for future social mobility and an eventual alleviation of those financial pressures. On top of this, the workers commonly grappled with fragmentations of their families as parents' untimely deaths, unforeseen injuries and illnesses, and migratory departures of those close to them took their toll not just emotionally but also by increasing economic urgencies for those left behind. If the neoliberal power formation depends on the cultivation, or at least the abundant presence, of a working class that is accustomed to laboring flexibly in whatever temporary opportunities present themselves, willing to accept low wages, and detached from hopes for a substantial increase in social well-being through upward mobility in workers' communities or even countries of origin, then these narratives show how such groundwork had been laid well before the 1980s.

For the people we interviewed, economic hardships tended to multiply as they entered adulthood, which in many cases happened just as Mexico sank into an epochal economic crisis. In talking about this phase of their lives and their resultant decisions about migrating to the United States, our interviewees formulated three distinct trajectories of identity, or what we might call three different kinds of neoliberal subjectivity, even though their stories about childhood had been more consistent with one another. One group of men described their plans to go to the United States as expressions of self-reliance, personal assertiveness, and moral autonomy, using language steeped in rhetorics of masculine individuality. The women we interviewed similarly underscored the self-determining features of their decisions about leaving Mexico: no sense of self-pity, of helpless victimization, or of having been forced to depart by overbearing forces characterized these stories. They also made it clear that these transitions always took place in the context of gender-specific, deeply felt obligations of direct care for family members and/or gender-based vulnerabilities to certain kinds of mistreatment. The other group of men, finally, used a different tone in speaking about the events leading up to their departures for the United States: a tone that exuded a sense of resentment over having been deprived of chances for upward mobility in Mexico through marginally but significantly better education.

I call these subject formations "neoliberal" partly to index them to the historical moment that the workers were describing when population mobility out of Mexico toward the United States began to surge in tandem with vast institutional changes commonly associated with the advent of neoliberalism in Mexico, such as state fiscal austerity measures, currency devaluations, downscaled social rights, and accelerating direct foreign investment. In addition, I mean in part to signal the persistence and fortification of this institutional environment through the later moment in 2002 when the workers spoke to us in the midst of their union movement against a transnational corporate goliath that had ridden the neoliberal wave to immense profitability. Yet I also put forth this provisional and plural schema of neoliberal subjectivities to invite skepticism about recent attempts by critical theorists to pin down a general template of the neoliberal subject. Brown, for example, contends that neoliberalism involves a historical, distinctive mode of moral-practical selfhood. It induces individuals, she argues, to become "rational, calculating creatures whose moral autonomy is measured by the capacity for 'self-care'—the ability to provide for their own needs and service their own ambitions" (2005, 42). Values deriving from market relations, for such subjects, furnish the exclusive epistemological framework for evaluating "all institutions and social action" (40). Michel Feher, in turn, posits not only that neoliberalism promotes subjective formations of this sort but also that "embracing" them, and then seeking to alter them "from within," is the only effective path toward "defying neoliberalism." Feher names the predominant neoliberal subjective form as "the notion of human capital." To see oneself in this way implies striving "to constantly value or appreciate ourselves" and thus taking the practical attitude "that everything I earn—be it salary, returns on investments, booty, or favors I may have incurred— can be understood as the return on the human capital that constitutes me" (2008, 26–27).

Such attempts to descry a latter-day, neoliberal "spirit of capitalism" that animates global society and its subjects, provocative though they are, run a serious risk of neglecting racially, culturally, and class- and gender-specific modes of neoliberal hegemony and counterhegemonic possibilities alike. This chapter sheds light on precisely these sorts of variations, demonstrating that these immigrant workers did not tell the stories of their prior lives in Mexico in ways that fed neatly or cleanly into the elaboration of neoliberal selfhood as the sort of all-encompassing, intensely disciplining, and stringently focused life project of self-capitalization that Brown and Feher envision. The irony and the enigma here is that workers who did not narrate their past in Mexico as a particularly politicized past, but instead stressed their individual efforts to pursue economic betterment for themselves and their families, went on to take such extraordinary political actions at Tyson/IBP.[4] It would be more in line with theories of neoliberal subjectivity if, for these workers, such distinctly privatizing responses to the rising pressures of neoliberalism in Mexico had foreshadowed more single-minded attempts to cultivate their worth as "human capital" after beginning to work in the United States. Alternatively, it might seem more logical if we were to hear, in this chapter, stories from these people about having come from politically involved families or about having gotten active in any of the popular movements that emerged in Mexico in the 1970s and 1980s as economic fortunes tumbled while the state and the long-dominant Partido Revolucionario Institucional (PRI) suffered new legitimacy problems. Instead, the people we interviewed stressed their abilities to exercise diverse kinds of self-care as individuals in the face of neoliberalism's onset and then remarkably went on to narrate their pathbreaking collective actions north of the border.

Ultimately, then, this chapter places the accent on the political *contingencies* associated with these immigrant workers' narratives about their past histories in Mexico. Although they were concerned with their dwindling economic prospects as they contemplated leaving the country of their birth and setting out for the United States, our interviewees mostly did not represent their reflections as a process of coming to see themselves more vividly and solely as human capital. Rather, a more finely tuned reading of their comments yields five different and more distinctive ways of making the past politically available for their contemporary contestations of power. First, by claiming agency for themselves as individuals even when faced with deteriorating economic circumstances that they knew were operating on a somewhat unfathomable social level, the workers provided a present-day reading of their past experiences that could feed directly into the union's discourse about developing group leadership, solidarity, and oppositional determination on the basis of smaller-scale, individual actions of self-assertion and interpersonal care. Second, the feminine-gendered dimension of this account of the origins of "the struggle," as Maria Martinez put it, could inform the movement's appeals to gendered conceptions of family responsibility and sisterhood as mobilizing themes in an organization that had a forcefully outspoken woman at its head and an indispensable corps of women activists. Third, those immigrant narrators who did, in fact, seem more preoccupied about the value of their lives as human capital, as they spoke about their decisions to move north, helped generate the discourse of dissent against the rank-and-file movement's mainstream in which most of these individuals, unsurprisingly, participated. This discourse proposed a form of worker activism that harmonized better with the neoliberal milieu because it eschewed direct confrontation with the owners and managers of private property.

Two additional political tendencies in this material stem less from the particular characteristics of the three main narrative currents and more from features they evoked in common. The fourth is this: although on the whole these stories did not clearly indicate that the workers were engaged in transnational or transborder forms of cultural, political, and economic life, their characterizations of Mexico as a site where certain kinds of agency were possible at least left the door open for their broader narratives of political struggle to transcend the bounds of the plant, the local community, the U.S. nation-state, and even the meatpacking industry. Fifth, and last, a limited number of common narrative streams emerged in these accounts of leaving Mexico, despite the wide range of regional and cultural differences within Mexico that characterized this group of workers; this bespoke the rising sense that as meatpackers in the United States, they would have to grapple with means of power that racially homogenized them as "Mexicans" and that thus required them to develop a discursive terrain of joint struggle that could express those shared experiences.

Hence, these records of immigrant workers' common sense *theorize* neoliberalism as providing enough flexible political space for the development of these multiple and differentiated self-conceptions of individual agency as well as for their expressions through both cross-border migration and, later, working-class activism. They thereby also *contest* neoliberal hegemony, in terms of the effects of narrativity discussed in chapter 1, by challenging a uniform characterization of the "homeland" of immigrant workers either as a space saturated by domination and mechanically forcing labor to go where capital bids or, at the other extreme, as a training ground for beginning to learn how to imagine one's very self as capital that one has a duty to make appreciate in value. And this contestatory character of the narratives comes from the way they render the ambiguity of migration, which after all is neither the decision to "stand and fight" nor, in any simplistic sense, acquiescence to power through flight from it.

Niños Trabajadores: Stories about Labor and Childhood

Concern for the rights and freedoms of workers would eventually galvanize political assertion by the people we interviewed, and for nearly all of them, labor was something they had been intimately acquainted with since their earliest years. They were born during the postwar industrial expansion in Mexico, and their stories of work during childhood bore witness that this phase of development did not distribute benefits consistently or equally among the population. National economic growth rates of 6 to 7 percent annually through the 1960s turned Mexico into "an industrial power, supplying its own needs not only in a broad spectrum of consumer goods but also in such strategic items as iron, steel, and oil" (La France 1986, 212). Yet prioritizing industrialization exacted a cost in the dwindling productivity of the agricultural sector where masses of poorer Mexicans, like many of those we interviewed, were attempting to make a living. Even before the 1982 crisis, government records showed that over 40 percent of the population lived on an income below the prevailing minimum wage and that a slight majority still had no running water (Lustig 1998). Food shortages in particular became an increasing problem for Mexico's poor working families in the 1950s through the 1970s, as declining government investment in agriculture led to diminishing domestic food production, increasing food importation, and higher priced food commodities (Sanders 1986). To be sure, many people did escape the most severe and tenacious poverty by participating in Mexico's mass urbanization and growing prosperity during these years, as the stories of several people we interviewed illustrated.[5] Nevertheless, gains in economic equality were slight and unevenly realized across the population.[6] Family economic insecurity meant that as children, the people with whom we spoke were expected to help generate income through labor from an early age.

Childhood labor had a distinctive texture in many of the stories we heard. In particular, such work was often woven together with serious loss in the family, commonly the death or departure of a parent. Typically, these individuals also had felt the need to do multiple kinds of labor rather than specializing in any particular area or trade, and they spoke very matter-of-factly about their readiness to do so. The ethos seemed to be that one took advantage of whatever work opportunities one could find to ensure that the family's needs were met. Equally, doing the work that had to be done invariably took precedence over the hopes that children would stay in school for more than a few years of basic education.

Esperanza Soto's story exemplified the confluence of these four elements: hard work from an early age, in lieu of formal education, in a family that shifted occupations when the need arose, and in the context of the loss of a parent. Soto was born in 1944 in a village called Los Trojes in the rural southwestern state of Michoacán. She had happy memories of her childhood despite the difficulties her family had faced:

In those times I lived in a very pleasant way, although somewhat in ignorance . . . a life of healthy ignorance. . . . I didn't have much schooling. My parents . . . tried to do the best with me and with all their children. . . . We were four women and five men. . . . My father lived from farming. . . . He had an orchard. He had fruits, different fruits. . . . It's just that, unfortunately, I was eleven years old when he died. And so it was left for us to keep working to keep living, because he wasn't there anymore. My oldest sister, she sewed. She was a teacher, at first, and later she got sick and couldn't continue doing that. Then she made clothes. And we all did too. . . . We made dresses, pants—all kinds of clothes to wear.[7]

Nina Garza had grown up in the same village and told us about the work she had done to help her father slaughter animals and to assist her mother in selling tortillas and pork *carnitas*. Previously, her father had delivered fruits and vegetables to ranches in the area, driving a team of donkeys and a horse. Then he had started a barbershop before switching to raising pigs and, with his wife, vending street food—until he began mistreating the family and ultimately abandoned them:

My father started slaughtering pigs to sell *carnitas*. And as we grew up we'd help him: to take care of the pigs, to shave them, to kill them and everything. He didn't hire anyone else to help him, just we children helped him slaughter the pigs and make the *carnitas* to go sell them on Saturdays and Sundays. Then my mother would make tortillas to sell—they sold the tortillas and the *carnitas.* . . . He started to drink and left with another woman. And he left my mother alone there, and there were still a lot of us little ones. And my mother always had food prepared for when he'd return; but when he already had another woman, he'd come back drunk and he'd just come back to treat us badly and to fight.[8]

Afterward, Garza recalled, her mother put her to work making palm furniture, having rejected the option of sending them to do domestic labor in other people's homes because it was common knowledge, she said, that these house "servants" were often "violated" by the men in the house. Like Soto, then, Garza ended up doing whatever kind of work presented itself so the family could survive, or as Garza put it, earning what they needed "to buy the clothing to dress ourselves." The absence of the family's father, although here through his dissolute and abusive behavior and abandonment of them rather than through death, put this ethos to a particularly stringent test. And as in Soto's case, for Garza, work was the clear priority over school: "They never put us in school; we never went to school at all. We just worked."

Among the people we spoke with were some who stated flat out that they had grown up in severe poverty. Felipe Ortiz told us that his family had been "very poor" and so he had worked "all day from dawn till dark" starting at the age of eight.[9] Jorge Hernández, a Mixtec from Oaxaca, had left home at the age of twelve to find work to support himself because his family was so desperate. Gilberto Rivera likewise had experienced devastating family dismemberment in association with extreme economic hardship. Rivera choked up with tears as he described his childhood growing up with his grandparents after his father had died when he was just a baby and his mother had abandoned him and his two siblings soon afterward. He remembered how he had only gone to school for about three years, since his grandfather needed help planting and "there was no money to buy the books." The grandfather had also "loaned him out" as a child to other area ranchers to work for them by taking care of sheep and cattle. Said Rivera, "They paid us with corn—they gave us money very rarely."[10]

Rivera stood out from our other informants, however, because he explicitly invoked his ability to find in difficult childhood experiences not only manifestations of sorrow and lack but also the seeds of self-worth and self-determining agency in the world. He told us that as an older child he had landed a more regular arrangement that gave him both his first experience of family intimacy and some basic material satisfactions:

In my childhood I suffered a lot for lack of money. It was a rare occasion when I could drink a cup of coffee, have a roll, because we didn't have anything even to buy a little packet of coffee, sugar. What I did was just to drink hot water and pretend it was coffee. . . . But after some time I met . . . a girl. We became friends and . . . we children would get together to play. And the mother of that girl told me that if I wanted I could work taking care of a cow. . . . They gave me food; we cleaned the stalls; we did the milking. And that was when I came to know what a roll was, a cup of hot coffee, what it is to be at the table together with people, with family. . . . As time went by I began considering myself part of their family. And so, thanks to God's help, I had the good fortune that all the people there loved me, they respected me; they told me that I was a hard-working boy *[un niño trabajador]*.

In these poetic terms, Rivera depicted the multifaceted deprivation that had been an indelible part of his youthful experience. He had grown up, as he explained, with neither pocket change nor a mother's love, an outsider to the family dinner table and the wage-labor economy alike, longing for real coffee and new clothes as well as human warmth. Yet in the home of his childhood friend (and employer's daughter), he had found not only respite but also "respect," and that respect was vitally connected to the family's recognition of his achievements and reliability as a *niño trabajador*. He claimed this identity and its allied sense of capable individuality with obvious pride.

As the exception that proved the rule, however, Rivera's story brought into sharper relief the more common narrative current that ran through the other interviews: not a search for self-respect and recognition from others through one's labor, but rather, more simply, the need to work as a bare, unavoidable fact of life. This attitude comprised a pronounced feature of the shared narrative about childhood labor whether the individual came from rural origins, like Rivera and the others previously quoted, or from an urban background, as did Isidro Gómez. Said Gómez bluntly, and in terms reflecting his childhood on the streets of Guadalajara, "In Mexico, you start working as a child . . . shining shoes, selling gum, washing cars, whatever it may be, trying to earn yourself a *peso*."[11] The people we interviewed also shared this disposition toward childhood work as part of the unalterable order of things regardless of their specific class location, which mostly became manifest only as the individual went on to talk about his or her educational opportunities as adulthood approached.[12] Even gender difference usually did not affect the need of the individual, as a child, to do work geared toward economic production and/or income generation for the family, although it sometimes affected the type of income-related labor done.[13] Most often, the comments of the women on this phase of their lives resonated with the men's remarks about the need- and opportunity-driven contingency of their labor. Thus, for instance, Ramona Díaz echoed Isidro Gómez when she remarked, regarding her childhood in Nayarit: "We worked in the coffee. In whatever [kind of work] could be done. When my dad had [a crop] that he planted, then we would help him to plant—whatever could be done."[14]

Individuality and the Decision to Leave Mexico:
Three Narrative Paths

As the people we interviewed described the paths that eventually led toward their migrations north of the border, their generally shared narrative—of a childhood that involved flexible labor as an inevitable condition of life, interrupted and unfinished schooling, and family fragmentations that increased the pressure to do "whatever could be done"—began to split into several divergent currents. While all our informants sought to portray the precipitants of their cross-border migration as one chapter in a highly individual story, and a story about coming into one's own *as* an individual, gender and class differences shaped the particular *form* of individuality that each narrative current presented. Their narratives also conveyed an unmistakable and varied sense of the communal and social contexts for these passages to a more determinate, adult expression of individuality: the family networks that had facilitated crossing the border, the mounting financial burdens that the epochal economic crisis imposed on them, the cultural atmosphere that promoted a sense that one could easily join the swelling ranks of people leaving their homes to seek better opportunities abroad. However, our informants also recalled this period of their lives in ways that suggested one of three trajectories toward acquiring distinction as an individual in the midst of interdependent relationships and social conditions: the path of self-reliant and morally autonomous masculinity, a route for women equally stressing proud self-determination but structured by gender-specific family responsibilities and vulnerabilities, and another avenue for men marked by dashed expectations for upward mobility within Mexico based on marginally but significantly higher educational opportunities.

Predictably, given the pall that spread over the Mexican economy during the 1980s when most of the people we interviewed departed for the United States, our interviewees tended to describe their later years in Mexico as a time of mounting, multiple hardships, especially in economic terms. The abrupt downturn of the 1980s dissolved the hopes of those on the margins of progress through industrialization while intensifying the housing, food, and employment insecurities of people passed by during the postwar boom. Underemployment, persistently low wages, and the lack of adequate public welfare supports to match the pressures of urbanization, even before neoliberal cuts in such services, meant that whereas virtually all the people we interviewed had worked to help support their families economically from an early age, now their children were even more likely to have to perform such labor (La France 1986, 220).[15] And whether or not our informants chose to refer to themselves as having been "poor," poverty, as measured by official statistics, mounted during the 1980s when most of them left the country, increasing by over 30 percent between 1981 and 1988 (Graizbord and Ruiz 1996, 385). During roughly the same period, wages fell by 42 percent and per capita consumption rates dropped substantially (Lustig 1998, 73; 1996, 159–60).[16] Massive increases in food staple prices contributed to advancing need, reflected in lower rates of food consumption, especially animal proteins (Lustig 1998, 87).[17] Housing conditions also remained sketchy for poor working families, particularly in cities; the recollections several of our interviewees had about housing-related frustrations preceding their movements across the border resonated with this more general condition.[18]

Characteristically and notably, one group of men we interviewed, as well as most of the women, downplayed the role of such mounting economic difficulties in their decisions to migrate to the United States. While they mostly acknowledged the reality of these pressures, they did not describe them either as preventing them from having realized expectations on which they had counted or as arising from any personal failings. To the contrary, most wanted us to see that even under adverse circumstances, they had managed, through intense effort and persistence, to carve out sustainable and satisfying lives for themselves and their families, at least for a time. Among the men with whom we spoke, Alejandro Méndez exemplified this posture especially clearly. Although he had spent his early childhood in the village of Joache in Jalisco, Méndez's family had then moved to Aguascalientes, and he had subsequently worked and lived in Mérida and Mexico City. Méndez emphasized that as he got older he had traveled alone through these places and others in Mexico looking for suitable and well-paying work, doing whatever jobs he could find. He also expressed mild contempt toward other Mexicans who, in his opinion, just were not looking hard enough for the good jobs that existed in their country, even though such jobs were fewer and tougher to find than in the United States. At a certain point, after spending nine years in the Mexican army, then working as a security officer in a bank, and then getting his license to be a bus driver in Mexico City, Méndez decided that it was time to "try his luck" and explore "new horizons" in the United States. Regarding his personal economic situation, he commented matter-of-factly and even somewhat breezily: "It wasn't very bad; but neither was it very good."[19]

Other men we interviewed spoke in similar ways about their decisions to leave Mexico, soft-pedaling any sense that dire financial circumstances had anything to do with it. Melquíades "Flaco" Pereyra, for example, said:

The reason that I came here wasn't a question of economics. Pure and simple, it was because I always liked to go adventuring; I liked to go wandering. . . . There's a certain part of me that likes exploring [laughing]. . . . It wasn't a question of economics. I played sports—I really liked soccer. . . . A friend of mine . . . began wanting to come to the United States. . . . He told me: "Don't you want to come with me?" I told him, "Yes, I'll leave with you."[20]

Pereyra went on to explain how his *fútbol* buddy had advised him to save his money for the crossing and how he had concocted a plan to fool his mother into giving him money by telling her that he needed it for school. The notion that the crossing was basically a youthful prank—an assertion of adolescent freedom, an adventure—paralleled Méndez's suggestion that coming to the United States was an expression of manly self-determination even though Pereyra did not avow a desire to improve his prospects for work and income, as Méndez did.

One individual who did tell us straight out that he had left Mexico under duress, though again not economic duress, was Isidro Gómez. His story is worth considering both for its idiosyncratic qualities and because of the basic features that align it with the common general narrative casting the decision to migrate as the result of autonomous, ethical choices. Gómez came to the United States, he said, partly because he had "the idea that life is a little easier here—nicer." Like Méndez, Pereyra, and others we interviewed, Gómez did not primarily attribute his emigration to financial need. Rather, he stressed that in immediate terms his departure was catalyzed by concerns about his personal safety arising from his political involvement in a movement of some three hundred peasants to acquire a government land grant to support their formation of a *comunidad agraria* (roughly, "farm collective," specifically for indigenous groups) in the late 1970s.[21] The movement challenged the prerogatives of local officials and a local property owner while at the same time broaching controversial matters of social oppression based on race. Explained Gómez:

I got involved in politics because I wanted to have lands taken away from a landowner on the outskirts of Guadalajara. There are many people there who don't have land to cultivate. We found out that this gentleman had lots of fields that he wasn't even planting. So I started getting involved with a group from San Martín Hidalgo, Jalisco, because I was from there, and I said, "We're going to take those fields away from him, for the people who don't have any." I'll tell you that personally, I had no interest in fields to plant because I grew up in the city. I don't know anything about the country—even here [in the United States] I don't know anything about it, and I live in the country! But it made me angry that there were lots of people who didn't have any lands, and this gentleman wasn't using them. . . . So many people hungry, and this gentleman wasting it all.

According to Gómez, after getting involved in the peasants' organization, opponents of this group began threatening him with violence and even death. "That's one of the reasons why I came [to the United States], too," he noted solemnly. What made this story exceptional, then, was Gómez's serious involvement in organized politics, a brand of activism that none of the other immigrant workers we interviewed appeared even to have considered. Accompanying this enthusiasm for politics, for Gómez, was also an explicit affirmation of communitarian ethics as well as an overt critique of state policy, in this case the lack of effective land redistribution mechanisms. At the same time, Gómez reaffirmed the broad outlines of the narrative he shared with the other men about individual initiative and agency grounding the decision to set out for the United States. He did this by underscoring his own moral autonomy in taking the side of indigenous peasants in their conflict with the landowner and local officials, stressing that he had no individual stake in working the land and lacked any personal knowledge, as a Mexico City urbanite, of these peasants' circumstances and ways of life.[22] That is, Gómez deliberately *dis*identified himself with this community, giving his political activism the cast of action taken on the basis of abstract principles, which he discerned through individual moral judgment rather than through any imperatives of his concrete social circumstances.

A parallel sensibility of personal fortitude, and of the ability to act freely and decisively *through* migration and in the midst of debates about whether or not to leave, emerged in the accounts of many of the women. After Alejandro Méndez's departure for the United States, Elvira Méndez spent several years supporting herself and her children by continuing to run the family meat and produce shop in Mérida. "The truth is that I didn't want to come," she said bluntly, "because I had work there. I had good work, and a good income." She also worried about the perils in the border zone that her young children might face. Although Alejandro pressured her during their eight-year separation to bring the children to the north, she refused to take that step: "I didn't want to come because my children were really little. And I [said]: 'How am I going to cross the border like that? With five children! I'm not leaving. If you want, when they're a little older.'"[23] Another aspect of her reluctance to leave Mérida, Elvira told us, was that there she had the support of a *comadre* who helped care for her children while she was working in the *carnicería*.[24]

Yet it was tough to keep the family market afloat, and after feuding with her stepmother (who was also her landlady) over their rights to the modest income it yielded, Elvira had to find new means to support her children (just as Alejandro's remittances stopped arriving, for reasons she did not clarify). So she moved to Cancún and spent her last two difficult years in Mexico working in the hotels frequented by U.S. vacationers and, without her *comadre*, relying on her eldest daughter both to care for the younger children and to supplement her own meager wages:

There were five of them. . . . My oldest daughter began helping when she started working, too. She was fifteen years old, and she could already work there. I had a boy, fourteen years old; he also started working there. And the other three little ones would leave for school by themselves. I would get up at four o'clock in the morning to make them their breakfast and I'd give them money for the taxi; they'd catch a taxi from there and they'd leave for school. When they came back that same afternoon, the three littlest ones would stay alone at home, but they already had food ready for them. I'd come back to the house from work at around seven or eight at night. . . . Those were two really hardworking years for me—because I had to leave the house to go work in the street.

For Méndez, the crisis point in Cancún came when her son suffered a serious accident in the street when a car ran over his foot and the boy nearly had to have his foot amputated. Alejandro immediately returned for a visit, his first in eight years, and that was when Elvira finally conceded that she and the children would come north to join him. Still, Elvira never painted herself as the victim of misfortune any more than did her staunchly self-reliant husband. "For my children, so that they could be with their dad, so they could get an education and everything, I came over here with them," she explained. Her story told of suffering and loss, but it had no tone of lamentation or self-pity. The sense she gave us was simply that she had done what she judged needed to be done, when it had to happen, and that was that.

Esperanza Soto's comments about the years leading up to her own passage to the United States had a similar ring to them. Shortly after they married in 1967, Soto and her husband had moved to Guadalajara and found jobs that brought in two incomes, from her work in a garment factory and his position as a police officer. Like Méndez, Soto emphasized that her life had been basically manageable and that she had not wanted to come north, even when her husband left for the United States: "As for me, I felt like we were doing well economically, the way we were living. But we also needed to buy a house and we knew well that with what we were making there . . . that it was really not enough to buy a house. So—he came here." In 1970, Soto was thus left alone with two very young children when her husband departed and found work in a Lamb-Weston food-processing plant in the United States. She remained in Guadalajara without him until she finally brought the children across the border in 1975. She only moved, however, when a family emergency combined with onerous economic circumstances to make it what she considered to be the right decision.

As with Méndez, this was a physical accident in her close family. One of Soto's sisters, with whom she shared parental duties, had married the brother of Soto's husband. When this brother lost most of his hand in an industrial accident at the cannery where the two men worked, Soto and her sister made their way northward as well.

Thus, the women's stories about the decision to emigrate in this major narrative vein expressed sincere reluctance about leaving Mexico, and they evoked the growing precariousness of life: the fraying of family bonds and the increasing proximity of grave physical misfortune. Yet they also described this decision as the right and good thing to do rather than merely as something forced upon the individual against her or his will. Within this basic narrative strain, in turn, palpable gender differences distinguished women's from men's stories. Whereas men and women alike discussed how they had evaluated their economic opportunities and living conditions in Mexico in terms of the welfare of their children, only the women mentioned certain other factors as having influenced their decisions about migration. Chief among these factors was the husband's desire to have the family reunited in the United States. Elvira Méndez resisted demands from Alejandro that she bring the children north before she thought it was safe to do so, as we have seen.[25] Nina Garza, by contrast, recalled how she had acquiesced when her husband declared, after living abroad for a couple years, "I've had it—I want to see my children grow up. Forget it all—shut the doors and let's go. It's now or never." "I felt fine, economically," Garza noted, echoing both Méndez and Soto and explaining how she had been satisfied with what she was earning by selling potted plants; raising corn, pigs, and chickens; and taking care of her home. But because her husband did not drink, treated the family kindly, and genuinely loved the children, she said, she acceded to his wishes. She did not exactly do this *against* her own wishes. Yet still, the meaning of both adjusting to circumstances beyond her control *and* making a principled, independent decision was qualitatively different for her, and for Méndez, than for either of their husbands. The men simply did not speak about conditioning their decisions about migration on the basis of independent actions taken by their wives and did not appear to have done so.[26]

Women's decisions to leave Mexico also seemed more contingent than men's not only on distinctive family or maternal obligations but also on specific kinds of mistreatment from family members. Juanita Castillo told us that her mother had done domestic labor in other homes to provide some support for her but sent her as a child to live with her cousins:

They told me, "I'm going to send you to school; I'm going to buy you clothes; I'm going to bring you here as a *babysitter* [English in original]." But no—that didn't happen there. They took me with my cousins, my aunts and uncles [did], and they put me in school there for one day and after that they didn't send me to school anymore.

Castillo tried to escape this situation by moving to her older sister's home in Mexicali as a young teenager, but her own sister made and broke the same promises about giving her an education and once more took advantage of her vulnerable position: "It was the same thing. . . . She just used me as a *babysitter*" [English in original]. Faced with the choice of staying there or returning to her mother who "had nothing," Castillo then accepted the invitation of a friend to join her on a trek across the border, even though they knew no one in the United States and had no money to bring with them.[27] Rosa Vásquez, in turn, was ostracized by the family and cut off financially by her father when she became pregnant as a teenager. When the Mexican economic downturn of 1979 hit, Vásquez told us, she thus was in a particularly difficult spot and decided that she would have to move north to support herself and her daughter. Even Vásquez and Castillo, however, stopped well short of portraying themselves as helpless victims who had been driven north by events wholly beyond their control. Instead, like the other women and in ways that were perhaps even more compelling given their particularly difficult circumstances, these two individuals confirmed their own abilities to steer an independent and confident course toward a better future.

Another group of men's narratives about the events leading up to decisions to migrate, however, stood out as lacking this expression of individual fortitude that both these women and the men I have discussed conveyed. These other interviews shared a sense that defeated expectations for educational, career, and class advancement had precipitated the crossing—and that these expectations had been slightly but significantly higher to begin with than they were for our other informants. Pedro Ruiz initially told us a fairly typical story of his childhood growing up in the village of Jilotlán, Jalisco, where he worked at a variety of agricultural jobs. He especially remembered a lot of time spent milking cows, getting up at three o'clock every morning "from a very early age" and doing it "all by hand."[28] Ruiz's account began to differ from the others, however, when he mentioned not only finishing secondary school but also enrolling in a *preparatoria,* a high school that can lead to university education, and working on his *bachillerato* degree. But Ruiz's family continued to face tight economic circumstances and so he kept working (by making rolls for vegetarian "hamburgers," a comical thing given his later job with the world's leading meat conglomerate). And the challenge of attending a distant night school after working from the early morning until evening ultimately proved too exhausting. Ruiz explained, with an air of dejection, that he had never finished his higher education and that *because* he had lost the opportunities a more advanced degree would have provided, he had decided to seek better-paying work in the United States.

Like Ruiz, Rafael Mendoza told us about his early life in Mexico in ways that signaled the opportunities he did *not* have as well as the work he had done. Mendoza recalled working as a child with his siblings to help his father pack boxes of fruit in his Michoacán village to be sold in the city of Toluca, closer to Mexico City. "We were a poor family, and we did almost every kind of work . . . whatever it is," Mendoza commented, "because we had no profession."[29] This last bit was a telling addition because it reflected Mendoza's engagement, like Ruiz's, in an attempt to gain specialized job skills through education. Mendoza had attained an unusually high level of education among this group of interviewees, having finished a *preparatoria* program as well as a vocational degree in the social sciences and then having completed two years of study in engineering, although this was not enough to earn him a certification. Yet despite this comparatively impressive record of accomplishment, Mendoza's efforts to translate his studies into a better occupational situation went unrewarded. In Mexico, he commented grimly, an education "is not a guarantee of a good job. . . . It was always the same: things go from good to bad."

These informants, in other words, had had opportunities to gain higher education and initiate careers, and their migrations north resulted when tangible benefits failed to materialize from these chances. They ironically emphasized what they *lacked,* in terms of educational achievements and occupational prospects, more strongly than the other immigrant workers who never had these opportunities in the first place. This tendency came through even more clearly in the comments of Diego Ortega. Here is how Ortega described his youth in Mexico City when, like many of the others, he had worked to help his family maintain itself economically:

> My father is a man *[señor]* who has worked in a thousand things; his profession *[oficio]* is that of . . . someone who makes furniture, fine furniture. But sometimes he didn't have work and he looked for work in other things: ironworking, plumbing—he did mechanical jobs . . . whatever opportunities came to him. He even began doing engineering. He worked a lot with engineers and sometimes he devoted himself to making plans, and in Mexico City he eventually made the plan for the first electronic station. And so . . . our situation, my father's situation, wasn't very stable. . . . My mother . . . started her own small business. Since she saw that my dad was struggling to find work, she started helping him. Although he didn't want that, she . . . started to make *dulce de guayaba* . . . and I went and sold them in the school.[30]

This story resembles others we have considered in the way it describes how the family used whatever means were at its disposal to produce a viable income, with help from the children. Yet Ortega distinctly wanted us to get the impression that his father had a social status above that of a common laborer, as a *señor* with an *oficio*, someone who had accomplished things of historical significance even though he appeared to lack formal qualifications. These comments only intensified the sense that somehow the family was not living up to its potential when Ortega then drew our attention to his own—foiled—striving to gain an advanced education in Mexico. He had completed secondary school, he said, but his application to complete a *bachillerato* was rejected, and he wound up in a vocational open school. He described the open school as being "like night school" in the United States and said that he was very dissatisfied with the educational opportunities offered there and disapproved of his classmates' lack of seriousness. Although he had hoped to learn computer skills, his family's means did not permit this, and so he settled, unhappily, for studying electronics and eventually left that program to help out in his father's home-based furniture manufactory. At that point, he grudgingly decided that searching for new opportunities in the United States was the best path to pursue.

Having traced the outlines of these three main narrative frames about individuality and the decision to migrate to the United States, I want to pause now and note that all these narrative currents gave expression to social and cultural forces that played into their individual reflections and choices. A paramount feature of these stories was that the decision to leave Mexico and preparations for the trip took place in a familial or kinship context. We have seen how this was explicitly the case for women whose husbands were already in the United States or wanted to go there, like Esperanza Soto and Elvira Méndez, or who faced pressing financial responsibilities for parents or children in Mexico, like Ramona Díaz and Rosa Vásquez. Yet even for the men who emphasized their individual daring and capacities for self-determination, it was clear that the option to move north of the border existed, in part, only because family networks were there to collect the cash for the person's crossing, secure the services of *coyotes,* and produce job and housing opportunities on the other side. For example, Isidro Gómez said that his whole family, on both sides of the border, had joined together to pool their funds and arrange his passage.[31] Beyond furnishing such practical means to make transborder crossings viable for individuals who were financially strapped and lacked experience with such treks, circles of family and friends often served as seedbeds where the idea of making a better life for oneself and one's own in the United States germinated. Said Gómez, for instance: "A lot of people in my family have emigrated *[Mi familia ha sido muy emigrante].* There are a lot of us in the family—uncles, cousins—who will really tell you about it. And that's how the idea grows that life is a little easier here, nicer."[32] Once they had made it to the other side, in turn, the people we interviewed often were able to rely on their relatives to smooth their transitions and provide a sense of continuity with their earlier lives in Mexico. About the town of Madera, California, where all four of his siblings had moved, where there was a hometown association for people from his village, and where he visited regularly, Ignacio Ramos said simply: "It's Oaxaca."[33]

Pedro Ruiz, like others with whom we spoke, also described how a broader, more diffuse cultural sense of mobility toward the United States helped propel his own decision: "At that time, yes, there was a lot of talk about it, and a lot of people were coming and going back. They talked about how over here you could earn a lot of money, and that life was different; and I wanted to come and find out, to see if I could get ahead, to help my family economically. And that's when I decided to come." Multiple people we interviewed used the term *ilusión*, or "dream" (but not in the pejorative sense of a false hope that the word *illusion* in English signifies) to characterize how they had anticipated acquiring the means for a better life in Mexico through work abroad. For Gloria and Pedro Ruiz, as well as for Isidro Gómez and Esperanza Soto, this *ilusión* had been to earn and save enough money to buy a house in Mexico in a housing economy of high and rising rents. Alejandro Méndez had hoped to compile enough capital to start a small business; Héctor Fernández wanted to invest in livestock. So the stories we heard about the precipitants of migration commonly evoked the sense that the air was full of news about the potential benefits of leaving, at least temporarily, for the United States and thus that these people saw themselves, to a degree, as part of a general cultural movement transcending their personal trials, disappointments, and ambitions.

Sometimes, the bleaker aspects of economic crisis poked through this more optimistic talk about making "dreams" come true. Ramona Díaz, for instance, spoke of how although her relatives had always worked in the sugarcane and banana plantations in Nayarit, "Now most of them have left those jobs, because in those villages there aren't enough [jobs for people] to live, and they always try to leave to look for something better." Rosa Vásquez likewise recalled a draining away of people and resources from the small village of Mascota in Jalisco where she had grown up, following the deterioration of the Mexican economy in the late 1970s. Francisco González spoke with audible bitterness about moving to the United States because of the 1980s economic collapse, which occurred just as he was entering his twenties:

Due to the crisis there in Mexico, you saw the way people dressed, the way they ate—it got really hard to earn your bread there in Mexico, your daily bread. . . . When I had the opportunity to come to the other side, then—then I gave it a try. . . . I didn't want to stay here. But because of necessity, the economic crisis that happened in Mexico, well, that makes us have to be here more years. . . . Here you'll notice people of all kinds: lawyers, doctors, teachers—we all come here out of the same necessity. If we weren't in need, we would be there. If they paid me the equivalent of four, five dollars an hour, I'd be in Mexico, I wouldn't be here. But there aren't those luxuries: in Mexico there aren't enough sources of work to survive.[34]

González was the only person we interviewed who described himself so bluntly and unequivocally as having been forced into abandoning Mexico because of sheer "necessity." Yet while this sense of having his personal fate driven by external factors beyond his control was much more extreme than we heard in the other interviews, the others, too, acknowledged various dimensions of an encompassing social context for their decisions about migration, whether economic, cultural, or familial.

Nevertheless, the clear accent in all the other workers' stories aside from that of González was on the distinctly individual elements of their roads toward cross-border migration, and more specifically on the realization or failure of a class- and gender-inflected process of self-determination. Having elaborated these various narrative permutations, I conclude this chapter by addressing the following questions: What do these constructions in hindsight of how the decision to leave Mexico came about, and how it expressed and actualized a person's identity as a certain kind of individual, suggest about the political dispositions of these workers with regard to neoliberalism today? How do these narratives theorize the structure of neoliberalism; and in doing so, how do they bolster and/or undermine the hegemonic operations by which neoliberalism achieves the status of something taken for granted or even legitimate and desirable for masses of immigrant workers in the contemporary United States? Finally, what reciprocally critical alliances of these narrators with other social groups and with theorists of the neoliberal turn would catalyze a politically innovative "criticism of common sense"?

Narrating Neoliberalism in the Aftermath of Immigration

Empirical accounts of neoliberalism's objectives, mechanisms, and consequences often have a tone that suggests an inexorable logic of domination. This is especially so when the narrative of neoliberalism focuses on watershed moments in the economic policies of nation-states. Telling the story of neoliberalism's rise in Mexico in this way, for example, usually means emphasizing themes like these: from 1970 to 1982, Mexico's foreign debt skyrocketed from $3.2 billion to over $100 billion, and in 1982, with its first major devaluation of the peso, Mexico became the first Latin American debt-burdened country to declare a moratorium on debt-servicing payments. Neoliberal reforms involved shifting from "import substitution industrialization (ISI)" to "an export-oriented industrialization (EOI) strategy promoted by opening the economy to foreign trade, massive withdrawal of public subsidies in most sectors of the economy, privatization of formerly state-owned enterprises, and, not least, a policy of controlling wages downward to attract new waves of foreign investment (partly to offset the effects of previously flown domestic capital)" (Otero 1996, 7). Other key steps included passage of a 1989 law that allowed 100 percent foreign ownership in the majority of economic enterprises; the 1991 amendment of Article 27 of the Mexican Constitution, effectively ending the revolutionary program of land redistribution through the system of *ejidos* and *comunidades agrarias* by allowing the privatization of these lands; and the passage of the North American Free Trade Agreement (NAFTA), followed shortly by another peso devaluation in 1994 (Otero 1996, 7–8; Bartra 2004, 23).[35] Prioritizing the accumulation of foreign investor capital while slashing government social spending meant a widespread reduction in economic chances and a hardening of the conditions of daily life for the great majority of Mexicans.

Our interviews certainly registered such rising hardships for poor and working-class Mexicans from multiple regions of the country. Nevertheless, as we have seen, the people with whom we spoke stressed their individual capacities to mull things over by themselves, to discuss options with others, to make independent decisions about their futures, and to act on them with determination and a sense of purpose. Their narratives about living through the advent of neoliberalism involved intensifying their efforts to take care of themselves and their own, and then, when this proved more difficult than they could manage, leaving the country to seek more lucrative jobs elsewhere. For the most part, however, and despite the key variations in emphasis and content that I have noted regarding gender-related factors or a person's possible sense of disappointed expectations, these were not narratives of being forcibly subjected to intolerable conditions that drove them onto the migrant trail.

At the same time, neither were they narratives that made much room at all for politically contesting the new circumstances wrought by neoliberalism through organized, collective action. This is all the more noteworthy because an increasingly opportune climate for such

political action arose in Mexico during the years when our interviewees were making their decisions about migration. Although these
individuals later briefly stepped to the forefront of immigrant workers
organizing for rank-and-file democracy in the United States through
their involvement with Teamsters for a Democratic Union, as I discuss
in chapter 5, in Mexico they had not been active in the efforts that
emerged in the 1970s and 1980s to foster union democracy and more
autonomy from the PRI and that spawned alternative labor organizations to the Labor Congress and the Confederación de Trabajadores
de México (Workers' Confederation of Mexico), which were so thoroughly integrated into the corporatist state (Middlebrook 1995, 256–
66; Cook 1996, 15–16). They had not participated in the efflorescence
of popular, social movement politics that occurred in the late 1970s
and early 1980s through the *coordinadoras,* organizations autonomous
from party control that originated among peasants and small farmers
as well as the urban poor (Fox 1994; Haber 1994; Cook 1996, 17).
Very few were indigenous persons, and those who were had not been
involved in the upsurge of "ethnically based rural organizing" that by
the early 1990s had become what Jonathan Fox calls "the most important kind of rural organization" (1994, 267–68) prior to the rise of the
Zapatista movement in Chiapas (Rubin 1997; Snyder 2001). Finally,
although the women whose stories are discussed earlier in this chapter all later became vital participants in the rank-and-file movement at
Tyson/IBP, they did not participate in the new social movements in
Mexico even though women played a pivotal role in the emergence
of such activism as older, corporatist systems for regulating popular
political action broke down (Stephen 1996).

Instead, the people we interviewed developed relatively more private strategies for dealing with their changing circumstances before
crossing the border to seek work and/or to rejoin family members.
Thus, it might seem appropriate to characterize them as neoliberal
subjects, in the ways conceptualized by Brown or Feher, and to see
them as having been constituted as such through their individually
and family-oriented adjustments to the economic crisis. Perhaps one
might read the avid determination that our informants associated with
their resolutions to seek better fortunes for themselves and their families, and the tremendous lengths they would go to in order to do so,
as evidence that they were at least experimenting with the notion of

prioritizing "self-care" as their primary ethical index. Maybe they even thereby embraced an idea of the self as human capital that they alone could make appreciate in value and that increasingly made migration seem the obvious path toward appreciation as economic crisis in Mexico deepened and personal finances flagged.

Yet this interpretive framework binds the reading of the interviews too tightly and ignores the ways that these narratives schematized alternative subject formations to the rubric of self-enclosed, rationally calculating personhood. That is, the variations among the three main narrative frames index politically consequential differences in the types and degrees of agency they envisioned. Political activists in Mexico these people were not; and their narratives of individual self-determination through work and migration certainly could have been conducive to their development as neoliberal subjects according to the formulas theorists have offered. Indeed, one group of narrators did veer in this direction as they spoke about their early lives before coming to the United States. For Diego Ortega, Pedro Ruiz, and Rafael Mendoza, one perhaps could say that the inability to elevate their net worth as human capital through education comprised the main frustration that set them on the migrant trail. However, even these individuals did not fit all that well the mold laid out by Feher. Although they migrated as a compensatory response to being blocked from appreciating the value of their human capital, they did not seem to expect that going to the United States would newly enable them to succeed as self-investors. (Much less did they bear out Feher's thesis about the possibility of reconstituting neoliberal subjectivity from within to counter the power of capital, since Ortega and Ruiz ultimately sought to undermine the rank-and-file movement in collusion with the company and Mendoza did not even participate in the strike.)

Meanwhile, the other two narrative frames carried ethical orientations that failed to coincide with the specific schema of accumulating the self's value as a "portfolio" of marketable characteristics (in Feher's evocative terms), despite their prioritization of the basic concern for meeting family and individual economic needs. Not only that, both were integrally related to the ways the workers narrated how their union operated and what it stood for in its manifest challenge to neoliberal corporate power. I explore this discourse about opposition through the rank-and-file movement in detail in chapter 5. Let me preview it here by noting, first, that the rhetoric of masculine self-reliance, self-assertion, and moral autonomy regarding previous decisions in Mexico, exemplified by Alejandro Méndez, Flaco Pereyra, and Isidro Gómez, proved distinctly amenable to being torqued in the direction of collective, confrontational struggle. As we shall see, the movement explicitly viewed group solidarity and militancy as further steps beyond, and commitments arising organically from, much lower-level moments of individual courage to stick up for oneself or for a fellow worker in the face of mistreatment from specific company officials. Second, the union's public discourse complemented its gestures toward manly self-determination with references to sisterly mutuality along with a vision of the union striving both *as* a family and *for* workers' families. Thus, what might appear at first glance to be Elvira Méndez's and Esperanza Soto's valorization of an apolitical and privatizing resolve to protecting one's own when economic times in Mexico got very tough, and hence a prelude to a feminine-gendered version of the ethical preoccupation of self-care, actually helped furnish another key ingredient in the union's recipe for involving and radicalizing workers.

Of course, even as a certain contingent of theorists has advanced the idea that subject formations are becoming ever-more narrowly constrained and tied up with market rationality in the neoliberal age, others have taken a contrasting tack and have investigated the transnational or transborder processes by which migrant populations come to acquire new identities and ways of life. Instead of homogenization or standardization, hybridization and multiplicity become the watchwords of such analyses. Thus, critical ethnographers have shown how cross-border migrants responding to the social disruptions wrought by neoliberal changes often live "transborder lives" in the sense of having cultural identities, kinship ties, financial networks, labor practices, or habits of geographic movement that keep them from conforming to any linear, teleological process of permanent resettlement and national reacculturation.[36] Rather, their actions and involvements situate them simultaneously in geographically distant local spaces. The further claim or implication is often that by eroding the presumed solidity of national spatial and cultural boundaries via their practices of everyday life, "transmigrants" *politically* challenge the neoimperialist presuppositions for the projection of neoliberal power (especially the notion of a racial hierarchy of culturally distinct nation-states with the United States at the pinnacle).

The stories about the precipitants of cross-border movement told to us by the Tyson/IBP workers do not particularly resonate with this model of subjectivity under neoliberal conditions either. In point of fact, the people we interviewed had followed a more traditional path of immigration to the United States than many other migrant workers do. Granted, most said that they still felt either essentially "Mexican" in their national identity or both U.S. American and Mexican. Many wistfully told us of the aspects of daily life in Mexico that they sorely missed, like greater respect by children for elders, a more active outdoor culture, or even the feel of the rain and the smell of the air in the places from which they had come. But especially following their legalization in the late 1980s through the Immigration Reform and Control Act, these individuals had made progressively fewer trips to Mexico, sent remittances more sporadically and often stopped sending them at all, and fell out of touch with people in Mexico with whom they had been close. One interviewee, Ignacio Ramos, did speak about a hometown association through which residents of his village of origin in Oaxaca solicited funds for municipal improvements from fellow villagers working in Madera, California, where he had previously lived; but he stressed that after coming to Washington State, he had entirely lost contact with this group.

Yet despite the absence of a robustly transborder existence among these workers, their narratives about life in Mexico still open up discursive space for conceiving of transnational political alliances that would challenge neoliberal capitalist power in more direct ways than novel constructions of transmigrant identity as such can accomplish. By construing the social terrain in Mexico where they had made their decisions about migrating as a space that allowed for their own expressions of individual agency, they created room in their broader discourse of immigrant worker empowerment for building lines of affiliation with political activists in Mexico. They did so even though they had not been politically engaged themselves in their country of origin. They also did it, we should note, in the face of a U.S.-centric discourse of "American exceptionalism" (often taken up, historically, by organized labor) proposing that especially in contrast to Latin American nation-states where corruption, cooptation, and authoritarianism fester, the United States is uniquely governed by the rule of law and enabling of active, competent democratic citizenship. Hence, yet again, the apparently strange conjunction between the workers' tellings of their prior histories in Mexico and their later acts of political assertion turns out to make more sense upon further consideration. The union made several intriguing moves to form alliances with groups that were engaged in energetic programs of transnational organizing. In the 2003 Immigrant Workers Freedom Ride, Local 556 collaborated with Piñeros y Campesinos Unidos del Noroeste (United Northwest Tree Planters and Farm Workers), which, as Lynn Stephen (2007) discusses, conducts its organizing not only in the farm territory of western Oregon but also in its members' hometowns in Oaxaca, Mexico. The Local also worked with a Portland- and Los Angeles–based group called Enlace that seeks to coordinate union strategies simultaneously in the United States and Mexico. The point is that these efforts had a discursive basis in the workers' narratives about exerting personal agency in response to ascendant neoliberalism in Mexico even though the narrators did not claim an activist past for themselves that would have given them specific, concrete skills for forming such alliances.

In sum, the immigrant workers we spoke with theorized the neoliberal condition, through their narratives about life before leaving Mexico, as open to transnational organizing even by subjects who were not identifiably transmigrants. They also conceptualized neoliberalism as the ground of various forms of personal agency that did not conform to any consolidated type of the neoliberal subject and that did not depend on affirming such a subject formation in order to wage opposition against a flagship neoliberal company. By narrating neoliberal power in these ways, then, our informants undercut the hegemony of neoliberalism in three distinct ways. First, they undermined the notion that neoliberal society admits of only a uniform brand of agency that demands embracing the notion of the self as human capital or an exclusivist ethos of self-care. Second, they refuted a defeatist version of neoliberal common sense that assumes that neoliberalism allows no agency at all to migrant workers but simply ensnares them in irresistible domination. Third, through the genealogical connection between their narratives of life in Mexico and their stories of radical democratic union activism in the United States, they also suggested a critical perspective on the idea that neoliberal transformations cannot be frontally opposed but only resisted indirectly or allusively through identity-making practices of everyday life. Or to put it in the language I used in the preceding chapter, the workers' comments had these contestative effects of narrativity: they theoretically construed the world of neoliberalism in Mexico in creative ways that solicited their innovative forms of action north of the border.

One last aspect of our interviewees' stories of their prior experiences in Mexico deserves consideration before we examine in the next chapter their accounts of crossing the border: the curious way that the stories about deciding to leave Mexico took on common narrative shapes even though their tellers came from such disparate locations within that country. The common narrative frames transcended and blurred differences of culture and geographic origin within Mexico. From their temporally and spatially removed position in an immigrant, working-class community in the United States, these individuals described a form of power that operated on an international and transnational level, depressing the fortunes for working-class Mexicans as a general population while opportunities north of the U.S. border gained attraction. By suggesting that a general fate enveloped the majority of Mexicans who did not possess enough capital to make the arrival of neoliberalism a boon, the narratives thus gestured toward a process of *racialization* that began in Mexico and assumed more determinate dimensions north of the border. The chapters ahead discuss this racializing dynamic, the biopolitical mechanisms it entailed, and the ways the workers' narratives both enabled and countered them in significant detail. Anchored in the operations of state, business, and legal institutions that functioned intensively within the United States, these racial power forms only appeared in their bare outlines in the portions of the interviews discussed in this chapter. In the coalescence of the main narrative frames about hardship in and departure from Mexico, however, we can at least subtly detect the border-overtaking processes that systematically render "Mexicans" a racially defined group with life prospects differentiating it from other groups. And we can anticipate how composing narratives about "the struggle" that could speak to these shared subjections to power, rather than being confined by regional or even national particularisms, would become both necessary and possible for the workers of Local 556.

3. Stories of Fate and Agency in the Zone of Illegality

IN CONTEMPORARY AMERICA, the politics of border control relies centrally on a politics of the body. Efforts to assert U.S. "sovereignty" by impeding and regulating the movement of undocumented immigrants northward from Mexico commonly evoke anxiety over the vulnerable body of the nation, whose corporeal boundaries are imagined as perpetually in danger of violation by immigrants. The "alien invasion" threatens to mainline drugs into the nation's veins, narcotizing Americans into such a stupor that they no longer care about freedom or the rule of law (Goldsborough 2006; Grassroots On Fire 2006). Significantly, in a special report by Lou Dobbs on a CNN reality show about Homeland Security agents, the drugs are smuggled into America by being hidden inside children's toys (CNN 2009). This disturbing image encodes a related fear: that a longer-term peril to the racially white character of the national corpus comes from the supposed influx of superabundantly fertile dark bodies from Latin America whose offspring will transform the country's racial demographics (Chavez 2008; Roberts 1996). Reports on rising pollution in the border region, in turn, complement these aspects of immigrant demonology in public discourse. They update historically entrenched concerns that Mexicans, riddled with diseases and lacking "an essential aversion to their own wastes," are choking off the life-support system for the American nation by fouling its environment as they inundate the borderlands (Hill 2006, 791).

Yet the long push for immigration control via the militarization of the U.S.–Mexico border not only has sought to refortify the fantasized boundaries of the U.S. national body—it also has mobilized a systematic array of techniques for controlling, directing, and influencing the safety and vigor of living, in-the-flesh immigrant bodies. That, at any rate, was the vision of power in the borderlands and other spaces of illegality within the United States that emerged from our interviews, as the people with whom we spoke moved on from describing their early lives in Mexico and told us about making their clandestine passages into this country. Toward the end of chapter 2, I suggested that insofar as a few generally shared narratives about deciding to come to the United States coalesced in the interviews, rather than a wider palette of culturally distinctive tellings reflecting our informants' varied places of origin, this signaled the beginnings of a process by which Mexicans became racially homogenized through cross-border migration. In this chapter, I delve into these people's narratives about their trials in venturing across the border and living without documents inside the United States. These narratives comprise a "theory in the flesh" regarding their subjection to a biopolitical regime of racial power that increasingly unfolded in these contexts. This power system not only produced certain regular conditions of bodily and psychological hazard for undocumented immigrants, it also yielded benefits for the physiological and mental well-being of the more racially privileged nonimmigrant populace, above all from the labor market segmentation and food production norms in the United States that border-control policies facilitate.

In considering these records of immigrant workers' common sense, I pay close attention to the shared conceptions of power they encode. I then provoke a reverberation between such congealments of narrative and critical theory, in this case Foucault's construction of the contrasting power modes of discipline and biopolitics. If, as I argued in chapter 2, the workers' narratives about their time in Mexico before coming to the United States both reinforced and contested the hegemony of neoliberalism, their stories about navigating the illegal zone at once fostered and challenged a more institutionally articulated and spatially specific mode of neoliberal power based in the biopolitics of border control. Thus, I chart the ambivalent relation of these immigrant worker narratives to the biopolitical formation in part by inviting them to invigorate the theoretical project of conceptualizing what biopolitics is and how it operates today. The novel theory of biopolitics that results then develops progressively in the chapters ahead.

Two basic narrative tendencies structured these portions of our interviewees' stories. On the one hand, these immigrant workers described existing in the illegal realm as a condition of utter helplessness and subjection to whims of fate that made multiple corporeal indignities and even mortal dangers loom before their eyes. To live in this domain was to yearn for deliverance from some higher power— "God" or "luck," as they frequently put it—while lacking any practical ability to determine their fortunes for themselves. It was also to feel forcibly confined to certain spaces and to a very limited scope of daily activities by a kind of stubbornly inscrutable coercion. Various aspects of these stories will sound familiar to anyone who has read other accounts of undocumented journeys across the U.S.–Mexico border in recent decades. Other authors have written about the trials of mothers who get separated from their children during the passage, the stress of waiting in what are euphemistically called "safe" houses for a relative to bring payment for the crossing, the predatory actions of *coyotes*, and "the sullying nature of border crossings" that comes from hiding in landfills or other filthy places along the way (Mahler 1995, 62–69; Coutin 2000, 57). Some writers have also described the shocking, life-threatening dangers on these trips, which were not uncommon problems on illegal border crossings even in the years before large-scale urban deployments of border security forces shunted migrant traffic into the Arizona desert (Mahler 1995, 71–72; Urrea 2005). The analysis in this chapter echoes these prior accounts but also asks more specifically what *stories about power* these immigrant workers were telling when they narrated such experiences. To a great extent, these individuals described themselves as being buffeted by unpredictable and arbitrary exertions of force that they had no choice but to try to endure.

On the other hand, the people we interviewed also expressed, more subtly but still detectably, the desire to control their own destinies in the process of migrating north and living everyday life without legal documents. They even conveyed a palpable sense of satisfaction when they succeeded in doing so in small but significant ways. This alternative account of power could be heard when our informants described how they had protested against *coyotes* who tried to abuse them and when they noted how they had struggled to master their own internal weaknesses and to withstand pain and hardship on the border passage. It was also audible when our informants told of employing various skills to stay concealed, to deceive those who might harm them, or to "pass" as ordinary U.S. Americans directly under the gaze of immigration officials. Again, we find resonances here with prior writings that bring to light Latin American immigrants' desires not only to escape death and misfortune but also to actualize some kind of personal agency or freedom in the very process of crossing illegally (Hondagneu-Sotelo 1994; Mahler 1995, 82). The difference, once more, is in my effort to distinguish the precise ways that the individuals we interviewed were speaking about power in the zone of illegality and to consider the implications of these narratives, both in this chapter and later in the book, for the hegemony of dominant political and economic institutions.

To say that hegemony depends, in some sense, on these narratives is to unearth the often-ignored connection that makes the *political* situation of the racially dominant nonimmigrant population partly contingent on the political agency of immigrant workers. The form of hegemony at issue here, in turn, is one that energizes and legitimizes a link on a *metabolic* level between these racially differentiated populations.[1] While our informants most directly described what it felt like and what it meant to them to be governed by the current regime of biopolitics, they also indirectly evoked the consequences of this power formation for more privileged population groups. For Foucault, biopolitics targets populations, while disciplinary power addresses itself to individuals. Biopolitics manages the levels of risks to people's life and vitality and applies a differentiating logic that exposes certain racially defined groups to higher risks of injury and death so that racially advantaged populations can thrive (Foucault 2003, 255–56; 1990, 139–44). Our interviewees' stories about traveling through and surviving within the domains of illegality graphically express the consummate effectiveness with which this mode of power has been applied to immigrants in our time. Although it lacks the explicitly eugenicist rhetoric that policy stakeholders employed a century ago to justify earlier schemas of biopolitics regarding immigrants, the current *implicitly* biopolitical regime makes physical and emotional traumas proliferate among members of the target population. And precisely this heightened vulnerability of Mexican immigrants to death and injury reaps benefits, metabolically speaking, for white native-born U.S. Americans. The racial vigor of the latter group may not be a matter of overt concern for state officials and interest groups, who argue for border militarization based on imperatives of national security, cultural integrity, and/or economic necessity. But white society's psychophysiological strength still is actively promoted by immigrant-policing activities that

allow nonimmigrants to scorn dirty and dangerous jobs with no benefits in favor of employment that carries health insurance coverage and
poses little risk of job-related injury and that, meanwhile, bring them
the nutritional value of a food economy premised on immigrant labor.

The narratives that emerged from the interviews bolstered this
power formation with the force of hegemony in two distinct ways.
Inasmuch as our interviewees portrayed the zone of illegality as a
place where immigrants were bereft of any ability to predict or alter
the whims of fate, they made the power that endangered them seem
impossible to resist. They thereby gave biopolitics a foothold in common sense. The submersion of individuality and heightened jeopardy of misfortune that was their lot became something they took for
granted, an inevitability to which they simply had to adjust. At the
same time, even when the workers departed from this narrative frame
and stressed their effective methods of hiding, passing, and strengthening themselves internally, they still, in a sense, reinforced the biopolitical apparatus. That is because their techniques to ensure their
own survival and successful entry into the United States, viewed in
terms of the macro-level effects of these micro-level practices, helped
routinize the stream of low-wage labor into the industries that produce
racial differentiation even as they produce apples, asparagus, and hamburger. Not only that: these practices, precisely because they worked,
gave the U.S. state more of a pretext to legitimize its deployments of
police and military power geared toward securing the "homeland."[2]
Or, to express it in Foucault's language, we might say that in the curious absence of an intensive, institutionalized regime of disciplinary
power aimed at forging immigrant subjects with "practiced bodies"
and self-regulating habits (about which I shall have more to say), these
workers took it upon themselves to develop microtechniques of the
self through their own informal networks.[3] These techniques ended
up promoting the ends of social production and political stability just
as efficiently and did so all the more effectively inasmuch as our immigrant narrators seemed personally invested in them as strategies of
individual agency that made unbearable conditions relatively tolerable.

Yet the part of the story underscoring our informants' self-
determining agency also mitigated the dour political implications of
the dominant theme regarding workers' utter helplessness in the face
of blind fate, which promised more certain submission in the face of

biopolitics. As I argued in chapter 1, the politics of narrative emerge more vividly when analysts pay attention to the complicated *memories of desire* that ordinary people's stories harbor, searching for the antagonisms and continuities among these various desires. The moments when our interviewees disclosed to us their tactics of self-protection and self-control thus enacted breaks in the chain of desire. They interrupted desires for deliverance from situations of peril, pain, and suffering borne in confused resignation. These moments interfered with the logic of victimhood that the narrative's more vigorous current implied, destabilizing the solid ground in common sense that the story otherwise gave to the uses of immigrants by capital and the state. As we see in subsequent chapters, these features of the workers' accounts also opened a path to more aggressive and collective challenges to state and corporate interests in the context of their union movement.[4]

Even apart from this genealogical link to narratives about worker solidarity, however, our informants' stories of the illegal zone evoke an alternative politics of justice for immigrants. Such a distinctive political approach would strenuously resist pragmatic efforts to segregate workers' rights from rights related to the immigration process (perhaps in a new legalization program that might emerge from Congress) or to enhance the rights of current illegal residents at the expense of increasing still more the already dismal risk of death and other traumas for those who will come across clandestinely in the near future. The politics of justice for immigrants suggested by these stories, furthermore, would deploy organizing strategies that grapple with the biopolitical implications of immigrant workers' bodily practices and narrative acts. These are precisely those aspects of the larger biopolitical formation that our storytellers theorized in the language of common sense.

Border Desires: Deliverance, Agency, and the Body in Stories of the Crossing

Clandestine travels across the U.S.–Mexico border, our informants suggested, involved the forced insertion of the migrant's body into bizarrely unfamiliar spaces and situations that gravely imperiled its safety and integrity while at the same time raising the prospect that the individual could use the body's malleable surfaces to express subtle kinds of agency. Of course, the most common story about the fate of the migrant's body in this illegal zone concerned the need to keep the body hidden from detection by the authorities. Here is Nina Garza, telling us how she and her family made their passage without being seen, while other mothers were not so fortunate, when the Border Patrol trained its searchlights on the area near Tijuana where these migrants were trying to make their way into the United States:

There was a place, like a valley. . . . It was all burnt—as if they had burned it on purpose so that the people couldn't hide there. But it was late there, it was getting dark, and more people were going in front of us: with little children in their arms. . . . And I was praying to God, praying to Saint Martin de Porres: "Cover us, dear Saint Martin, cover us with your cape." . . . Then *la migra* appeared, and me praying—my children too and my husband. . . . "For sure, now," we said, "they've caught us." . . . And a helicopter came, up in the sky, and came down on the side where the ladies with children were going. And they say: "Stop. Stop right there." . . . Thank God, they didn't see us in that little place, where we were hiding. That's why I say that God really does exist.[5]

As Garza described the eerie burnt-out landscape, her frantic prayers, and the imperious voices commanding the parents carrying small children to halt in their tracks, she clearly suggested that what happened in this place was well beyond anyone's ability to predict and that only divine benevolence could have ensured the family's safe crossing. When intervention came from above, it was either going to be *el Señor* [the Lord] or *la migra;* but either way, the migrants themselves were helpless supplicants down below. The only self-determining capacity Garza herself seemed to have in this situation of extremity came from the power of prayer (and this could be seen, sympathetically, as an emboldening albeit ambiguous form of agency rather than an utter disavowal of personal strength).[6] But the picture that emerges most starkly from her account is that of bodies running for cover as searchlights from the darkening skies light up the blackened ground, bodies caught in the glare and rendered immobile, and the even more exposed and defenseless bodies of little children.

Esperanza Soto provided a parallel account of how her body seemed at the mercy of random events, and of agents far more powerful than she, during her cross-border trek. Soto alluded to experiences of disorientation with excruciating corporeal and psychological dimensions alike. Somewhere near Tijuana, Soto told us, in the darkness, the *coyote* took her, her husband, and the others in their group out to a beach:

We got to the water's edge. Then my husband said to him: "Are we going to cross through the water?" He told him, "No, no, no," he says, "it's just a few puddles, it's not much." . . . So we went on. Then we started going into the water, and we go further in and further in, and when I felt the water reach all the way up to here [points to her chest], I said: "No, I can't walk anymore." . . . [But] we went on that way for about an hour and a half. . . . We got out of the water but from there on we started going on in nothing but mud. . . . And when we got out, we came to a place that was like a little town, and I suppose it was on this side [in the United States]. At that point I didn't even know where I was, because I had already . . . reached the limit of what I could bear. . . . I thought we had gotten out, but still no. We had to walk for another hour. And once again it was through pure mud.[7]

The image Soto painted of wading through the deepening water and trudging through thick mud in the middle of the night, led by *polleros* who obviously had lied to them, grimly encapsulated the situation to which she and many others attested: literally having no idea what to expect next, never really knowing where they were, and not even being able to gauge the severity of the dangers at hand. Here the body's *movement* across the border ironically lands it in a predicament of *immobility:* mired in mud. And the irony of Soto's spatial disorientation is heightened inasmuch as popular rhetoric about "controlling our borders" naïvely presumes the existence of a stable, clearly perceptible border where immigrant bodies determinedly shift from one exclusive space into another. Other episodes in Soto's migration saga underscore these dynamics, such as her recollection of hurtling down a California freeway in a van crammed with the bodies of other illegal migrants:

We got in and he was carrying about fifteen people in that van. It was hot, hot. . . . It was summertime. And from there we drove for a little while and more people kept getting in. I think we stuffed around fifty people in that van. We were going along with some on top of the others, and in there nobody could talk, nobody could say anything. You had to be totally quiet. . . . I was also lying down—all of us were like that. . . . And on this side, on this side of my body here [points], a part of the van was touching me that was getting very hot. . . . I'm guessing it was, like, part of a wheel, because it was giving off extreme heat. It gave me a blister, but what could we say? Nothing. And this young guy was driving, but I really think we had to have been going eighty or ninety miles an hour . . . way too fast.

Released, at last, from the van, the couple were taken into an abandoned and empty house near Los Angeles where they spent almost
three days with nothing to eat or drink, seated on the bare floor with
a large number of other people. ("It stank, from all the people who
were in there.") There they awaited the arrival of the person who was
supposed to pay for their journey; and, Soto emphasized, they were
not permitted to go outside or even to open a window until this person arrived.[8] Deprivation of nourishment, then, along with repeated
immersion in repugnant situations of much-too-close contact with
many other bodies, complemented the general sense of bodily confinement, immobilization, and disorientation in Soto's account.

A different, sexualized kind of intrusion on the body—but also a
chance for the migrant to deploy her body tactically to accomplish her
own ends—figured in our interview with Elvira Méndez. Having
crossed the border successfully, albeit with great anxiety because of
her *coyote's* insistence that he take her children across separately from
her, Méndez found herself packed into a station wagon with her kids
and their guides:

They put us in there: my oldest daughter and me in the front, right, with the
driver, and the three other children in the back, and another man in the
back. . . . But at night, my oldest daughter told me: "Mom, this man is grabbing
my leg." And he was smoking marijuana. It frightened me. . . . I couldn't tell
him, "Stop. Let me out." And I couldn't say anything because I thought if I
said something to him maybe he would take us to a different place. . . . [But]
at a gas station where we stopped I told her: "Get out, my daughter." I sat down
myself in the middle—excuse this word, I'm going to say a bad word—I sat
down there [and said]: "OK, you motherfucker, now you just go ahead and
grab *my* leg!" . . . No way they were going to touch me, me who's already an old
lady. And from then on things were calm.[9]

As Méndez recounted the hardships of her journey north, she plainly
wanted us to see that she had endured extreme bodily indignities
comingled with, and often directly brought on by, panic over her
daughters' vulnerable bodies. At times she needed badly to urinate but
was unable to do so and could scarcely walk because of the pain.
"Dying of thirst" and desperately hungry while hiding in an apartment, Méndez refused the coffee, water, and hamburgers that she was
offered because of "the fear that they might put something in a drink
to put me to sleep because they wanted to violate my daughters." Nor

did she let herself fall asleep, for the same reason. Yet at the same time, Méndez just as obviously hoped we would grasp that she had *put herself* through this hell quite intentionally. She had actively renounced sleep, food, drink, and the relief of urination, disciplining her own body to avert any potential calamities. She made it known, too, that when things got rough, she could rely on her own wherewithal to change the course of events by interposing her "old lady" body in between her daughter and the *coyote* with the wandering hands. (Méndez's self-deprecating diffidence here, along with her demure apology for using crude language, made the bold self-assertiveness of this moment even more pronounced.)

Méndez's story manifested a tension between conflicting *memories of desire:* between the tacit desires reflected in descriptions of personal, embodied agency like this and the more explicit longings to be delivered by transcendent forces from the perils, confusions, and corporeal indignities of cross-border journeys. Locating the friction that expressions of agency create within Méndez's remarks pulls into view similar elements in the other workers' stories. Esperanza Soto, for instance, mentioned several small but crucial ways that she and her husband had manipulated their clothing to maximize the chances that their border-crossing attempts would succeed, buying sturdy work boots and sewing a check inside the collar of her husband's shirt. And somewhat like Elvira Méndez, they had intervened forcibly to scold and shame *coyotes* who were cruelly disregarding their clients' bodily needs and integrity, even after initially being told to stay silent or at least feeling that they "couldn't say anything." Soto told us how they had "demanded" that the van driver slow down and stop "putting in danger the lives of all [the] passengers." Likewise, she said indignantly, she had threatened to "report" the *coyotes* in charge of the safe house because of the "injustice" of the way they were treating the people inside.

Strategies for passing as legal travelers comprised another set of techniques of self-management through which our interviewees asserted some control over things that happened on the migrant trail, in these cases specifically by altering the play of appearances surrounding migrant bodies. Gloria Ruiz conveyed the sense that this realm of the visual was open to her reconstructive abilities, for example, when she told us this humorous story about how she barely avoided making a key tactical error as she prepared to cross the border through the official line of cars "with supposedly good papers" provided by a *coyote:*

I went quickly to get some pictures taken for the papers they were going to make me—a visa. And the same blouse that I was wearing to go across, was the same one in the picture—"Oh, no, no [the *coyote* said]! Change your blouse!" So we dashed out to buy clothes. . . . I went [across] with a man in a car, this way, like it was normal. . . . I was really lucky, thank God; I didn't have any problem.[10]

Another comical story about passing was the one Diego Ortega told about his wife's illegal crossing:

They brought her across through the line; they gave her a false visa. . . . And what this person did to get her across is he got together a lot of children and put them in the car—from people he knew—and he said to the children, "When you go to cross, start making a ruckus. You: cry. You: yell. You: talk." So when they got to the line, he said to my wife, "You, pretend like you're sleeping; you're sleeping, and you've got a headache." And they went through the line, and this person knew how to speak English well. He was an American citizen. So they arrived at the line, and the [agent] peeked in and said, "OK, what's going on?" "My wife and my children" [responded the *coyote*]. And they started crying and shouting, "Daddy, Daddy!" "Wait, wait, here are the papers" [said the *coyote*]. They started doing that, and the [agent] said, "Move along, move along."[11]

Whether it was playacting or dressing the part of a legal crosser, strategies of bodily comportment and adornment to influence others' perceptions belonged to the repertoire of personal abilities our interviewees claimed in their stories about navigating the border zone. Against an inescapable backdrop of indeterminacy and, to some extent, fearful contingency, such techniques of the self gave these immigrant workers ways to elude capture and achieve their purposes—as well as a concrete basis for *seeing themselves* as capable of doing so, as their patterns of narration demonstrated.[12]

Up to this point, I have considered mainly the stories of women we interviewed. Their shared narrative frame, in which subtle references to individual agency insistently contest the theme of involuntary subjection to whims of fate that dispose of migrant bodies indiscriminately, has a distinctly gendered quality. The gender-specificity of these stories centrally derives from the immediate responsibility many of the women had for bringing children across with them—a duty not one of the men shared—along with the risk of sexual abuse. The vulnerability of the women's own bodies to becoming exposed, disoriented, immobilized, and debilitated through injury, pain, hunger, thirst, and sexual aggression was thus always intimately connected to the violable bodies of others. (And the terror of being compelled to cross the border separately from their children, an ordeal on which both Méndez and Soto dwelt in the interviews, thus also produced a special torment for women.)[13] But just as chapter 2 showed how preimmigration experiences and decisions often became venues for claiming and asserting a gendered form of individuality, so the maternalist bent of many of these border-crossing stories suggests that gender differences provided a substantive basis for the articulation and action of an embodied self capable, at least in limited ways, of conditioning its own environment. In other words, these women suggested to us that it was *through* protecting their children in tense moments during crossings, and indeed through brightening their children's futures by undertaking such grueling voyages at all, that they had held at bay the chaos, inscrutability, and physical menace of the situations they encountered.

Readers familiar with Mexican cultures or cultural studies may also sense some manifestation here of the feminine side of what is often known as the *macho/María* identity dualism. The phrase expresses a cultural tendency for gender identity to take shape according to a dichotomy that opposes a feminine norm of patient, willing, and self-sacrificial suffering for the sake of others (as modeled by the mother of Christ) to a fearlessly self-reliant and physically robust masculinity that is essentially unencumbered by any intimate ties. Just how widespread these Mexican cultural notions of normal masculinity and femininity really are, however, is a matter of no little debate.[14] Moreover, even though a number of the men narrated their border-crossing ordeals in ways that generally conform to the *macho* figure, I advise caution against reading the narrative material in this chapter as evidence that this particular group of Mexican immigrants, much less Mexicans or Mexican Americans in general, necessarily embraced these identity constructs. Such skepticism is needed not only because my methods were not aimed at empirically characterizing these habits of everyday life, which are the concerns of cultural ethnography, but also because the stories we heard were the products of intrinsically *political* dialogues with these immigrant workers rather than transparent records of their "authentic" experiences. That these individuals employed these cultural categories thus signals that, consciously or not, they turned to such notions in an effort to communicate with us and to advance the political projects activated by their narratives. They may have drawn on these conceptions precisely because they were deeply sedimented currents of shared common sense in Mexican and Mexican American cultures. Additionally, or alternatively, they might have thought we were more likely to support their movement at Tyson if they appealed to us using traditional images of gender identity. Within the context of my analysis as a whole, in any case, what must be kept clearly in view is that the workers expressed *their accounts of power* in the illegal zone in gendered terms, depicting both how power acted upon them in gender-specific ways and how they exerted gender-specific forms of agency. To anticipate an argument I shall elaborate at the end of this chapter, this suggests that these narratives hold the particular potential to help theorists conceptualize the formation of hegemony in which immigrant workers participate as pivotally involving not only class dynamics but gendered elements as well.

With that said, it is important to recognize that in many ways the men's stories of cross-border travel closely resembled those of the women in that the former involved a similar mixture of assertions of embodied personal agency and longings for rescue from dire circumstances that seemed to place the individual's body entirely under heteronomous control. These men may not have had children in tow as the women did, but they were in no sense immune to the corporeal hazards of the border zone and the emotional panic they provoked. On the whole, the men we spoke with had more frequent brushes with death than the women did as they made their way through the borderlands. Isidro Gómez, for example, told us how his misfortunes had begun when he became separated from his group of travelers after border security forces ambushed them:

The Border Patrol came upon us, and then a helicopter. Then people were running everywhere—you don't know where you're going—and I ran, I ran to the right as fast as my feet could carry me. It's the kind of thing where you don't even know where you are, in the hills; and then there are the dangers, like coming upon snakes, or something, in the dark. . . . I threw myself into a deep stream, all alone. And I said, "Now what do I do? Where do I go? What am I going to do here? I have no idea." And I held on and kept walking, until off in the distance I saw two shadowy figures. And you get scared, because you don't know if it's going to be good people or bad people, you know? And I approached, and I said [to myself], "Well, whatever happens, happens, right?" They were the same ones who had been there before [in the group], a man and a woman, and I asked the man, "And now what do we do?" "Well, I don't know," [he said]. . . . I tell him, "Well, let's keep walking, by the stream, down that way, and see what happens."[15]

Ultimately, Gómez found additional members of his group as well as one of their guides, who ended up leading them back to the highway and taking them to Los Angeles in a van. Yet it was the fact that he "spent the whole night walking and walking without knowing where [he] was going" that stayed with Gómez most strongly, and his emphasis on the "traumatic" quality of this experience of disorientation echoed comments from certain women, such as Esperanza Soto. Gómez noted that he felt very fortunate that he had not run into even worse "dangers" that he knew existed in the border region, such as being assaulted by Tijuana gangs. "I was lucky, thank God," he said, reiterating the common refrain we heard among so many others. Yet this still did not diminish the terror, he told us, of "walking all night without knowing where I was."

Other men we spoke with described moments during their cross-border ventures when their lives were even more obviously in peril. Gilberto Rivera told us that after he had been placed in a holding house in San Diego and kept without food or drink for many hours, the *coyotes* herded him along with about a hundred others into a trailer in the middle of the night:

We drove for about a half hour, and we had the feeling that we were starting to run out of air. We were breathing, but it was hot air, steam, like in a sauna. The trailer had no air conditioning, it just had a little hole in the floor, and when it was running along a little bit of air came in. But all these desperate people wouldn't keep to one side so that the air could come in; they all wanted to be in front of the little hole. And then the desperation of all these people started to spread to the others. There were about seven children in there; there were about fifteen women. And it didn't matter to anyone whether there were children, whether there were women; what we all were trying to do was to breathe air.[16]

As the panic inside the trailer swelled, Rivera and his friend resolved that it would be better to be caught by *la migra* than to suffer possible death by suffocation in the fetid trailer, so they fled, "soaked with sweat," when the driver stopped at a weigh station. The Border Patrol apprehended them and deported them to Tijuana, he said, where they went around to restaurants begging food: "We had to eat the food that the customers left, although we were ashamed to do it; but we had to eat." Rivera emphasized not only the severe physical hazards of the migrant trail but also the damage to his (and others') personal dignity that suffering bodily deprivations entailed, including the integrity of behaving ethically toward others as well as the individual's sense of self-reliance.

While Rivera's *coyotes* had nearly caused the asphyxiation of their trailer passengers, Felipe Ortiz's *polleros* abandoned him and left him to fend for himself on two separate undocumented trips across the border. In the guide's absence, Ortiz remembered, situations soon arose that put his life in jeopardy, although for different reasons on the two occasions. The first time, Ortiz said, he had been caught in the hills soon afterward and deported, and it was the border security authorities who subsequently put him in fear for his survival:

They caught us there and they took us to Chulavista, to a jail there; and later from there they took us to Tijuana. And [then] . . . they took us in an airplane to León, Guanajuato, Mexico. And I wasn't from Guanajuato and that's where they took us. And it was an airplane where they carry animals. The seats were like beach chairs, and there was manure from the animals in there, in the airplane. I was really afraid because the airplane, outside, was broken—it had holes in it, but it had patches that were advertisements for Coca-Cola and Pepsi-Cola. And so, now, later, I've gone in the airplane and it doesn't take long for an airplane to get to Guadalajara or Aguascalientes now, it takes about two and a half hours, three hours, and that one took about six hours. . . . It made me really afraid.[17]

Ortiz's pulse-quickening (but low-velocity) flight in the broken-down aircraft, back to an unfamiliar location in Mexico far from his home in Zacatecas, recalled both Rivera's trailer incident and Esperanza Soto's hair-raising ride in the van. Like these other episodes, it evoked a sense of the body's confinement, degradation, and exposure to a sharply elevated risk of sudden death. (And again, the body's distress took on a distinctly ironic quality inasmuch as Ortiz got flown back to Mexico under the banner of the global soft drink industry whose products have an easier time crossing national borders.) That heightened precariousness of life became all the more extreme in one of Ortiz's subsequent trips back across the border. Hungry, thirsty, and exhausted after being abandoned yet again by their *coyote*, the luckless Ortiz recalled, he and some others finally quit their hiding place in a tunnel and went looking for something to quench their thirst:

> We started walking again, to ask for water at some houses that were there, in La Jolla, California. That was when we were calling out to [a person we saw] that we wanted water—a man, we saw that he was drinking, like, coffee, because you couldn't see his face; [but] you could see his hand. . . . We called out to him that we were very thirsty, and asked him to give us water. That was when he grabbed a weapon and was pointing it at us through the window. And we ran.

Nor was Ortiz the only worker we spoke with who had had a firearm pulled on him—Pedro Ruiz actually had come under fire from gun-toting vigilantes:

> I remember that we walked about six or seven hours on foot through the hills. When we crossed the fence dividing Mexico and the United States, we went through a hole. . . . We came to a field where there was a path, and there were some people there who blocked our way. . . . These people started telling us move along, and when we were going along suddenly three or four other people with rifles came out, and they shot at us with the rifles. . . . They started cursing at us. . . . My thoughts in that moment were, "I'm not going to turn around so they don't hit me in the face," so they hit me in the body. . . . I ran, I ran, I ran. We got to the fence; we didn't find the hole; we went over the top of the fence. We ran and when we saw a place where there was tall grass, we hid ourselves. . . . We waited until they had gone, and went back—but thinking that they had killed the other two people who were missing, or something.[18]

Ruiz added that he and the other three men he was with never found the two who were missing, so they kept moving ahead with their journey. But he had sustained the most fearful brush with unpredictable hazards along the border, including mortal dangers and deadly violence, of any of the people with whom we spoke.

Yet as with the women's stories, these men's accounts of the illegal zone not only stressed situations of extremity that completely eluded the individual's agentic capacities but also, in certain moments, indicated the storyteller's ability to influence the outcome of events and to protect the safety and security of their bodies. Ruiz's account was a case in point, and a remarkable one at that, given the severity of the danger he had encountered. Ruiz told us how he and two other men later had been stuffed into the trunk of a car and taken down a highway toward their destination. This episode initially seemed to put the accent once more on the immigrant body's immobilization, humiliation, and forced exposure to unforeseeable and uncontrollable hazards. However, the tone of the story changed when Ruiz described how he had tried to bolster the spirits of one of his fellow travelers in the trunk of the car when this man began moaning in pain from muscle spasms that had begun to plague him after he had been unable to move for an extended time. Urged Ruiz: "'Now, you can take it, because you know you want to make it to the north.'" He then added, matter-of-factly: "That's how we gave ourselves courage." Ruiz sought to make things just a little better for the man lying next to him in the trunk by offering words of encouragement. And he did it, not coincidentally, by prodding this man's sense of manly bravery, ambition, and ability to tolerate pain.

Just as the women often found resources for self-assertion in gendered aspects of their experiences, above all their responsibility for their children, the men likewise turned to facets of gender identity to fuel their own deployments of individual agency. And as in the women's stories, so likewise in the men's narratives: these sporadic but significant moments produced an important tension with the countervailing narrative current that stressed the person's helplessness and confusion. Melquíades "Flaco" Pereyra told us another story of a border-crossing adventure that evinced these kinds of contrasting elements. Having traveled up to Tijuana from their home in Culiacán, Sinaloa, Pereyra and his friends embarked on a labyrinthine journey through unsavory parts of the city, searching for one of the boys' relatives so he could arrange for a friend who was a *coyote* to take them across the border. Pereyra thus reiterated the theme of spatial disorientation we heard in the accounts by Isidro Gómez as well as several of the women: "We had no address [for the friend's half-brother]; we had no idea where to go."[19] After they finally located the man they were seeking, things only got worse:

We walked for about . . . four hours, walking in the hills. We got to the mountains; we slept there in the mountains. . . . It was very cold—very, very cold. I couldn't sleep it was so cold. . . . From there, they transported us to—I think it was San Clemente, or San Isidro—someplace like that. . . . It was a place where they threw away the garbage from the city. That's where we were, for one day and one night. . . . I never encountered [the Border Patrol]. Nor was I ever arrested by *la migración*. That is, I was lucky; I crossed cleanly. . . . We didn't have any mishaps at all. Thank God we didn't—because there sure are plenty of dangers. . . . They assault you, they rob you, they kill you.

Pereyra thus dwelled on the themes examined earlier: that the winds of fate subject the migrant's body unwillingly to harsh suffering, putrid surroundings, and manifold calamities.[20] Yet there was still a tension in his story between these components and his statement that at least he had not slouched back home to his mother like a "loser," as he put it. In part, as I noted in chapter 2, crossing the border seemed to have served as a masculine rite of passage for Pereyra, who loved "wandering" and saw it as a kind of youthful adventure. Consequently, there was a dimension of *positive struggle* in his story: the struggle to act like a man and to meet his adversities head-on, taking shrewd advantage of the limited resources that he had. For instance, Pereyra told us that his and his friend's personal connection with the *coyote* from Tijuana had allowed them to travel across the border free of charge. This also made it possible, he noted, for them to pass the time outside when they were waiting in a safe house during one stage of their journey. "But the other people sure couldn't leave the house," Pereyra stressed. "They had to stay locked up [*cautivadas*, literally 'held captive'] there, until they talked to their relatives, the people who were going to pay." It was obvious that some of the time, Pereyra himself had felt like a captive; but he also saw himself as acting strategically and manfully to augment his freedom of movement in both particular situations and through migrating as such.

While almost all the men we interviewed frankly acknowledged their tremendous fears about suffering bodily harm or even death while crossing the border, Alejandro Méndez stood out from the rest in that he bluntly denied feeling any such fright whatsoever. Here was a more pronounced expression of the stereotypically *macho* sensibility. In describing his passage across the border, Méndez extended the self-concept he had articulated in discussing his original choice to migrate to the United States as a matter of seeking "new horizons" and "trying his luck" rather than being driven by dire need:

I wasn't afraid of anything at all. No, I wasn't afraid. I came having made up my mind to cross and if things went well, fine; and if they didn't, I'd go back.

Fear? Fear? No. . . . Since I had been in the army—well, you lose your fear. There, you bet you're afraid, and it takes the fear out of you. Or it's like: when you decide to do something, you're going to do it, for better or worse. . . . And so that was the way I decided, I said: "OK, if I don't make it across, I'll just go back."[21]

Méndez's air of supreme confidence, his soldierly decisiveness and resolute commitment to action regardless of the consequences, contrasted sharply with the many of the others' avowals of near-paralyzing anxiety. Notably, however, Méndez did not claim to have been able to anticipate what would happen when he tried to cross the border. Nor did he tell us that his military training had given him any practical, technical resources for making the crossing successfully. Instead, he stressed his cavalier disregard for the outcome of events. In these ways, his account actually reaffirmed the sense in the other stories that crossing the border exposed the migrant's body to deeply contingent events that were beyond the individual's capacity to steer in any particular direction. Méndez dealt with this problem by turning inward and drawing on his military training to expunge, or perhaps simply to disavow, any residual fear he might have had. In a sense, then, his strategy of self-management in the illegal zone placed in even sharper relief the body's outward vulnerability to violation.

Just as Méndez was exceptional in denying any anxiety about his personal safety while crossing the border, a few other people we interviewed seemed not to have encountered any serious assaults on their bodily well-being along the way. Even though Rogelio Salazar's *coyote* inexplicably lost his way, for instance, Salazar did not feel that what he had gone through in his cross-border passage had involved any severe hazard or stress.[22] Rosa Vásquez had crossed with what seemed to be only mild inconveniences: a half hour walking through the hills, running "a little bit," hiding "a little bit when a helicopter passed by," and getting temporarily soaked when she waded through a canal.[23] Diego Ortega said that he had gone with people who "knew the way" and thus he "didn't have bad experiences."[24] Such accounts, however, went against the grain of the interviews as a group. Yet as we have seen, even when our informants underscored their exposure to seemingly random forces capable of doing them great bodily harm and incapable of being foreseen or resisted, they also doubled back on this narrative current by adding indications of self-satisfaction at marginally influencing their difficult circumstances through practices of physical comportment and visual manifestation, techniques of emotional self-mastery, and express moral indictment of other agents who disrespected their bodies.

Living *Encerrado* and the Arts of Hiding

Our informants' characteristic intertwining of conflicting desires, between avowals of personal agency and the notion that only God or fortune could stave off disaster, often of a sort that was impressed in their very flesh, continued in the stories these immigrant workers told about their years living and working in the United States prior to becoming legalized. For some of the people we interviewed, inhabiting the realm of illegality inside the United States felt like being imprisoned: they emphasized the keenly physical as well as social immobility that characterized their lives and the way this condition seemed forced upon them by powers beyond their control. Others, however, told us with evident pride about the techniques they had honed for making their way through everyday life while undocumented, stressing their abilities to exercise self-determination even under these difficult circumstances. Elvira Méndez gave voice to both tendencies when she described how she once had eluded the INS during a raid on the eastern Washington orchard where she was picking apples:

I was on the ladder. So I come down the ladder—me, the first time in my life that that had happened to me! That I get down and run, but with the whole bag of apples here [points to her lap]. And my son-in-law catches up with me and tells me, "No, man, get rid of that." Because my son-in-law already knows; he's been there longer [than I have], and he doesn't have papers either. . . . I threw away the bag and we started running. We got into a box where they store apples. . . . The people from *la migra* came by and they didn't see us. But they stayed there waiting for the people working on the ranch to come out. The helicopters passed by above us. . . . [The ranch] only had one exit and my son-in-law told me: "Now I sure think we're going to go to Mexico for free." [She laughs.] . . . "Wait," he told me. "Wait; we're going to wait a little bit and we're not going to move, and hope nothing happens." . . . And after an hour he got out, and he tells me: "We're going to the car," he says, "and I'm going to try to find a way out." . . . I was wearing a *gorra* [farmworkers' hat], and everything. I took off my *gorra;* I put on makeup and I acted like I was just visiting *[turisteando],* so that *la migra* wouldn't suspect anything when we went by in front of them. But, thank God, since we waited a long time, when we left the people from *la migra* had already left the road. . . . But they were gong along on the highways waiting for the people, and [my son-in-law] hid in the hills, in the paths and everything until we arrived here. . . . Thank God I was lucky.

As the first few lines in this passage illustrate, Méndez presented these experiences as though they were completely out of the ordinary. Her dismay at the indignity of it all was palpable, even as the sheer strangeness of it made her laugh, somewhat uncomfortably, as she recounted what had happened. Yet by emphasizing the ways she depended on her son-in-law to escape detection by *la migra,* Méndez also conveyed that these apparently exceptional events were, in fact, woven into the fabric of her everyday life and relationships. The son-in-law evidently knew the drill for handling such situations because he had "been there longer," and so he could share this practical knowledge with Méndez. In this story, he was schooling her, informally but effectively, in what I call the arts of hiding. The sense that Méndez's agency had evaporated, which she indicated by laughing grimly at the absurdity of having to spend an hour cooped up inside an apple box as well as by thanking "God" that she had been "lucky," thus mingled with a different kind of storyline. In this alternate narrative stream, Méndez explained how she had learned novel tactics of bodily comportment and placement, and how she had begun to develop a newly critical awareness of key spaces within her social landscape that undocumented workers could exploit to make their daily lives functional. The former included postures and forms of dress enabling one to pass as an ordinary U.S. American, while among the latter were the interiors of apple crates and the paths off the main highways.

Some immigrant workers we interviewed privileged one of these two narrative strands over the other. Ramona Díaz gave vivid and anguished testimony to the sharp, ever-present sense of confinement that living without documents within the United States had entailed for her, when we asked her what she missed most about her earlier life in Mexico:

The biggest difference is that here you spend all your time shut in *[encerrado].* That's what it is—you go to work and you come back; you spend all your time shut in *[encerrado].* It's not like in your own country. Because in your own country . . . you spend all your time outside. And not here. Here you do everything shut up inside *[encerrado].* . . . You come home from work tired and you have to do things at home. . . . And then when a person comes who doesn't have papers, who is afraid that *la migra* might come—it's even worse! And then, you need a car for everything, and you don't over there. . . . It's really hard to be a person here . . . with no papers and not knowing how to drive.[25]

We should take special note of Díaz's insistent repetition of the word *encerrado* to describe the general condition that she and others like her have faced. This term not only means being shut inside a closed area but additionally carries connotations of being imprisoned or trapped and is also used to describe the caging or fencing-in of animals such as livestock. Díaz thus dramatically underscored the feeling of physical immobility and constraint that living in the condition of illegality created for her. Héctor Fernández echoed Díaz's comment that both the ever-present fear of *la migra* and the comparison to prior life in Mexico made this problem especially acute: "What I missed most was the freedom, to go out without being afraid that they were going to catch you."[26] He also confirmed the observation of Díaz's husband that undocumented immigrants lived in fear of not only the INS but also local police, who would often do the work of immigration officials although not authorized to do so.[27] Echoed Francisco González: "Here the police have us registered. . . . Here you feel more imprisoned *[enjaulado]* than in Mexico. In Mexico you feel more free in every single way."[28] Both González and Fernández thus amplified and further specified Díaz's evocative comments about the immigrant body being forced into confined spaces. They underscored that living *encerrado* was an effect of multiple agencies of the state and represented this situation as a heteronomous fate well beyond the individual's control.

Meanwhile, the resonances between these immigrant workers' comments about life in the U.S. interior and the border-crossing narratives indicate how the zone of illegality stretched through time and space to encompass both episodes and domains. The Díaz, González, and Fernández interviews, for example, brought to mind Flaco Pereyra's remembrance that his fellow travelers had been "held captive" by their *coyotes* in the border way stations, along with the other stories our informants told about spending long, painful hours and even days locked up inside abandoned houses, shuttered inside dank apartments, or trapped within airless vehicles. Together, these accounts suggested that the situation of living *encerrado,* as a core constraint upon migrant bodies in the situation of illegality and as a condition forced upon the person unwillingly, really had begun along the border. On the U.S. side, moreover, the power that applied itself in this manner to migrant bodies was again distinctly gendered, as our informants described it. Following a cryptically allusive remark by Díaz, her husband clarified that when she had come across for the first time as a young woman, relatives had taken her in but then mistreated and exploited her: "Taking advantage of the fact that she didn't have documents, they kept her as a house servant without paying her. And after doing the housework she went to go spend her labor in the fields." Prior research on Mexican immigrants suggests that such personal exploitation of women by family members in the United States occurs fairly frequently, even though this was the only instance we heard of a person enduring this sort of treatment (Hondagneu-Sotelo 1994).[29]

Journalists and political advocates routinely refer to undocumented migrants and their families as being "invisible" or flitting, wraithlike, through the "shadows" of everyday U.S. society. Susan Bibler Coutin goes so far as to argue that these workers are made to disappear into a space of "nonlocation" and "nonexistence" insofar as "many of their daily practices must be clandestine," including "such commonplace actions as working, traveling, and driving" (2000, 31–34).[30] Yet when immigrant workers like Díaz, Fernández, and González narrate their experiences, they describe the unwanted *placement* of the body in specific, palpably *present* situations of confinement. These locations are often out of sight from mainstream culture, to be sure, but they still possess a concrete particularity and physicality that the standard notions of the undocumented as apparitions haunting empty nonplaces in the seams of ordinary society do not quite capture.

At the same time, the rhetorical conventions that situate undocumented immigrants in ephemeral places-that-are-nowhere discourage an awareness of the techniques for asserting personal agency to which our informants frequently called attention. Pedro Ruiz, for instance, elaborated on the theme of strategic self-regulation through "passing" that appeared in Elvira Méndez's story of the raid on the apple orchard. He told us this story about how he had avoided capture during an INS incursion on a warehouse in Los Angeles where he had begun working after illegally crossing the border:

La migración raided the place once. . . . They didn't let us run away; they didn't give us any warning, that is, that they were coming to ask us questions. . . . The women started to run; they started to cry. Some started tearing up the wire mesh fence, because the plant was surrounded with wire mesh. And me, what I did was I stayed right there at my job, working. . . . I remember that my *compañero* started coughing; it was a nervous cough. And what I did [was to say]: "Go to the bathroom." I sent him to the bathroom, I said, "because you're going to make them discover me." And I wasn't worried. . . . And they passed by alongside me, and I kept working as if it was nothing. And . . . they didn't interrogate me at all. I just stayed there working. They took away about forty people.

These comments resonated clearly with Alejandro Méndez's martial strategy of emotional self-control as well as Ruiz's own exhortations to his companion in the trunk of the car (during his border crossing) to steel himself internally and manfully bear with his pain. Here, as well, Ruiz matched such inward self-regulation with the confident management of outward appearances in ways that were more flexible in terms of gender. He avoided discovery simply by *acting* as though he had nothing to fear, like Elvira Méndez preparing to pose as a visitor to the orchard; and he accentuated his disciplined command over his own body in contrast to others who manifested physical symptoms of fear and anxiety when the agents suddenly broke into the warehouse.

The most remarkable stories about using these kinds of corporeal and affective techniques to diminish the pressures of *la vida encerrada,* and ultimately to escape from it entirely, came from Rogelio Salazar. We marveled as Salazar recounted how he had been able to walk unimpeded through airports and thus to fly back and forth between the United States and Mexico "three or four times," even before he obtained his own proper legal documents:

RS: Well, I got lucky, because I went through the line and I came in a plane. That is, I just dressed nicely. They didn't ask me anything. . . . I went through the airport, and the immigration officials are there. . . . They didn't question me. . . . [Speaking as though this were an adventure] I always was lucky with that.
PA: Were you very afraid of the officials, in those moments?
RS: [Very sure of himself] No. That is, what I did was that I dressed nicely. . . . With a nice haircut, well dressed, and . . . when I put my suitcase down I'd quickly go pick it up. Because I was going to say that some people put down their suitcase and forget about it. And they get nervous, and the officials notice that. They say, "Something's wrong here." . . . I never gave them anything to notice.

Just as Elvira Méndez had described eluding the INS agents in the apple orchard by donning makeup and doffing her telltale farmworker's hat, so Rogelio Salazar explained how he had evaded detection by visually fitting in to the normal scene in the airport. By his account, he had adopted specific techniques of bodily comportment and certain ways of handling objects. He added, furthermore, that he had applied these same methods in more mundane circumstances: "I've always driven cars that are more or less nice, that don't arouse suspicions, either. . . . I've never called attention [to myself]." Salazar then told us how he had deployed a similar practice of passing when he took the U.S. citizenship examination in 1997, making himself seem proficient in the ways of U.S. American mainstream culture even though he had very limited English abilities and could barely read and write in Spanish:

RS: I tell you, I have always, always had luck with these things. . . . And I say that I was lucky, too, because I—I never went to school. I know this—I can't read or write well, or quickly. . . . What I did was I found out all the questions [on the examination] and I started writing them down. That is, I wrote them the way they seemed like they'd come out in Spanish. That is, in English, but I read them in Spanish, you know, so they'd stick with me better, or more easily [i.e., he sounded out words that were written in English using Spanish pronunciation, and wrote them down that way]. . . . The exam was in two weeks. . . . It's a hundred questions . . . that you have to study because you don't know which ones they're going to ask you. So that's how I did it: all those days I got home from work, and I made myself write. . . .

PV: Well then, it wasn't luck. It was because you really studied the questions.

RS: Well, yes. That is, I say it was luck because—I don't know. What I'm saying is, doing it that way wasn't so hard for me. I guess I believe that it's all a matter of, if you want to do something, you can do it.

For Salazar, "passing" the examination thus occurred in two senses. Not only did he perform successfully on the test but he did so by, in essence, posing as a normative naturalization applicant. Just as he had modulated his dress, physical demeanor, and material accoutrements in airports and while driving, in this instance, he had displayed his skill in manipulating the malleable surfaces of linguistic sounds and texts. He had thus won himself new freedom from the condition of living *encerrado,* notwithstanding his reiterated and far too modest disclaimers about just having been "lucky," which my assistant astutely pressed him to reevaluate.

Work in the Zone of Illegality

If bodily confinement and physical self-representation through passing were the signature themes when our interviewees talked about their brushes with immigration officials inside the United States, their experiences of labor both reinforced this narration of power in the illegal zone and elaborated it further, adding new complexities. The great majority of the people we interviewed had spent their years as illegal residents working for U.S. agricultural firms, mostly picking, sorting, and packing fruit or vegetables and pruning plants. The memories of desire they voiced about this period of their lives, looking back from their later situations as workers in the slaughterhouse, were sometimes quite unexpected. Especially since the mobilization of the United Farm Workers (UFW) movement in the 1960s, union organizers and farmworker advocates have drawn attention to the severe plight of agricultural laborers. The difficult circumstances they face involve multiple and intersecting problems such as low wages, a lack of benefits, routine contact with toxic chemicals, dangerous exposure to high heat, deplorable housing conditions, physical and social isolation, and educational barriers for farmworkers' children due to all these factors as well as their families' often transient lives (Griffith and Kissam 1995; Martin 2003). Given these well-known hardships, it was something of a surprise to hear more than a few of these immigrant workers talk about their days "in the field," as they generally referred to this period, as a relatively happier and better time in comparison to their later lives as employees of Tyson/IBP.

Alejandro Méndez, for example, depicted his years working in the fields during the 1980s as a period when he had trained himself to work with tremendous efficiency and with lucrative monetary rewards, at least for a while, in comparison to his later position at the meat plant:

I say that I worked seasonally, but when there weren't lots of people, we worked almost the whole year. Because I worked whenever I could, pruning and replanting Christmas trees. . . . And so I practically worked from Monday to Monday. . . . And I earned up to a thousand, a thousand five hundred a week. What I earn now, I earned in one day. . . . I got fifty, forty, thirty dollars an hour at a minimum. That was depending on how motivated you were. . . . Then more people started to arrive. They started lowering the wages a lot. . . . Pruning blackberries, I'd get $1.75, $2.25 with the trimming. I used to do that in seconds. In just seconds, I would earn myself those two dollars. . . . It was quick. Then they started paying me fifty cents, for trimming underneath. I said: "No. That doesn't work anymore." . . . From there I switched to the slaughterhouse.

For Méndez, the fields thus furnished an individual proving ground, a place to hone his physical skills to the point where they brought him exceptionally high wages as well as prodigious self-satisfaction. Performing such work at lightning speed, the body could be active and productive, validating concretely Méndez's belief in his exceptional individual autonomy. This, in turn, grounded Méndez's allied confidence in his tactical abilities to negotiate favorable hiring arrangements with employers even though, he admitted, shortages or surpluses of farm labor ultimately determined his wage levels more potently. Yet while hovering visibly in the background, this sense of a more massive and irresistible institutional power that set the conditions of daily life still did not overshadow the opposing dynamic of self-assertion via well-crafted techniques of the body that Méndez spotlighted in this portion of his interview.

While other workers did not similarly speak about farm labor as offering this sense of personal achievement and fulfillment, they did suggest other ways that work in the fields involved a loosening of the tethers binding immigrant bodies. Ramona Díaz, for example, described her experiences in the fields as having mitigated the acute sense of physical restriction and isolation, of living *encerrada,* that otherwise pervaded her daily life. Through her work, it seemed, she had found a measure of relief from the oppressive feeling of forced confinement inside interior spaces, as this exchange between us indicated:

PA: How was the work at IBP, in comparison to the work in the field?
RD: Well, it's really different. It's very different to walk around working in the field, because you feel free. You do your work, but even so you have the air. You're walking, even if the sun is beating down on you, you know. And also, there aren't the same kind of supervisors that there are at IBP. . . . Because the supervisor just isn't right there with you like they are here [at IBP].
PA: And is the pay very different?
RD: That too. That's very different, too. That's the reason why you sometimes restrain yourself when the supervisors tell you things, do things to you . . . because in the field you earn very little. And here you work yourself to death more, but the wage is a little more.

The sense of freedom Díaz associated with work in the fields had several dimensions, as she described it. She felt at liberty, she suggested, because she was physically able to move about in the open air. In addition, she could work without the burdensome sense of bodily restriction that came from the claustrophobic nearness of supervisors' bodies at the slaughterhouse and that at IBP kept her silent in the face of abusive authority. (Echoed Rogelio Salazar: "In the field, the supervisor hardly ever came near me. He just came and looked to see how much I was doing. Sometimes he told me to ease up a little.") And by saying that working in the fields meant working at her own pace rather than working herself "to death," Díaz implied, somewhat like Alejandro Méndez, that such work had provided more of a chance for her to act in a self-determining way than laboring at the beef plant later would be.

Other people we interviewed, however, stressed more heavily the vulnerability of their bodies to discomfort, pain, indignity, and even traumatic injury that laboring in the fields involved. Pedro Ruiz's remarks partly resonated with those of Alejandro Méndez when he spoke about finding real satisfaction doing the difficult job of cutting asparagus and earning good money during the period of the farm labor shortage.[31] However, he went on to tell us about an incident when his work in an orchard suddenly left him "blind" for several days, from causes that he could only suspect but never knew for sure, beginning on the day that he became a father (with his wife, Gloria, adding some vivid details at the end of his remarks):

PR: When my girl, my first girl, was born, I was out pruning and I don't know what it was that hurt us, but five of us had to go to the hospital. For five days I couldn't see anything. There had been a big snowfall, and the trees had snow on them and when you were pruning the branch, snow would fall. And the sun came out, and steam started to rise up. And I don't know if that was what hurt us, or if the tree had a chemical that hurt us. My eyes swelled up; I couldn't see my wife. And that very day her water broke. I had to take her to the hospital at, like, two in the morning and sometimes I had to slow down because I couldn't see. And they took care of her, and another nurse took care of me because my eyes were burning.
GR: With the road full of snow, and he's asking me, "Am I going the right way? Am I going the right way?" And me, with really strong pains.

This episode struck me as particularly poignant because the evaporating chemicals that temporarily blinded Ruiz not only caused him corporeal pain and the fear for the future that went along with it but also thwarted his ability to act in line with his sense of masculine identity at such a critical moment—ironically, just when his wife was supposed to be the one with the vulnerable body in pain that he would protect. He didn't say for sure, but I also wondered later if this meant that he was prevented from gazing at his newborn child at the moment of her birth and what additional sense of hurt this might have provoked.

Gilberto Rivera likewise remembered suffering from exposure to cold weather, although with less dramatic consequences. For Rivera, the supervisors' lack of intensive involvement with the workers came across more as cruel disregard for their pain than as the trust in their ability to manage themselves that Díaz and Rogelio Salazar had recalled. Ordered to perform an irrigation job in subfreezing temperatures, Rivera told us, he had asked in disbelief: "How am I going to water the plants if it's so cold?" The manager replied, "If you don't want to do it, go home." Jorge Hernández, in turn, held down two tough physical jobs at the same time and worked around the clock, sacrificing sleep to support himself after he arrived in the United States as he picked apples by day and labored at a sawmill by night. Not that sleeping would have been easy in any case—as Hernández recalled, with a wry chuckle, he had endured absurdly crowded living conditions in a shack that he and some other workers rented from the grower who employed them: "It's a little room, a really small one like this, six feet wide, and there are six or seven people in there. They put in a double bed for us, and there you are, piled up in there, like chickens." Again and again during our interview, Hernández repeated: "I know what it is to suffer the work in the fields," or something similar to that.[32]

There were a few among our interviewees who had worked in industrial or service jobs rather than, or after, working in the fields. These individuals expressed neither the sense of confronting quite such physically taxing and hazardous circumstances nor the contrasting feeling of gaining more free space for the body under the contained (encerrada) condition of living to which migrants otherwise were subjected. Instead, they painted a vivid portrait of working life that was highly contingent on an unstable labor market and that demanded a versatility, adaptability, and submissiveness of body and mind to changing and often disagreeable conditions. At one point or another, Rivera told us, he had held down jobs roofing, cleaning, working in a small retail store, helping a church-based theater troupe, and laboring in a nuts and sweets factory. In this last job, he and his coworkers had put up with routine verbal abuse from the supervisors until at one point he shouted back: "We are workers, we are not slaves; it doesn't give you the right to insult us this way!" Isidro Gómez had experienced a similar string of short-term, low-paying, exploitative jobs, moving from an abysmal garment shop in Los Angeles to a seasonal fumigating business before finally landing a steadier job in a tire factory. Juanita Castillo at first could only find an eight-hour-a-week job packing carrots but then made what seemed to her like a step up to a minimum wage job in a chicken slaughtering and packing plant.[33] Rosa Vásquez had earned minimum wages in a fast food restaurant, where, she noted, the turnover was extremely high and the work was intensely pressured.

Overall, then, the shared currents of common sense about power that materialized in our informants' stories of crossing the border continued to characterize their comments on working life in the domain of illegality. On the one hand, as these narrators described things, making it past the border zone and finding work perpetuated or intensified their bodies' susceptibility to injurious, undignified, sullying, and precarious circumstances. Gilberto Rivera's story of being treated like human chattel in the factory provided an apt and disturbing follow-up to his account of nearly dying while being herded across the border with other immigrant workers in the unventilated trailer. Bodies were crammed into compressed spaces and too-close proximity to one another, whether in vehicles near the border piloted by Esperanza Soto's and Elvira Méndez's *polleros* or in the shacks where farmworkers like Jorge Hernández lived, as he put it, *como pollos*. Isidro Gómez's peregrinations through the informal labor market of immigrant Los Angeles called to mind his painful story of wandering alone through the border hills after losing track of his *coyote*. And the blinding panic to which Pedro Ruiz testified, in those milliseconds after he heard the first gunshots whiz by him near the border fence, seemed a depressingly fitting prelude to the sudden attack of pesticide poisons in the orchards that had left him literally sightless.

On the other hand, these people continued inventing and deploying bodily practices to leverage at least a marginal degree of self-determination once they had made it to this side of the Rio Grande. The process of learning key techniques of self-concealment, self-assertion, and self-regulation that had begun in tense moments near and beyond the border—Gloria Ruiz's last-minute search in Tijuana for the right blouse to wear, Elvira Méndez's tongue-lashing of the lecherous *pollero,* Rogelio Salazar's maneuvers under the noses of immigration officials in airports—went forward in the realm of undocumented work. Thus, when Ramona Díaz talked about "feeling free" as she labored in the fields, when Pedro Ruiz talked about appearing calm and avoiding capture in the warehouse raid, and when Alejandro Méndez recalled doing his pruning job "in seconds," they narrated a form of power in the illegal zone that was susceptible to their own small but significant attempts to exert agency. And with this shift in the story about power came an equivocation in the language of desire: between a sense that the individual yearned *to be set free from an oppressive fate,* and a notion that the same person wanted *to demonstrate and cultivate capacities to augment substantive, embodied forms of freedom for himself or herself.*

Immigrants' Narratives and Biopolitics by Other Means

How, then, might the stories these immigrant workers told about power in the zone of illegality, and the memories of desire that their stories encoded, relate to the narratives that critical theory constructs or invites regarding power in this domain? As surveillance technologies on the border proliferate, as the network of immigrant detention facilities expands, and as public anxieties about the contaminating effects of mobile Mexicans on the health of "Americans" continually resurface (witness the brief but acute hysteria over the swine flu epidemic in 2009), it makes sense initially to ponder what our interviews say about immigration as the scene for mechanisms of *discipline.* The advance of disciplinary power through its application to immigrants has a venerable history in the United States. Ali Behdad, for instance, describes how the early twentieth century witnessed the "medicalization of immigration control" (2005, 138). The U.S. Public Health Service, equipped with the research of eugenicist intellectuals, began requiring newly arriving immigrants to undergo medical diagnostic procedures that officially classified individuals as healthy or diseased while unofficially marking them all as, at the very least, suspected of physical degeneracy (Behdad 2005, 133). For Mexicans, as Mae Ngai observes, the consequences of this shift were particularly humiliating:

Inspection at the Mexican border involved a degrading procedure of bathing, delousing, medical-line inspection, and interrogation. The baths were new and unique to Mexican immigrants, requiring them to be inspected while naked, have their hair shorn, and have their clothing and baggage fumigated. Line inspection, modeled after the practice formerly used at Ellis Island, required immigrants to walk in single file past a medical officer. These procedures were particularly humiliating, even gratuitous, in light of the fact that the Immigration Act of 1924 required prospective immigrants to present a medical certificate to the U.S. consul when applying for a visa, that is, before travel to the United States. (Ngai 2004, 68)

Precisely this quality of excess, however, signals the political rationale for these procedures. The point was to enact a process "that clearly demarcated one society from another," stabilizing new constructions of national identity by creating a new geographic border that was inscribed on the individual bodies of immigrants (68).

More recently, Behdad notes, deployments of military force have made the border into "a privileged locus where the state's disciplinary practices can be articulated and exercised" (2005, 145).[34] Border agents' inspection manuals entangle agents and "aliens" alike in "a detailed system of identification, description, and categorization," thus rehearsing the "political anatomy of detail" that Foucault theorized as a central element of disciplinary power (151). Like the panopticist prison, the border's surveillance apparatus induces self-regulation because "the prospective border crosser must never know whether he or she is being observed at any particular moment, but must be made aware that the possibility always exists" (158).[35] Insofar as border militarization takes the form of "low-intensity conflict," as Timothy Dunn characterizes it, this process also lends itself to the diffuse yet pervasive style of disciplinary power. Not only does this approach intensify surveillance; in addition, it distributes power and responsibility among a growing multitude of state and even private voluntary agencies (Dunn 1996, 58–60, 98–99).[36] Finally, the explosive expansion of the immigrant detention industry not only helps fuel this dispersion of power but also creates the stark prospect that soon immigration control will no longer be merely analogous to the prison—it will adopt the carceral model as its core, explicit principle.[37]

The immigrant narratives about the domain of illegality considered in this chapter, however, convey an understanding of power that downplays the role of disciplinary mechanisms in a rigorous, specific sense. For Foucault, the "docile bodies" that discipline creates are not only "submissive," perpetually exposed to observation, taxonomically ordered, and "tractable and obedient" (Behdad 2005, 164). They are also *practiced bodies* in the sense that "discipline increases the forces of the body (in economic terms of utility)" even as it "diminishes these same forces (in political terms of obedience)" (Foucault 1979, 138). The body's activities are not just controlled—they are also made more efficient and productive. Moreover, Foucault sees the individual as not simply compelled or habituated to comply with certain institutional conditions but also as trained to regulate herself according to an internalized moral sensibility about the very "truth" of who she is, for instance through confessional practices (Foucault 1990, 58–70). Our informants simply did not depict power in the border zone, or in the domain of illegality inside the United States, as functioning according to these principles of *intensive individuation*. The people we spoke with did not indicate that they had been subjected to sustained programs of surveillance, examination and diagnosis according to precise schemata of classification, or regimens of training to induce self-regulation and to develop practiced bodies. Nor did their stories convey any sense of an urgent need either to perform adequately in such contexts or to be relieved of these sorts of pressures, whether they were talking about crossing the border or living and working without documents in the U.S. interior. The portions of the narratives that concerned work life were notable in one sense precisely because of the frequent slackness of disciplinary norms in these employment situations, as these immigrant workers described them.[38]

Instead of representing power in ways that would suggest such processes of individual normalization, this group of immigrants characterized power in this zone according to patterns that made it more closely resemble Foucault's conception of *biopolitics*. Foucault defines this mode of power in direct contrast to discipline, even while arguing that modern societies have tended to deploy both kinds of power in complementary ways:

Disciplines, for their part, dealt with individuals and their bodies in practical terms. . . . Biopolitics deals with the population, with the population as a political problem, as a problem that is at once scientific and political, as a biological problem and as power's problem. . . . The mechanisms introduced by biopolitics include forecasts, statistical estimates, and overall measures. And

98 Stories of Fate and Agency

their purpose is not to modify a given individual insofar as he is an individual, but, essentially, to intervene at the level at which these general phenomena are determined, to intervene at the level of their generality. The mortality rate has to be modified or lowered; life expectancy has to be increased; the birth rate has to be stimulated. . . . In a word, security mechanisms have to be installed around the random element inherent in a population of living beings so as to optimize a state of life. (Foucault 2003, 245–46)

Applying these life-promoting strategies to populations makes it possible to "distribut[e] the living in the domain of value and utility" (Foucault 1990, 144). Biopolitics thus promotes the general productivity of society in ways that "can be articulated with" discipline but that differ substantively from it (Foucault 2003, 250). However, Foucault also recognizes that states and societies do not seek to enhance biological vitality—or, as he puts it, to "invest life through and through"— for all populations equally (1990, 139). In fact, modern societies with sophisticated programs of discipline and biopolitics have also developed vast machineries for causing the deaths of mass populations through war, genocide, and other means. Faced with this apparent contradiction, Foucault argues that racism is a structural requirement for societies employing strategies of population management through biopolitics. Regarding racism, Foucault writes: "It is, in short, a way of establishing a biological-type caesura within a population that appears to be a biological domain. This will allow power to treat that population as a mixture of races, or to be more accurate, to treat the species, to subdivide the species it controls, into the subspecies known, precisely, as races" (Foucault 2003, 255). Once this division is in place, racism enables the "killing" of the groups that "are threats, either external or internal, to the population and for the population" (256). It sanctions lethal, mass-level strategies aimed at "the elimination of the biological threat to and the improvement of the species of the race" (256). Foucault adds: "When I say 'killing,' I obviously do not mean simply murder as such, but also every form of indirect murder: the fact of exposing someone to death, increasing the risk of death for some people, or, quite simply, political death, expulsion, rejection, and so on" (256).

Foucault's reflections on biopolitics provide a fitting preliminary framework for characterizing the primary dynamics of power, vis-à-vis undocumented immigrants, in the zone of illegality. However, a certain reformulation of this concept is also necessary to grasp the specific ways that immigrants encounter biopolitics in the United States today. Most importantly, the major current discourses about immigration generally do not achieve their biopolitical effects through explicit appeals regarding the racial health and vigor of the population. In earlier times, precisely these sorts of outright eugenicist considerations determined U.S. immigration policies. The "medicalization" of immigration not only exerted discipline upon individual immigrant bodies, as Behdad argues, but also sought to promote the health of the native white population by sequestering it from diseased, darker immigrant masses—and declared itself to be doing so. The popular writings of Alfred C. Reed, a physician and leading public health official at Ellis Island in the early twentieth century, epitomized this overt concern about "safeguarding the nation against contagious diseases from abroad," as Behdad puts it (2005, 133). By supporting the medical diagnostic, therapeutic, and quarantining operations in immigration regulatory facilities, Reed intoned, citizens would help the country "'wage war against the powers of ignorance, indifference, disease and degeneracy'" (1913, 314).[39]

Even today, the anxiety that disease-bearing immigrants from the south might infect and weaken the national *corpus* resounds in certain discourses about immigration, but now there is a reticence about saying this in plain language. In 1980s news stories about environmental deterioration near the U.S.–Mexico border, Sarah Hill argues, "characterizations of the border's degraded environment became a surrogate for immigration-writ-large through depictions of trespassing, soiling, and contaminating matter and bodies that appeared to threaten the integrity, safety, economic security, and hygienic future of the American nation" (2006, 780). Yet here a process of *coding* substitutes the symbol of the dirtied natural environment for the "self-soiling" immigrant who presents the implicit hygienic threat to "America." This rerouting of meanings, which dissimulates the racist logic of power, illustrates the common tendency in biopolitical discourse regarding immigration today.

The twenty-first-century bipartisan consensus about the need to "secure our borders" does not explicitly raise the specter of germ-infested immigrants contaminating white America, but it exudes biopolitical consequences in full measure.[40] As the stories of our informants clearly show, even back in the 1980s when most of them entered the United States, crossing the border illegally meant that for this population subgroup, the ordinary conditions of life—finding sufficiently remunerative work, ensuring adequate schooling for children, keeping families together—involved undergoing extraordinary risks of physical and emotional trauma and even of death. Protecting the country against incursions by those who erode the rule of law and jeopardize the survival of a uniquely American "common culture," however, rather than giving the nation prophylaxis against disease, are the main tropes of current immigration "reform" discourse. To be sure, nativists implicitly raise eugenicist anxieties when they accuse immigrants of soaking up precious public welfare resources and, in particular, rage against immigrant women for driving up state expenditures on prenatal care and hospital childbirth services. As Dorothy E. Roberts notes, such vitriol in the campaign for California's Proposition 187 certainly suggested that immigrants are not worthy of the aids to reproduction that the dominant racial subpopulation deserves (1996, 207). Even so, the express rationale for denying immigrants access to reproductive health services has been the purported need to preserve a unified, inherited national *culture* rather than to promote the health and vitality of "authentic" Americans.[41] Indeed, proponents of tighter immigration restrictions and more vigorous border enforcement often have sought to suppress public attention to the health-related needs of undocumented immigrants altogether by insisting that the only meaningful lens for understanding this population is as transgressors of the law.[42]

The project of border militarization, in turn, employs methods of population management that strikingly resemble the techniques Foucault associates with biopolitics. The state directs the border zone in terms of populations and policies that are conceived of and evaluated through the generalizing medium of statistics. These labors of calculation measure how many undocumented crossers are apprehended by the U.S. Border Patrol each year, how many illegal travelers have entered the country despite border enforcement efforts, how many people without documents have died in waterless deserts or airless boxcars, how much public money needs to be invested and how many Border Patrol agents must be commissioned to boost "security" on the border, and how many new beds and prison cells are required for the growing network of immigrant detention facilities.[43] The state takes these aggregate measurements, adjusts them to one another, and promulgates policies that distribute life opportunities and mortality threats to immigrant populations in the aggregate. It renders immigrants vulnerable to death by compelling them to negotiate the hazards of clandestine border crossings in order to find sustaining work. In steering processes of everyday life for the undocumented within the United States, in turn, the state employs strategies of intimidation and deterrence to induce the undocumented population to confine itself within a certain spatial grid, thereby reinforcing its racially differentiated program for promoting the social increase of "value and utility." The state thus makes sure that this population is for the most part only present and active in spaces devoted either to generating economic value or reproducing its own labor power (which it accomplishes with negligible public assistance).

Crucially, biopolitics operates in this way with respect to undocumented immigrants not *in spite of* the fact that the legally resident population benefits from a different palette of life-promoting institutional interventions but rather as a (tacit) means of *enabling* the racially privileged population to thrive corporeally. By ensuring through policing tactics that undocumented immigrants are confined mainly to jobs in the informal economy such as farm labor, biopolitics gives the racially dominant group the discretion to decide that there are certain jobs it simply "cannot or will not do." These, of course, are the jobs that carry neither health insurance nor actionable occupational safety and health rights while also involving higher than usual health and safety hazards. (Thus, the unspoken condition of that singular moment when a legally resident white man gazes into his newborn child's eyes for the first time is the higher probability that an undocumented farmworker like Pedro Ruiz will barely be able to make out his minutes-old daughter's features because of the pesticides that have stolen his sight. Likewise, the greater incidence of birth defects and miscarriages for farmworkers' children are the preconditions for lower risks of both kinds in the U.S.-born white population.) These jobs are also the occupations in which workers subsidize public health benefits for others that they themselves will never enjoy, through the Medicare deductions from their paychecks.

The metabolic link that biopolitics forges between the racially privileged legal population and undocumented immigrants also arises from the latter's production of the food that nourishes the former. Here, to be sure, the bodily benefits accruing to the dominant group are more equivocal. On the one hand, because of cheap farm labor that poses no serious, organized obstacle to agribusiness's structural dependence on poisonous, fossil fuel–based fertilizers and pesticides, U.S. American consumers enjoy a bonanza of food commodities. These products provide plentiful and diverse nutrients and are available in wide selection throughout the year, thanks both to the sweat of farmworkers for export-oriented growers in Mexico and South America as well as to the exertions of cannery, produce warehouse, and frozen-food immigrant workers in the United States. On the other hand, the same chemicals that debilitate workers' bodies contaminate the apples and frozen asparagus that consumers eat. Moreover, bales upon bales of inexpensive farm commodities help generate a food economy in the United States and other developed countries that runs on massive overeating and yields the well-known by-products of ill health, from diabetes and heart disease to sugar-related mental problems. Even so, what the racially privileged lose in terms of these hazards they likely recoup by having more stable health insurance, broader public social benefits, and less dangerous jobs of their own.

The stories of immigrants in the illegal zone examined in this chapter not only expressed what it meant to these people, as unique individuals, to become systematically exposed to such racist biopolitics—they also conveyed *theories* of the constitutional elements of biopolitical power in what Gramsci reminds us is the already "critical" mode of common sense, although this itself is open to "critical renovation" through contact with theory from other quarters. And these conceptions of power, to return to a point I raised in the introduction to this chapter, both represent and exemplify the active but ambiguous role that immigrants play in constituting the domain of "illegalities," which turns out not to be simply the creature and administrative object of the law and the state. One major feature of power in the illegal realm that these narrators descry, when they engage in the narrative strain stressing the migrant body's subjection to looming forces beyond the individual's ability to control or predict, is quite simply the extensive catalog of miseries and compromises that the biopolitical formation incessantly produces for immigrant workers. But another component, perhaps more easily overlooked, is the storytelling capacity of immigrant workers themselves. Insofar as our informants positioned themselves as profoundly at the mercy of an inscrutable fate and emphasized the anxieties and physical traumas that had been thrust upon them, for example, they told their stories in ways that were likely to confirm the intrepid advance of biopolitics. In this dimension of the narratives, to borrow a musical metaphor, resignation was the tonic key. Crossing the border was essentially an experience of loss, a series of shamefully distressing corporeal trials that had been painfully withstood and were better forgotten. But in a sense it seemed impossible to forget, since this response to the dangers and humiliations of the border furnished an abiding genealogical precedent for interpreting experiences in later stages of the journey through the zone of illegality. These included, for example, the further encounters with biopolitics that set the patterns of spatial self-enclosure involved in living *encerrado* as well as the harsh working conditions and endemic unreliability of the jobs these people performed. This pattern of narration, in short, tended to make inevitable, though no less lamentable, the stripping of the individual's agency to determine the bodily impact of migration.

At the same time, it is important to consider how the uneven power relations characterizing the interview situation itself, which I considered in chapter 1, may have been implicated in the sotto voce and equivocal terms with which our informants described their practices of self-concealment and self-regulation to us. For example, Rogelio Salazar's failed attempt to deflect my research assistant's attention away from his own agency in developing such techniques could be seen as evidence of a further experiment with the art of passing, with the aim being to pass *before our eyes* as an immigrant with little control over his own circumstances. The curious tensions in so many of these immigrant workers' stories between attributing their good fortune to fate and describing their deliberate actions to elude capture and accomplish other goals, such as in the accounts provided by Elvira Méndez, Esperanza Soto, and Pedro Ruiz, could also be read in this way. In other words, these individuals very well could have been layering their exposures of various practices of hiding, passing, and righteous resistance with a form of verbal camouflage. Dismissing their successful navigations of the state's surveillance apparatus as just plain *suerte* might have been a defensive tactic for directing attention away from abilities that are more potent the less well understood they are by people in privileged positions of social power. These individuals may have deliberately downplayed their real capacities for avoiding capture because of the power differential characterizing the interview situation, or they may have done this simply out of habit, or both. Without insights from more sustained ethnographic study of these individuals and their culture of everyday life, it is difficult to resolve these thorny questions regarding their intentions and motivations. However, it is important to acknowledge that their narratives may have functioned in this political mode because it invites skepticism about too hastily or unequivocally viewing these stories as serving the *status quo*.

The people we interviewed theorized an even more varied and ambivalent range of features within the biopolitical apparatus when they called attention to their capacities for performing various kinds of work on their environments and themselves. When these immigrant workers noted the multiple practices of body and soul that they had adopted to get across the border and to remain undetected while living illegally in the United States—particular ways of dressing, tactics for staying out of sight, habits of movement, precautions for carrying means of payment, strategies for locating human smugglers—they were showing us how they had developed a regime of effective microtechniques of the body and its visual, audible, and otherwise sensible accoutrements. They had done this, moreover, through loose networks of association they had developed when neither the state nor employers sought to incorporate them into more formal schemas of disciplinary power. These institutional entities neither educated them in new bodily habits that certified them as new Americans nor trained them in the productive skills they would have needed to acquire practiced bodies, nor tried to inculcate the desire to regulate and motivate themselves in accordance with official norms. Thus, in the context of this disciplinary vacuum, these immigrant workers generated self-regulatory practices for themselves through their unofficial tutorials with *coyotes* during border crossings as well as via the informal relays of communication among fellow travelers and kin about how to avoid abuses by unscrupulous *polleros* and escape capture by *la migra*. Similar kinds of practical training also happened through informal employment-related networks, as workers taught one another techniques for maximizing their take-home pay while evading *la migra* in the fields or for locating jobs in the fluid labor market for contingent workers.[44]

In an important sense, the workers' stories about their arts of self-concealment and self-management, as well as their techniques of personal resistance against immediate forms of aggression, revealed an array of buttressing joists within the biopolitical structure. By deploying this practical knowledge, our interviewees fortified the state's ideological position as the guarantor of the law's force and the protector of American culture. Doing so enabled them to get across the border and thus to reproduce, as a population, the problems of lawbreaking and cultural destabilization—problems the state has set itself up to solve as a way of legitimating its uses of power and problems that, as I have argued, rationalize implicitly biopolitical consequences. Furthermore, by training themselves in techniques for staying invisible in plain sight, modulating their internal emotions and physical responses, and lashing out in righteous indignation at those who posed face-to-face threats, these immigrants helped the state perform these other problem-solving tasks more efficiently, with no need to pay the political and financial costs of official disciplinary programs aimed at them. Instead, the state could limit itself to circuitously crafting the conditions in which discipline through unofficial channels would arise, just as it indirectly promoted biopolitics. As the workers' microtechniques enabled them to migrate successfully and to stay concealed once inside the United States, moreover, they also made it possible for companies dependent on immigrant workforces to count on a reliable stream of inexpensive labor from the south. They thus reinforced the contributions of the racially segmented labor market and the industrial food production and distribution system to the general management of racially differentiated life and health prospects.

This point comes through with added clarity when we take another close look at the politics of the stories these immigrants told about times when they engaged in acts of resistance during their crossings and the understandings of power that these narratives of self-exertion both presupposed and obscured. The people we interviewed directed these oppositional acts against external or internal forces that operated at close range and had an immediately palpable quality. Thus, it was in relation to individual *coyotes* that some of the women issued moral condemnations of personal conduct, confronted would-be perpetrators of sexual abuse, performed defiant acts of generosity in moments of dire deprivation, and sewed checks into their clothing to avoid getting robbed. The men, by contrast, tended to take up an inwardly directed battle that focused on the self and its recalcitrant weaknesses: the test was to stave off fear, to bear up under intense physical suffering, to keep a grip on manly aspirations, and to fire the resolve of one's comrades to do likewise. (Gilberto Rivera's defiant outburst in telling his boss that he was a "worker" and not a "slave," after making it across the border, was the one departure from this pattern.) In both cases, channeling struggle toward either the smuggler or the self *displaced* oppositional energies that otherwise could have been leveled at the larger institutions that had created these terrains of power and resistance in the first place: the state and capital.

In addition, by telling stories that communicated a genuine and occasionally keen feeling of pride and a sense of emotional investment in having deployed these tactics of self-regulation to good effect, our informants were in some degree feeding biopolitics by making it seem tolerable and justifiable in their own eyes. With the aid of this current of common sense, that is, they could imagine a mode of action under biopolitical domination that at least reserved for them a small quantum of self-determination. In other words, their storytelling about retaining a modicum of agency in the zone of illegality helped give *hegemonic* force to implicit biopolitics, a foothold in ordinary people's everyday habits of thought and action beyond its roots in the statements and policies of government and business institutions. By narrating affirmatively their own successful practices in response to the contingencies of the journey across the border, the depredations of the *polleros,* the dangers of capture both during and after the crossing, the conditions of work in the underground economy, and their own internal fears and frailties, these people were helping to constitute the condition of illegality in ways that promoted—again, implicitly—biopolitics on the wider social level. This too, then, comprised a key part of the critically renovative moment of the workers' narratives vis-à-vis critical theory: exposing the all-too-convenient advantages for biopolitics that stem from immigrant workers' storytelling even when it accentuates their agentic capacities, not to mention when they position themselves as hapless victims.

Nevertheless, the Tyson/IBP workers' accounts of their bodily microtechniques still signaled important moments of rupture and self-negation within the biopolitical formation. The facility that Rogelio

Salazar and Pedro Ruiz showed with techniques for passing as legal travelers and workers, for example, enabled them not only to evade the state's surveillance but also to make that power revert back against itself. They did this by making the authorities' procedures of observation become precisely what prevented them from detecting these immigrants' illegal presence, turning these formulas of visual appraisal to the immigrants' advantage. To note this is not to deny that the state's legitimation operations and the employers' labor projects still gained substantially from immigrants' abilities, through these tactics, to keep working in the United States. It is to acknowledge, nevertheless, that power did not function exclusively in this way, since these situations provided contexts wherein immigrant workers could cultivate their abilities to redirect the flows of force and take an active role in the constitution of their world.

Meanwhile, by *narrating* power's operation in this way that recognized the migrant's active, generative abilities within the sphere of illegality, at least as an individual placed within an informal network of affiliation, the workers disrupted the hegemonic force of the other current within their narratives that put them in the spot of abject helplessness and paralyzing fear. They also set up something like a resonance board for the adjacent portions of their narratives that stressed organized, collective action through the rank-and-file movement, which I examine in chapter 5. The politics of this segment of the interviews, dealing with this particular stage of their shared experiences, thus paralleled and confirmed that of their stories about life in Mexico that I considered in chapter 2. In both cases, we heard the workers describing modes of individuality and psychophysical agency that contained the germinal potential to grow into narratives of power-in-solidarity, given the right political nutrients. In neither phase of their stories did these individuals express desires for explicit political opposition to the national or transnational institutions that orchestrate biopolitical power on a grand scale. Yet here, just as when they described the circumstances under which they had set out on migrant paths, their stories of acting to enhance the freedom of and limit the damage to their bodies in the zone of illegality laid the groundwork for more incisively counterhegemonic patterns of narration.

Before moving on to discuss the subsequent stages of their personal life stories, dealing with their experiences at the slaughterhouse and with the union movement, it is worth noting that a radical response to biopolitics in the current age of mass immigration stands to learn much from these narratives, as such, about life and travel in the domain of illegality. As cotheorists of power, the immigrant workers we interviewed spotlight the need for any counterhegemonic politics of justice for immigrants to speak directly to those dimensions of the implicitly biopolitical formation that they uniquely pinpoint. Creating a new legalization program, for instance, which at this writing is on Congress's agenda, certainly would alleviate the burdens of living *la vida encerrada* for undocumented immigrants who are already in the United States. Such a policy innovation would be a truly momentous achievement given the hard and bitter struggle against the forces of nativism that it would entail. However, even this seemingly far-reaching reform would not change at all the biopolitical operations exerted on new border crossers. Indeed, if the legislative politics of the Immigration Reform and Control Act (IRCA) offer any tea leaves in which the future of immigration reform can be read, the price of easing bodily and social constraints on illegal workers who currently reside in the United States may well be to ratchet up even further the exposure to "killing," in Foucault's grimly inclusive sense, of new clandestine travelers across the border. The critique of power encoded in these workers' narratives further suggests that any immigration reform package that sunders immigrants' legal rights to immigrate from their rights *as workers* would similarly fail to shift the ground under the biopolitical formation significantly. Immigrant farm laborers need practical, actionable rights to safer and healthier working conditions as well as enforceable political rights to assemble freely and form unions if immigration reform is to mitigate the racial differentiation of the population's prospects for life and vitality.

At the same time, the critical political message of these immigrant workers' narratives of the illegal realm extends beyond the reconstruction of legal rights and toward strategies of counterhegemonic organizing. Such political practices ought to include efforts by immigrant workers to refunction the narrative habits and bodily microtechniques that, as I have shown, comprise ways that they themselves bolster current-day biopolitics. Fighting for justice for immigrants would have to mean much more than, say, conducting fact-based workshops on the law for undocumented workers, as useful and necessary as such sessions are for many people. It would also mean multiplying the forums where migrants can more freely share their stories of navigating the border and the illegal zones within the United States and where they can sort through the political complexities of their experiences of victimization and self-determination in those domains. Where the techniques of action and narration divide into gendered kinds, furthermore, immigrant justice groups should use such forums to develop the critical potential of gendered ways of seeing, experiencing, and refunctioning power rather than superimposing a gender-neutral discourse over this diverse narrative field. Ultimately, seeking justice for immigrants must involve concerted efforts not only to recognize how immigrant workers individually contest and redirect the flows of biopolitics through bodily techniques of freedom but also to assemble these micropractices into collaborative incursions against the biopolitical apparatus.

4. Labor, Injury, and Self-Preservation in the Slaughterhouse

HAVING GROWN UP in Mexico doing an assortment of odd jobs to help their families scrape by, and having kept afloat financially north of the border by laboring in the fields, orchards, or other areas of the informal economy, the immigrants we interviewed found their lives to be dramatically changed when they gained legalization and began working at IBP. With over 1,500 employees at its Pasco facility, IBP was much larger than any workplace these individuals had ever entered before. And more than just a source of income, it was its own world with its own culture—even its own popular mythology. Melquíades "Flaco" ("skinny guy") Pereyra remembered the dread with which he anticipated his job there after opportunities in local canneries dried up as winter approached in 1987:

I had heard a whole lot of talk about IBP. There were three guys living with me, and those three were working at IBP . . . they didn't talk about anything else but IBP. About the work, and how their hands hurt; how their backs hurt. And—and it was horrible, really, to hear them talk. . . . The way they were talking, I imagined that this job was just for strong people. . . . They told me, "Don't go; you won't be able to do it. You're really skinny; you're just a little guy." . . . I had no other option. I struggled for two months to get an easier job, where I could, but they were all gone, the time was up, and I had to go to IBP. I went to IBP; I applied. And when I arrived the person who interviewed me says: "And you, how much time do you think you're going to last here?"[1] I told him, "Well, I don't know. Maybe a year; maybe two years. I don't know." . . . I started working at IBP. And I regretted it very much. I regretted it a lot; I regretted it because it was hell to work inside there.[2]

There was something all consuming about working at IBP, as Pereyra's reminiscences about his housemates illustrate. There was also something frankly debilitating about it. Part of what made the job seem to colonize the rest of everyday existence was the relentlessness of the pain and exhaustion people experienced from working there. The job at IBP was a far more regular and formal kind of employment than these immigrants previously had obtained. Yet while it offered relatively greater economic stability, it also promised newly acute insecurity and vulnerability of a brutally physical nature. In exchange for dependable wages, benefits, and the chance to labor under a roof instead of out in the field, the workers urged us to see, they had to work in a state of constant crisis as they battled to stave off complete bodily devastation.

After abandoning work in the fields and surviving the manifold anxieties of life in the illegal zone, individuals like Flaco Pereyra and his housemates had entered a new terrain within the biopolitical formation involving a fresh set of difficulties for immigrant workers. The meatpacking industry had constructed this social space for immigrant workers as part of the historic overhaul of its hiring practices, production methods, marketing priorities, and capital accumulation strategies—a process inaugurated, as journalist and author Eric Schlosser terms it, by "the IBP revolution" in the 1960s. IBP's engineers designed an innovative, highly automated production process that used a variety of emergent technologies and enabled a much more thorough division of labor. IBP's cattle "disassembly line" thus vastly reduced the company's reliance on skilled, unionized, U.S.-born workers while making possible much faster rates of production and far higher volumes of output. At the same time, IBP and the other beef industry giants cut production expenses (e.g., by lowering cattle transport costs) and reduced exposure to union pressures by relocating their facilities from major cities like Chicago to little country towns like Wallula, Washington, or Greeley, Colorado (Schlosser 2002, 153–54).[3] Wages in the meat industry fell precipitously, losing 50 percent of real value in the last quarter of the twentieth century, with deunionization and the loss of union militancy as key factors in this shift (Apostolidis and Brenner 2005; Craypo 1994, 70–79).[4] Immigrant workers, in turn, provided a logical and increasingly plentiful new labor source to take jobs that no longer compensated their occupants at levels acceptable to the U.S.-born, jobs that in any case were popping up in sparsely populated areas distant from urban, working-class communities. With the acceleration of immigration from Mexico and elsewhere in Latin America following the termination of the Bracero program (which analysts say stimulated undocumented immigration in the long run by enabling the growth of migrant networks and reinforcing immigrant workers' role in U.S. agribusiness), the 1965 immigration reforms, and then the advent of economic crisis and neoliberal transformations, U.S. slaughter-houses' dependence on immigrant labor increasingly became a key structural feature of the industry.

This chapter probes the stories that the rank-and-file activists from Tyson/IBP told us about the relations of power they encountered when their lives became centered within this domain specially reserved for immigrant workers. I initiate this discussion in an experimental mode, approaching these stories from a couple of different theoretical angles to see how closely they match the conceptions of power one might *expect* to see given the meatpacking industry's drive toward rationali-zation of the labor process as well as the workers' own life transition from the informal to the formal labor market. Since the focus here is on the mobilization of consent or opposition to power through specific features of a factory work environment, I first turn to the pathbreak-ing industrial-sociological theory of Michael Burawoy as a potential model for the production of consent at Tyson/IBP. Burawoy's Grams-cian analyses of the hegemonic ramifications of the organization of work stress the consent-making forces that flow from routines on the job that lead the worker to experience work as a realm where she or he makes meaningful individual choices. Our interviewees' narratives about labor and power at the slaughterhouse, however, contrast might-ily with this vision of consent through individualist, strategic commit-ments to perpetuating the "rules of the game." I show that this is the case even when the workers spoke about aspects of the work environ-ment, such as the preferential hiring system for current employees, that in principle could have nurtured the disposition of competitive individualism conducive to consent in the mode analyzed by Burawoy. Nor do our informants' accounts of their experiences on the shop floor or with the plant's injury treatment protocols accord well, I argue, with another conception of power that one might anticipate would aptly describe this work environment: Foucault's theory of disciplinary power. Fitted out with many of the trappings of a classic disciplinary apparatus, from intensive surveillance of workers to a detailed classi-fication of individual production roles and a highly elaborate system for diagnosing and rehabilitating workers rendered dysfunctional by their injuries, in practice the work environment at the factory as nar-rated by these workers seemed to thwart discipline's realization at every turn.

In contrast to both Burawoy's notion of consent based on individuals' habitual pursuit of personal benefits through strategic choices and a Foucauldian conception of power that yields docile laborers through discipline, our narrator-theorists offered a vivid image of despotic domination that was generated simultaneously by formal management policies, informal subversions of those production standards by the company, and directly personal and physical intimidation by supervisors. They told us shocking accounts of how supervisors shouted at them in rage to get them to keep up with the chain, which was invariably set at inhumanly high speeds. The managers, they said, arbitrarily forced them to do jobs they did not want to do or had not been trained to perform, compelled them to work past quitting time and into their breaks, and even refused to let them leave the line to go to the bathroom. Between these pressures and the added strain of having to labor in persistently understaffed workstations, most found it impossible to avoid getting injured or developing job-related health problems. At this point, their situation of powerlessness only intensified. Thus, the workers described in excruciating detail how supervisors had denied them referrals to the infirmary and how nurses at the plant had redirected them hastily back to work with "fistfuls of ibuprofen." When their injuries became unbearable, they further explained, the company made them go see handpicked doctors who issued temporary work restrictions instead of prescribing therapeutic care. Once assigned to "light duty" at the plant, they met with a fresh round of degradations and physical hardships that they believed were intended to compel them either to quit or to work despite being hurt. In short, the predominant picture the workers painted of their workplace revealed a domain where they were the unwilling, ignored, and abused objects of a tyrannical power that appeared to pride itself on always finding new ways to torment them.

At certain moments within this narrative of power, however, the seemingly intrepid domination of the workers by the company broke down. Now and then, in the creases between their laments about being mistreated and deprived of all autonomy, the workers would note how they had found small ways to make their labor a little less damaging to themselves. They would say, for example, that they had learned to do work not only on cattle carcasses but also on their own bodies: religiously applying skin creams and washing themselves when the labor process made contact with infectious matter inescapable; training themselves in habits of movement on the shop floor to minimize their exposure to lacerations from coworkers' knives; and sometimes medicating themselves with drugs and alcohol to dull the pain and boost their stamina. At times, our informants would also insist that they had gained the courage to confront and repel the most immediate, personal forms of violation by yelling back at their supervisors—and, more dismally, by shouting at one another to keep pace with the chain and to stave off worse treatment by the managers. So whereas the main storyline about life in the slaughterhouse projected a deep desire for relief from pain and rescue from victimization, this other narrative strain evinced a different type of yearning. It assumed a stronger, more abiding sense of the workers' ability to construct a viable working environment for themselves, even under severely beleaguered conditions.

This competing narrative about power in the slaughterhouse had ambiguous political and theoretical implications that corresponded closely to those emanating from their stories about the domain of illegality. When the workers told us how the labor process forced them to endanger their bodies, how supervisors commanded their job performance with imperious authority, and how the company responded to their injuries with cold indifference or outright hostility, these stories of abject humiliation once again bespoke the enactment of biopolitics by nonexplicit means. In other words, they conveyed in the everyday language of common sense (in the Gramscian meaning) what it was like to be subjected to the social discourses that impose special bodily and psychological costs on nonwhite immigrants, thereby promoting the physiological well-being of the racially privileged group without acknowledging this goal. These discourses include, first, the prevailing wisdom that the U.S. economy needs immigrants to do the jobs that Americans cannot or will not do, which leaves unspoken the higher risks of physical and emotional trauma that go along with jobs like meatpacking. Second, the consumerist fantasy conjured by the meat industry, where bodily vigor increases through daily intake of industrially produced meat made sanitary by technopharmaceutical practices, conducts biopolitics by other means even though it says nothing overt about race. To guarantee cheap prices while legitimizing sanitization by antibiotics and irradiation rather than through slower and more hygienic production methods, the industry depends on the sweat of immigrants who accept low wages and churn out vast volumes of meat products by working themselves far past the point of injury. Third, the racial differentiation of prospects for physically safe and emotionally healthy employment occurs through the public policy discourse, vacant though it is of explicitly racial language, that counts on employers' voluntary initiatives to implement the rights and duties enshrined in the Occupational Safety and Health Act of 1970. When the workers portrayed themselves as laboring under despotic power that brooked no resistance and ground up their bodies just as surely and mechanically as they themselves ground meat into hamburger, they were contributing to a *theorization* of these multifarious dynamics of biopolitics today. They characterized with excruciating precision the multiple dimensions of bodily distress for the racially subaltern that this biopolitical apparatus effects as well as the oppressive sense of inescapability that, for them, accompanied these power operations.

This notion that persistent suffering on the line at Tyson/IBP was simply inevitable, in turn, combined with other aspects of the workers' narratives about work at the plant to *augment the hegemony* of the biopolitical formation they described. Inasmuch as these narrators conceived of themselves as having no option but to endure the harms that these conditions generated, they embedded the mechanisms as basic facts of life in their everyday common sense, just as they had done when discussing their exposure to humiliating, disorienting, and corporeally imperiling forms of danger and mistreatment on their clandestine border crossings. Or, to refigure a phrase coined by Burawoy, these worker-narrators subtly aided the growth of what we might call "hegemonic despotism" at the plant. Burawoy invokes this ominous notion to describe a shift in the main institutional strategy for cultivating organized labor's consent to state and capitalist authority in advanced capitalist countries during neoliberal times:

The interests of capital and labour continue to be concretely coordinated, but where labour used to be *granted* concessions on the basis of the expansion of profits, it now *makes* concessions on the basis of the relative profitability of one capitalist vis-à-vis another—that is, the opportunity costs of capital. . . . The reproduction of labour power is bound anew to the production process, but, rather than via the individual, the binding occurs at the level of the firm, region or even nation-state. The fear of being fired is replaced by the fear of capital flight, plant closure, transfer of operations, and plant disinvestment. (Burawoy 1990, 149–50)

Burawoy thus gestures toward the pattern I discuss in this chapter involving the deactivation of individuating mechanisms and the adoption of company strategies aimed at the workers as a mass population. However, the Tyson/IBP workers' accounts of power at this plant extend and diversify the terrain on which it is possible to discern the efficacy of power in the mode of hegemonic despotism. According to these narrator-theorists, this hegemonic field includes not only the class political-organizational dynamics to which Burawoy refers but also the characteristic structuration of the labor process, the guiding rubric of its complementary system for handling injured workers, and—crucially—certain aspects of the workers' own narrated "common sense" regarding the ways that biopolitical power functioned at the slaughterhouse.

In turn, by drawing our attention to the microtechniques they had developed to gain some prophylaxis against the torrent of hazards and degradations at the slaughterhouse, the workers in some ways fortified the biopolitical regime even further. By training themselves and one another in various arts of self-preservation on the job, these immigrant workers complemented macro-level corporate strategies for orchestrating beef production, marketing, and consumption with micro-level preparations and adjustments by individual bodies and minds. They thereby helped to ensure the overall continuity and functionality of the system. Insofar as they also suggested that learning these techniques made them feel like competent employees who had a degree of control over their situation, they added an extra dose of *consent* to the implicitly racist discourses on which the industry depends concerning "immigrant jobs," healthy carnivory, and employer voluntarism in occupational health and safety. Or, to put it in terms I introduced in chapter 3, they facilitated the link on a metabolic level that entwined their labor-related and immigration-induced bodily suffering with the biological flourishing of the racially dominant population.

Yet at the same time, it is important to note that by telling us about the habits they had cultivated for deflecting harm and abuse at the plant, these immigrant workers were interrupting their own preferred narrative about being simply at the mercy of cruel managers, callous doctors, and the chain itself. Minute and forlorn though these strategies of self-defense were, they were not trivial. They proved that the workers saw some alternative to viewing themselves as helpless victims of authoritarian practices completely beyond their control. And this alternative view not only disturbed the tendency of the more prominent part of the narratives to promote biopolitical subjugation by making it seem a fait accompli, it also created a different sort of genealogical antecedent for the stories they would tell about their collective actions to change their union and power relations in the plant. In other words, instead of only being able to draw on a mentality of resentful victimization, in the context of the rank-and-file movement the workers could also find resources in their narrated experiences of work on the line for fashioning stories of self-determination aimed at transforming the institutions around them.

Individualism, Careerism, and Choice in the Work Environment: Means of Consent?

To a surprising extent, as we saw in chapter 3, the individuals we interviewed had found elements of satisfaction in their work in the fields before coming to IBP. Especially in hindsight, having experienced the working conditions at the slaughterhouse, they had appreciated the lack of constant and physically overbearing supervision as well as the chance to work in the open air. One might surmise, nevertheless, that the workers would have come to find more valuable kinds of freedom and contentment in their beef-processing jobs. IBP offered them a far more formalized and predictable world of employment than they had experienced as farmworkers. As long-term contractual employees for a major corporation, might they not have viewed their meatpacking jobs not only as means for earning a weekly paycheck but also as stable, structural features of their lives? Could they perhaps have invested themselves personally in mapping out a career trajectory with the company or at least in crafting informal strategies for making their work yield maximal advantages to them over time? And if so, then might they thereby have gained a novel sense both of their own ability to succeed through occupational advancement and of the value in doing so?

Michael Burawoy's singularly influential, Gramscian analyses of what he calls "the politics of production" suggest the pertinence of posing these questions when we begin to evaluate the circuitries of power at the slaughterhouse as the workers described them. Burawoy investigates the ways that the organization of work in industrial settings elicits workers' consent to capitalist relations of domination in both site-specific and broader social dimensions. This hegemonic dynamic often occurs, he argues, when processes in the work environment induce workers to gain a sense that they are making autonomous, individual choices about the work they do, such that work makes them feel capable and brings them diverse, concrete benefits. At a machining plant Burawoy analyzed, for example, workers had become skilled at maximizing their individual take-home pay and solving practical problems by cultivating advantageous relationships with supervisors and other workers, such as auxiliary workers who could help them produce at high rates by supplying them expeditiously with materials. In other words, the workers had learned how to play a "game," which Burawoy called "making out," that brought them tangible rewards. It boosted their wages, alleviated their boredom, increased their sense of psychological self-worth, improved their status in the eyes of fellow workers, and staved off excessive fatigue (Burawoy 1979, 64, 85). At the same time, they had acquired a desire to perpetuate the game so as to keep these positive benefits flowing. And by acting on this personal investment in the game's continuance, they furnished a very practical, day-to-day form of consent to both the immediate authority of management and the capitalist order in general (85–86). Yet precisely because both these specific dynamics of production and the broader capitalist framework depended on workers' consent, and because workers themselves generated the game that ensured their compliance, workers retained the ability to reorganize these processes in more democratic and self-determining ways. "As an instrument of critique," Burawoy writes, "the game metaphor implies some notion of an emancipated society in which people make history themselves for themselves, self-consciously and deliberately" (93).

How closely did the dynamics of hegemony at Tyson/IBP, as the workers described them, parallel this model of consent through "making out"? Did workers actively invest their energies in their jobs in the strategic, plan-oriented, highly individualist ways that Burawoy stresses? The comparison might at first seem ill advised because at Tyson/IBP, meatpackers were paid hourly wages rather than the piece rates that Burawoy's machinists earned. In any given job, the worker's wage remained the same regardless of how fast she or he worked and irrespective of the actions of coworkers. Nevertheless, Tyson/IBP and the machining plant shared one key process for letting workers make choices about their jobs and career paths: an "internal labor market," or a formal protocol for making open jobs initially available just to current employees and only subsequently, if left unfilled, to workers hired from the outside. Burawoy emphasizes how this institution stimulated competitive individualism among the machinists by activating their desires to develop specialized capabilities and to prove themselves by gaining open positions over coworkers (Burawoy 1979, 104). On the surface, the "bid job" system at Tyson/IBP seemed likely to do the same thing. According to Flaco Pereyra, workers had three days to bid for an open job before the company would hire from outside the plant. Workers who transferred to new positions were supposed to receive the training they needed while also undergoing a "qualifying" evaluation. There was a competitive dimension to the bid job process, as indicated by a limitation on transfers from slaughter into processing as well as by the value workers placed on the preferential treatment in bidding that came with seniority. At union meetings to determine priorities for the 2004 contract campaign that I observed, it was clear that many workers valued this system as a conduit to higher pay and a device for exerting more individual control over their working conditions, and they wanted to repel any effort by the company to eliminate it.

The stories the workers told us in the interviews, however, made the bid job system seem highly dysfunctional and poorly equipped to nurture the processes of individualization and consent that, for Burawoy, internal labor markets tend to promote. Their desires for establishing a career track at the slaughterhouse and for competing against other workers in this venture were tenuous at best. When the workers we interviewed used the bid job system to their advantage, they tended to do so not to *achieve* any positive aspirations for career advancement or self-improvement but rather to *escape* a dangerous or distasteful situation. Rogelio Salazar, for instance, worked in slaughter and had been kicked in the face twice by cows during the killing process, when he had performed an especially hazardous task while working on the first leg (the first limb to be handled following the killing of the animal). He decided to exercise his bid job options after the second injury landed him in light duty for another term of nearly nine months, put him in a neck brace, and caused major dental damage resulting in surgery to remove a tooth that had died after being driven up inside his face: "After that . . . a supervisor told me that if I wanted, I could move to the second leg and if I wanted, I could sign up for that; so that's where I stayed. I didn't want to be over there [on the first leg], because they probably would have kicked me again. That is, it was for my safety that I wanted [to switch], that I moved over here."[5] As Salazar emphasized, his primary desire in using the bid job system was to protect himself against further blows from the hooves of dying cattle; and he added that he did not find the job on the second leg more appealing than working on the first leg. Neither competition with other workers nor any hope for the achievement of personal career objectives played a role in his action.

Elvira Méndez used her bid job rights as an exit route from another difficult situation, in her case a conflict with a fellow worker. The conflict did not stem from competition over mutually desired goods but rather from perceptions of unfair treatment tinged with racial resentments. Méndez was dissatisfied with her initial job at IBP, partly because she had to work the evening shift when she wanted to be home with her family but mainly because of unfair treatment by her supervisor—"*un chino*," as she called him, using the slang common among these Mexican immigrant workers when they referred to the Asians at the plant, who were in fact mostly from Laos and Vietnam:

He made me go look for pieces [of meat] that were coming down the other line . . . and bring the meat back. And he only made me do it because my coworkers were two *chinas*. I was the only *mexicana* working in that job, and my supervisor was a *chino*. And besides making me go get that meat, he made it so that the pieces that I had to pull got all backed up, so that when I got back everything would be all piled up. . . . Then there was a bid job in the morning [shift], called "tri-trim," and I signed up for it and I got it. . . . I wanted to leave from that line and go to another line because I was really tired of that *chino*.[6]

In part, Méndez wanted us to see that she used the bid job system strategically to gain greater remuneration and satisfaction from her work: working tri-trim took her a step up in her wage grade and was easier work, as she explained, and it also meant working the shift she preferred. Yet her job transfer seemed more powerfully motivated by the racially inflected conflict she had with her supervisor, which she interpreted as an example of the Asian workers' imputed tendency to be pushy and protective of their own kind rather than cooperative with the Mexican workers. When new conflicts with an Asian coworker erupted in her new position, Méndez told us, she was quite willing to have her bid job rights temporarily suspended so she could move back to her old job and not have to work with people she considered repugnant. Méndez thus turned to the bid job program repeatedly, not out of an ethos of competitive individualism but rather to negotiate the racial antagonisms in which she was embroiled at work. Nor did she ever indicate that the internal labor market had prompted her to try to distinguish herself as a productive, uniquely skilled, and successful individual.

Both Elvira Méndez and Pedro Ruiz also suggested that the company undermined the bid job system's ability to lead workers to see themselves as exercising free choice in important aspects of their working lives. Ultimately, Méndez had been able to switch to a day job in tri-trim where her pay increased to grade three, her tasks (and coworkers) were more agreeable to her, and her family time was better protected. No sooner did this happen, however, than the managers abruptly transferred her back to special trim. Said Méndez: "They don't let you say no. [They say,] 'You have to do it. . . . If you don't want to do it, go home.'"[7] Méndez thus wanted us to see that far from institutionalizing a process of what Burawoy calls "participation in choosing," the company often simply disregarded workers' efforts to secure individually selected job roles via the bid job system. Ruiz told us of a similar experience when his supervisor one day peremptorily declared that he would have to make a certain cut with a knife, but without a protective glove, in addition to the task designated for the bid job that he had been awarded, which had not included handling a knife. Ruiz saw this as blatantly contravening his reasonable expectations that his job would stay the same after he signed up for it and also as endangering his safety and negating his capacity for self-determination at work.[8]

Appraising Tyson/IBP's bid job system from a more general perspective, another key factor cannot but have interfered dramatically with this program's efficacious operation as a means for gaining workers' consent to the relations of production: the extremely high turnover at the plant, as reported by multiple workers and union officers and as circumstantially indicated by the tremendous injury problem. According to Flaco Pereyra, the company was taking on ten to fifteen new workers from outside the plant every week, even during the production and sales trough caused by the 2004 Mad Cow disease incident in a nearby eastern Washington town, and twenty to thirty outside new workers per week during better times. By these figures, the plant would have been replacing over 5 percent of its nonmanagement workforce every month.[9] Ramona Díaz confirmed: "[New] employees arrive all the time, and . . . they don't stay. . . . Sometimes ten or twenty come in; one stays, or two stay."[10] Echoing Díaz, Diego Ortega explained how he had been that one person out of twenty who hung on and clarified a major reason why turnover was so high:

Personally, I never had done one of those jobs. . . . It really was hard for me because sometimes, since you don't know how to sharpen the knife, sometimes you use force, pure force, and then your hand starts hurting. . . . In general, almost all the new people who come in, like me, have their hand start hurting. . . . When I arrived in the morning and grabbed the knife and started cutting, right away my hand would start to get numb—it would start falling asleep. And it hurt, and you can't hold on to the knife because you feel all numb, like when [your muscles] are giving you spasms. . . . They teach you to inspect [for contamination], and how to cut the meat, but they pretty much don't teach you to sharpen [the blade].[11]

Shortly, I discuss in greater detail the mutually aggravating problems that made few workers want to remain employed at Tyson/IBP for very long, especially those related to injuries on the job, the lack of training to which Ortega referred, and abusive supervision. I also consider workers' charges that the company actively sought to purge its labor force of injured workers by a variety of means. The main point here, however, is that if turnover was as high as these workers claimed it was and as circumstances suggested, then it would have been impossible for the bid job system to generate widespread effects of consent among the workers simply because the composition of the factory's workforce would have been changing so rapidly, with few workers staying long enough to derive any tangible benefits from their bid job rights.

Finally, the failure of the internal labor market to generate a competitive-individualist disposition among most workers was manifest in the fact that very few people we interviewed wanted to develop a career path at Tyson/IBP. Virtually no one seemed satisfied with their job, even those who had used their bid job rights to get it. (Two notable exceptions, tellingly, were Rafael Mendoza, who as a machinery

maintenance specialist earned wages well above those of the processing and slaughter workers, and Ignacio Ramos, who described himself
as a "supervisor's assistant.")[12] Instead, we repeatedly heard expressions of despair about being trapped at the slaughterhouse because of
simply having no other options, especially because of lacking English
abilities. Rogelio Salazar articulated the general attitude of these workers succinctly when he said, "These jobs are basically for people who
don't know how to do other things." Both Salazar and Ramona Díaz
felt stuck at Tyson because they could not speak English and had very
limited job prospects; and in the case of Salazar and many others, limited literacy augmented this problem. At the same time, these very
issues likely induced some workers to leave: research shows that a lack
of English skills among immigrant meatpackers drives up turnover
because workers cannot realistically aspire to supervisory positions
(Gouveia and Stull 1995, 102). Either way, the language barrier was
bound to aggravate the bid job system's dysfunctionality as a mechanism for building workers' positive commitments to a career path with
the company.

The injury problem, in turn, both directly led some workers to stay
at the plant when they had no desire to be there and indirectly contributed to this result by inhibiting them from gaining the English
capacities they needed to pursue other options. Ramona Díaz explained
that since her injury, she had been unable to "leave to look for another
job outside" because she was battling the company to pay for her treatment. Felipe Ortiz faced the same difficulty as well as the inability to
do physical jobs elsewhere because of his injury and said that this
was why he just "bore with" his job in the rendering department, where
he worked in temperatures of "up to 130 degrees in the hot season."[13]
Meanwhile, the accumulated pain and exhaustion of working on the
line thwarted even the most earnest efforts of workers who attempted
to learn English through classes offered at the plant, as Alejandro
Méndez explained in these vivid terms:

The job sucks everything out of you—all your energy, to put it that way,
because the job is really hard. What a difference, when you work in a job that,
when you leave, as they say, you go home satisfied. You leave tired, because no
job is easy. But it's very different to leave work tired than to leave work in pain.
That is very different. Because fatigue is one part of it, but the greater part
isn't fatigue—it's pain, from doing the same job that is so repetitive. To the

point where, the people, when we get home, we lie down, and we can't sleep—we get up right away. Our fingers, our hands fall asleep from that same pain. The next day we get up with hands that are in pain and that have fallen asleep, making little movements to try to get the blood flowing. That's why I say that this job is hard; it's not a matter of leaving work tired. You leave work injured.[14]

Méndez had tried taking English classes at the plant, he said, but to his "shame" he would sit there just "nodding off" like all the others.[15] Juanita Castillo had attempted to refresh herself by going home and eating before attending an evening class at the local community college. Yet she still fell asleep in class because she had been up since four o'clock in the morning and was exhausted from the day's work.[16]

Overall, the workers' stories indicated not only that the internal labor market at Tyson/IBP did not encourage the workers to feel that they could make "real choices" about their day-to-day activities within the labor process at Tyson but also that they felt a general inability to determine the long-term trajectories of their working lives. If the work environment at the slaughterhouse, as the workers described, was not a scene for "manufacturing consent" according to these sorts of positive inducements, habits, and attachments, then how, alternatively, *was* power in this institutional arena structured?

The Antidisciplinary Labor Process: Supervision, Speed, and Staffing

Knowing something of the historical development of work processes in meatpacking through the IBP revolution and its aftermath, we might speculate that even if the work atmosphere at Tyson/IBP did not prompt workers to see themselves as freely deciding agents, it still might have involved *individuating* processes of other kinds linked to mechanization and the division of labor. It seems quite plausible, more specifically, that routines of *disciplinary power*, along the lines theorized by Foucault, would have accompanied the industrywide turn toward prioritizing "throughput, efficiency, centralization, and control" (Schlosser 2002, 154). In plants where workers' physical movements are measured by fractions of seconds and output levels are precisely engineered, perpetual monitoring would seem necessary to ensure the coordination of workers' bodies with the plant machinery and with one another. For Foucault, discipline efficiently distributes responsibility for such monitoring among officials in authority, technologies of surveillance, and the individuals whose productive behaviors are the explicit focus of the disciplinary matrix. Discipline thus effects *normalization* in the sense of generating self-regulating subjects who know that at any time they might be being watched to see if they are conforming to norms governing their bodies and minds and who therefore strive to realize the productive behaviors and attitudes expected of them. In part, disciplinary power at a plant like Tyson/IBP would lead workers to develop "practiced bodies" by honing the specific skills needed to qualify themselves for certain spots within a complex taxonomy of jobs, fitting themselves into an individuating schema of classification. It also would imply therapeutically addressing those incapacities of musculature and character that comprise deviations from set standards (which also help constitute them as particular individuals or "cases"). Such individuals might not be persuaded of their abilities to exercise "free choice" regarding their daily jobs and their long-term careers, like the machinists whom Burawoy studied. But they might nonetheless be integral to the type of docile and efficient labor force most conducive to meatpacking companies' strategies for achieving phenomenally high rates of production and consumption.

Yet the workers' commonsense theorizations of power did not confirm this Foucauldian line of sight any better than they ratified the perspective suggested by Burawoy. One primary way that their accounts of power in the shop floor departed from the model of discipline was by stressing the manifest and immediately coercive presence of domination as opposed to more subtly insistent, spatially dispersed, and not necessarily even detectable mechanisms that, for Foucault, are all the more effective for *not* presenting themselves as irresistible sovereign might. Foucault's theory of discipline indicates how even quite intensive supervision may not necessarily be experienced by workers as oppressive or abusive. Foucault describes the characteristic way that modern techniques of surveillance become all the more potent by becoming dissociated from particular individuals and from direct bodily force:

The power in the hierarchized surveillance of the disciplines is not possessed as a thing, or transferred as a property; it functions like a piece of machinery. And, although it is true that its pyramidal organization gives it a "head," it is the apparatus as a whole that produces "power" and distributes individuals in this permanent and continuous field. . . . Thanks to the techniques of sur-veillance, the "physics" of power, the hold over the body, operate according to the laws of optics and mechanics, according to a whole play of spaces, lines, screens, beams, degrees and without recourse, in principle at least, to excess, force or violence. It is a power that seems all the less "corporal" in that it is more subtly "physical." (1979, 177)

The norms of supervision at Tyson/IBP, according to the workers' stories, thrust into reverse this intensification of discipline through power's dispersion into the organization of physical space. Rogelio Salazar decided to seek a leadership post with the union after his dis-may mounted at the abusive way supervisors were treating the work-ers: "It made me really angry to see how the supervisors treated some people—how they yelled at them really horribly, how they bawled them out, almost like the only thing they didn't have was something [they could use] to hit the person."[17] Diego Ortega described verbal and physical mistreatment alike:

This supervisor, when I first started working there, really yelled at the people. Sometimes he yelled words like, "So you can't do it? If you can't do it, tell me so I can help you"—he said it this way, like he was really mad. Then he'd say, "And if you can't do it, there's the door and you can leave. Just go home." And sometimes he came by and, joking, he gave you a slap on the back—jok-ing, according to him, but he would hurt you. . . . And sometimes he yelled at the people, calling them "animals" . . . snapping his fingers or sometimes shov-ing them.

The slaps and pushes that Ortega describes seem to have been outside the norm, but the torrents of verbal humiliation were not, especially before the rank-and-file movement revitalized the union.[18] Ramona Díaz haltingly conveyed her outrage and disbelief at hearing one of her managers explicitly use dehumanizing language to characterize her and her coworkers:

He told me, "Look, you all are . . . like a disposable cup. A—a disposable plate," he said, "that you use and," he said, "you throw in the trash. . . . We take a person, and if we don't like him because of something or whatever it may be," he said, "we give him a certain amount of time. If we don't like him," he said, "we throw him in the trash."[19]

Juanita Castillo echoed both Díaz and Ortega in describing how super-visors often assumed an overbearing, capricious power over their sub-ordinates, denying them vacation requests if they did not get along

with them personally and threatening to fire them if they did not follow orders.[20] Said Flaco Pereyra: "They yelled at you; they humiliated
you. It was hell to work there. It was like being in a prison."

Not much like a prison from the pages of *Discipline and Punish*,
though. Instead of the disembodied, sanitary lightness of power that
Foucault so vividly evokes, workers at Tyson/IBP met with open hostility, taunts, and whimsically sadistic ploys of authority. The practice of
denying workers bathroom breaks typified the latter tendency. Juanita
Castillo told us how this had happened to her:

> Sometimes they don't want you to go to the bathroom, either. *How can you not
> go to the bathroom?!* It's a necessity, if you have to go to the bathroom. . . . If you
> say . . . to your supervisor: "I need someone to come help me right now, *right
> now,*" he leaves and forgets about it.[21]

Esperanza Soto similarly described the anger and embarrassment she
and others felt when faced with this situation, and elaborated on why
it occurred:

> The problem was also about going to the bathroom. . . . Those who were not
> allowed to go, did it [i.e., urinated] right there. It happened to me and it also
> happened to other people. And don't you think it was just a few—it was a lot.
> It's just that those are things that you don't tell other people because it's
> embarrassing. . . . One time that happened to me. No one came to relieve me,
> because there—in packing—if another person doesn't come to relieve you,
> you can't leave . . . because if no one comes, all that product goes and falls on
> the floor. . . . And that day, I was telling them many times that I wanted to go.
> And when I saw no one was coming, I left—and they made me go back. Then
> there was nothing else I could do; I left there completely soaked.[22]

Soto reflected that while she really didn't mind how hard the work was
physically, she found such appallingly disrespectful treatment impossible to bear: "The work didn't bother me. What bothered me was . . .
how they treated the people. . . . Sometimes, moral pain hurts worse
than physical pain. That wounds [you] more deeply."[23] For her, the
injury to her sense of dignity went even further when supervisors she
later told about the problem refused to take it seriously.

At Tyson/IBP, then, workers wanted us to see that supervisors routinely abused them and thus that the more depersonalized, less "corporal," and more subtly ubiquitous supervisory norms consistent with
the inculcation of discipline manifestly failed to operate. Other core

elements of the labor process, in turn, fortified this antidisciplinary dynamic as well as the pervasive sense on the shop floor that things could erupt into sheer chaos at any time despite the elaborate structure of official rules supposedly governing the labor process.[24] Chief among these factors was the pace of production, or what the workers called the speed of the "chain"—the mechanical apparatus that carried carcasses, or portions of them, through the factory to be worked on at the various stations.

Untenably high chain speeds, according to the workers, lay at the root of a multitude of interrelated problems, including the denial of bathroom breaks, the injury issue, and many others. Exact figures for chain speed are hard to ascertain because they are privileged information of the company. However, it is well known that chain speeds in the United States tend to be far more rapid than in other developed countries and have risen dramatically since the 1960s. According to a union representative for the United Food and Commercial Workers, line speeds went up by 50 to 80 percent during the 1980s (Stull and Broadway 1995, 68). Eric Schlosser reports even more drastic increases since then: "The old meatpacking plants in Chicago slaughtered about 50 cattle an hour. Twenty years ago, new plants in the High Plains slaughtered about 175 cattle an hour. Today some plants slaughter up to 400 cattle an hour" (2002, 173). A *Washington Post* reporter who interviewed Temple Grandin, a renowned expert in meat industry slaughter practices, confirmed that line speeds "now approach 400 per hour in the newest plants" and that chain speed was 309 animals an hour at IBP's Pasco facility (Warrick 2001, A1–A2). Francisco González, a worker with fourteen years' experience at the plant, estimated the rate to be closer to 330 cows per hour when he spoke with us. Ramona Díaz put the figure at just over 250 cows per hour but said that the rate had increased by over one-third since she had begun working at the plant around 1990.[25] Steve Bjerklie explains the close relation of pressures to increase line speeds to the structural tendency in the industry for firms to operate with low profit margins as well as to related conditions of fierce competition that are reflected in the recent corporate consolidation of the industry under the domination of just a handful of companies, including IBP and Tyson (1995, 42–43).

Not only did the speed of the chain make it extremely difficult for workers to keep up, thus providing ample pretexts for the supervisors to yell at them or to refuse to let them use the bathroom; in addition, it created conditions under which workers were likely to become injured. In other words, far from generating the *practiced* bodies of docile subjects who were thoroughly absorbed in their productive activities, the work environment at the plant yielded *debilitated* bodies of subjects who were hounded into silence through direct intimidation and pain and who were often expelled from the site of production altogether. No fewer than 90 percent of the workers who participated in a thorough survey of the plant's workforce in 2001 judged that "chain speed contributed to the accidents and injuries in their work area" (Apostolidis and Brenner 2005).[26] For Ramona Díaz, as for most others, it was the speed of the chain even more than the lack of training that precipitated injuries, especially those from using dull knives: "You're racing around, and you don't have the chance to sharpen the blade."[27] Ismael Rodríguez stressed how handling large and heavy pieces of meat under severe time constraints deepened workers' vulnerability to injury: "That piece of meat weighs between forty, forty-five pounds. You have to turn each piece about three times; sometimes in a minute and a half you have to finish that piece."[28] Elvira Méndez told us that since she worked with relatively smaller hunks of meat, she had to process each piece in even less time: "We had about twenty-three seconds to finish a piece. [Sarcastically] Not minutes! Over there, there are no minutes. . . . For larger pieces, yes, there are minutes, but in what I had to do—I'm not very sure, but it was seconds, not minutes."[29] Francisco González specified that the company imposed precise time limits of "fourteen seconds, eighteen seconds, twenty seconds, depending on which piece it might be." Méndez had sustained serious injuries in her hand, arm, and shoulder as a result of performing repetitive motions at superhigh speeds; and González described in harrowing terms how his coworkers' wrists and fingers had gotten locked up from grasping their iron hooks all day as the chain raced along, to the point where they needed surgery.

Elvira Méndez also said that the understaffing of her workstation had contributed to her injuries, and this was another prominent theme in the workers' stories of their lives on the cattle disassembly line: being deprived of necessary assistance in a futile battle to do the jobs forced upon them by the absence of coworkers. In this way, too, the company systematically undercut the processes by which workers might have experienced the continuity, predictability, and manageability of their jobs that would have enabled them to cultivate practiced bodies and efficient, stable habits of self-regulation. About three-fourths of the workers surveyed identified understaffing as a "contributing factor" to injuries in their area of the factory (Apostolidis and Brenner 2005). Regarding her first job trimming fat from pieces of meat, Méndez insisted: "There have to be three people on that job, and sometimes they left just two of us there. You're still finishing one piece and another one comes. Sometimes they all piled up on me."[30] These comments were resoundingly typical of what we heard from many of the workers, both in the extended interviews for this project and in the shorter follow-up interviews related to the survey. Jorge Hernández also emphasized that, ironically, injuries caused by short staffing aggravated the staffing deficit: "These days there are lots of injured people; where they have to have six people to do the job, right now they have three. . . . Those three people who are doing the job can't last three months because they get hurt, too."[31] Even when the company said it would remedy the dangerous consequences of short staffing, it did not necessarily follow through. Gloria Ruiz, for instance, noted that she once had been transferred to a job where "a lot of people had gotten injured" and the company had therefore increased the official number of staff in the area but that Tyson then had not fully staffed those positions. Understaffing, Ruiz thus believed, along with "the speed of the work, repetitive movement, the chain and all," had caused the injuries to her back and waist that she suffered soon afterward.[32]

Sometimes, being pressured to do the work of others on top of one's own responsibilities meant being assigned new tasks without warning, preparation, or compensation. Like Pedro Ruiz, Rogelio Salazar told us how this had happened to him:

I remember one time they took me to the office to tell me that I sharpened my knife really well, and that I really could give one more cut, to help the other worker who was next on the line. I told the supervisor: "If I'm doing my job well, why—why do I have to do more, if you're not paying me to do more?" He tells me, "OK, if you don't want to do it, I can fire you." "No way, if you think you can fire me for that, go ahead and fire me." And I kept on doing the same thing.

The company's appeal to his sense of pride in doing his job proficiently, Salazar suggested, was wholly disingenuous and quickly turned into a bare threat to do what he was told or suffer extreme consequences. Salazar, who helped lead the strike in 1999 and later was elected a shop steward in the union, firmly resisted this tactic of intimidation. But it is easy to see how workers with less self-confidence, fewer years experience at the plant, and illegal or noncitizen status would have found it more difficult to refuse such orders. For his part, Pedro Ruiz felt that he had no alternative but to do as he was directed when the supervisor added the task of making a knife-cut to his regular job of hanging cow intestines on hooks.

If, in the words of Rogelio Salazar, the company always seemed to "demand too much," it also gave too little in return by depriving them of the pay they were owed. Besides informally manipulating job specifications, supervisors routinely pressed workers to keep working into their break periods and after the ends of shifts without any additional compensation.[33] Esperanza Soto explained:

They made us work extra hours and without pay. Because, for example, if the time came to leave for lunch, it didn't matter to them: you could be working five, ten minutes more and we ourselves would pay them for that time. . . . Many people . . . their work was really piling up in there, and the supervisor came and told them: "You're going to leave only when you finish your work." . . . Because when the time to leave was going to come, a lot of product arrives. . . . So at the end you had to pick it up to be able to leave. And then they'd say to you: "Seven minutes. The first seven minutes aren't paid." And at the end it wasn't seven; it could be ten. . . . For the most part, in that place, what a minute is, is a quantity of product that comes out. So there is where you start to see . . . the way they make money with you.[34]

There is an intriguing resonance between Soto's comments here about the way workers experienced time on the production line and Elvira Méndez's sardonic remark that at the plant, "there are no minutes." As theorists of political economy going back to Marx (1976) have noted, the subjection of workers' labor power to precisely timed operations and its measurement for compensation in terms of time have been defining elements of wage labor for most industrial workers. These processes have further intensified in modern factories geared toward mass production.[35] In terms of the contemporary experiences of Mexican immigrant workers, anthropologist Roger Rouse (1992) notes that one of the ways that working life characteristically becomes more "proletarianized" for such people is that they face the new demand of working on the clock, such that both the rhythms of each working day as a whole and their specific movements on the job are precisely regulated in terms of segments of time. In different but complementary ways, Soto and Méndez were both saying that they felt acutely and understood consciously, in the midst of their work, the functional *failure* of this core element of the rationalization of work at the factory.[36] For these workers, the scrupulous, scientific determination of time-and-effort ratios by the engineers thus was routinely subverted as the labor process unfolded, as work expanded into time segments that were supposed to lie outside the boundaries of laboring time, and as the amount of effort expected during each parcel of work-time swelled beyond formally designated limits. The company's unexplained and uncorrected failures to include workers' overtime wages in their paychecks further exacerbated the former problem.[37] Meanwhile, the latter problem emerged both through the effects of understaffing, as Elvira Méndez suggested, and through chain speed-ups without corresponding wage increases, as Ramona Díaz emphasized.

By depicting a wage relation that was imploding from within, the workers furnished yet another sign that discipline, in Foucault's specific sense, would not be a fitting way to characterize the predominant relations of power in the slaughterhouse. Instead, the unreliable system of payment complemented other structural problems, including the company's routine flouting of staffing protocols, the operation of the chain at impossibly high speeds, the dysfunctions of the bid job system, and the phenomenon of supervisor abuse, to generate a work environment where, according to the workers' theory of power in the plant, a frankly arbitrary and despotic form of authority was constantly negating the disciplinary potential of key processes. This was true of both the labor process and the political apparatus of job rights in which productive activities were ensconced (since both bid job procedures and staffing levels were part of the collective bargaining agreement along with wage rates). Rather than a normalized individual with a practiced body oriented toward developing and monitoring the self in prescribed ways while attaining normative satisfactions, the subject that emerged in the power domain conceptualized by the workers was absorbed by the anxious and often terror-filled quest simply to shield herself from harm and to make it through the day.

Injury and the Mocking Semblance of Worker Rehabilitation

The arcane sequence of referrals, examinations, diagnoses, and temporary job reassignments in which injured workers typically became ensnared was another major domain of practical experience at Tyson where one would have expected to hear the workers talk about intensively individuating forms of intervention. As with the other elements of the organization of work, the system for handling injuries had all the trappings of a disciplinary matrix. A whole network of health professionals affiliated with the plant existed, and these medical personnel could have avidly sought medical knowledge about the injured worker. They could have ordered reasonable and extensive physical examinations and diagnostic tests, classifying the worker as a certain type of case depending on the results and using that "power-knowledge," as Foucault calls it, as the basis for subjecting the worker to a tightly controlled process of therapy and retraining. In this way, they could have tried to endow the worker with a renovated, practiced body so that this individual could become fully exploitable again within production operations. In addition, the routines for handling injured workers could have fortified the disciplinary aspects of the company's approach to preventing injuries in the first place, which was to rely mainly on workers' use of personal protective devices (PPDs). Injuries on the job could have provided occasions to reinforce both the individual worker's commitment to using such equipment diligently and that person's skills for handling it effectively.

Yet in the narratives of the people we interviewed, the treatment apparatus at Tyson/IBP never seemed remotely intended to produce any of these disciplinary effects. Instead, we encountered a different narrative about power—power that did not aim to forge a practiced body with an attendant moral conscience through subjection to regimens of observation and rehabilitation but rather that prodded the worker into either abandoning the job or continuing to provide productive labor despite severe bodily pain. Spurning opportunities to generate power-knowledge, delaying rehabilitation indefinitely, and thus dispensing with the potential psychophysical and ideological advantages of these processes alike, the company instead appeared just to want to squeeze the labor out of our informants for as long as they could tolerate it and then to discard them as damaged goods.

According to 2002 data from the U.S. Occupational Safety and Health Administration (OSHA), to which the company is required to report all employee job-related injuries that rise above a certain threshold of severity, 27 percent of the workers at the plant experienced a "nonfatal occupational injury [or] illness involving days away from work, restricted work activity, or job transfer." This put Tyson's Pasco plant in the worst quartile of all meatpacking plants in the country, for which the rate was 10.3 percent. It also means that the rate of serious work-related injury at this facility was nearly ten times the rate for workers in all industries in the United States that year, which was 2.8 per 100 workers (Apostolidis and Brenner 2005).[38] Even these disturbing figures, however, almost certainly understated by a wide margin the incidence of occupational injuries and illnesses requiring treatment beyond first aid. In the 2001 survey of workers at the plant, an astounding 78.7 percent of respondents "reported work-related health problems" during the previous year (Apostolidis and Brenner 2005).[39]

The workers attributed the frequency of their injuries to a host of entrenched and interrelated problems at the plant. They stressed above all that ultrahigh chain speeds caused the injuries in both direct and indirect ways. Fast-moving lines induced excessive bodily effort, demanding repetitive motions on heavy and sometimes only partially thawed pieces of meat at an exceedingly rapid pace, at times in stressful positions. The speed of the chain also made it hard to find the time to keep knives sharp while simultaneously exacerbating the understaffing issue. The result was a story that resonates clearly with multiple accounts in the scholarly, journalistic, and advocacy literatures about meatpacking: an epidemic of job-related musculoskeletal disorders (MSDs), especially cumulative trauma disorders (CTDs) such as carpal tunnel syndrome (Broadway 1995, 20; Compa 2005, 33–38; Schlosser 2002, 173; Stull and Broadway 1995, 63–64).[40] The intense speed of the chain also imbues the production process with a distinctly chaotic character, which is reflected in the high incidences of laceration injuries in the industry as workers pressed beyond their limits end up cutting themselves and their coworkers (Compa 2005, 38; Stull and Broadway 1995, 72). Furthermore, both the hectoring from supervisors to keep up with the chain and the imperatives generated by short staffing, according to the workers, led them to overstrain themselves and caused injuries and health problems.

Yet another major cause of job-related injuries at Tyson/IBP's Pasco plant, as Juanita Castillo and others noted, was the problem of floors made slick with fat, water, and blood:

A lot of people hurt themselves. They fall—the floor is slippery. . . . I've also fallen, myself. And more when I was pregnant with a child—I fell down two times. In there, there is fat mixed with water; so sometimes they put down salt, and when there's no salt, you fall.[41]

Ramona Díaz, Rosa Vásquez, Alejandro Méndez, and Nina Garza all had fallen and sustained back injuries for precisely the same reasons.[42] Of course, chain speed contributed to these problems, too, because the need to move rapidly across the floors made it less possible for workers to step gingerly on these dangerous surfaces.

Meanwhile, the workers depicted the company's approach to injury prevention as both faulty and disingenuous. Tyson/IBP followed the historical norm in American industry by dealing with health and safety hazards mostly through providing PPDs rather than by altering the technical aspects of the production processes that created the hazards in the first place.[43] The workers made it clear that while their protective gear may have shielded them from some common types of injuries such as lacerations, it did not prevent the MSDs that stemmed from the speed of production and other factors intrinsic to the technical organization of the work process. They emphasized that the company did not even seriously value this limited, relatively inexpensive health and safety regimen, pointing out that they had had to file a lawsuit against the IBP to wrangle payment from it for the time they spent carefully putting on and taking off their protective gear. (In court, the company had sought to avoid these financial losses by claiming that this equipment was just "clothing," which cast further doubt on the company's dedication to its own injury prevention plan.)[44] In addition, Esteban Múñoz stressed, the company had reclassified certain pieces of protective gear (plastic sleeves) as optional rather than required and even had taken them away from workers once it perceived that it might be compelled to pay for "donning and doffing" time.[45] To Múñoz and others, this further exposed the firm's lack of interest in making a coherent effort to ensure workers' safety.

The questions of injury causes and preventions aside, there were routine procedures at Tyson/IBP for dealing with workers who got hurt on the job: for diagnosing disorders, treating them medically, and arranging programs of rehabilitation involving adjusted work requirements and continued monitoring for designated periods of time. The first source of examination and treatment was the infirmary at the plant, which was staffed by qualified nurses. Subsequent referrals to physicians and/or for tests might follow. Company health personnel opened a formal case for each worker who sustained a serious injury to document the individual's condition and the specific steps taken in response. If all went as was presumably intended, the worker received the professional care she or he needed to resolve the problem medically as well as the time and adjusted working conditions necessary to heal without further incident. And indeed, several workers we interviewed told us that this was exactly what had happened to them. Rogelio Salazar had no complaints about the treatment he had received for either of his two head injuries. Isidro Gómez likewise confirmed that he had been given appropriate treatment when he had been cut on the finger by a coworker: "They've always been nice to me. They paid attention to me and they took care of me and they reexamined it every day."

Gómez acknowledged, however, that his cut was not a deep one and that the wound had healed within a week. The vast majority of other workers we spoke with had sustained more serious injuries, and unlike Rogelio Salazar, they had been very dissatisfied with the company's responses. The problems began on the shop floor. A major reason the injury data from OSHA and the figures in the survey differed was likely the underreporting of injuries due to supervisors' adverse pressures on injured workers. According to workers, this was a systematic problem at the plant, and it is a documented characteristic of the meatpacking industry as a whole (Compa 2005, 52–54). The survey found that even when workers reported an injury or health problem to a supervisor, they more than occasionally met with resistance in getting referred to the plant infirmary.[46] According to the survey results, "more than ten percent of work-related health problems identified to supervisors were never referred to the plant infirmary and nearly a quarter were referred more than a day after the problems were reported" (Apostolidis and Brenner 2005). Esperanza Soto endured several months of pain and numbness while her supervisor kept putting off sending her to the infirmary. She finally took the risky step of insisting on going to the infirmary even without a referral. At that point, the supervisor relented and agreed to make the referral. Even then, however, she was pressured to conceal the supervisor's earlier unwillingness to report this clearly serious injury:

ES: I hurt one of my hands and I told my supervisor, and I had to keep telling him for about three months. But he would say to me: "Tomorrow; next week." Or else, it would be because someone had gone on vacation, so when they would come back. . . . And so the time passed. Until my hand lost all strength: the knife would get loose in it and I wouldn't even notice. Then . . . I told him: "If you don't take me to the infirmary, I'll go by myself." Then he told me: "OK, I'll take you on Monday. But . . . you're going to tell my supervisor . . . that you told me about this on Friday after work." . . . Then I said to him, "I'll say what you want me to say."

PV: Why do you think the supervisor wanted you to say that?

ES: Because they're supposed to take you in on the same day you tell them about it. . . . And if I say that I've already been telling him about it for months, they're going to discipline him.[47]

As Soto noted, once injuries went unreported for a certain amount of time, threats directed at supervisors from above made it that much less likely that the injury eventually would be reported. This tendency of higher management to "blame" the shop floor supervisors for "not being careful" when workers under their watch got injured, Rosa Vásquez surmised, was the reason her supervisor had refused her request to go see a nurse about a back injury, putting her off by saying: "'You know that I really can't do anything because they are not going to believe us. They're just going to say that you did it to yourself in some other place.'"[48] Alejandro Méndez informed us, moreover, that the company relied not only on sticks but also carrots to minimize injury reporting:

One time I had a burn. I burned these two fingers. . . . I put the knife into the sterilizer. I was really careful, you know. But then I pulled it out on one side and then the water jumped out and burned me. In those days, if we didn't have accidents for a full three months, they gave you a free meal. . . . I kept working for a while, like maybe fifteen minutes. But I saw that I couldn't work anymore, because . . . my fingers swelled up with blisters. And so they took me to the infirmary. Yeah, they took me finally, because they saw that I couldn't do it. The supervisor got really mad at me, because it was my fault that we didn't get that free meal.[49]

Dutifully reporting injuries like the ones Méndez, Soto, and Vásquez suffered and swiftly sending injured workers to the infirmary could have been the first step in a rationalized process of restoring these workers' physical health and compiling systematic, individualized records regarding the fitness of the plant's workforce as a whole. In the stories the workers told us, however, the conflict over referrals to the infirmary usually initiated a sequence of occasions when the company recoiled from intensive, rehabilitative interactions with the injured.[50] Here and at subsequent moments in the process, managers applied personal pressure that deflected responsibility onto individual workers for dealing with the bodily debilitating consequences of meat-packing work.

Sometimes this effort to saddle workers with the blame for their own injuries and health problems took more active, and ugly, forms. Juanita Castillo remembered what had happened immediately after she cut her finger (the first of two times):

All the leads were around me, and they were telling me that it was my fault. I felt like they were pressuring me, and I was really angry. I wanted to cry, I was so mad, because everybody was blaming me for something that I didn't do. . . . I don't know why they get so angry. All I know is that they were blaming me and telling me it was my fault because I was, like, in a hurry, wanting to go home, and I didn't watch what I was doing.[51]

Castillo also spoke indignantly about how supervisors accused workers who fell on the slippery floors of injuring themselves by not wearing proper shoes or racing around too quickly.[52] Esperanza Soto had once experienced even more prolonged, demeaning, and intrusive pressure to declare that she herself was responsible for a work-related health problem:

It was when I was in packing that they were giving us the dirty, wet gloves . . . and they gave me an infection in my fingers. . . . It went on for twenty days, more or less; they took me to the office up to two times a day, waiting for me to say that it was my fault. Then they took me to their own doctor. But it didn't do anything because I didn't get any better. . . . They asked me some questions but about unrelated things: they even asked me about my mother's medical history. . . . They asked if my mother had had abortions. And if I had had abortions. I don't know why they asked me those questions. . . . I think it was to intimidate me. And later they asked me how many times a day I washed my private parts; if I cleaned the yard; how many children I had, and if they were still

living at home. Things that had nothing to do with the matter. And what kind
of soap I used when I bathed or when I washed my private parts. What body
creams I used. Whether I was a sleepwalker, whether I was putting my hands
on the walls without noticing it.[53]

As a devout and traditionalist Catholic, Soto must have found especially galling the bizarre insinuations that she and her mother had had
abortions and that somehow her skin condition was related to sexual
promiscuity. Here, the effort to dump responsibility for work-related
injuries and health problems onto the shoulders of the workers took a
particularly cruel twist; but the overall pattern that linked this story to
what Castillo said, for example, persisted.

It could be argued that by telling us how managers led workers to
feel at fault for their own injuries, our interviewees were in effect describing a company strategy for implanting a disciplinary norm through
workers' informal routines rather than through formal, officially designed procedures. Yet the workers' narratives should make us view
such an assumption skeptically. Not only did they depict the company
as wholly unwilling to expend any of its resources on systematically
disciplining them—in addition, by their accounts, Tyson/IBP did not
even value the workers' health-related self-regulatory actions as a cost-
free by-product of supervisory routines. As Juanita Castillo told her
story, for instance, the supervisors who reviled her after she cut herself
had absolutely no interest in whether she either cultivated an earnest
attitude of personal responsibility for her own health and safety or
became better skilled at avoiding such lacerations. Nor did the managers who taunted Soto intend to train her in new habits of hygiene.
While surely not opposed to any practices the workers might have
developed to stave off injuries and health problems, the company's
predominant disposition toward such self-disciplining behaviors by its
immigrant employees, according to these narratives, was one of indifference. Like "disposable plates," they suggested, they could simply be
replaced whether or not they managed to avoid bodily debilitation on
the production line. Thus, although disregard for workers' injuries was
a standardized element of the plant's work environment, this meant
less that the company was making a concerted effort through negative
means (i.e., humiliation and intimidation rather than formal training
programs) to elicit disciplined action by the workers than that the
company saw workers who got hurt as a nuisance to supervisors and a

drag on profits and did not care whether they stayed or left. That, at any rate, was the story the workers told about power in this context, and it is this narrative of power that most concerns us here.

The workers reiterated this story of meeting with heedlessness and accusation instead of conscientious therapeutic attention when they described their visits with company medical personnel. Nearly 60 percent of the workers surveyed reported that they did not "receive the expected level of medical attention" in the plant infirmary (Apostolidis and Brenner 2005). Again and again in the follow-up interviews, workers testified that the company nurses most commonly gave them "a fistful of pills," usually ibuprofen, perhaps treated them with some ice, and then sent them back to work right away or after very little rest (hence eliminating the need to write up an OSHA report). In our more extended interviews, as well, multiple workers also characterized their treatment in the infirmary in ways that echoed Elvira Méndez's summary description: "Ibuprofen and ibuprofen; 'and go back to work.'"[54] Esteban Múñoz told us that when a cow fell on him, injuring his shoulder, he was simply given a bag of ice and told to return to his workstation. When workers received superficial attention to their injuries and were too hastily returned to the production line, sometimes their injuries would multiply, deepening their misery. Geraldo Morales recalled, for instance, how after one of his fingers locked up from repetitive motions, he was referred to the infirmary, given ibuprofen and a brace, and then sent back to work the same day. Later that day, the knife Morales was attempting to use, but which the brace and the injury prevented him from gripping securely, slipped out of his grasp and lacerated his foot.[55]

Delayed referrals to physicians comprised another element within this narrative of plant officials' systematic disregard for the seriousness of workers' injuries. According to the survey, barely 20 percent of workers treated in the infirmary were referred to physicians; and almost 40 percent of those workers received the company's grudging permission to see a doctor "weeks" or "months after [they] needed to see a doctor," about 20 percent in each category (Apostolidis and Brenner 2005). Pedro Ruiz said that the infirmary personnel typically waited three to four weeks to see if an injury was serious enough to warrant a physician referral. Rosa Vásquez told us the following grim stories about workers who had to wait even longer:

Despite my own injuries, there have been people who have suffered more. They've left there injured. Once I happened to see a young woman who had had a very heavy lid fall on her—it was a real blow—they didn't even take her to the doctor, they just put her on light duty. Until they saw that she wasn't getting better—months had to go by—then they took her to the doctor. Her health was getting worse and worse—instead of getting better, she was getting worse. Around the time of the strike, she went to them and they took her, almost carrying her, because she couldn't walk. And me, it almost made me want to cry, to see it, [thinking]: "How could it be possible that this is happening here?"

Vásquez went on to say that once she had seen a young man who had injured his back on the job "weeping from the pain" because the company waited for "months" to send him to the doctor and that the man eventually had quit in utter discouragement.

Injured workers told us that the gauntlet of mistreatment often extended into doctors' offices. There, the ritual of dispensing pain-reduction and anti-inflammatory pills, deferring further treatment until after a follow-up appointment, and getting the person back to work as quickly as possible frequently continued, especially with the physicians to whom the company referred workers. Elvira Méndez explained how she had injured her shoulder and arm due to repetitive motions with extremely high chain speeds and persistent understaffing in her work area. She urged us to look at her injured arm, and we could clearly see that it was swollen to about twice the size of her well arm. When she finally went to see a company doctor after waiting six weeks for a referral, Méndez recalled, this is what transpired:

The doctor said to me, "Let's see, lift up your hand." Well, I couldn't lift it up. . . . "Take these pills to alleviate the pain." "OK." "You're going to be on light duty." . . . And I took them but I didn't get any better. . . . They hadn't given me [physical] therapy. I kept on going: every month, month and a half, two months, they took me. And on the second visit: "How are you feeling?" "Well, the same." "Lift up your hand; make this movement. OK, you can go now." . . . The doctor spent two or three minutes with us, and said, "Everything is fine. Keep doing this; these are your restrictions. You have an appointment in two or three weeks . . . no let's make it six weeks." He gave me the same restrictions, the same pills. . . . I tell you, I couldn't even lift up a bottle of milk because of the pain in my arm—I couldn't bend it, or anything.[56]

Whether in the hands of the infirmary nurses or in the examination rooms of the company doctors, the story was the same: the point of these contacts with medical personnel, the workers insisted, was to provide minor alleviation for the symptoms of the injury while prompting them to work through the pain as long as they could bear to do so. Tyson/IBP made little or no effort, however, to rehabilitate the worker's body so that it would be better suited to her or his role in the labor process.

Many workers also strongly believed that the company was systematically interfering with doctor–patient relationships when workers got injured on the job. Agustín Peña and Federico Reyes told us that for examination and treatment of job-related injuries conducted at the company's expense, a Tyson official rather than the worker made the appointments and corresponded directly with the physician, invariably only in English. Reyes, who spoke only Spanish, had been mailed a letter in English describing a doctor's diagnosis of industrially related muscular strain along with "preexisting" arthritis, which he could not read and had brought along to show the students of mine who interviewed him. This document explicitly stated that the physician's evaluation "does not constitute a doctor–patient relationship or privilege."[57] Alejandro Méndez noted, likewise, that when an injured worker went to see a physician, "they also make you sign a paper where they tell you that they can send a representative from IBP to see the files of the doctor or the lawyer you have. And then, if the operation doesn't turn out well, if I want to fight with them over the case, they have the right to go into the files of the lawyer and the files of the doctor."[58] Méndez spoke in even more blunt terms about the company's interventions in the doctor–patient relationship when he talked about his wife Elvira's injury and the alternatives workers pursued when company-selected doctors denied them effective treatment:

The doctors—they've sold themselves. . . . And a proof of that is my wife . . . with her arm, so she can't wash a dish or do a simple little job like that—her hand swells up like this. . . . She was trying to get herself taken care of by the doctors of the company—which is who gives her the doctor. All they want is to have control: [of] the lawyers and the doctors. . . . There are people who need operations and they don't operate on them because the company doesn't want to pay. . . . There are people who need operations and they get operated on with their own means, God knows how—looking for [public] medical coupons or I don't know what. . . . But the company got away with it: they whip you into shape by not curing you in this way. They give you the doctor and the doctor orders you to work. What kind of doctor is that?[59]

Because they did not trust the doctors to whom they were referred by Tyson/IBP and were not getting suitable treatment from them,

Méndez told us, workers sometimes visited a physician located in the town of Colfax, over two hours by car from Pasco. This doctor had a reputation for listening to the workers more carefully, examining them more thoroughly, and prescribing more effective treatments. The company tried to prevent workers from going to Colfax, however, as Alejandro Méndez, Elvira Méndez, and Gloria Ruiz all noted, by refusing to pay for the visit, denying the worker time off to make the trip, and/ or refusing to recognize that doctor's diagnosis and recommendations as valid.[60] In addition, company personnel intimidated, harassed, and threatened retaliation against workers who asked for referrals to this other doctor or received treatment from him, as Elvira Méndez and Esperanza Soto reported.[61] According to Francisco González, supervisors sometimes even gave out disciplinary tickets and threatened to fire workers who sought help from any physicians other than those on the company's list.

The climactic moments of injured workers' stories of their ordeals at Tyson/IBP usually involved their assignments to light duty. Responsibilities on light duty were supposed to be less physically taxing than the worker's normal job, thus presumably giving the worker time to heal before returning to her or his regular post. The survey found that "more than a third of Tyson workers report that they have experienced problems when on light duty. These problems included higher levels of supervision than normal, verbal harassment by supervisors, unwarranted disciplinary write-ups, or abrupt changes in their shift schedule" (Apostolidis and Brenner 2005). Regarding the latter, Elvira Méndez spoke impassionedly about how she was forced to work on Sundays while on light duty, when she desperately wanted to be home with her family.[62] Juanita Castillo described how higher levels of supervision were involved on light duty:

They're always checking you to see what time you get back from break, what time you get back from lunch, if you get back late. If you get back late, they reprimand you or—one time a woman arrived late and they fired her. . . . She had only arrived about five, or three minutes late. It's that they go around looking for an excuse to fire us.[63]

In the narratives of these workers, the realm of light duty took on Kafkaesque qualities. Injured workers told us how they had been given jobs with no evident purpose other than to expose them to added policing and punishment. Both Elvira Méndez and Felicia Domínguez, for example, said that they had been ordered to spend all day writing down the numbers on the tags of cattle being slaughtered, one by one, even though they knew that this information was of no use to the company. At the end of the day, Méndez's supervisor would toss her recorded results in the trashcan right in front of her eyes.[64] More exhaustive and arbitrary performance criteria, along with relentless surveillance, increased the chances that injured workers would run afoul of those in authority and become liable to reprimands, seemingly by design. Recalled Domínguez:

> They think that if you're on light duty, you're on light duty to not have to do the work. . . . They're there watching you; they have a little book and a pencil. . . . You're checking and you're writing down what they told you to write down as the cow goes by, and in that time that you're looking at your hands or you're looking over that way or whatever, they're checking on you and they're saying, "Pay attention to the cow. Don't look anywhere else." Or, "How many do you have?" "So, let's see, I have twenty." "No, twenty, that's wrong. How come you have twenty and I have twenty-five?" I mean *they're* just checking up on what *you're* checking up on, just to see if you're working or not.

Not only had Domínguez's light-duty supervisors used her make-work on light duty as a pretext for bearing down on her and issuing reprimands, they had also been hypervigilant and suspicious about her requests to go to the bathroom, a problem that Gloria Ruiz had experienced as well. The worker's vulnerability to being scolded and fired also increased, Pedro Ruiz and Manuel Guzmán explained, through another particularly cruel machination: company medical personnel would give workers on light duty elaborate and precise job restrictions such as limits on heavy lifting or on doing certain kinds of movements; light-duty supervisors would ignore those restrictions and demand that workers do jobs they were not supposed to perform; then the workers would be given tickets for not complying with their work restrictions.

Light duty, according to the workers' stories, seemed set up not only to make the weight of authority unbearably oppressive but also to make injured workers' physical working conditions so repugnant or harsh as to be intolerable. These degrading conditions reached a series of extremes in Elvira Méndez's narrative of her time on light duty. After sustaining a hand injury, Méndez was ordered to paint and clean the factory's "basement," a subterranean chamber of horrors that she described as "A repulsive place! A foul-smelling place!" Here, Méndez was forced to wade through vast quantities of cow excrement and fat, amid swarming cockroaches and worms as well as the dead fetuses of slaughtered, pregnant cattle.[65] Juanita Castillo, Alejandro Méndez, Rosa Vásquez, and Gloria Ruiz all spoke of spending long hours trembling in the cold without being able to move enough to keep warm.[66] Other workers emphasized how light duty often exacerbated their physical injuries and/or precipitated new health problems. While on light duty after arm and hand injuries, both Elvira Méndez and Juanita Castillo had been told to paint walls using only the one well hand, which predictably then began to hurt as well.[67] Gloria Ruiz's supervisors had made her lift heavy objects, which she said aggravated the injury and the pain in her back that had led to her light-duty assignment in the first place (although she had chosen to bear with the pain for nearly two weeks before seeking reassignment because she "was afraid of light duty"). Her husband, Pedro, told us of how he had had to use his injured fingers doing his light-duty task:

On light duty they put me in a job checking the jaws of the cows, to make sure they didn't have any contamination, but they told me: "You don't have to use this [injured] hand, put it inside your pocket." But how can I check the meat that way? . . . I had to pick up a piece this big, open it on one side, make sure it had no hair, waste, or anything like that, and turn it onto the other side, but I couldn't do it with one hand. I was forced to use two hands.

A big problem with light duty, then, was that the tasks workers had to do usually were not light at all. As Elvira Méndez sarcastically quipped, "There is no 'light' duty there."[68]

Gloria Ruiz thus spoke aptly when she poetically termed light duty "a martyrdom, a crucifixion [un calvario]," except that this tortuous path involved no eventual redemption. For Felicia Domínguez, light duty amounted to a mechanism for getting people to work while hurt so that the company could avoid dealing earnestly with the physical debilitation caused by the labor process: "It's like they give you those jobs as a punishment. That's why a lot of people, they say, aw, they'll just put up with the pain. It's better to do that than to be on light duty." Alejandro Méndez echoed Domínguez's words: "For me, they are zones of punishment. . . . You just can't stand the cold, so you think, better to work all injured than to be here enduring so much cold."[69] The survey confirmed:

There is widespread sentiment among surveyed workers that these difficulties are not coincidental, and that Tyson is using these methods to discourage other workers from requesting light duty assignments when they have been injured. . . . Close to two thirds of surveyed workers believe that the company mistreats workers on light duty for this purpose. (Apostolidis and Brenner 2005, 9)

Of course, there was another option for injured workers besides sucking it up and staying on the job, as Méndez dourly noted:

You keep on having this illness, and there are two things you can do: either you take yourself back to work or you yourself decide that it's better for you to leave [saying]: "This lousy company, those dirty rats, they aren't helping me get better at all, and they're not fixing anything for me. It's better if I just leave. So I don't hurt myself even more." And they leave, injured. Injured![70]

Guadalupe Flores had chosen that option, quitting her slaughterhouse job and turning to Medicaid to "get some relief" and finally to begin to heal.[71] But in these cases, as Alejandro Méndez emphasized, the company "got away with it," ducking the costs it would have incurred had workers stayed on and ultimately succeeded in their demands that the company pay for appropriate treatments. Ramona Díaz, Felipe Ortiz, and Elvira Méndez all told us how they were struggling to do this by remaining in their jobs; but as Ortiz put it, "Now I'm a problem for them."[72] In short, workers who got injured said they knew how the company wanted their stories to end and believed Tyson/IBP used light duty to force this conclusion, in which the worker, finally beaten down by pain and frustration, simply quit.

Hegemonic Despotism and the Narration of Biopolitics

In the workers' primary account of their work lives at the slaughter-house, the institutional channels for dealing with workers' injuries combined with the labor process along with the apparatus of wage payment and bid job transfer rights to constitute the general matrix of power relations. All these fields within the matrix projected a semblance of discipline. Yet time and again, in this dominant narrative of power at the plant, the potentially disciplinary instrumentalities of the company refrained from addressing the worker in an individuating manner. One would have expected that after becoming legalized and entering a technologically and organizationally modernized factory, especially given the historical trajectory of the production process in meatpacking, these immigrant workers would have described a decisive shift away from the general absence of formal normalization that characterized the condition of illegality. Almost invariably, however, they spoke of situations in which more intensive discipline appeared to materialize only to dissolve itself from within.

In the process of narrating this self-cancellation of discipline, however, our informants also brought into view another form of power that operated in Tyson/IBP's work environment even as discipline receded: biopolitics. It was not their fate, they made clear, to develop practiced bodies, identities harnessed to a schema for classifying worker types, or self-regulating temperaments, at least through formally institutionalized procedures. Yet the promotion of economic productivity and social harmony through industrial food manufacturing still required crucial things from them as a *population*. Narrating their experiences as undocumented immigrants, the workers had told us of being herded into the dark hills along the border, compressed into the hidden spaces in vans and automobiles, packed into holding houses, driven away from the main roads patrolled by immigration officials, and funneled into the fields, orchards, and garment-making shops where immigrant labor was in demand. As I argued in chapter 3, these stories, and the elevated risks of physical and emotional trauma they bespoke, reflected the subjection of this immigrant population to biopolitical management, albeit couched in social discourses that did not explicitly justify the treatment meted out to immigrants in terms of benefits for the health and vitality of the national population at large. The accounts of work life in the slaughterhouse, in turn, carried forward and underscored this story about immigrants' subjection to biopolitics by implication.

These narratives portrayed an industrial environment that systematically deformed workers' bodies, crushed their spirits, and drained their vigor, *en masse*. Foucault writes that biopolitics aims to "invest life through and through" and thereby enhances social "value and utility" (1990, 139, 144). However, such power treats different mass, racially defined categories of human beings distinctly; it is a racially discriminating "power to *foster* life or *disallow* it to the point of death" (138). In narrating their mortally dangerous journeys through the hills and deserts, in airless vehicles, and into the sights of rifle-toting vigilantes, the workers emphasized their disproportionate vulnerability to what Foucault calls "indirect murder: the fact of exposing someone to death, increasing the risk of death for some people" (2003, 256). Likewise, as they told us about their work killing and processing cattle—their culture of dread and lament regarding pain and injury, the practical inescapability of these torments, the formulaic distribution of generic palliatives to injured workers in lieu of individual rehabilitation, the expectation that they would follow supervisors' orders regardless of their own desires and abilities—they were showing us how it felt to be the target of biopolitical strategies "disallowing life" so that a racially more privileged population could thrive.

As in the zone of illegality, however, so likewise in the political economy of meatpacking biopolitics functioned through implicit rather than explicit means. One can see this by considering some of the major social discourses that are coupled with the production processes described by the workers. For instance, the stories in this chapter amply illustrate why slaughtering and processing cattle are among those jobs that "Americans cannot or will not do," as the popular refrain goes. They also light up in Technicolor the terrible costs that workers in these jobs pay in terms of their bodily health, physiological vigor, and emotional well-being, even when they have moved out of "the fields" and into regular industrial employment with health insurance and other benefits. The racially privileged white population reaps the benefits of these expenses, in one way, by retaining the discretion to abjure such jobs in favor of occupations that involve much lower risks of injury and death, in the complex sense meant by Foucault. Public rhetoric about which jobs are suited for immigrants as opposed to the native-born helps produce these biopolitical distinctions without promoting them overtly.

Similarly, the meat industry's public relations discourse about how beef belongs at the core of a healthy American diet functions biopolitically but makes no obvious appeals to fears about white racial degeneracy caused by contact with immigrants in the way that corporate discourses about industrially produced food in earlier ages of mass immigration once did (Bobrow-Strain 2008). Tyson, for example, packages its products not only in shrink-wrap plastic but also in the pages of a story, legible on the company's Web site (www.tyson.com), about how eating lots of meat gives the body protein to make it strong and upholds the values of family, faith, and community. A subtext of this story is that Tyson scrupulously ensures the healthfulness of the nation's food supply by making certain that its products are inspected to keep them free of spoilage, by exploring new technologies like irradiation to minimize food-borne contaminants, and by publishing clear and easy-to-follow instructions for how the moms and dads who cook the meat can do so responsibly and hygienically. Tyson thus in effect christens all good family folks as "Team Members" in the project of building a physically hale and emotionally stable nation through their habits of meat consumption. Yet the unofficial presupposition of this discourse is that the *official* Team Members—the immigrant workers in Tyson's factories—will work themselves to death. Only by destroying their own health and vitality can these workers churn out the massive volumes of beef products that allow the company to keep prices so low and consumption rates so high (the latter, to be sure, being a mixed blessing for the cardiac health of overfed Americans). And only when workers show that it is possible to labor at inhuman speeds can the industry's reliance on a consumer-oriented, technology-intensive, and pharmaceutically based approach to food hygiene, rather than a slower and more careful process of production that would prevent contamination from occurring in the first place, come to appear rational and uncontroversial.[73]

A tacit form of biopolitics also provides the practical subtext for the leading trend in policy discourse about occupational safety and health. As political economist Charles Noble argues in his history of OSHA, the Occupational Safety and Health Act of 1970 originally supplied ample legal grounds for requiring employers to make far-reaching technological, physical, and procedural changes to fulfill their general duty as articulated in the Act "'to furnish . . . employment and a place of employment which are free from recognized hazards that are causing or are likely to cause death or serious physical harm'" to employees (1986, 95). Noble further explains:

Engineering controls, that is, changes in the technical organization of the production process, are generally more effective means of controlling hazards than what specialists in the field call *personal protective devices* (PPDs), such as dust masks, hard-toe shoes, and ear plugs. Engineering controls are also considerably more expensive than PPDs. Understandably, employers prefer to avoid them whenever possible. (24)

A secular, increasing tendency to defer to employers' structural interests in this regard set the parameters for public policy regarding the staffing and funding of OSHA essentially from its inception through the Reagan years. The first President Bush launched a major project at OSHA to develop a national ergonomics standard, continuing through the 1990s with the full support of the Clinton administration and resulting in the issuance of the new standard after much anticipation in 2000. However, Congress abruptly repealed the law in 2001 following the Republicans' return to executive power. In any case, this standard still would have left employers with wide discretion over when and how they conducted ergonomics evaluations of their facilities as well as over the procedures, timelines, and substantive aspects of plans for implementing consequent changes (Hecker 2001; *Congressional Digest* 2001, 131–33). As it happens, Washington State more recently developed an innovative ergonomics standard that occupational safety and health specialists viewed as potentially establishing a major precedent for other states to follow. The law establishing the standard, however, was repealed in 2003, before it was ever implemented, by a voter initiative campaign led by the food-processing and construction industries.

The common discursive thread running through these repeated rebuffs of attempts to enhance workers' occupational safety and health rights was the notion that *voluntary* employer programs were more conducive to companies' economic viability and worker health and safety alike. But this discourse, along with its typical complementary assumptions regarding the preference for PPDs over engineering alterations, carries unspoken biopolitical implications. It means that the racial sorting of immigrant workers into the most dangerous occupations, like food processing and construction, can proceed apace, blanketed by the comfortably color-blind assumption that all employers will respond similarly to the market incentives for preventing workplace health and safety hazards.

The workers' stories about sustaining their daily doses of pain, humiliation, and hazard on the job thus collectively reflected the effects on them, as a population, of these racialized biopolitical discourses. Biopolitics on the level of the political economy, translated into popular narrative, took on the form of a *despotism* that made the semblance of autonomy in their jobs a joke while forcing them to withstand a multitude of injuries that were physical and "moral," to recall Esperanza

Soto's term, alike. More than this: insofar as the narrators depicted themselves as utterly incapable of resisting the power that oppressed them and having no choice but to adjust to its imperatives, they lent a *hegemonic* quality to the processes that mortally threatened and racially subordinated them as well as to the public policy and public relations discourses in which these processes were enfolded. Such hegemonic despotism penetrated right through to the common sense of these immigrant workers. It anchored biopolitics in their practically expressed "consent" by making the racially differentiated patterns of vulnerability to injury and illness seem like obdurate, immutable realities that simply had to be endured and accommodated.

Workers' Microtechniques and the (Limited) Instability of Biopolitics

Nevertheless, as our informants painted this image of power as despotic, they added occasional counterstrokes that complicated its visage. Even while biopolitical mechanisms inexorably and tacitly generated their effects, this alternative current within the interviews suggested, the workers had adopted a variety of techniques for accomplishing certain goals and fulfilling specific desires of their own, just as they had earlier developed arts of hiding and passing, along with strategies for battling their own frailties and the aggressions of *polleros,* in the zone of illegality. With the responsibility for escaping injuries and health problems being thrust upon them and with no way to stay fully out of range of abusive supervisors, workers developed special practices for minimizing the harm that came to them. Jorge Hernández, for instance, told us about how he had taken measures to protect himself after realizing that he was regularly being exposed to skin ailments in his job in the slaughter area. Hernández worked in the area where the animals' filthy hides were removed and placed into tubs that were supposed to be treated daily with salt and chlorine:

But they never put it in—they [only] put it in every month. . . . I didn't get hives or anything, but all the workers there get hives. . . . The cows are animals that—who knows what state they're in when they arrive. There are some that come in with diseases and all that. And that's what makes you break out in rashes, in hives on your arms. But I always, every break, I put alcohol on my arm, or if I don't then when I get home I put on creams and salt water, this way, so I don't get an infection. And I tell everyone at work, I tell them what to do so they don't get hives, rashes, all that. I sure tell them, but I think they don't do it because they get them.

Hernández thus asked us to see that at his own time, initiative, and expense, he had taken steps to combat the health hazards to which the company routinely subjected him, presumably with the intention of minimizing its costs and maximizing the speed of production. He presented himself, with discernible pride, not only as a leader acting out of concern for his peers but also as someone who stood apart from them by dealing more adeptly with the risks of work-related disease.

Hernández and other workers also seemed to want us to see them in similar ways when they described their efforts to shield themselves and others from verbal assaults by the managers. Earlier, we saw how Rogelio Salazar refused to let himself be intimidated by the supervisor who threatened to fire him if he did not start making an extra knife-cut without any additional pay. Similarly, Alejandro Méndez, Rogelio Salazar, and Esperanza Soto all emphasized how they often exhorted fellow workers not to let supervisors shout at them or force them to work into breaks or past the ends of shifts.[74] For his part, Hernández insisted that he would not tolerate supervisors yelling at him or his coworkers and claimed single-handedly to have put an end to such abuse from the supervisor on his line:

I told him no, he might be a supervisor but with me he wasn't going to go around yelling all the time. . . . And after that they asked me to forgive them. . . . And since then they've never said anything to me. I just hear it when they shout at other people. And I go and I tell them, "Why are you yelling at him? That person is not here for you to be yelling at them. You're here to tell them how to work, not to go around shouting." Then they calm down right away; we've had about eight months now and they haven't said anything to us.[75]

Like several notable others, Hernández thus developed a narrative persona that joined together his analytical initiative to appraise health hazards at work, his practical cultivation of techniques of bodily self-care to respond to these dangers, and his firm resolve to stand up for himself and others in the face of repressive power.

Nina Garza did something very similar when she spoke of avoiding further injuries beyond two major ones by developing a precise, critical knowledge of the hazards posed by specific spaces on the shop floor. She confined herself to those areas least likely to place her in harm's way and urged others to do the same:

> I still keep telling them where they should go, not to go close by the places where the knives are. Before they used to cut their hands going by, because they use the knives like this, they put their hand down and they cut them. There's no need to go by those places; you can make a turn. There's [also] no need to go by where all the fat is thrown down; you can make a turn. That's where people slip; they fall.

Garza also told us how she once had been injured when a Laotian worker launched a huge hunk of meat through the air toward a nearby conveyor belt, hitting her squarely in the face and knocking her unconscious. No sooner had she come to than her supervisor began excoriating her for getting hurt by not paying attention to what was going on around her. But Garza retorted: "*You're* not paying attention. When the accident happened and I got hit, it's because the belts were full of meat—the chain is too fast, there were boxes everywhere you looked. Why do you think they couldn't get me out of there?" Garza even took the side of the man who had thrown the meat at her, who had injured his hand in the conveyor belt several days before the incident and had thus become "a problem" for the company, in Ortiz's evocative words, when her supervisors coaxed her to retaliate against him:

> So then they wanted to fire him. Then when he hit me, they wanted me to say that he had done it on purpose, and that that's why he had hit me. Then I said, "If I couldn't even tell where the blow came from, how am I going to accuse him?" They wanted to fire him because out of a group of workers they set one against the other.

Like Hernández, then, Garza narrated an identity for herself that welded together solidarity with fellow workers, self-assertion in defense against the company's depredations, and a keen sense of her own personal capacity to recognize dangers on the shop floor and keep herself safe through techniques of her own devising.

There were variations in the types of work on the self, the gestures of engagement with others, and the forms of individual distinction the workers described as they unfolded this counternarrative of personal agency under the shadow of despotism. For example, Gilberto Rivera put a special spin on the message we had heard from Hernández about encouraging other workers to protect themselves physically and psychologically at the plant when he explained why he routinely gave coworkers "advice" on how to avoid getting injured, overworking themselves, and being shouted at by the supervisors: "They've asked me why I get involved in other people's business, why I don't just take care of my own job. Above all, it's because of my past. We are the same people, and if he doesn't defend himself because it makes him afraid they're going to fire him, it hurts *me*."[76] Here, Rivera grounded his sense of obligation to help fellow workers make the work environment more secure and humane in a feeling of common Mexican cultural identity. This was in contrast, notably, to Garza, who had made a point of telling us that she tried to get along with all her fellow workers, regardless of their racial or ethnic background, to prevent the company from sowing division among the workers based on such differences. Rivera also supplemented his vision of moral responsibility for helping coworkers develop strategies of self-defense with a frankly (self-)critical view of more destructive, self-medicating bodily practices, which we had heard occurred at the plant but about which the workers generally did not comment:

I've seen people who take drugs inside there—cocaine, pot. In my experience, and I'm still sorry that I used those drugs—it helps you physically. There are people who use them because sometimes it really helps us and sometimes we use it because it makes us feel good, it makes us forget all the problems we have. . . . There are people who use them because the work is hard and with the drug they don't feel anything at work. It helped me because when I drank beer, the next day I woke up with a headache, with no desire to do anything, and I could tell I had a hangover. Then when I started taking drugs, I noticed that the people didn't say anything to me, I noticed that the drug takes away the effects of the beer, it gives you a lot of energy and I worked happily—but it's the opposite.

Rivera credited a resurgence of his faith in God and, consequently, a more determined personal will with enabling him to leave such "vices" behind. Such inward forms of moral self-regulation thus also belonged to the repertoire of microtechniques that these immigrant workers applied to themselves to carve out a terrain of self-determination within the hostile environment at Tyson/IBP, along with self-medicating measures (healthy or unhealthy), habits of bodily movement, and practices of personal objection in the face of abusive supervision.[77]

This palette of microtechniques, then, constituted a crucial, additional feature of the biopolitical formation that our interviewees theorized through their stories about working life in the slaughterhouse. Just as when they described the zone of illegality, so likewise when they spoke of working at the plant, they insistently qualified their predominant account of power as essentially despotic with subtle references to their own techniques to influence their surroundings. In both phases of the narratives, these arts of everyday life included direct confrontations with the immediate agents of repressive power: earlier, the *coyotes;* here, the plant managers.[78] They involved efforts to boost the courage and stamina of traveling companions or coworkers—think of Pedro Ruiz urging his fellow stowaway in the trunk of the *pollero's* car to take courage and remember how badly he wanted to make it to the north; and then think of Garza and Hernández exhorting their coworkers not to let their supervisors intimidate them. Among these arts of the self were also practices of instrumental value in eluding the antagonistic forces in one's immediate environment, such as tactics for hiding and passing while crossing the border without documents as well as, later, routines for taking care of one's body after work hours (and, very importantly, skills in sharpening one's blade correctly and managing time before work to make that possible). Additionally, these arts could take the form of struggles to overcome one's internal moral and physical weaknesses, as the affinity between Alejandro Méndez's boasting about having mastered his fears along the border and Rivera's battle against substance abuse illustrates.

One more art of self-preservation, less noble than these others but just as significant, needs to be mentioned here: the habits the workers developed for repelling the abusive treatment they often seem to have leveled at one another. Just as Elvira Méndez's strategic use of her bid job rights to get away from racially different coworkers bespoke the reality of prejudice and conflict among workers, so likewise workers often responded to oppressive supervision not by turning on the managers but by turning against other workers. According to Flaco Pereyra, they did so as a regular part of the job, joining in the supervisors' vituperations and even preempting them:

If someone's not doing his piece, I'm going to get into trouble. Lots of times the meat piles up and you have to help them, or pressure them. Lots of times your coworkers push you, even though you're part of the same thing they are. . . . You're forced to do it just to survive, because of the work. Because they're shouting at you, "Pull it, you fucking son of a bitch!" They start attacking you that way—and you have to defend yourself. Even if you're a respectful person, you reach your limit—you have to defend yourself. If you don't, they'll eat you alive.

Pereyra's story put a darker spin on the notion of worker agency that came out in the stories by Garza, Hernández, and Rivera. To be sure, as Pereyra noted, a certain kind of cooperative mentoring could result from the rigors of the labor process and the problem of insufficient training, as more experienced workers showed the ropes to their newer coworkers. Most often, however, workers got frustrated with one another, and this aggravated the anger and tension already brimming over on the shop floor. Ironically, the curses they flung back and forth among themselves crossed lines of racial, ethnic, and linguistic difference, generating a shared jargon among the workers of mutual insult and hostility. As Pereyra put it with desultory sarcasm, the Bosnians and Vietnamese never really needed to learn Spanish, the dominant tongue on the shop floor, because "they understand well enough what *pinche madre*" [roughly, motherfucker] means.[79]

This particular micropractice shows especially vividly how the workers contributed to the stability and productivity of the biopolitical schema by cultivating their range of techniques for self-protection at the slaughterhouse. Yet the same thing was also true of the workers' other microtechniques of the self. By keeping infections and injuries at bay as much as they could, and perhaps also by rebuffing supervision that had become so egregiously abusive that it threatened the functionality of the labor process, they facilitated the company's production goals under the overarching conditions of speed, understaffing, and injury risk that are structural factors in meatpacking. One might also say that although the company failed to capitalize on the disciplinary potential of its production and rehabilitation operations, and did not even seem disposed to try to provoke discipline indirectly, the workers still regulated themselves in ways conducive to the firm's and the industry's overall objectives—and, more broadly, to the biopolitical formation with its public policy, corporate public relations, and "immigrant jobs" discourses. In short, in this aspect of their narratives, the people we interviewed further elaborated their theorization of biopolitics by drawing attention to the fortifications this power formation receives from immigrant workers' informal practices of self-protection.

Here, furthermore, our informants underscored a theme that had emerged when they spoke of their journeys in the zones of illegality, as discussed in chapter 3. Just as unofficial immigrant networks had carried out, to some degree, the disciplinary operations that the state or other major institutions refrained from conducting vis-à-vis immigrants in the illegal domain, so likewise in the slaughterhouse, informal chains of communication spread knowledge and training in tactics for protecting oneself and others.[80] In the previous chapter, I argued that when these immigrant workers then deployed their arts of hiding and passing, resisted the predatory actions of *coyotes,* and fought against their own internal wavering in the face of uncertain hazards in the illegal domain, they were partly facilitating the advance of biopolitics. They offered the state a handy pretext for pursuing further border militarization by making it to the other side in contravention of the law; and by arriving ready and able to work, they also kept open the spigot allowing immigrant labor to flow into the jobs that Americans cannot or will not do. Our informants' tactics of survival and mutual aid in the slaughterhouse, acquired through parallel means, yielded very similar effects. They validated in practice the assumption that if "Americans" refuse to perform various kinds of dirty and dangerous labor, like meatpacking, then immigrants will "naturally" step in to do them. They also practically enabled the highly dysfunctional system for producing vast quantities of meat at dizzying speeds, so that it could feed the voracious beef protein requirements of the population without letting decontamination processes compromise output volume and consumer prices. In addition, their techniques for protecting themselves and others from harm helped maintain the myth that meatpacking employers should be trusted to evaluate and solve occupational safety and health problems responsibly on their own—precisely the assumption that has deferred fulfilling the promise of the Occupational Safety and Health Act of 1970. They thus reaffirmed the racially differentiating consequences for themselves of higher mortality and morbidity that these implicitly biopolitical strategies portended, along with their attendant benefits for the racially dominant population.

Furthermore, by the evident satisfaction and pride they expressed in having figured out ways to make the job sustainable even under extremely harsh conditions, the workers additionally reinforced the biopolitical schema by imbuing it with an aspect of *consent,* again as they had done in their stories of the migrant trail. Once more, we see how not only the practices the workers discussed in the interviews but also their distinctive *ways of narrating power* could weave key threads through the fabric of hegemony. The workers' references to their capacities of self-regulation and self-preservation certainly differed in tone from their more dire and hopeless depictions of arbitrary, irresistibly abusive power at the plant. Yet the former still complemented the latter in an important sense by generating another narrative current that had its distinctive uses to power. And this narrative practice by the workers, like the techniques of action they were narrating, had both immediate significance for the company and wider ramifications for the wider biopolitical apparatus. Speaking about the work environment as a place where workers *were able* to stick up for themselves and avoid the worst of injuries, if they really tried, could not help but add at least qualified support to Tyson's public-relations rhetoric about offering workers opportunities for individual fulfillment through jobs and careers with the company. (This stopped well short, however, of validating the company's disingenuous evocation of ethical relations of mutuality between it and its employees through its jargon about Tyson Team Members.) Meanwhile, the narrative stream regarding the efficacy of workers' self-defensive tactics supplied a diffuse, de facto type of buttressing to the broader capitalist-cultural disposition to view technically rationalized and financially profitable business operations as compatible with the maintenance of workers' personal dignity.

Nevertheless, it is still the case that the differences in the memories of desire characteristic of the dominant storyline about work in the factory, on the one hand, and the subordinate narrative strand emphasizing techniques of self-protection, on the other hand, mattered politically. The former were principally desires to *receive* better treatment by the company—fairer wages, more respectful treatment, more adequate staffing for their workstations, higher quality health services after getting injured, and bona fide career options. But the comments regarding workers' techniques for self-preservation and the protection of others reflected a more ambitious desire to modulate the contours of the work environment through their own plans and practices. When they spoke in these terms, the workers seemed to want to prove themselves capable of taking responsibility for themselves and others alike, to act as people who were able to shape their life conditions at least in small and immediate ways. These genealogical elements, like similar features of their stories of clandestine migration and working in the fields without documents, and even like the claims of individuality they had made about their decisions to leave Mexico in the first place, complicated the political dynamics of the workers' stories of power at Tyson/IBP. In particular, they interfered with the logic of resentment that the dominant narrative strain encouraged: the politically pacifying tendency to see the company (or, before it, the Border Patrol, or the *coyotes,* or the economic collapse in Mexico) as holding the exclusive capacity and responsibility for constructing the environment that injured their bodies and souls and to view its might as simply overwhelming.

As episodic, isolated bouts of self-assertion in the face of the chain's relentless motion, these counterthrusts against hegemony were admittedly only anticipatory of any substantial transformation of power relations at the plant. Thinking back on Jorge Hernández's late-afternoon self-ministrations with skin cream, or Nina Garza's choreography of safe walking routes on the shop floor as knives whizzed around her, it is hard not to see such demonstrations of agency as mournfully small and of very limited consequence. As I argued in chapter 1, however, political narratives can unleash the potential to transform social relations when an organized movement exists to sort through their genealogical features and bring the most promising antecedents to the fore. In the next chapter, then, I examine the workers' stories about mobilizing a rank-and-file collective force in response to the dismal circumstances at the slaughterhouse as well as the deficit of democracy in their union. When the workers described their grassroots and legal campaigns to address these problems, how did their stories about power-in-movement compare to their accounts of power in the work environment at Tyson/IBP and in the zone of illegality? How did they position themselves with respect to formal regimes of disciplinary power, in particular the domain of the law that they entered as unionists? And in what ways did their stories of collective struggle perhaps intensify the challenge to the intrepid and indirect orchestration of their experiences by biopolitical imperatives that, in their accounts of the illegal realm and the labor process at Tyson/IBP, remained still only a matter of incipient potential?

5. ¡Nosotros Somos la Unión! Immigrant Worker Organizing and the Disciplines of the Law

As THE NEW CENTURY DAWNED, the misery wrought by the meatpacking industry following the IBP revolution and borne disproportionately by immigrants began to catch the public's eye. This was partly because of the splash created by Eric Schlosser's best-selling exposé *Fast Food Nation* (2002) along with his related articles in *Mother Jones* (2001) and *The Nation* (2004).[1] Commonly seen as a latter-day cousin of Upton Sinclair's famous muckraking book *The Jungle* (1926 [1906]), which revealed the agonies of immigrant workers and the dangers to consumers in the meat industry during the Progressive Era, *Fast Food Nation* riveted the eyes of aghast readers on the ways the beef-processing industry systematically disregarded the health and safety of its employees while showing comparable indifference to contamination problems in its products. A less frequently read but still highly publicized investigation of the meat industry by the international organization Human Rights Watch (HRW) followed close on Schlosser's heels. Released in early 2005, the HRW report excoriated Tyson and other mega-meat firms for violating international law, U.S. law, and human rights by exposing workers to occupational safety and health hazards as well as by denying workers' fundamental rights to freedom of association in unions.

In addition to these journalists and advocates, however, immigrant workers themselves stepped forward to bring what had been happening inside U.S.-American meatpacking plants out into the open. In 1999, after several years of organizing that began at a low level but gathered intensity and militancy, the largest wildcat (extralegal, non-union approved) strike by meatpackers in at least the last quarter-century broke out at the IBP plant near Pasco, Washington. Shortly thereafter, immigrant workers at an even bigger Tyson/IBP beef-processing facility in Amarillo, Texas, as well as another large beef plant owned by Cargill/Excel in Fort Morgan, Colorado, staged briefer but still notable walkouts. The leaders of the movement for rank-and-file union power and industry reform in Pasco were directly involved in these other actions as consultants on tactics for democratizing local unions and changing power relations on the shop floor. This string of actions garnered the attention of the national media, in part through the workers' efforts to link their experiences of bodily debilitating chain speeds to inhumane slaughter practices but also because these events suggested a growing mobilization of immigrant protest forces. While the *Washington Post* pursued the former angle in an article on the "brutal harvest" wrought by "modern meat" (Warrick 2001), the *New York Times* highlighted the latter theme in a story about "The Latest Example of Immigrants Packing the Picket Lines" (Verhovek 1999), both of which featured the workers of Teamsters Local 556.

This chapter examines the stories the immigrant workers at Tyson/IBP told about their ventures into political activism. The brief version of the workers' mobilization goes as follows. By the mid-1990s, the workers at the plant had fully absorbed the wretched consequences of "the IBP revolution": plummeting wages, increased speeds of production, harsher supervision, and multiplying health and safety hazards. The company still tolerated the union's presence, but only because the officers had made it standard practice not to stir up trouble for management by pursuing individual workers' grievances, much less by organizing the workers to put collective pressure on the firm. Those officers were white non-Hispanics who did not speak Spanish, while the Latino proportion of the unionized labor force had mushroomed to about 85 percent with most being Mexican immigrants who spoke limited or no English. Also, the workers overwhelmingly lived in Pasco, near the plant, in a small urban area where Latinos had become a rising majority of the local population; meanwhile, the principal union officer lived and supervised the union's office thirty miles away in Walla Walla, where he was well regarded among the town's (80 percent majority) white community and where none of Local 556's main industrial employers were located.

Realizing that they were on their own if they wanted anything to change at IBP, a small group of immigrant workers began to meet informally in Pasco around 1994 and 1995. They coalesced around two key leaders: Diego Ortega and Maria Martinez. While Ortega himself had emigrated from Mexico (and we heard portions of his story about those experiences in chapters 2 and 3), Martinez had been born and raised in California in a Mexican American family; it was she who ultimately led the movement from its main mobilization through its defeat. She was fully bilingual, and she felt intimately connected to immigrant workers because she had grown up poor, in a very large family, with her schooling interrupted and her long-term prospects for social advancement limited by the need to help the family financially by doing farm labor. In the fields, she had worked side by side with immigrants and came to know how to "speak their language" in many subtle ways, not least by enduring with them the contempt of certain Mexican American schoolmates whose families scorned such work. Martinez was also an exceptionally charismatic leader with a rare gift for putting workers' outraged sense of injustice into bold public words, words that reverberated in the gut and that made management sit up and take notice.

At the outset, however, the workers' efforts were quieter and more low key. They began by meeting in Martinez's basement to mull over their mounting problems with abusive supervisors and unresponsive union officers as well as injuries that seemed impossible to avoid and that never got better even after seeing the doctor. A key leap forward occurred after Martinez sought help from Teamsters for a Democratic Union (TDU), a movement that since the 1970s has actively promoted rank-and-file democracy within the International Brotherhood of Teamsters (IBT, or as the workers referred to it, "the International").[2] Applying TDU's well-honed grassroots organizing strategies led to better attended meetings in a Pasco public park, an expanding network of supporters built line-by-line inside the factory, and then a 1998 mobilization to change the local union's bylaws to permit the direct election of shop stewards (the union's main representatives inside the plant), which brought Martinez into elected office for the first time. Its hackles raised, IBP shuttered the shop steward's office inside the plant. The workers reacted by turning toward more disruptive tactics. Eventually, in the midst of a contract renegotiation dispute in 1999 in which IBP was seeking to eliminate the workers' pensions, tensions boiled over. One day that summer, after the company summarily fired workers who had engaged in a planned work stoppage to protest the speed of the chain, a small group of workers walked off the job. They were followed almost immediately and (somewhat) unexpectedly by most of the other workers at the factory. *La huelga* (the strike) had

begun, illegally and in blatant defiance of the principal officers' conciliatory approach, and it manifested in stark terms the amazing degree
of solidarity and militancy the rank-and-file movement had attained.

The strike, which lasted six weeks, did not preserve the workers'
pension—but it broke the back of the Local's inherited leadership.
The movement consolidated its command of the local union in the
2000 elections that ousted the "old guard" and replaced them with
Martinez, Ortega, and other crucial leaders in the strike. Prevailing
over a sustained effort by the International's regional body to squelch
this unruly upsurge in rank-and-file power by nullifying the elections,
the new officers immediately democratized the Local's internal structure and vastly multiplied the opportunities provided by the union for
participation and politicization. The union also began chipping away
at the entrenched problems at the factory. By most accounts, the new
union's efforts to train workers to stand up for themselves when facing
illegal firings, refusals of medical referrals, inadequate medical treatment, and shouting supervisors yielded real changes in these areas.
The problem of supervisors denying bathroom breaks to workers ceased
to be an issue. And beyond cultivating a more resolute disposition
among workers to resist unfair treatment by managers in directly interpersonal ways, the union undertook longer-term legal and political
projects. Chief among these efforts was a lawsuit to get the company to
compensate workers for the unpaid time they spent "donning and doffing" their elaborate protective equipment. Rather than an exclusive
affair for attorneys acting benevolently on workers' behalf, the lawsuit
became a vehicle for the Local to enact its TDU-based strategy to keep
building rank-and-file participation and leadership through individual members' step-by-step activation, in this case through a campaign
to sign up as many workers as possible to be coplaintiffs.

Thus, the spirit of *political education and movement* continued to
animate Local 556 even after the strike and even after the reformers
became engaged with forms of action more densely regulated by institutional and legal norms. As I discuss in the Conclusion, this spirit
waned as the strike receded into past history, as the absurdly rapid
turnover of the workforce left the union with dwindling numbers of
political veterans in its ranks, and as the exigencies of navigating
bureaucratic and legal processes diminished the militancy of the officers' vision to a certain degree. After Tyson purchased IBP in 2001

and then implemented a coordinated strategy to bust the union, the rank-and-file movement began to face challenges it was ill equipped to meet—challenges that eventually resulted in the local union's destruction and the termination of political activism at the plant. In this chapter, however, I focus on the ways the workers conceptualized the movement's remarkable rise to power and the ethos of radical democratic politicization that they were still actively cultivating among themselves in 2002 when we performed our interviews, despite the simultaneous emergence of counterdiscourses and environmental mutations that ultimately proved deeply damaging to the movement.

In the interviews, we asked these individuals to tell us their accounts about how the movement among the rank and file at IBP had begun, what they remembered about the strike and the rank-and-file takeover of the union that followed shortly thereafter, and how they conceived of what the union meant and what it was capable of doing. We listened to them speak about both their individual experiences and their roles in the movement as well as their judgments about the core leaders' successes and failures. Here, I emphasize how the stories of the stalwart reformers diverged from those of the counterreform activists. The former offered a symbiotic conception of the relation between their struggles to learn and exercise their legal rights and their efforts to mobilize themselves as a self-determining movement that sought a creative role in both constituting the work environment and operating the union. The counterreformers, by contrast, after having been devoted comrades of the reformers in mobilization before and during the strike, later veered toward a much more domesticated and one-sided conception of the union that stressed the workers' lack of independent capacities and their desperate need for remedial intervention by the state.

In the conclusion of this chapter, I argue that this latter tendency reflected the disciplinary consequences of the workers' increasing entanglement with legalist modes of authority—precisely those normalizing effects that Wendy Brown's (1995) critique of liberal-legalist activism would lead us to anticipate. For Brown, activists who stake their movements' successes on the pursuit of substantive legal rights undermine their own efforts by exposing themselves to the law's disciplinary mechanisms. They thereby fall into the pattern that Brown, following Nietzsche, dubs "the politics of *ressentiment*." This disposition involves becoming attached to one's wounds and vulnerabilities as the basis of a bitterly defensive and self-blocking political identity and thus yearning for authority to compensate the harms done and punish the perpetrators rather than desiring to create a new world for oneself. Starkly evident in the narratives of the counterreformers, the politics of *ressentiment* had left its traces even in the accounts of the dedicated reform activists at Tyson/IBP insofar as they drifted away from extra-legal experimentation after the strike and came to center their efforts more exclusively on invoking the law's protective, compensatory, and retributive functions.

Deeper complexities of these immigrant workers' political common sense, however, emerge with the help of genealogical inquiry into both the breaks and continuities between these individuals' accounts of their political activities and their stories about power in the other key domains discussed in earlier chapters: the political-economic and cultural circumstances spurring emigration from Mexico, the realms of illegality along the border and in the U.S. interior, and the work environment in the factory. These other aspects of the workers' stories signal the limits of Brown's theory of legalist activism, pointing to a richer conception of political mobilization in the context of the law that avoids capitulation to the politics of *ressentiment*. Certain genealogical antecedents in the workers' stories about their experiences as undocumented immigrants and as participants in the slaughterhouse labor process, especially their tendency to depict themselves as vulnerable to catastrophe and virtually helpless in the face of capricious and despotic forces, fueled the embrace of legalist discipline that especially characterized the counterreformers' discourse. Still other anterior moments in these narrative genealogies, however, above all their accounts of developing subtle techniques to protect themselves and others and thus to exert a modicum of agency in determining the events of their lives, provided narrative resources for stories of union struggle that more strongly emphasized the self-generative and world-transforming capabilities of ordinary workers. When these narrative impulses toward a more generative political disposition took on *collective, institutional* aspects in the context of the workers' accounts of their joint efforts to reform Local 556 and fight back against the company, they nourished political alternatives to the machinations of biopolitics that subjugate immigrant workers in the United States today.

Stories about the Antecedents of Rebellion

From a wide-angle view, the development of the workers' movement at Tyson/IBP seemed to follow a trajectory that led from early unity and strength to eventual division and weakness. The stories the workers told us about their experiences with organizing, however, were marked by disparities over how to conceive of the movement's goals and accomplishments from the very beginning. A chief difference, most vividly manifest in the competing narratives of Maria Martinez and Diego Ortega, concerned the question of whether workers had the desires and capacities needed to improve their own circumstances at the plant or whether the point of organizing was to solicit the beneficial intervention of institutional authorities capable of demanding that the company alter its behaviors, above all the state and the law.

By common consensus, it was Ortega who led the workers in their first serious venture into activism. This was a battle in 1994–95 to oust the chief shop steward, Marta Pérez, from her position as the union's key representative in the plant after workers wearied of her unresponsiveness to their concerns. Ortega described a work environment at that time, as we saw in chapter 4, where supervisors both verbally and physically abused the line workers and where rumors circulated that several women had even "lost their babies" from doing excessively heavy lifting, being exposed to dangerous chemicals, or being forced to work in positions unsuited to their bodily limitations during pregnancy.[3] He got angry and started organizing with the rank and file after the company charged him a high replacement fee for some protective metal sleeves that had been stolen from his locker—and after the union officials, to his shock, joined the company in "attacking him" rather than "defending" him. What the workers needed, Ortega believed, was guidance from the state and knowledge about what the state and the law could do for them:

Then we decided to go ask for information from another place, so they could give us an orientation. . . . We started telling the people to come to the meeting of injured people, which [the Washington State Bureau of] Labor and Industries was going to have. . . . They gave us flyers to give out. And people came to the meetings . . . but a lot of them didn't even understand what Labor and Industries is, or anything like that. No one knew. And they explained. But a lot of people didn't really get a sense of what was happening in the meeting. . . . That was how we started informing ourselves more about those who were injured and the rights of the worker.

Several aspects of the way Ortega told this story are noteworthy. Above all, Ortega expressed a fervent optimism about state intervention as the crucial means for solving the workers' problems. In this account, the state reached out to people who were in a woeful and vulnerable condition, not only being abused but also only dimly understanding how the state could help them even when they were meeting face to face with public officials. They needed "the authorities," as Ortega put it elsewhere in his interview, to "defend" them, to "inform" them, and to "orient" them; and even when the state did this, they seemed incapable of being moved very far. The *agency* of change resided with the state and with an elite corps of activists, most of all with Ortega himself.[4] Gendered imagery played a significant role here, moreover, for Ortega cast himself as the responsible masculine leader who responded to the plight of ordinary workers, typified by the pregnant woman whose vulnerable body was not receiving the special protection it was due. Similarly, Ortega described how he and several other (male) leaders recruited an unwilling Maria Martinez, "convinced" her to join the fight, and "pulled her in," essentially to be a front-person for the movement that they were really directing behind the scenes.

Martinez acknowledged that at first she had been reluctant to plunge into worker activism, having been burned by an earlier venture of this sort.[5] However, Ortega persuaded Martinez to join the new fight that was brewing. Martinez told us a different kind of story than Ortega did about how the workers initially mobilized, a story that gave a different cast to the relations of power in play. For Martinez, the workers' push to organize began in earnest when several processes coincided: an upward spike in popular participation in local protest activities, an increase in contact with rank-and-file democracy activists within the Teamsters international union, and Martinez's own accelerating involvement in the International's politics as a rank-and-file reformer. Martinez and Ortega reached out to the leaders of TDU, including Ron Carey who was by then in his final months as IBT president during the International's brief and exceptional reform period. A pivotal event, Martinez and others told us, was the arrival of veteran California TDU organizer Joe Fahey to facilitate a mass meeting of 300 workers in 1997 in a Pasco public park. The more she learned about TDU, the more she realized that the organization's rank-and-file values resonated with her own self-developed approach to leadership and the more convinced she became that activating—and following—the rank and file was crucial to change at IBP:

I got interested and involved because the workers wanted to do something about it. . . . The workers always saw that I stood up to myself and really, the supervisor never did anything to me. . . . And I used to work in the line where the majority were men, where there were all men except, like, two of us women. . . . And then Joe Fahey sponsored me to a TDU convention. *That's* when I found out what TDU was all about. . . . I started learning a little about what the Teamster history was all about. . . . That's when we started organizing people . . . to change our bylaws, to have the right to elect our stewards. . . . We got three hundred people to this Local, to vote on our bylaws. We changed the bylaws.

Like Ortega, Martinez stressed how organizing the workers began as a learning process. She also talked about making an appeal to certain kinds of authority, in this case the international Teamsters leadership under Carey as well as provisions in the local union's charter that made the Local's bylaws amendable by a vote of the membership. But the similarities between their two stories mostly ended there. When Martinez reflected on the workers' early rank-and-file gatherings, the workers did not appear as people who remained dull-witted and impermeable to what officials "explained" to them. Rather, she presented them as people who began talking about their difficult situation and who attracted the commitment of leaders like Martinez because they themselves wanted to take action. As a leader among these workers, correspondingly, Martinez motivated others by setting an example of resolute self-defense in the face of potential abuse rather than by securing aid from above and from outside for people who could not help themselves (and explicitly defying stereotypes about women as needing such protection by others).

The differences between the *kinds* of educational endeavors that Ortega and Martinez described were also telling. While for the former the workers desperately needed a *legal* education, for the latter what opened new doors was a *political* education. As Martinez explained, this meant gaining knowledge about the history of the labor movement and what ordinary workers had done for themselves through their organizations. This political learning process, to be sure, involved venturing into legalist domains: changing the Local's bylaws to democratize its electoral procedures and filing the first of two wage-and-hour lawsuits against IBP, which enabled Martinez's own rapid rise to national prominence as TDU's vice-presidential nominee in the 1998 IBT elections. Yet the point of these legalist and electoral ventures was not simply to secure authoritative interventions from above to solve the workers' problems. In addition, it was to enable the workers to re-fashion their union organization from below so that it could become a means and a medium for their collective empowerment. Thus, the effort to change Local 556's bylaws not only brought new rights and protections but also *built the grassroots organization* by mobilizing hundreds of workers to turn out at union meetings. They caught the old guard completely by surprise, because the officers never advertised their meetings or expected members to show up.[6] As envisioned by Martinez, then, political education did not simply inform workers about the technical imperatives of a system of power that the educators administrated in the way that Ortega suggested. Rather, the educators in Martinez's story counseled the workers in tactics for creating new constellations of organized power for themselves through popular mobilization in the context of legalist struggle.

Regarding the subsequent buildup to the 1999 strike, the stories told by Martinez and Ortega again intertwined to a certain extent while retaining some notable disparities. Ortega told us about how he had organized a major work stoppage in 1998 after his fellow activist, Héctor Fernández, was threatened with company retaliations for his role in getting workers to complain to managers about the slippery floors in the plant. By then, as Ortega noted, the workers' struggle had expanded to encompass not just the indifferent behavior of union officials but also "the things the company was doing." This broadening of the workers' goals, along with the widening of their repertoire of methods to include coordinated direct action, represented a shift in the characterization of ordinary workers in Ortega's version of the story. No longer helpless supplicants for state intervention, they appeared more as a collective force gaining the ability to act on its own behalf. Nevertheless, Ortega continued to stress the pivotal character of his individual role in inspiring the protest, sometimes making it seem as though it was only through his personal exertions that workers were motivated to take part in the resistance. He also underscored that before letting the work stoppage go forward, he had submitted an official complaint with state officials and filed a grievance with the company "to have the protection from the two sides for the workers." Added Ortega: "When we stopped [working], the company wanted to retaliate, but we had the papers from Labor and Industries saying that we were protected." Characteristically, his emphasis was on the workers' need for state authorities to protect them from the company.[7]

Like Ortega, Martinez and her allies stressed how the workers had constructed a network of resistance outside the formal union apparatus and on the shop floor as momentum gathered before the cataclysmic strike of 1999. Yet these accounts lacked the anxiety Ortega expressed about ensuring protection and guidance from authoritative institutions, even when they self-consciously mentioned the workers' need to secure their *rights* through legalist means like collective bargaining. Following TDU's vision of popular democratic unionism, Martinez and other key activists such as Alejandro Méndez, Rogelio Salazar, and Esteban Múñoz orchestrated a "campaign" to bring rank-and-file voices to bear on the 1999 contract negotiations, once again turning a legal process into the basis of group activation.[8] Recalled Alejandro Méndez:

At first we started chatting with people there among the lines: "Hey guy, this or that is happening. The contract is going to expire soon. If you want a change and if we want to get rid of all those abusive things the company is doing to us, so that we have no right other than working like donkeys, that's the only right we have—if you want, we're going to have a meeting, Maria, me, and everyone. And so-and-so, from TDU, is going to come and they're going to give us some guidance. If you want, those of us people who feel like it and want to have a change are going to be there—people who at least want to fight a little bit—for a raise. . . . A year before the contract expires, the union should already be holding dialogues with the company about the contract and what benefits we want—that is, getting us to agree on what benefits are going to stay.[9]

On the one hand, when Méndez referred to workers' "rights," he meant, in part, the simple and limited notion of the worker's right to a fair wage and decent benefits, a right that is contingent on the collective bargaining agreement. On the other hand, Méndez's evocative and sardonic comparison of the worker to a *burro* (donkey) suggested a more sweeping, universalistic vision of fundamental human rights that the company had been violating by treating the workers no differently from animals. The worker had the right, Méndez seemed to be saying, to treatment by the company that was neither abusive nor crudely instrumentalist. This conception of workers' rights certainly was consistent with Ortega's desire that workers take advantage of state-based legal and administrative resources protecting them from physical hazards at work and compensating the injured. Yet the *politics* of lodging rights claims differed in the two accounts. In Méndez's story, the people needed orientation from labor organizers like those from TDU, but this seemed to be more of a tool for the workers to use at their discretion than requisite training in predefined channels of worker action. The terms the two men used to describe their modes of interaction with fellow workers to bring them into group meetings, moreover, contrasted in interesting ways. Ortega stressed his own actions to get fellow workers to fall in line: "I called them all to a meeting and I spread the word, 'We're going to the cafeteria.'" Méndez, by contrast, emphasized the collective, participatory aspect of these endeavors as well as the importance of appealing to a coworker's personal will: "We started chatting there among the lines [saying] . . . 'If you want, we're going to have a meeting.'"

"The Chain Stopped": Stories of the Strike and Its Aftermath

Despite the tensions between the various interviews, the political sensibilities of the workers' stories tended to converge when they told us about the events immediately precipitating the strike, the walkout itself, and the first heady weeks on the picket line. Although the fault lines reemerged in the accounts of why rank-and-file solidarity had begun to dwindle after that, the narratives we heard from all sides conveyed the keen sense that a moment of truly remarkable common purpose and collective spirit had materialized among the workers as the summer of 1999 began. Neither chagrin at being denied ineffable human rights of the sort transcending merely legal formulations, nor pragmatic intentions to secure designated contractual rights, seems by itself to have motivated this extraordinary phase of unity and resolve. Rather, simultaneous and mutually reinforcing desires for these two different kinds of rights, both abstract and concrete, fueled this phase of the Tyson/IBP workers' movement. Likewise, the workers proved themselves able to muster a versatile assortment of tactics in their struggle, encompassing disruptive and constructive elements alike. Here again, it becomes clear how this movement crystallized a unique constellation of activism geared toward building autonomous rank-and-file capacities undertaken in the midst of, and by means of, engagement with the law and the state. We can also vividly see how, for a time, the dedicated reformers' propagation of this strategic ethos held full sway over the movement as a whole.

Part of the fabric of motivations contributing to the strike was the accumulating sense of injustice among the workers, which they described in terms of the company's constant violations of their basic human rights and disregard of their fundamental human dignity. In this way, other workers elaborated the line of thought in Alejandro Méndez's sarcastic reference to the workers only having "the right to work like donkeys" at IBP. When I asked Rogelio Salazar whether going out on strike had been a difficult decision for him, he responded, "No! No, because—it's that you get tired of—that they always . . . want to keep their shoe on your neck, always want to treat you as if you were a—a cockroach. And a moment comes to you when you say, 'Well, whatever happens, happens. That's enough.'"[10] Prior to this exchange, similarly, he had explained that when he and other workers pressed their cause under the slogan of "Respect and Dignity," they meant that the company "should treat you like a human being, not like an animal." Esperanza Soto likewise told us how a profound moral intuition had made her "feel" that fundamental human dignity and basic justice were at stake in the workers' situation and that this moral feeling distinguished her from coworkers who were urging a strike without having the commitment to see it through:

You start to get, like, a resentment. And you say, as I have said many times: "My God, will there never be justice here, as should be done here?" Because you saw some things that were *unjust* [slowly emphasizing each syllable of the word *injustas*]. And all that keeps building up and ultimately came crashing down in the strike. . . . I felt the obligation to invite [the other workers] to go out. . . . I felt that I had made the decision [speaking with great conviction]: "If they fire me, or whatever happens, I'm decided, whatever may be. But I want to see justice in this place." . . . A lot of people, maybe without thinking, were saying, "There has to be a strike." [But] I knew that it was from here on the outside, not from there [gestures to her heart]. "A strike is not easy [I told them]. I've never been on strike, but I've heard that a strike is not easy."[11]

When justice was denied, Soto seemed to be saying, a person could sense it in the form of an acute moral indignation. "Resentment" against being stepped on like insects, or forced to "work like donkeys"— in any case, being treated like subhuman beings—generated an impetus to call a halt to such a situation and to demand that justice be done. Only if one's stated desires for action were rooted authentically in this feeling, furthermore, would one have the resolve to shoulder the heavy burdens that a massive act of protest entailed. As both she and Rogelio Salazar told the story, then, there seems to have been almost an instinctual human desire for freedom that kindled the workers' resentments until eventually it was inevitable that, as Salazar put it (citing Melquíades Pereyra), "the bomb [was] going to explode."

Yet the activists' stories of these crucial weeks in the trajectory of the struggle at Tyson/IBP also contextualized these yearnings for justice, articulated in the register of abstract moral right, within concrete power dynamics concerning the workers' organization, the union–management relations at the plant, and the wider politics of food production. The coordinated, TDU-style grassroots campaign to amplify the rank and file's voice in the collective bargaining sessions, these narrators urged us to see, helped *compose the terrain* where the workers generated the political energies and developed the moral sentiments expressed in the strike. While Ortega provided few details about this chapter of the struggle, he did note that the workers had "done other things" before the strike, including staging the work stoppage for which he had sought legal protection. About this key phase of the workers' mobilization, when she was still working on the line, Martinez remembered:

MM: We used to tell people [in processing]: "At ten o'clock, we're all going to . . . hit the table, the metal table, with our hooks." Slaughter did the same thing. They would bang the knives. We used to make noise at the same time so the company knew there was . . . something built between us, slaughter and us . . . during our campaign. We did rallies outside the plant. We did rallies inside the cafeteria. There was a time we just bought a bunch of, like, fifty balloons . . . and everybody signed the balloons. "Respect"—we just had one week of "respect" . . . a week of "safety," and we had stickers on.
PA: But this is without the support of the union?
MM: Right. We did it ourselves. . . . We had one sticker that said, "Ready." You know, we just put "ready." And the supervisors and the managers were, like, "'Ready'—what does that mean?" So people would respond, "We're just ready." You know, we taught them, you just respond, "We're ready. Whatever comes, we're ready."

The campaign to which Martinez referred was the effort to win a fair contract in 1999. Part of what inspired the workers' mounting militancy, in other words, was the hope for tangible gains in these formal negotiations. In particular, the workers sought contract language ensuring them better treatment from supervisors, higher wages, and the retention of benefits the company was threatening to revoke, above all a pensionlike program where senior employees would receive a small bonus in their checks that was set aside for retirement. At the same time, the workers also were after changes that would have interfered more boldly with the company's property-based prerogatives to determine the organization of production. Specifically, they wanted some authority over the operation of the chain, as one of my exchanges with Martinez showed:

MM: I think one of the most important matters would be the chain. You know, we didn't want to have full control of the speed of the chain. But we wanted to be able to stop the chain. . . . Years back, Paul, when . . . we were all stacked up, the USDA . . . would stop the chain. . . . When there was abscess on the tables . . . you just come and wipe it off the tabletops. We wanted to be able to stop the chain, and be able to make sure . . . people were not afraid to stop the chain. And there was a lot of animals. People needed to have the right to stop the chain and not to work on the live animal. These were our demands, and [for] better raises.
PA: Was it also the ability to stop the chain if someone got hurt?
MM: Right. . . . I remember there was a time when somebody fell. They didn't stop the chain. They just moved her aside and picked her up. They just moved her aside.[12]

Martinez placed in the foreground the practical-political struggles where workers' more abstract moral feelings about being denied justice or human dignity took on concrete points of reference. She underscored the mobilizing effects that stemmed from these demands for specific rights, as the workers advertised their "readiness" to defy the bosses: visibly, through wearing stickers; audibly, by banging their knives on their worktables; and also, as Esteban Múñoz told us, through personally confronting managers, such as when "some fifty people from slaughter, apart from [additional] people in processing" descended on a collective bargaining session to "put pressure on them."[13] Moreover, Martinez invoked the broader political context that gave further concrete particularity to the workers' battle for respect and dignity, namely, the movement's hopes of cultivating alliances with consumers worried about meat contamination as well as animal welfare activists concerned about the humane treatment of cattle in the plant.

Together, then, these workers told a story of the buildup to the strike where the apparently spontaneous stirrings of the human heart against palpable injustice and inhumanity in the plant arose within a very deliberately constructed context of organized movement-building and legalist contestation. In addition, this was a story about cultivating collective power that intertwined constructive and negative tactical dimensions. Rather than confining themselves to communicative approaches geared toward prudent, effective bargaining (i.e., aimed at finding common ground or achieving mutual understanding with management, such that jointly acceptable contract terms could be finalized), they actively sought to disrupt the linguistic and sensory field in the factory and to confuse the company about what they intended to do. Their injection into the work environment of noise, both literally through clanging hooks on tables and in the sense of semiotic rupture, was a tactic woven into their contestation of power through formal, legal processes rather than disjoined from or opposed to it.

The fuse that lit the bomb on the day of the walkout, then, had been burning for quite a while; and to some extent, the metaphor belies the substantial degree of preparation the workers had carried out by developing a diverse repertoire of tactics; a set of concrete, particular goals; and an idiom of moral sensibility. Alejandro Méndez provided the most specific account of that fateful morning when he and the other workers on his line achieved what must be judged the pinnacle form of self-assertion in the struggle against the company because it involved not only a reactive refusal to comply but also a momentary, positive enactment of workers' capacities to reorder the production process for themselves. His words are worth quoting at length because of the vivid story they tell:

They were starting to speed up the chain more and more and more. *So we said,* *"We're going to work at our own pace* [emphasis added]. If they speed up the chain, let the pieces [of meat] just fall down there. Let them fall! And let's do it all lines together. United." Then the supervisors and their bosses, and everyone, started running around like, like crazy people. They didn't know what to do with so much meat here, meat there, meat everywhere, all along the line. And after a while, the place was just full of meat. That is, with bones, big pieces there. Why? Because the chuck-workers let the whole pieces go by. The loin-workers: whole pieces. All the little jobs— *"Let's go, let's work more slowly, the way that seems right to us* [emphasis added]. . . . And then, they started taking people out by twos and threes. . . . They were going to start firing them. . . . It was in my line that they took out one or two, loin-workers. And in that [line], well, I was the last one in the line. . . . So I just said to the people . . . "They've taken two. Let's all go out, the whole line. And whatever happens, happens. Every-one out, or everyone in." Then the people . . . [said], "Let's go out." Then [the managers] started saying, "No." They started shutting us in, not letting us leave. They shut the door on us. They didn't want to let us go out into the hall-way. . . . Now they wanted to keep us locked up that way like slaves, by force! We are free. We are not slaves. Even so we got into the hallway and to the other, second door, which led outside—they were putting a chain on it with a pad-lock, to keep us from getting out. [We said,] "How do you think you're not going to let us leave? Either take those things away or we'll break the windows. But we'll get out one way or another." Then they started looking scared because they were used to their word being the law, 100 percent. What they said was done. Whether it was in violation or whatever it was, it was done. And to see that the people weren't responding anymore, that they didn't care a bit about any of them, all the supervisors—they thought they'd better go hide because, well, we were going out.

As Méndez told his story, the firing of two workers that most imme-diately precipitated the strike did not just involve a mundane incidence of supervisor irritation at workers who got injured or did not keep up with the pace of production, of the sort discussed in the previous chap-ter. Instead, these workers were fired because they willfully had stopped yielding to the company's compulsion of high-speed labor through its operation of the chain and had started working at a pace they deter-mined for themselves. They had done so, moreover, in planned collabo-ration with the whole line of workers in processing where Méndez was working. The most dramatically confrontational moment in the work-ers' mobilization thus involved two remarkable kinds of political ex-periences: collectively organizing themselves and using this combined strength to seize control temporarily of the production process. In other words, before the moments of *negation and refusal to comply*—when "the chain stopped," as Martinez succinctly and resonantly phrased it, as workers ceased doing their jobs and walked out of the plant—this story included some crucial moments of *positive action,* in particular taking the initiative to perform work in an autonomous way regardless of the pressures of the chain.[14]

As Martinez noted, this audacious maneuver was only fleeting. The workers, she said, "didn't want to have full control of the speed of the chain" in terms of their collective bargaining goals, although they were seeking the right to stop the chain in exceptional circumstances. But for the most part, their deployment of constructive, creative political energies as they operated in the terrain partly constituted by the law and the state was directed at developing their capabilities as a movement rather than reorganizing production by ending management's unilateral discretion over chain speed. For his part, Alejandro Méndez gravitated toward rebellious imagery of "slaves" bursting their shackles, invoking an Exodus-type narrative of leaving the oppressors and their "law" behind rather than elaborating his vision of workers founding a new order with a new law for themselves. Breaking the chains temporarily laid on the factory doors moved to the center of the story, displacing the theme about workers superseding the power of the chain (i.e., line speed) that had exerted far more continuous and pervasive effects on their bodies and minds. Still, the very fact that workers temporarily commandeered the production process at all emblematizes the political complexity and generativity of their scrupulously developed combination of legalist initiatives and organizational mobilization.

While the walkout and strike might seem on the surface to have been essentially acts of refusal, albeit grand and dramatic ones, the workers' stories of these events also indicated the vast array of practical tasks and the extent of political education needed to carry these endeavors forward. Staying on the picket line for six long weeks involved cultivating the strike force as an organized collectivity, building on the coordination that had been developing on the shop floor and in the public parks of Pasco. Ramona Díaz, for example, recounted the mundane but important jobs that she and others had performed to ensure the continuing vitality of the workers' organization during the strike:

We put ourselves in charge of taking role of the people. . . . We took it by lines and we were always getting the signatures of those who were present, and for those who didn't go, for what reason they weren't going. . . . And helping . . . to pass out food, to give people something to eat; we went around there doing whatever could be done.[15]

Many of the activists we spoke with, including some who later sided with Ortega against Martinez, described other ways that they had greased the wheels of the workers' organization, often by serving as conduits for communication among various groups of workers. Héctor Fernández claimed to have formed the original "network of communication" inside the plant and to have kept it going during the strike.[16] Rosa Vásquez told us that Ortega had relied on her to communicate with workers who spoke no Spanish, especially immigrants from countries outside Latin America, since she had learned English.[17] Esperanza Soto recalled how she had first informed Maria Martinez that the two workers had been fired and then had gone around the other lines to relay the word that all the workers in the plant were walking out. And Rogelio Salazar noted that the workers divided responsibilities for staffing the picket line according to a schedule they invented: "We started working in shifts: one day some people, the next day others." Beyond these mundane but crucial organizing tasks, furthermore, the striking workers carried out a variety of more sensational efforts to build their ranks and garner community support. They drew over a thousand to a Mass that a priest celebrated on their picket line, mobilized two thousand workers and supporters to march through the streets of Pasco, protested outside U.S. Department of Agriculture offices, and even took their actions to Seattle and Portland.[18]

Waging the strike clearly saddled the workers with the need to make special personal exertions and to handle acute difficulties in their family lives. Rogelio Salazar described how he had felt to be outside the plant on the day of the walkout, in the withering midsummer heat of the eastern Washington high desert:

We were there almost the whole day. I don't remember what time we went out. . . . It was early in the morning. And, well, we stayed there almost the whole day—outside. And I remember that one young woman fainted from the heat of the sun. Because we weren't even drinking water, or [eating] food, or anything.

In turn, Pedro Ruiz recalled shivering in the nights he spent at the workers' encampment outside the plant gates: "I remember that at night it got cold; we just covered ourselves with our coats. We had to be there twenty-four hours, because a person had to keep walking all night long."[19] His wife, Gloria, told us how especially since they had only recently arrived from Mexico and had incurred "some really tough expenses" in moving, they were hard-pressed financially during the strike.[20] Pedro Ruiz explained: "The union gave [each worker] fifty dollars a week to support us. By the end, in June, we . . . went in the morning to pick cherries and in the afternoon we went to the strike . . . because we had to pay the rent and get food to eat." Rosa Vásquez had also found it a real hardship to make ends meet during the strike, even though she was less economically vulnerable than the Ruizs because of her knowledge of English; she noted that losing the chance to earn "a nice paycheck for overtime" had been particularly hard. As a single mother of several children, one of whom had Down syndrome, Juanita Castillo felt the strain on her responsibilities as a parent especially acutely: "It scared me. I said: 'What's going to happen if . . . they fire us, or . . . if we're going to be out there for a long time?'"

On the whole, a core assumption informed these accounts of the strike: that the workers, even as they pursued a better contract, were seeking to bring about changes at IBP through their own exertions rather than simply yearning for the state or some other powerful authority to establish justice for them. None of the activists narrated these events in ways that suggested any strong desire to get the state to intervene on the workers' behalf, a desire that, as we have seen, prominently figured in Diego Ortega's story of the workers' earlier mobilization. To be sure, several people, among them Ramona Díaz and Pedro Ruiz, expressed dismay at the stingy payments the IBT was disbursing from its strike fund and believed they had deserved stronger support from the International. Yet on the whole, legal, state, and union-bureaucratic mechanisms seemed either beside the point or antagonistic to the workers' endeavors. Rather than turning to the state's law to rescue them, the workers saw themselves as confronting a situation in which the managers' word "was the law, 100 percent," as Alejandro Méndez put it, and in which they needed to challenge that effective but unwritten law directly—and, for a brief instant, in which they could impose a new regime of production for and by themselves. Although none of the workers ever suggested that the strike force seriously considered resorting to violence (other than the property destruction involved in the threat to get out by breaking windows), several emphasized that when people walked out of the factory, they took their knives with them, along with other equipment. They likewise noted that a pivotal moment came when they agreed to go back inside later that day to turn in their gear.[21] The fact that these rebellious workers were essentially *armed*, with tools for butchering cattle that easily could have served as weapons, could not have been lost on the company and local law enforcement agents.

To be sure, the legalist aims of the collective bargaining process remained firmly ensconced within the workers' motivations for protest. Furthermore, the strike only violated the law during its first few days, after which the union's officers capitulated to the overwhelming resolve of the membership and the strike was declared legal on the grounds of an impasse in contract negotiations. Yet the workers knew full well that this legalization of their strike brought them few practical advantages in terms of either support from the state or leverage within the International. In at least two instances, the police intervened in ways that undermined worker solidarity and weakened their attempts to win broader support. According to Rogelio Salazar, a regional IBT official called in the police to break up a rally the workers were holding at a local racing facility, preventing speakers from talking and turning the event into a "disaster." Manuel Guzmán, who in 2002 headed the ticket opposing Maria Martinez's Respect and Dignity slate in the Local 556 elections, told us how police also had been stationed at the plant to ensure safe passage for the cars of people who, like he, were crossing the picket line to work:

That time when we arrived there, the people were in the road that goes in to IBP; they were there with flags; they didn't want to let the cars go inside. But little by little we were going in; they had to start opening the way. But when we had gotten ourselves inside, since they were carrying flags or something, they scratched up our car because they were pressed up against the car so tightly. The first day was when they just did that; then later the authorities were there. The police came over there and I think they ordered that every time a car passed by they had to open themselves up to leave the way clear.[22]

Guzmán also described how the company had given workers who had stayed on the job favorable treatment: offering them new work gloves daily rather than only once every three to four weeks; bringing them coffee and rolls; letting them take breaks at their own pleasure and for longer time periods than usual; allowing them to work extra hours with full overtime pay; and paying them a full day's wages in return for a promise to visit the picket line and vote to end the strike on one day when a pivotal ballot was taken. And although threats of plant closure are illegal during contract negotiations, Esperanza Soto reported that the company persistently warned workers that it would close the plant or curtail operations and work hours if they did not accede to the company's demands. Thus, in spite of the fairly quick conversion of the wildcat into a legal strike, this did not mean that the workers soon put more faith in the idea of resolving their problems through normal institutional channels. To the contrary, as they portrayed the power relations governing the scene of the strike, they stressed how forces antagonistic to their cause persisted in ways both formally exercised by the police and informally applied by the company with the state's tacit permission.

Almost without exception, the workers' stories of the strike described the heady, initial days as an inspiring and unprecedented demonstration of unity among the workers. This was true, for example, even of Diego Ortega, who recalled: "We were all working together" to fight the company. It also featured in the words of Rogelio Salazar, who said, regarding the workers' determination that they would stay outside the plant after the walkout:

> It wasn't a decision of Maria, or of Flaco, or of any other person. Rather it was Maria who asked them, "What do you all want us to do, go in to work or not go in to work?" And everyone shouted with one voice: "No! We're not going in to work!" So what the people asked for was done.

Both Rosa Vásquez, who later (temporarily) joined Ortega's dissenting faction, and Esteban Múñoz, who remained a stalwart ally of Martinez, depicted the strike force as including non-Mexican immigrant workers and African Americans at the factory and as making active efforts to do so, in part through their own efforts as people with bilingual abilities. Múñoz, for instance, told us that Bosnian, Russian, Laotian, and black workers all had participated in the strike, explaining:

> More than anything, what we were trying to do at that time, is to have . . . one person from each group who knew how to speak the language of the other people and who also knew English. And we would communicate to that person what was happening and that person was in charge of telling all the others.

The few, rare divisions with regard to the strike that the interviews illuminated seemed to stem from differences of occupational status and location within the plant. Ignacio Ramos, who said he worked as a supervisor's assistant, participated in the strike out of loyalty to his fellow Mexican "countrymen" but felt as though the movement leaders never really trusted him.[23] Neither Rafael Mendoza nor Manuel Guzmán, who worked respectively in the machinery maintenance and rendering departments (which were much smaller than slaughter and processing, and in Mendoza's case much better paid), took part in the strike; yet neither disputed the overriding sense from our conversations that the strike had involved a massive upsurge of the great majority of workers at the factory.

The stories diverged more decisively, however, when it came to describing and explaining the gradual decline of that unity as the weeks went by and the company still refused to make meaningful contract concessions. As Juanita Castillo put it, "Little by little they started going back in, two or three [at a time]. . . . Our spirits went down. . . . Our morale declined . . . each time we saw a person going in." According to Castillo, the divisions among the strikers sprang from disagreements regarding Maria Martinez's leadership that had been stirred up groundlessly by various antagonists, including probusiness conservatives within the local Latino community.[24] Others who remained aligned with Maria Martinez, like Esperanza Soto, drew attention to the company's role in suppressing enthusiasm for the strike. Soto told us that IBP had done this, in particular, by blaming the loss of the workers' pension on the strike even though the company had planned to eliminate this benefit before contract negotiations began.

Some workers who had helped wage the strike, however, started to believe the gossip about Maria Martinez's supposedly self-serving ends and viewed her aggressive, confrontational style as evidence that she no longer had the workers' best interests at heart. Some even questioned why they had gone out on strike in the first place. Pedro Ruiz, for instance, had this to say about how and why the strikers' unity dissipated:

PR: At the beginning [we were] really united: flags, marching, shouting. And afterward it started dying out little by little, they started going back in; [there were] quarrels, fights, accusations. . . . So that the people got disillusioned bit by bit, that the time kept passing by. . . .
PA: Could the leaders have done something different?
PR: I think, yes, they could have. . . . If there had been leaders who negotiated, who got to know the people from the plant, then there would have been a

fair agreement for the worker and I think that what happened, a strike, wouldn't have happened.

As Ruiz narrated these events, all Maria Martinez did was "shout and shout" instead of working congenially with company officials to accomplish what workers really needed.[25] Similarly, Ortega insinuated that Martinez was trying to manipulate the workers into acting against their interests for selfish reasons and criticized what he saw as her unwise disregard for state benefits that could have aided the struggle. He described the final decision to ratify the contract and go back to work as follows:

> For political reasons, it was decided that we had to go in. We had to go back because the strike was arriving at a limit, and this quote-unquote "limit" supposedly could create a bigger problem. I was opposed to that, because . . . a limit was arriving when the unemployment agency couldn't keep holding back the money of the worker . . . the time limit for unemployment to deny you benefits. And before that time limit arrived, it was decided to go back in. So it looked bad to me, because we were going to have more support of money for the worker.

On the surface, there appeared to be a tension between Ruiz's and Ortega's stories: Ortega seemed to be advocating renewed militancy among the workers, while Ruiz wanted the leaders to work more collaboratively with the company. The parallel feature of the two accounts, however, lay in the way both fundamentally doubted the possibility of an autonomous workers' struggle. In each narrative, the vigor and fruitfulness of the workers' efforts remained contingent on their cooperation with institutional authorities, either the company or the state.

When these and other dissidents who later parted company with Martinez and the other activists told their stories about the rising discord among the workers after the strike and the rank-and-file takeover of the union, this theme would harden and become more pronounced. In contrast, while the union's main activists would also come to emphasize even more strongly than in the strike phase the project of teaching workers to understand and employ their legal rights, they would continue to stress the integration of such legalist strategy within a more encompassing program for inspiring workers' collective responsibility and agency for determining their own futures.

We Are the Union! Stories of Power and Rights in Local 556's Post-Reform Era

As we have seen, regardless of their ultimate political alignment within the Local, the workers' stories of how the rank-and-file movement at IBP germinated and built to its climax in the strike all emphasized the mission of educating workers about their legal rights and pursuing the enforcement of those rights. Thus, the workers described their quest for empowerment, not entirely but still significantly, as an effort to enhance their electoral rights by using their local union's charter and bylaws strategically. In turn, after the strike, they used their new voting powers to eject the old guard leaders from their posts and install Maria Martinez, Diego Ortega, and other key activists as new officers of Teamsters Local 556. And when the IBT, in an attempt to thwart the rise of this TDU-affiliated movement, sought to nullify the Local's election, the activists took their case to the administrative courts of the National Labor Relations Board (NLRB) and by 2000 had prevailed.[26] Meanwhile, the workers continued prosecuting their wage-and-hour lawsuit against the company.

Nevertheless, interwoven with these accounts of legalist activism in many of their stories was a profound sense that securing and enforcing rights was not merely an end in itself. For the people with whom we spoke, especially those who remained allied with Martinez rather than siding with Ortega, legalism was also a means for accumulating solidarity and activating an increasingly broader corps of leaders within the rank and file. The goal, in other words, was not simply to receive protections and compensations from juridical authorities. It was also to develop workers' capacities to organize themselves and to struggle for justice in the workplace and in the labor movement.

Sometimes, the workers characterized their exertions to effect changes at Tyson/IBP in ways that veered close to placing a narrow and unequivocal trust in legal means. This was surprising given the audacity of their legal trespass at the start of the strike as well as their movement's history of having grown up outside the union's formal apparatus. Perhaps just as oddly, it was Alejandro Méndez, who had been on the line that staged the protest that catalyzed the walkout, who articulated this embrace of legalism in the sharpest terms:

A company always has to base itself in contracts or some document that pro-
tects you . . . because that is what helps you protect yourself, to demand a right.
That they don't violate that right. And that's where I try to grab hold of that.
And if I keep studying a little more, the state law, the federal law, rights I
have—well, it's a lot better, you know. I defend myself better. . . . To me, any
supervisor who wants to intimidate me, doesn't intimidate me. They shout
at me—I shout at them. . . . If a grievance has to be made out, I make them
out. . . . Lots of people have seen how they used to take me to the office, how
they gave me tickets [demerits]. [I say to them,] "Do you all see how it's the
opposite now? Now I'm the one who gives tickets to them." Why? Because I
have the power to give them to them. But how? Because I'm also studying my
rights a little with Maria.

In some ways, what Brown calls the "politics of *ressentiment*" seemed
to have a real presence here. In line with this political disposition,
Méndez emphasized self-defense against abuse and violation instead
of working to restructure the social conditions producing this mistreatment in the first place. He also envisioned himself as having
power in a way that involved *trading positions* with those who tried to
intimidate and reprimand him rather than *changing the terms* of those
power relations: he became the punisher rather than the one pun-
ished, and it was the ability to punish the guilty rather than to create
something new that he appeared to desire most strongly. In a basic
sense, moreover, Méndez spoke as though the law were the golden key
that sprang the lock, opening the door to a new political space where
bosses would give workers the respect and dignity they demanded. The
aspiration to build a movement enabling workers to recast their conditions of labor for themselves, by contrast, seemed rather distant from
his comments.

Yet as the last few lines in this interview excerpt subtly suggested,
Alejandro Méndez's legal education took place neither in a political
vacuum nor in a political context defined exclusively by these dynamics of resentment. Studying one's rights, learning how to deploy them
in practice, and accumulating the courage to act on them were all processes that the workers' organization promoted in systematic ways and
as a collective project. Leaders like Maria Martinez became tutors facilitating the workers' self-educating strategies rather than professional
providers of services to a passive rank and file. In turn, key activists
like Méndez actively sought to set positive examples for their coworkers who were less self-confident by showing them how they really could

change their conditions of work for the better through a combination of individual initiative and group solidarity. Thus, the shift from a temporary experimentation with extralegal strategies of protest in the dawning hours of the strike toward a more sustained focus on legalist activism did not require sacrificing the sense that the workers' movement could be self-determining and could generate new and different class relations at the plant. Nor did it portend the abandonment of direct action tactics. In the fall of 2002, Martinez amassed a crowd of several hundred workers to protest the company's removal of flyers advising workers about their immigration rights, in the midst of a new effort by the company to harass workers regarding their immigration status. When management tried to bar Martinez from the plant in retaliation, Esperanza Soto and others led a group of activists into the offices of human resources managers and demanded that Martinez be permitted to return immediately.[27]

The reform activists in Local 556 frequently encapsulated their vision of a self-mobilizing, legally *and* politically self-educating rank and file by announcing what became a core slogan of their movement, along with the phrase "Respect and Dignity." This oft-repeated motto was *¡Nosotros somos la unión!* or, in English, We are the union![28] Although not all the workers interpreted this catchphrase in precisely the same way, there was a prevalent understanding of what it meant among them. Elvira Méndez tried to distinguish this political ethos from what she saw as the misconceptions of fellow workers who seemed stuck in a traditional mentality about the union. These others, she argued, wrongly saw the union as a set of professional service agents to whom the members related as needy clients rather than as the organizational context for a collective, grassroots-democratic project of ongoing popular education and mobilization. Explaining how she had sought help from Maria Martinez to navigate complicated rules for getting Tyson's permission to see a physician of her choice rather than a company doctor about a job-related health problem, Méndez noted:

They think that because Maria is the [Secretary-]Treasurer of the union, they think that she is the union.[29] She is the [Secretary-]Treasurer of the union, *but we all are the union, not Maria, not even the shop stewards. All the teams of workers* [emphasis added]. . . . People want someone to do for them the things they should do. And that's not right. You always have to do your part if you want things to turn out right. It's like a home. I could come to my home and just stay there sitting around all the time, like I have nothing to do. Let's say my children are there. If I set the example of standing up to do something, they've all got to get up to help. If I don't do anything, then they're all just sitting there. But you have to start, too, to do things. . . . If I'm interested in them helping me, and the lady tells me, "You know what? Write this letter"; and right away I go look for some way to write the letters. Sure, I don't know English, but [I ask]: "Can you help me, John Doe, or Maria, to put it into English?"[30]

Méndez thus was seeking to get the company to respect her right to choose her own doctor in an atmosphere where the company was openly hostile to workers who tried to claim this right. But far from simply invoking the potency of the law to protect her from harm, Méndez saw this process of rights claiming as part of her own long-term political education through involvement in the union. So she emphasized how important it was for her to take the initiative to ask for Martinez's assistance and to propel the process forward herself rather than to take the position of a supplicant who expected union officers to fix things for her, as she said some of her fellow workers tended to do.[31]

Méndez's conception of what it meant to say "We all are the union" thus wound together several crucial themes, all of which helped compose the distinctive model of worker activism that the union attempted to instill following the rank-and-file takeover: personal responsibility, a sense of the individual's real capacity to change her own working conditions for herself, reliance on the legal-technical guidance of union officers who had come up through the rank and file, and participation in a collective endeavor that maintained internal solidarity and motivated the members to take action. Other workers reinforced these same principles in their accounts of the union's ambitions under the new leadership. The main job of those leaders, Esteban Múñoz confirmed, was "to teach the people that you have a voice in the union—that you *are* the union. We, the workers, are the union, not the officers. . . . We are the ones who can make the changes." When we asked Ramona Díaz who the most important leaders in the union were, she immediately responded, "All the people are important, right?"

Likewise, these workers and others emphasized that such collective, radically democratic action depended on a political education that involved learning how to deploy one's rights self-protectively in tense situations on the job. According to Múñoz, supplying such a political education had been the principal achievement of the reformed union:

The company knows now that the people won't let anyone get away with anything. Why? Because . . . now we know more about our rights. . . . The officers that were there before, from the union, didn't give us information. . . . They kept us in the dark, you could say, because we didn't know anything. . . . Because it didn't interest them whether the people knew how to defend themselves. Because the only thing that interested them was getting the people's dues, and all that. They never gave us a meeting or said, "Come learn this; we're going to teach you this."[32]

Díaz, like Múñoz, reached for metaphors about a newfound sense of sight to describe how things had changed with the ascension of the rank-and-file movement. Martinez, she said, had "started opening our eyes because before they would make us cry every time, there, in the office. . . . I've learned a lot with them." In turn, Nina Garza credited the union with helping workers learn to overcome their fears, bolstering their courage to defend themselves and one another, nurturing a spirit of mutual commitment among them, and fostering the desire to become even better educated and more able to stand up for themselves—and, above all, to *speak for themselves* in a power environment where the workers' lack of English contributed to their subordination:

When I started working there, I was afraid of letting a piece of meat fall because I saw that they fired other people who let the meat fall. It really scared me because I said, "Right now it's them, and soon it will happen to me." . . . So time went by, and by going to the meetings I have learned not to be afraid: to speak, to try to go to school a little more to try to learn more English and understand a little more, and not to need an interpreter when they take me to the office. . . . The one who is affected is the one who should speak because he is the one who is feeling something; the interpreter isn't feeling anything. And that is the reason to go to the meetings, because you have to learn so that you don't feel alone.[33]

Notice once more how for Garza, as for Alejandro and Elvira Méndez, practical contexts for claiming concrete rights in direct conflicts with managers, in association with the group-organizing context provided by union gatherings, provided the crucial terrain where she took part in this process of political education.

Just as this coupling of legalist struggles over concrete rights and group mobilization had shown itself in the rank-and-file movement's collective projects prior to taking over the union (e.g., the 1999 contract campaign), so this pattern of activation continued in the period after the strike. Hence, the union carried forward its agenda in the courts by filing a second wage-and-hour lawsuit on the same terms as the first, demanding the payment of back wages owed to workers for the uncompensated time they spent putting on and taking off their protective equipment. And as I mentioned previously, beyond stimulating enthusiasm for the union through the promise of eventual monetary rewards secured by attorneys, the lawsuits provided further occasions to mobilize new leaders within the rank and file through efforts to get as many workers as possible to sign on to the suits as plaintiffs—and then to get some of those people to recruit still others, thus teaching activist skills to a new and ever-expanding cadre of supporters. The union acted in similar fashion after a horrific incident when a young man working in slaughter had most of his arm severed by a giant mechanical scissors machine with a broken safety device. Pressing forward on the legal front, union leaders demanded a state investigation of the incident that ultimately found the company to have been negligent in its responsibility to maintain the hock cutter in good working order and secured over $60,000 in compensation for the man (Levin 2005). But at the same time, activists used the shocking event and its aftermath as a way to cultivate new leaders by recruiting workers to give testimonies about the incident. For most individuals, taking this step required mustering no little courage in the face of possible retaliation by management. Thus, like the wage-and-hour lawsuits, the coordinated response to this "accident" ended up being far more than a mundane bureaucratic operation. It also furnished a key scene of political training.

One interesting variation on this story of collective action based on individual responsibility and political education deserves consideration before moving to an examination of the counterreformers' narratives. A certain embrace of personal sacrifice figured prominently in the workers' stories of the strike, especially those of the women, and to some extent this theme of suffering and self-renunciation for the good of others persisted in the core activists' accounts of the reformed union. Ramona Díaz thus told us: "There are times when I run around with my children because I come and take them with me and bring them along, running to all the meetings, to the strike—wherever it is, they've gone along with me. And it's a lot of sacrifice sometimes." This conjunction of dedication to the union and women's self-sacrificial care for the family also came through when Esperanza Soto reflected on the qualities that made Maria Martinez, in her eyes, a model leader:

> Above all, she has a heart for all the people around her. That is really important: that she does what she does from the heart. And that it doesn't matter to her whether she sleeps or doesn't sleep, whether she eats or doesn't eat—it doesn't matter to her; trying to defend the workers, she is ready at all times.

Soto underscored the feminine-familial dimension of such self-renunciation both by privileging the "heart" as the organ of moral sensibility, as she did in her comments on the strike, and when she added, regarding Martinez: "I don't see her as a leader; I see her almost like a sister."

The activists' conceptions of political education through the rank-and-file movement, then, were gendered. Even when men invoked the notion of self-sacrifice, as Jorge Hernández and Alejandro Méndez did, they did it in ways that reflected more typically masculine presuppositions about sacrificing oneself *for* the family, providing *for* the family, and stoutly defending the family when it was suffering.[34] The women, by comparison, more commonly evoked a sense of the union struggling *as* a family: as sisters, in the emotionally charged words of Esperanza Soto; and as parents and children who were coparticipants in the struggle for change at Tyson/IBP, as Elvira Méndez's analogy of the union to a home and Díaz's story of bringing her children with her to various union events both conveyed. (It bears noting here that children of all ages were virtually always present and welcome at the union events I observed, from health and safety workshops to contract campaign meetings, picnics, and rallies. Díaz's husband invariably attended these meetings, too, and conveyed clearly that he felt part of the struggle even though he did not work at Tyson/IBP.) Such comments resonated with aspects of these women's stories that I considered in preceding chapters, especially their narrative about how their decisions to leave Mexico were contingent on husbands' choices, responsibilities for the direct care of children, and gender-specific forms of mistreatment. "Understanding the struggle," to recall the evocative phrase spoken by Maria Martinez, had always involved conceiving of their projects of immigration and labor in familial terms. Here we see that a parallel understanding infused their narrative about union activism as well.

In short, the vision of rank-and-file democratic action summed up in the slogan "¡Nosotros somos la unión!" and favored by the most dedicated activists over the long term was both internally differentiated and highly integrated. The stories that expressed this political ethos consistently depicted efforts to learn and apply concrete rights as stepping stones within a more broadly cast project of political education that catalyzed a synergy between increasing personal responsibility and growing collective capacities and sympathies. For many key women leaders, in addition, family commitment supplied the affective force and the analogic imaginary that bound together these elements of individualism and collectivism, of legalism and innovative democratic action, of rights claiming and power exertion.

Injured Workers and the Politics of *Ressentiment*

Not all the worker-activists at Tyson/IBP were fully committed to this rich and inventive vision of rank-and-file democracy. Shortly following the NLRB administrative court decision to uphold the Martinez slate's election to head Teamsters Local 556 in 2000, Diego Ortega, who had won a vice-president post with the reform contingent, broke from Martinez and her other allies. Another key organizer during the phase leading up to the strike, Héctor Fernández, joined him, and they set about building a new coalition antagonistic to the Martinez camp. When we interviewed Ortega, Fernández, and their supporters, they were in the midst of an unsuccessful effort to unseat Martinez and those aligned with her in the union's 2002 elections. Ultimately, as I discuss in the conclusion, they would help the company and the IBT bring down the union, belying their protestations to us that they supported the union while opposing Martinez and her comrades. Although those battles were a couple of years away, there were palpable intimations of the road that lay ahead in the stories they told us about where the workers' movement had gone wrong, how the union had betrayed the workers' trust, and how members of the rank and file should have viewed their organization and its leaders.

According to these counterreformers, Martinez and her allies had diverged from the proper way to prosecute workers' interests by becoming overly entangled in partisan wrangling within the IBT because of unseemly self-serving motivations. They accused the reformers of getting too caught up in union "politics" and using their offices to leverage personal privileges rather than to solve workers' pressing problems. "The union doesn't resolve anything," Héctor Fernández spat out contemptuously, adding: "All we know is that every month the company deducts the union's dues from us." As far as Fernández was concerned, TDU was no more than a vehicle for a self-interested cabal to take control of the IBT: "They came and they changed our course completely, for the sake of internal [IBT] politics; they left the members worse than before. It looks to me like this organization has ambitions for power in the International." Diego Ortega also asserted that Martinez and her crew had taken the workers' cause down the false path of "political" involvement, although he spoke in more measured terms about TDU:

At the beginning we were getting good results, because we were focusing ourselves on the real needs of the worker. But then, for political reasons, the Local has been diverting from the interests of the worker. And it has been focusing itself on fighting, on being partisan: "I'm TDU and you're Hoffa." . . . TDU isn't bad. TDU is OK because it teaches a lot. I learned a lot from them; but what I think is that when . . . the government has the power, it's not like you're going to change things with your faction: you have to work within the system so that the worker has more power. . . . We are talking about the laws of the state of Washington, and that those laws sometimes focus on IBP. . . . And you don't need to change your party, or your religion, or anything. You have your vision, and you have your ideology, whatever it may be—defend it, but you always have to work within a system.

What Gutierrez favored, then, was a more legally efficacious mode of action that, for him, necessitated a *depoliticized* form of struggle. By reducing "politics" to factional bickering, he and Fernández thus bracketed out the very idea of political education of the sort that the slogan We are the union! encapsulated.[35] As we have seen, Alejandro and Elvira Méndez certainly were committed to "working within the system" and working with the law, too. Theirs was a form of engagement, however, that recognized the currents of domination moving through those legal processes: the supervisors that verbally abused workers despite their contractual rights to respect and dignity, the managers who intimidated workers into seeing the company doctors when they got hurt. Their notion that workers needed to mount a self-driven movement of opposition to those dynamics of power was nowhere to be found when the counterreformers spoke to us. Instead, we heard a much more uniform faith in using "the system" and a tendency to denigrate the confrontational, agitative elements of activism that the reformers employed as a lot of yelling and no "real" action.

Ortega thus sought to make conformity to legally prescribed modes of conduct the modus operandi of worker activism. Accordingly, his and the other counterreformers' narratives encouraged the assumption that any agency that mattered, in terms of improving workers' circumstances, rested firmly in the hands of public administrators and others in positions of authority. When Ortega described the buildup to the strike, he emphasized the pivotal meeting held by the Washington State Bureau of Labor and Industries (BLI) to inform the workers regarding their rights. This stress on the critical need for action by state officials and other elites reverberated through the stories of Ortega's allies when they catalogued the union's failures. When I asked Fernández to explain "the best way to fight for changes" in health and safety matters like the hazards posed by slippery floors and ultrahigh chain speeds, he responded flatly: "I think it's best to file a lawsuit. It's good for the government to come in and take action, so that it sees the things that are happening. There's no other way the company will concede anything." Fernández told us that he was in the midst of a lawsuit of his own alleging that the company unfairly had denied him light duty and fired him after he had gotten injured and that he also had filed an application for disability insurance. It seemed like a lonely fight, read against the stories of other workers who had found in the union not only a repository of technical assistance with legalistic, bureaucratic negotiations but also a source of encouragement and mutual motivation to work together to change conditions at the plant so that the injuries would not happen in the first place.

Pedro Ruiz, in turn, evinced a parallel sensibility about the need for elites to address the workers' situation. Even though he had participated in the strike, he seemed unable even to imagine that a long-term rank-and-file mobilization through political education might be possible. Somewhat wistfully, Ruiz remarked:

If I could help all the people, I would do it with pleasure—if I could, if I had the means or the power. But, I'm telling you, sometimes there are problems that we have. If I had had the opportunity to study, if I had been a lawyer—that's what I mostly think—I would have helped the people. Because I see so much need in the company, and many people are trying to get help and they don't get help from around them because since the company is powerful, they get them all [i.e., lawyers] to go along with them. It's difficult when the company is powerful, when it has a lot of money.

When Juanita Castillo, Ramona Díaz, Isidro Gómez, and Esperanza Soto told us about helping out as the workers waged their strike and as the union planned health and safety workshops, they emphasized the mundane but crucial tasks that were vital to the workers' collective self-organization. These jobs also exemplified the individual's responsibility within this enterprise: taking roll, passing out leaflets, facilitating communication among different production lines. In contrast, the only kind of help that seemed consequential to Ruiz was an attorney's professional expertise, a form of agency that virtually none of these ordinary immigrant workers could reasonably have hoped to wield even in the distant future.[36]

Similarly, Manuel Guzmán, who did not even support the strike and who headed the ticket opposing Martinez in 2002, told us proudly how he had lodged complaints about hazards related to faulty conveyor belts in the rendering department with the Washington Safety and Health Administration, the BLI, and the NLRB. He claimed that these were "the first complaints that had been made in that department" and added: "I also started to contact politicians. I have political contacts. . . . We met a senator from here, from the state of Washington. . . . What we think is, it's better if we look for support—support not just like what you get from coworkers but also the authorities, too, or politicians." Just as Guzmán had relied on "the authorities" to protect his car as he crossed the picket line every day during the strike, he likewise stressed soliciting aid from state "authorities" to address health and safety problems at Tyson/IBP. To be sure, although Guzmán noted that he had filed his BLI complaint "as an individual," he did mention that he and other workers had met with the state senator as a group; so there was at least some sense here of a collective project. Yet as Guzmán continued his remarks, it became clear that his alternative vision of collective activity differed sharply from that which Martinez and her fellow activists imagined in their vision of political education.

Ortega, Guzmán, and their allies had named their counterreform group Organización de Lastimados Ayudando (Organization of Injured Workers Helping Others), and they used the motivational acronym

OLA (Spanish for "wave"). When we asked Guzmán who the group's leaders were, Guzmán responded emphatically: "There are no leaders here; the leaders are all the people." Although he qualified this by acknowledging that most members thought of Ortega as their leader, he insisted that OLA had named officers merely as a formality so that it could establish its nonprofit tax status. Thus, OLA seemed to share with the Local at least the patina of rank-and-file democracy. The group's name, which evoked the image of a dynamic movement swelling from below, augmented this vaguely egalitarian sensibility. But when Guzmán began to specify the members' activities and the types of assistance they offered, these political-activist overtones rapidly faded away:

> We give a lot of help to the people who are on light duty, and we don't focus on anything else but that. . . . We raised money; we were helping the people that the company stopped [from working], whom they fired, or whom the doctor stopped them from working—who didn't have any money coming into their homes. We were giving them food; we were helping them to pay their bills or whatever. . . . That is our goal; it's not to be an attack group, but rather a helping group. A group that has no relation at all either with IBP, or with the Local, but rather is there to help the people who don't have any income.

According to this story, OLA essentially provided charitable donations to the needy rather than carrying out political education. Principles of mutual aid and self-organization certainly had a role in Guzmán's story about OLA, since he told us that these injured workers raised funds on their own initiative (e.g., through raffles) to help others who were injured like they were. Nonetheless, this was not a story about learning how to become a more capable, individually responsible agent through studying one's rights or in any other way. Nor was there any ambition to enhance the workers' abilities to control their own situation through direct struggle with the company. Just as Ortega and Fernández explicitly denounced political contestation in favor of a bureaucratic-technical approach to solving workers' problems, so Guzmán vehemently repudiated the idea of engaging in contention with either Tyson/IBP or fellow union members. Rather than offering political education, on the terms of this narrative, OLA prompted its participants to embrace their identities as needy injured workers, to seek fellowship with others who would confirm those identities, and to develop nonconfrontational initiatives in the form of aid that had a distinctive whiff of paternalism.

The OLA faction's criticisms of Martinez and the activists working with her predictably faulted them for not behaving like benevolent stewards of the members' welfare. Guzmán and Fernández accused the Martinez cadre of letting time drag on without taking action on piles of grievances that workers had submitted to them for help in getting them processed. Said Fernández: "There have been complaints lasting up to a year and the union doesn't resolve anything, when there is a contract that says that a grievance process has thirty days to be resolved."[37] Notice here how Fernández spoke about "the union," by which he meant simply the officers, and how different this conception of a union sounded from the idea of the union in the main activists' stories when they reflected on the motto We are the union! Guadalupe Flores could have been any of the workers about whom Elvira Méndez and Juanita Castillo shook their heads, dismayed by their attitudes toward Local 556's officers, when she said:

Maria hasn't helped me at all in any way. . . . She hasn't done anything for me. I [have done it] all alone, for myself. I told her that I chose the doctor that I'm going to; I went to apply for welfare; I'm covering myself with Medicaid. I told Maria, and she told me that she was going to write a letter to call a lawyer, and she never sent me the letter.[38]

Although Flores depicted herself as able to take steps on her own to deal with her problems at work, what was starkly missing here, in comparison to the reformers' stories, was any sense that her interaction with Martinez could have become a learning experience that increased her individual capabilities.

Accompanying this sense within the OLA faction that the current union leaders had been ineffective were darker implications that they had betrayed the workers for their own private gain, a backlash nourished by an undercurrent of resentment that had existed since the days of the strike. Flores, for example, descended into paranoia when she accused Martinez of seeking her secretary-treasurer post so she could drive a new car and go on frequent vacations (an outlandish claim, since Martinez not only had slashed her own salary in half upon gaining her office but rarely took time off of any sort, even to get a decent night's sleep). In a similarly aggrieved tone, Pedro Ruiz charged that

Martinez and her loyalists were secretly colluding with the bosses to cover up workers' problems, such as his own battle against management's demand that he add a knife-cut to his job without any additional training or compensation:

> The representative of the union goes out and he stays there chatting with [the managers] inside, behind closed doors, and they don't tell me anything about what is going on, but the matter stays inside the plant. I want it to get outside, so that Labor and Industries notices how they treat you—but most of the problems happen and stay inside the plant, between them—representatives of the union and those who are in charge of the plant. . . . They wash their hands of anything that happens.

For Ruiz, the reform leaders not only had been unwilling to prosecute the workers' grievances—they also had crossed over to the company's side and, like Pilate trying Jesus, shared the guilt for others' suffering while disingenuously attempting to evade it.

In general, then, the counterreformers' narrative about the union's betrayal of the workers and diversion from more prudent courses of action brought together two core characteristics: a conception of ordinary workers as deeply reliant on state and legal professionals to effect any changes at Tyson/IBP and a profoundly resentful suspicion of the motives and abilities of the union officers. They viewed the latter as responsible for soliciting authoritative interventions as well as for fostering more humane company policies through cooperative negotiation with the state and the company. Precisely in the same measure, they perceived rank-and-file workers as lacking responsibility for learning how to help themselves through a more politicized, educative style of action. These key features of the narrative fed off one another, as these comments from Héctor Fernández vividly illustrated:

> Maria—since we're in disagreement with them, she doesn't talk to us. . . . The shop stewards who came in, since she put them in from the very start, she has them under her thumb and they are the only ones who have information about her. . . . They don't help the workers, because Maria said that they had to teach themselves on their own—that they have to learn on their own the process that they have regarding their rights, like through the contract. *That's like tossing a child in a swimming pool to teach him how to swim.* [emphasis added]

Impulses toward infantilization, paternalism, and resentment thus mingled at the center of these stories from Martinez's foes. The more helplessly dependent on elite agents the workers felt themselves to be, the less able they were to express their own thwarted desires for personal and collective agency in any terms other than disparaging the ethics and capacities of the leaders whom they fantasized as having joined with the company in victimizing them.

Biopolitics, Discipline, and the Genealogical Antecedents of Activist Narratives

The preceding chapters examined the narratives told by the immigrant workers of Local 556 about how they traversed the institutional terrains of Mexico at the dawn of neoliberalism, the zones of illegality at the border and beyond, and work in the slaughterhouse. I have shown how, when these people told their stories about power in those domains, they tended to generate two different narrative strands in tension with each other. One of these currents portrayed ordinary individuals as caught in the thrall of overwhelming, inscrutable, and unchallengeable forces that, seemingly with the force of fate, determined whether they would live or die on the border and arbitrarily commanded their bodily exertions on the shop floor even after legalization. In these aspects of their stories, the workers expressed a sense of what it felt like to be the racially designated objects of a tacit kind of biopolitics. More than this, they made a novel and critical contribution, through the effects of narrativity accompanying their common sense, to the capacities of politically engaged activists and intellectuals to theorize the workings of biopolitics today. This form of power systematically exposed them as a group to heightened risks of death, injury, and trauma, albeit usually without explicitly broadcasting any intention to promote the health of the dominant population at immigrants' expense.

The other narrative current called attention to these individuals' abilities to devise, disseminate, and deploy informal techniques for presenting or caring for their bodies, confronting immediately present sources of abuse and repression, and controlling their own fears and other emotions. In this strand of the narrative, immigrant workers brought into view the ways that they responded to the absence or self-undermining of disciplinary power, whether in relation to the state's border enforcement and immigration authorities or to the orchestration of the labor process and the wider work environment at Tyson/

IBP, by developing their own microtechniques of individual and inter-personal agency. As we have seen, the stories about these latter capa-bilities added further complexities to the workers' theorizations of biopolitics. They showed how the biopolitical formation depends not only on the mass-regulatory mechanisms that enhance immigrants' vulnerabilities to injury and "killing" (in Foucault's specific sense) but also on a range of practices that immigrants themselves perform and in which they school one another informally. In addition, I have argued that insofar as these patterns of narration presented domination as a condition to which workers could adapt in a way that left them some hope for self-determination, they further reinforced the regime of biopolitics by supplementing it with the force of popular consent. Yet this narrative stream also harbored a germ of resistance to this dynamic of consent because it eroded the taken-for-granted quality of the more prominent storyline regarding workers' helpless victimi-zation. Thus, this dimension of the interviews prevented any easy con-junction between the workers' narratives about power and the forms of common sense needed to ensure the *hegemonic* force of the implic-itly biopolitical, public discourses that structured the workers' lives. These discourses included popular rhetoric about "the jobs that Amer-icans cannot or will not do," the bipartisan commitment to "securing our borders" and boosting immigrant apprehensions in the U.S. inte-rior, the meat industry's public relations talk about the healthy (beef-eating) American family, and a voluntary employer-based approach to occupational safety and health policy.

The institutional power environment surrounding the workers began to change in fundamental ways, however, when they entered into their combat with the union "old guard" and with the company through means that often depended on *legalist* strategies. As activists in the rank-and-file movement and later as committed unionists, these immigrant workers began engaging much more intensively with juridi-cal institutions like the state and federal judiciaries, administrative courts, the company's grievance process, union bylaws and constitu-tional provisions, and collective bargaining processes. These legalist struggles exposed the workers to state-based disciplinary power in unprecedented ways. They saw themselves, in the evocative words of Alejandro Méndez, as eagerly "grabbing a hold" of their legal rights and wielding them to defend themselves against the full slate of horrors and indignities they endured at Tyson/IBP. But as Wendy Brown warns, the very assumption that the law is a neutral tool in the hands of the activist is part of what makes the liberal-legalist mode of activism so insidiously effective as a means of discipline. The danger of legalist activism from Brown's perspective is that the process of claiming legal and administrative rights *normalizes* the individual, re-creating her as the type of person that the law and capital prefer her to be. The individual herself helps accomplish this reconstitution of identity as she defines her struggle and acts on it along the lines established by the juridical authorities. And the sort of person that fits best with the legitimacy requirements of the law, the state, and capital, Brown argues, is a person so deeply preoccupied with the injuries he has suffered that wounded-ness becomes the very basis of his identity and his orientation toward politics. Mired in resentment toward those whom he sees as having perpetrated such harm, this wounded individual fervently seeks authoritative intervention from above to provide compensation, to ensure his future protection, and to exact retribution from the evildoers. In their reign over psychopolitical space, moreover, these yearnings crowd out desires for more ambitious kinds of freedom. Such desires, for Brown, would depart from the logic of *ressentiment* by aiming to recompose the world in partnership with similarly disposed allies—to reshape the institutions that generate hazards so that the specter of injury never materializes in the first place (1995, 26–27).

Major historical trends in the development of labor law and public policy in the United States since the New Deal have fortified the institutional basis for the structure of political desires that Brown describes. Growing more intense during the recent neoliberal era, these tendencies have elaborated the *disciplinary* apparatus for members of the working class in ways complementing the *biopolitical* mechanisms I described in chapters 3 and 4, thus constituting a more complete and internally differentiated social strategy of biopower. Analyses of U.S. labor law and the labor movement in recent decades suggest that legal and state-administrative processes with regard to unions have turned decisively toward enabling employers to thwart union-organizing campaigns by making violations of union rights pro forma. These practices not only have contributed to the secular and huge decline in private sector unionization rates, they also perpetually consign labor to the *political disposition* of the aggrieved party seeking recompense and retribution for such legal misdeeds. HRW has reported that while the NLRB originally spent most of its time administrating union elections (i.e., positive efforts by workers to realize new forms of political freedom by forming and operating their own organizations, albeit under legal auspices), now over 80 percent of its efforts are devoted to investigating unfair labor practice claims, which themselves multiplied from several hundred a year in the 1950s to over twenty thousand annually in the 1990s (Compa 2000, 8, 26). According to HRW, this is because employers have become more brazen about violating labor laws, more tenacious in using opportunities for delays in investigations embedded in NLRB regulations, and more sanguine about the prospects of any remedies that may eventually materialize. At the same time, persistent (and bipartisan) cuts in social spending reduced the NLRB's full-time staff from three thousand to fewer than two thousand between 1980 and 1998 (26). Concludes HRW:

> Many employers have come to view remedies like back pay for workers fired because of union activity as a routine cost of doing business, well worth it to get rid of organizing leaders and derail workers' organizing efforts. As a result a culture of near-impunity has taken shape in much of U.S. labor law and practice. (10)

The judiciary, too, during the past half-century, has trended increasingly toward skepticism or outright rejection of union rights while boosting private property rights and individual union members' adversarial rights against their own union organizations. Traditionally considered a bastion of protection for employers' property rights prior to the reforms of the 1930s, the courts were studiously avoided by the New Dealers in favor of administrative bodies such as the NLRB as institutional vehicles for advancing the rights of workers in their unions. It was in the courts that the first major challenge to the New Deal regime of union rights emerged in a 1938 decision *(NLRB v. Mackay Radio & Tel. Co.)* granting employers the right to hire permanent striker replacements, although this case law precedent was never invoked until the changed political climate of the 1980s made it feasible to do so (Gottesman 1996, 293–96). In 1956 *(NLRB v. Babcock & Wilcox Co.)*, the high court opined that enforcing the National Labor Relations Act (NLRA) required respect for a principle of "accommodation" between union rights and private property rights, even though the act does not mention the latter (299). This provided the precedent whereby the Court, in the 1992 *Lechmere v. NLRB* case, confirmed employers' rights to exclude union representatives from company parking lots (302–3). Thus, when Local 556 activists were forced to adopt the inefficient method of going house to house to gather support for retaining their union in the 2004–5 decertification struggle, which I discuss in the conclusion, they were living the legacy of these earlier moves by the judiciary. Likewise, the fact that the key activists at Tyson/IBP in Pasco were mostly legalized immigrants along with a few Mexican Americans, but did not include any undocumented workers, may have reflected the Court's recent, pathbreaking decision to exclude the undocumented from the NLRA's protections in the 2002 *Hoffman Plastic Compounds v. NLRB* decision (Compa 2005, 118–21).[39]

Even as the courts have dialed back employers' obligations vis-à-vis unions, they also have fortified the rights of individual union members to launch complaints against their unions. Since the 1930s, the basic framework for adjudicating union-related conflicts has shifted from the industrial pluralism preferred by New Dealers toward a new and more classically liberal preoccupation with individual rights. Hence, for example, on fair representation issues, the courts formerly addressed these questions with reference to the equal protection clause of the Fourteenth Amendment, attempting to ensure that no groups of workers, especially racial minorities, suffered discrimination by their unions (Schiller 1999, 23–30). Yet more recently the courts have reinterpreted the duty of fair representation, changing it "from a method of protecting groups against discrimination by unions to a way of ensuring that unions treated individual workers fairly" (65). In a parallel manner, the judiciary has also elaborated members' rights not to have their dues support political candidates not of their own choosing as a category of the right to free expression, whereas previously the courts had assumed, in line with pluralist logic, that organizational rights were essential for individual workers to have any meaningful voice at all in political matters (65–71). Congress helped underwrite this transition in 1959 by passing the Labor Management Reporting and Disclosure Act, which furnished a novel "Bill of Rights of Members of Labor Organizations" and specified a union's "fiduciary duty" to individual members (58–59). As time has gone on, both Congress and the courts have increasingly closed the door on the use of union dues to support political campaigns and union projects beyond those narrowly related to collective bargaining.[40]

Multiple features of this institutional environment thus can be seen as nudging—or wrenching—workers toward skepticism about collective action, deference to management, clientelistic reliance on the state, and a preoccupation with individual grievances against unions and employers alike when they try to address problems in their workplace through legalist strategies. More and more, that is, to struggle for workers' rights through legalist means has involved meeting a proliferation of inducements to don the disposition of *ressentiment* that Brown and others have discerned of late in the women's, gay and lesbian, and black civil rights movements (Brown and Halley 2002; Brown 1995). Of course, the state's turn against the labor movement has made many workers and organizers utterly cynical about the utility of employing the law to pursue justice in the workplace, as recent experiments with union organizing through informal card check campaigns rather than official NLRB elections illustrate. Yet an abiding disposition in the movement still exists to fight rearguard maneuvers and cling to whatever resources from the state still remain, as Burawoy (1990) notes in his analysis of unions' priorities in the era of "hegemonic despotism" that I discussed in chapter 4. Given the historical trajectory of U.S. labor law and policy, this posture lends itself to the politics of *ressentiment*—and precisely this discursive tendency comes through graphically in the narratives of the counterreformers at Tyson/IBP. Lacking the reformer narratives' enthusiasm for political education, these stories emphasized workers' vulnerability to mistreatment by both company and union officials and their inability to help themselves in any way other than by soliciting authoritative state intervention to bring the company to heel. As the counterreformers abandoned their concern for strengthening the autonomous power of union organizations, took a more conciliatory approach to the company's managerial authority and property prerogatives, and stressed conflicts between aggrieved individuals and their union heads, they brought their stories into line with key disciplinary tendencies in the development of U.S. labor law and public policy that extend back for decades but that have intensified with the advance of neoliberalism. Or, to return to Foucault's categories, those who rejected the reform movement exemplified the effectiveness with which these normalizing operations of the law and the state could supplement the biopolitical administration of the working population.

What is also important to note but less immediately apparent, however, is that there were potent genealogical antecedents in the workers' narratives about their experiences in Mexico, in the zones of illegality, and in the slaughterhouse for these counterreform stories of cynicism about mobilization, deference to elites, and condescension toward ordinary workers. Counterreform activists like Diego Ortega, Héctor Fernández, and Pedro Ruiz, along with some nonaligned and politically passive workers like Rafael Mendoza, narrated the long trajectory of their experiences in ways that made these filial relations manifest. In particular, as I noted in chapter 2, these individuals were especially prone to describe the events precipitating their departure from Mexico with reference to their injured sense of entitlement to upward mobility (or, in Francisco González's case, as a burgeoning national economic crisis that drove him out of Mexico wholly against his will).[41] This was notably unlike the workers whose otherwise similar claims of individual autonomy in making momentous decisions about migration did not include this two-sided frustration at having failed to advance one's fortunes in accordance with one's prospects *and* having been deprived of something one was due (or having been driven to emigrate by heteronomous forces).

Nevertheless, virtually all the workers we interviewed contributed abundantly to the capacious reservoir of narrative material that irrigated the resentments that Ortega and his clan sowed among their coworkers. Thus, the counterreform stories of the union leaders' betrayals and of the need to approach the state as meek supplicants reactivated the narrative yeast in other generally shared aspects of the stories about life in Mexico prior to migration, especially the individualizing, privatizing, and apolitical (although, as I argued in chapter 2, incipiently political and transnational) tendency that characterized each of the three main permutations of identity I discerned in those portions of the interviews. Recall, in addition, the common approach to narrating passages across the border that portrayed immigrants as beseeching spiritual powers for deliverance from terrifying circumstances beyond their control as they sought to escape discovery by Border Patrol searchlights, asphyxiation in barely ventilated vehicles, disorientation in the dark hills, and the bullets fired by vigilantes. This narrative tendency, in which our informants all engaged to a significant degree, also was available to feed the more docile and resentful strand of narration about the union. Also functioning in this way was the narrative of power-as-despotism in the slaughterhouse—the storyline lamenting workers' futile efforts to keep up with the chain, their constant exposure to injuries, their mute endurance of supervisors' capricious conduct, their frustrations with the callous indifference of company medical personnel, and the seemingly inevitable "martyrdom" of light duty. Thus, the workers' own common sense about power in Mexico, on the border, and in the plant had prepared them in all these ways to approach their novel identities as legally entangled, rights-bearing individuals in the manner of people needing protective and compensatory care from authorities who exercised full sway over their conditions of life and whose rules therefore had to be followed without question. Precisely this genealogical thread found keenest expression in the narratives about the union's missteps and the workers' supplicant position vis-à-vis the authorities that the people allied with Diego Ortega and OLA created.

Just as these ways of narrating power in the zone of illegality and the work environment of the slaughterhouse nourished the story about the union told by the Ortega faction, so in contrast a second genealogical line of affiliation was available to the workers who propounded the main narrative within Local 556 of what the workers had done and still hoped to achieve. By stressing the individual's responsibility and capacity for improving his or her own circumstances in the face of adversity, all three main narrative currents about deciding to emigrate from Mexico formed tributaries to the discourse of *respeto y dignidad,* which as we have seen in this chapter, successfully harnessed such assertive individualism to the collective endeavor. Likewise, a common sensibility connected the women's stories of contemplating cross-border migration, in which they affirmed their personal autonomy through fulfilling responsibilities to loved ones by delaying or undertaking migration, with their familial narrative about the union as a sisterhood based in commitments of the heart and extending values of mutual accountability cultivated in the home. In turn, when the workers spoke of mustering the courage to confront *polleros* who mistreated their children, the inner fortitude to endure fear and physical pain, and a palette of kinetic and sartorial techniques for eluding discovery in the domains of illegality, they further strengthened their narrative foothold for resisting the legalist disciplines they encountered as unionists. They gained additional wherewithal on the terrain of common sense for deflecting the subject-constituting forces of the state and the law that prodded them to see themselves as vulnerable clients of a protective, compensatory, and retributive state apparatus (albeit an apparatus that has offered workers ever-weaker safeguards, compensations, and enforcement capabilities with the advance of neoliberalism but precisely thereby has augmented the sense that workers are lucky to get any scraps that fall to them). And our informants did this once again when they made sure we appreciated their self-designed habits for protecting themselves and others amid the hazards constantly buffeting them at Tyson/IBP. These filaments of narrative, then, coalesced as an alternative set of antecedents that could be recapitulated and refashioned in more ambitious ways in the story of political education that the motto We are the union! encapsulated. Such education, as we have seen, sought to realize the political purchase, on individual and organizational levels alike, of the conceptions and practices of power that bespoke at least micrological forms of opposition to neoliberalism and biopolitics in these other realms of narrated experience.

One key point needs to be emphasized here: there was no necessary logic by which the stalwart reformers were bound to let these specific genealogical antecedents, rather than others, come to orient their politics. In just the same way, no causal necessity determined that the activists who broke with Martinez would let their politics be informed more thoroughly by genealogical strands that prioritized the desire for deliverance from despotism and calamities brought on by blind fate. For the most part, the workers' stories about crossing the border, living without documents in the United States, and working at Tyson/ IBP exhibited important aspects of both genealogical tendencies. So, for example, Gloria and Pedro Ruiz narrated their experiences in the domain of illegality in ways that sometimes drew attention to their proficiency in the arts of passing and techniques of masculine self-control, respectively, but they ended up supporting Ortega. In turn, Esperanza Soto and Isidro Gómez were stalwart allies of Maria Martinez, who also stressed how profoundly helpless they felt when various problems with their *coyotes* put them in fear for their very lives. Thus, there was no simple correspondence between the way a given individual told the story of navigating the zone of illegality or the work environment at the slaughterhouse and her or his eventual political posture toward the union.

Precisely the congealment of shared forms of common sense *on the collective level,* however, is of greatest interest to me here. That is because these innovative narratives about workers' self-mobilization, and the organizing activities they developed in conjunction with such common sense, finally presented a genuine hope for challenging power *in the sphere of social discourses and institutional agendas.* They raised the prospect, more specifically, of reworking power relations on the terrain of biopolitical strategies and neoliberal initiatives aimed at mass populations, formations of power that can only be transformed through political initiatives that organize groups of people in alternative ways. Such a possibility was notably lacking in the accounts about individual and interpersonal techniques for improving family finances, evading harm, disciplining the self, and protecting others that we heard in the aspects of our informants' narratives examined in the preceding chapters. I argued that in some ways these techniques interrupted the facilitation of neoliberal reforms and biopolitical schemas that came from positioning the narrator as the passive plaything of unforeseeable and unalterable whims of fate or despotic caprice. But these subtle subversions of hegemony only reached the point of threatening viable opposition to social practices on an institutional scale in the context of the rank-and-file movement and its narrative about workers' self-organizing in symbiotic relation to legalist struggle. Internally conflicted this narrative may have been, and vulnerable to domestication through the law's disciplines it certainly was; but it still represented the genuine prospect of substantial institutional change through immigrant workers' individual *and* collective agency.

These new political possibilities materialized not only in the union's particular actions but also, and in more promising respects, in the alliances it cultivated with other institutional actors. New prospects thereby arose for contesting each of the circuitously biopolitical discourses I have mentioned. So, for instance, in 2003, Local 556 anchored the southeastern Washington State coalition to coordinate local events for the Immigrant Workers' Freedom Ride (IWFR), which promoted immediate legalization of the undocumented and a quick path to U.S. citizenship.[42] In this way, the union took tangible steps in alliance with other unions as well as church and student groups to build an alternative policy agenda beyond immigration restrictionism and to articulate a new public language about immigration that did not prioritize (or even mention) "securing our borders."[43] The Local also pushed back publicly, in league with other groups, against the common policy approach that defers to employers' prerogatives to devise methods for ensuring occupational health and safety. Local 556 joined with student and religious organizations that same year to battle the voter initiative abolishing Washington State's ergonomics standard, and in 2002 sponsored a community meeting in a large and overflowing hall where the workers spoke out about the injury problem.[44] At this same event, the workers shared their platform with activists who were concerned about the lack of humane treatment for the animals being slaughtered at Tyson, partly on the basis of secret video footage they had obtained of live animals making it past the killing area.[45]

In addition, the workers took steps to build coalitions with consumers challenging the industry's claims about the healthfulness of its products, exposing the links between the marketing of mass-produced beef and the biopolitical subjugation of immigrant workers that the companies' public relations talk has occluded. The union's list of speakers at a 2005 rally included Eric Schlosser, who spoke out about the connections between food-borne illnesses and the production practices that maimed workers at the plant. And the workers pursued these links further by forging ties with labor and consumer groups in transnational and local arenas alike, as the conclusion discusses. In 2004, Local 556 President Melquíades Pereyra traveled to Japan, where Tyson does a large portion of its foreign business, to cultivate these sorts of alliances. The union also helped form a small nonprofit organization in the city of Walla Walla called Safe Work/Safe Food, one principal officer of which was a small producer of pasture-finished meats; a local organic farmer helped publicize the group's and the union's activities through her newsletter.

Casting a very dark shadow on all this encouraging potential, however, was the harsh fact that none of the Local's political initiatives lasted very long and that in the end, the union itself went down to bitter defeat. The destruction of the union, as I explain in the conclusion, occurred in 2004–5 through the combined machinations of Tyson, TDU's inveterately hostile opponents in the International's Hoffa leadership cadre, the Bush administration's NLRB appointees, and of course the OLA faction among the workers themselves. Meanwhile, legislative and popular support for tighter restrictions on immigration and a more punitive approach to the undocumented rose rather than fell in the wake of both the IWFR and the spring 2006 immigrants' rights protests.[46] The state ballot measure repealing Washington's ergonomics standard passed easily in 2003, and there has been no serious attempt to develop a new policy along these lines. With the union having gone bust and one leg removed from the labor–consumer alliance represented by Safe Work/Safe Food, finally, this group abruptly demobilized. The immigrant workers' stories in this chapter testify to the impressive magnitude of what our interviewees accomplished as well as the roads their movement might have traveled had it outlasted the onslaught of 2004–5, which it nearly did. They show that even when the workers found themselves, as activists before the law, operating in a newly intensive disciplinary environment that gave biopolitics more consistent support than in either the sphere of the labor process or the domain of illegality, they still were able to contest the dynamics of hegemony and offer their own transformative vision. But were there perhaps elements within that very counterhegemonic enterprise and the narratives that informed it—and those that worked against it— that helped bring on the demise of their visionary projects?

Conclusion:
Immigrant Workers and Counterhegemony

I BEGAN MY EXAMINATION of the Tyson workers' narratives at the beginning of chapter 2 by discussing an evocative statement that Maria Martinez, the principal leader of the workers' movement, had made when we interviewed her toward the end of 2002. We spoke to Martinez shortly after her "Respect and Dignity" slate had triumphed by a landslide in the first round of elections following the rank-and-file takeover of Teamsters Local 556 in 2000. Buoyed by heavy turnout, the Martinez group had soundly beaten the so-called Reform slate organized by Diego Ortega, garnering over 70 percent of the vote. Yet when we talked with Martinez in the aftermath of her victory, she was worried that the vigor of the workers' movement was abating. In particular, she sensed that there was something about the union's vision that the younger, U.S.-born, more recently hired workers fundamentally did not and perhaps could not grasp given their life circumstances. "They don't understand the struggle," Martinez had remarked apprehensively. These new workers hadn't grown up in Mexico or seen their family's hardships multiply as economic conditions slid downward. Nor had they known what it was to bear the humiliations and traumas of crossing the border or the miseries of laboring on the farms while living *encerrado* and hiding from *la migra*. Without this experiential basis, she implied, it was hard for them to gain any critical perspective on the enticements Tyson offered in exchange for their refraining from lodging any protests against the manifest abuses of the slaughterhouse.

Within a few years, events proved Martinez's concerns to have been well founded: in early 2005, after a grueling but failed campaign to win a new contract and to repel an effort to bust the union, the members of Local 556 voted to abolish their own organization. In this conclusion, I step back from a detailed consideration of the workers' narratives and consider the legacy of these stories for immigrant workers' counterhegemonic struggles in light of the union's eventual downfall as well as its prior achievements. Since the union's decline occurred after the interviews were done, telling this story requires that I shift modes of writing. Thus, in the first part of what follows I move away from a style focused on how the workers expressed to us their commonsense conceptions of self and world in various contexts of power toward an account of events based on my own observations of their denouement as a continuing observer of their efforts and as a supportive community activist.

I then confront questions that stand at the intersection of immigrant worker activism and contemporary critical theory. First, I revisit the critique of liberal legalism by Wendy Brown and others that I discussed in chapter 5. What does the inability of Local 556 to survive amid the disciplinary pressures of its legalist entanglements, despite the radicalizing energies of the narrative strain regarding political education, suggest about the very possibility of sustaining this kind of dually invested struggle? Are legalist endeavors such as lawsuits, contract-based grievances, appeals to state regulatory authorities, and collective bargaining processes simply a dead end in this neoliberal age? Or does the experience of the Tyson workers show that stauncher efforts can and must be made to wrangle radical democratic consequences from within engagements of the state and the law by doing something else, simultaneously, to nourish the spirit of political education?

Finally, moving beyond the matter of legalist struggle: what exactly qualifies as counterhegemonic politics in the context of contemporary biopolitics and in the midst of the transformations wrought by neoliberalism? What is the particular role of immigrant workers within broader coalitions that contest these modes of power, given the ambivalent effects of their narratives? If biopolitics administrated by the state and private corporations is also partly the creature of immigrant political narrators, then what do those storytellers and their allies need to do to set alternative flows of power in motion? And if these biopolitical mechanisms, reenvisioned through the prism of immigrant workers' narratives, serve as key components of the historical project of neoliberalism, then what does this analysis suggest overall about strategies for reversing the neoliberal tide?

The Destruction of Local 556

The forces that eventually accomplished the downfall of the Local began to gather in the aftermath of the 2002 union election. When the faction that called itself Obreros Lastimados Ayudando (OLA; Organization of Injured Workers Helping Others) failed to unseat the Martinez cadre, the counterreformist workers resorted to tactics of opposition that ultimately proved devastating to the union. These actions baldly belied their claims that they supported the union but saw it as ill served by its officers. Following the 2002 balloting, Manuel Guzmán, who had run to replace Martinez as principal officer, began conducting a petition drive calling for a union decertification election in accordance with National Labor Relations Board (NLRB) protocols for such a procedure. With the rapid turnover at the plant, the persistence of frequent injuries and low wages, and the formidable challenges under these conditions of cultivating a sustained culture of enthusiasm for the union, the dissenters collected the requisite number of signatures (30 percent of the plant's unionized employees) to force a "decert." At that point, Tyson stepped in and launched a full-scale drive to destroy the union. (The company also promoted Guzmán to supervisor [Levin 2005; Lilley 2005].) Labor law in the United States plainly permits companies to use union elections as opportunities to rid themselves of worker organizations. Thus, while the decert campaign superficially appeared to be a contestation among workers over whether or not they wanted a union, in fact it predictably became a struggle waged by the union and its supporters against the overwhelming corporate might of Tyson. Union organizers told me how their hearts had sunk the day they saw black limousines pulling into the plant parking lot, bearing representatives from corporate headquarters in Little Rock, Arkansas, who had come to coordinate the company's antiunion push.

The situation was even worse than this. Sensing blood in the water and eager to be rid of the troublemakers in Pasco who were allied with Teamsters for a Democratic Union (TDU), the Local's parent organization, the International Brotherhood of Teamsters (IBT, or the International), under leaders loyal to the "business–unionist" approach of Teamsters President James Hoffa Jr. decided to aid the company's cause. Instead of throwing its muscle behind the campaign to save the union, the International began relentlessly harassing the Local. In early 2004, an IBT representative arrived in Walla Walla and set up camp in the Local's headquarters. There he proceeded to comb through the Local's files fishing for evidence of bureaucratic missteps that would supply evidence for charges by the IBT against the local officers of mismanagement and incompetence.

It is a testament both to the enduring strength of the rank-and-file movement and the union's inspirational culture of political education that even in these dire circumstances, the Local actually prevailed in the initial decertification election that was held in April 2004. The margin was quite slim—708 to 657—but it saved the union, and TDU organizers claimed that it was also Tyson's first-ever defeat by a local union in an election of this sort (Levin 2004). Tyson, however, appealed the election results on the grounds that union representatives had unfairly influenced workers' votes through improper conduct on the day of the election, in particular by wearing union hats in the area near the cafeteria into which the line of workers waiting to vote had extended. The union had to keep fighting to prevail against decertification—just as it had plunged into another full-scale contract campaign, because the 1999 collective bargaining agreement, forged in the furnace of the strike, was set to expire in late spring 2004.

While the reformers hoped to make their struggle for a better contract the basis for gaining support against decertification, the company and the International moved strategically to make the negotiations work against the Local. Tyson refused to make significant concessions and plowed ahead with its goal of downsizing (or "chickenizing") the workers' health plan. Inherited from IBP and reflecting the more generous deal traditionally offered to beef workers, Tyson sought to bring this package into line with the more humble benefits offered in its chicken-producing sector. The IBT then used the company's intransigence as a pretext for additional accusations that the Local was failing to pursue the best interests of the rank and file. After the workers' contract expired in May 2004, the company, in compliance with the law, stopped automatically deducting members' dues from their paychecks. With the Local now in bankruptcy and the officers and staff working around the clock for no pay, the International not only withheld financial support but also continued to tighten the screws by soaking up precious staff and financial resources through the audit.

Meanwhile, the appeal of the April election kept working its way through the NLRB bureaucracy. The regional body of the NLRB threw out the company's appeal, judging it to be without merit. But when Tyson took its appeal to the (Bush) presidential appointees on the Board itself in Washington, D.C., it met with success: the Board nullified the election results and mandated that a new election be held in

February 2005. The combined assault on the Local by the IBT and Tyson then intensified. Tyson held captive-audience meetings and used its vast resources to distribute videotapes or DVDs to all workers in Spanish and English that exhorted them to abolish the union (Levin 2005). Officials with the International furnished Tyson with quotations for the company's campaign videos and literature in which they denounced Maria Martinez and urged a vote to decertify Local 556 (Teamsters for a Democratic Union 2005). But perhaps the greatest impact came from Tyson's decision to lay off roughly four hundred workers at the plant for a temporary period of six weeks, citing the drop in Japanese demand for U.S. beef because of the Mad Cow disease scare. Tyson still paid those workers for thirty-two hours per week while the plant was closed (Lilley 2005). On the one hand, this experience made the company appear beneficent because workers were getting paychecks while the company was absorbing losses; on the other hand, the layoffs undoubtedly reminded workers of the company's ultimate discretion over whether they had any jobs at all. Fears that a union victory would lead Tyson to close the plant further multiplied when the main Spanish-language newspaper in the region, *La Voz*, began printing articles warning that this would occur and accusing Martinez of malfeasance in office.[1] Although it would have been illegal for Tyson to have directly threatened plant closure as a consequence for a vote preserving the union, union leaders and their attorney alleged that company officials had distributed at least one article from *La Voz* making this threat to workers at the plant (Lilley 2005).[2]

As the workers noted in their conversations with us, even during the strike, the mass commitment to the movement had begun to ebb from its high point on the day of the walkout that started the six-week protest. Now, five years later, Martinez and the other leaders knew that another strike was out of the question because commitment was lacking both within the union and among its allies outside the factory gates. Rank-and-file meetings to coordinate the combined effort to win a superior contract and to deflect decertification drew a regular crowd of about seventy-five attendees, yet support in the wider base of workers was growing more tenuous. Concerned that any far-reaching demands to reform the labor process causing worker injuries and health problems would fail to resonate with an electorate worried about losing their jobs, the union leaders and activists gravitated toward demanding marginal wage increases and preventing significant benefit cutbacks. And they relinquished their politically visionary goal of inscribing in the contract a mechanism to give the workers more control over chain speed, which they sought to do by having the company formally recognize a *worker's* right to refuse to do excessively rapid work that would endanger *consumers'* rights to safe meat products.

Similarly, the Local's outreach beyond the factory gates reflected substantial creativity and initiative as well as tactical retreats. Community support for the Local had waxed in nearby Walla Walla but waned in Pasco, where most of the workers lived and where the Mexican community was much stronger and more numerous. Nevertheless, Local 556 redoubled its efforts to maintain and build the public campaign, netting over ten thousand signatures on support petitions from churches, colleges, and other community groups and drawing crowds of over five hundred to two separate, major worker-community rallies in Pasco and Walla Walla (Teamsters for a Democratic Union 2005). The union even extended the reach of the public campaign across the Pacific Ocean. Led by Melquíades Pereyra, a delegation traveled to Japan to meet with consumer and labor groups in an attempt to raise pressure on Tyson to concede to new contract provisions that would better protect workers and beef consumers alike. However, the union flinched when it came to the decision about how strongly to emphasize the relation between worker health and safety hazards and food contamination risks for the public closer to home.[3] Knowing the company's deeper sensitivity to criticisms on the latter issue and therefore its propensity to react by shutting down negotiations entirely (and to blame this on the union for bringing up the problem of dirty meat in the first place), the Local narrowed the focus to exclude this coalition-building issue.

Utterly depleted of resources and facing a rank and file that was increasingly frustrated over the contract's delayed resolution, in the February 2005 rerun of the decertification election, the union lost by roughly one hundred votes out of nearly thirteen hundred ballots cast (690–586). Within a week, Melquíades Pereyra and Esperanza Soto told me afterward, the company fired a number of injured workers, suspended seniority rights that had been specified in the now defunct collective bargaining agreement, and sped up the chain. Plant manager Ray McGaugh observed, however, that in accordance with "Tyson's core values and code of conduct," the company had instituted a chaplaincy offering "pastoral care and counseling" in the plant. And in a rhetorical move that audaciously obscured the memory of what the union had struggled for by appropriating its language, an industry publication added: "Plant management also continues to update and improve workplace safety and the overall working environment, through programs such as the company's 'dignity and respect' training" (Institute for Agriculture and Trade Policy 2005).

Lessons Learned: Workers' Struggles, Legal Struggles, Immigrants' Struggles

In chapter 5, I briefly surveyed the grim trajectory of recent labor law and federal policy with regard to union rights. In certain clear ways, the destruction of Teamsters Local 556 rehearses a pattern that has become depressingly common in this context, especially in terms of the company taking advantage of the lopsided rules of NLRB processes and the NLRB's very weak powers for deterring unfair employer practices. But were there also, perhaps, aspects of the workers' own approach to their struggles that proved self-defeating? One might easily think so, calling to mind the dynamic of self-destruction that Wendy Brown associates with the politics of *ressentiment,* discussed in the previous chapter, and noting that the union ultimately was dissolved through decertification by its own members. It is arguable, in other words, that precisely *because* the organizers cast their lot more and more with struggles on terrain prearranged by the law and the administrative state—collective bargaining negotiations, NLRB elections, government investigations, and lawsuits—they sealed the union's doom. Instead of expanding the cadre of leaders and mustering support for more ambitious goals that would have involved *challenging and newly creating the institutions themselves,* the activists increasingly found themselves on the defensive, fighting to minimize their losses and eventually losing the battle to keep the union itself alive. If Brown's theory is valid, then the movement's downfall can be traced to a constriction of the activists' aspirations for freedom. As these workers' desires came to focus more on legally based rights, and as unionists became skilled in the disciplines and routines of legal-administrative action, Brown would suggest, the overarching relations of class and state domination became less accessible to critique and less capable of motivating oppositional politics.[4]

Yet the union's demise was neither so steady nor so uniform as this interpretation would have it. As we have seen, even as the informal rank-and-file network and popular uprising became an official union organization, and into its waning months, the union pressed forward with truly novel experiments that stretched the boundaries of what "official union business" normally means in the United States. These initiatives ranged from Pereyra's overseas trip to build coalitions with Japanese workers and consumers to the union's cultivation of the local Safe Work/Safe Food community support network to the pathbreaking attempt to bridge the consumer–producer divide by enshrining in the contract a new right of workers to defend the rights of Tyson meat consumers.

In terms of tactical lessons for future immigrant worker organizers, then, the snuffing of Teamsters Local 556 does not hold the unequivocally dour message for legalist unionism that it initially might appear to offer. Precisely because the workers of Local 556 who led the drive for safer work, better treatment, and a democratic union invested themselves in struggles that presupposed the prior disciplinary power of the state and the law, they gained access to what Gramsci would have called an "effective terrain" where their visions and affective sensibilities for radically reconstructing class, racial, and gender relations could start to coalesce. And the political desires and practices of freedom that germinated on that terrain simply did not conform neatly to the resentful subjectivity conceptualized by Brown. Rather, as I show especially in chapter 5, elements of a radically democratic politics grew from within the context of the workers' juridically oriented initiatives. Hardly straightjacketed by the politics of *ressentiment,* the workers' common sense pointed toward the transformation of capitalist relations of production while also challenging related structures of racial and gender subordination, albeit not wholly consistently and in ways that often stayed within the symbolic register of narrative and remained unrealized in sustained, collective efforts to alter institutions.

The wider message of this study as a whole, however, concerns the tendencies toward freedom of a different kind of strategic ecumenism: not just the melding of legalist and extralegal contestation but also, and more crucially, the blending of labor activism and organizing around justice for immigrants. To many progressives, this probably sounds like nothing new. I would argue, however, that we need to understand more carefully the complex *reasons* why these sorts of alliances are necessary as well as the narrative *practices* such political engagements would do well to foster. Certainly, workers who are secure in their legal status and shielded from Immigration and Customs Enforcement raids are likely to be more assertive in defending and extending their rights as workers. Likewise, it is obvious that immigrants who become emboldened by standing up to their bosses are better equipped to advance the cause of reconstructing immigration policy to reflect norms of justice. Yet what my foregoing narrative critique shows most vividly is that activists ought to cultivate organizational spaces where immigrant workers can speak out loud and share with one another and with allies their *stories* about immigration, work, and political action. By such means, the diverse and often unconscious genealogical connections that workers construe between the different strands of their narratives, such as those I explored throughout chapters 2 to 5 and particularly at the end of the last chapter, can become audible material for reflection. What Gramsci called the "criticism of 'common sense,' basing itself initially, however, on common sense" can grow into a matter of routine, popular-democratic, organizational practice, as the tensions among divergent narrative tendencies emerge and invite consideration. Immigrants' narrated practices for micrologically adjusting the biopolitically wrought conditions of clandestine border crossing, life in zones of illegality, and manufacturing work, can thereby inform and inspire actions of collective self-assertion with regard to immigration and labor alike.

Aside from the union's outreach in Japan and its experimental proposal for workers' defense of meat consumers' rights, another telling sign of the persistence of radical sensibilities in the political culture of Local 556, even toward the bitter end, was the union's increasing embrace of a public discourse about immigrants' rights. This discourse came through loud and clear when Maria Martinez and several others spoke at the union's events to host participants in the fall 2003 Immigrant Workers Freedom Ride (IWFR), which I discussed in the introduction. It also informed the Local's resolve a year earlier to help mobilize a grassroots national campaign to collect a million postcards demanding augmented immigrants' rights and to deliver them to Congress. And while this push for national legislative reform was underway, the union strove to beat back repressive measures targeting immigrant members close to home. Besides rebuffing Tyson's move in late 2002 to call workers into supervisors' offices to question them about their immigration status, as I mentioned in the previous chapter, activists also conducted a major political education campaign for members who worked at an eastern Oregon Lamb-Weston frozen foods plant when the company began firing workers after receiving Social Security "no match" letters for them. These activities opened up new spaces for *narrative* work to take place regarding labor and immigration *together.* Thus, for Local 556, linking activism against mistreatment on the shop floor with efforts to address injustices in the immigration system had at least a germinal political significance that transcended the immediate benefit of forming pragmatic, instrumental coalitions among scattered leaders and constituencies. This coupling of immigration and labor politics surely can yield similar benefits for immigrant workers' movements today and in the future.

Through the prism of this narrative analysis, one can see more clearly the significance of the political projects undertaken by unions that have most energetically pursued justice for immigrants in association with more traditional efforts geared toward workers' power and rights on the job. Two prime examples of such innovative organizing exist on the U.S. West Coast: the array of organizations that has sprung up in association with Piñeros y Campesinos Unidos del Noroeste (PCUN; United Northwest Tree Planters and Farm Workers, the main farmworkers' union in Oregon) and the partnership between Teamsters Local 890 and the Citizenship Project in the Salinas Valley of California. Initially, the foe of the United Farm Workers (UFW) in the much publicized "labour war . . . in the fields" during the 1970s, a struggle for jurisdiction in farmworkers' unionist efforts, Local 890 later came under the leadership of a homegrown rank-and-file democracy movement supported by the UFW (and independent of TDU). The reformed union then commenced a naturalization effort in 1995 after California voters passed Proposition 187, which denied major services to undocumented immigrants. Organizer and sociologist Paul Johnston articulates the ethos that has guided this ongoing initiative as "a radical vision of citizenship that includes an expansive approach to unionism"—radical and expansive, both in terms of including workers' social rights within the notion of being a citizen and in the sense of rejecting a model of "client processing" in favor of an approach based on "organizing methods" to train leaders and promote "community self-defence" (Johnston 2004b, 86, 89). The Citizenship Project has defined citizenship as an active process of work rather than simply a legal status, as its slogan aptly expresses: *La ciudadanía es más que papeles* ("Citizenship is more than papers") (91). "Active citizenship," according to the vision at the Citizenship Project, meant not only that volunteers would provide direct services but also that in doing so they would nurture the growth of the activist corps. They would kindle new participation and leadership on the part of others while also bridging the union's formal organization and the complex social and geographical community where it was situated.

Activists in Oregon, by contrast, began by organizing for immigrant justice, with the founding of the Willamette Valley Immigration Project (WVIP) in 1977 "to provide legal representation for undocumented workers," and then later based an effort to unionize farmworkers on the trust and communication built by the WVIP. Even after organizers formed PCUN in 1985 to seek collective bargaining agreements with growers, they relied on projects geared toward immigrant rights and services, especially through local forums and legalization assistance after the passage of the Immigration Reform and Control Act, to fuel enthusiasm for labor activism (Stephen 2007, 243–44). And as with Teamsters Local 890 and the Citizenship Project, so also in PCUN's case, the mutually strengthening relationship between immigrant justice activism and labor organizing has occurred under the banner of participatory democracy. For example, PCUN's interest in promoting self-determining, collective action by ordinary immigrant workers and their families became manifest when the community group Voz Hispana (Hispanic Voice), which PCUN helped found, mobilized over eighty residents to attend school board meetings where they persuaded officials to institute new educational activities about César Chávez and the farmworker movement (251–52). Women from PCUN have formed their own organization, Mujeres Luchadoras Progresistas (MLP; Progressive Women Activists). Like Local 556, MLP has nurtured activism by cultivating a sense of "family feeling" among participants even as they gain new confidence in performing political work traditionally done by men, such as public speaking (256–57). PCUN has also done pathbreaking transnational labor organizing, sending representatives to meet with Mixtec workers in their Oaxacan hometowns when they return there during the winter months and to educate others in the community about the union and the labor movement (248–49).

The Citizenship Project and PCUN thus both have demonstrated similar commitments to the process of political education that the Tyson/IBP workers described in their narratives, while moving well beyond Local 556 in jointly articulating immigration and workers' struggles in public rhetoric and organizational innovations alike. In all three cases, one sees a resolve to treat rights-based engagements with public authorities not as ends in themselves but rather as a basis for building a grassroots movement, a radically democratic politicization of family bonds, the welding of the impulse toward individual self-defense with an ethos of collective struggle, and the determination to view working-class immigrants as the architects of their own futures. One can readily imagine that the former partisans of the slogan *¡Nosotros somos la unión!* in Washington State would have found welcome companions in struggle today among those in California who proclaim that *"la ciudadanía es más que papeles"* if Local 556 had survived, just as they likely would have found an ample basis for deepening the alliance with PCUN that had begun with the 2003 IWFR. However, it is also important to stress the far more extensive development of *organizational structures* for political pedagogy in the Salinas and Willamette Valleys and, therefore, the proliferated opportunities in these other places for reaping the harvest of acts of political narrative like those examined in this book. What the Citizenship Project uniquely has had in partnership with its parent organization Local 890, and what PCUN has enjoyed in collaboration with groups like Voz Hispana and MLP, is a self-constituted and institutionalized forum for intermingling stories of power about immigration and work. Local 556 took only the first faltering steps toward initiating such a forum with its occasional involvements in immigration-based activism.

Yet understanding the politics of narrative that informed the struggle at Tyson/IBP enables a broader perspective on the potential and achievements of the California and Oregon networks alike. Nourishing the tactical, opportune cooperation between immigrant justice and labor projects that has produced such impressive numbers—the contract priorities won, naturalization applications approved, and volunteers recruited—are, quite likely, crucial processes of narrative cross-fertilization.[5] At the very least, these immigrant worker networks have prepared the way for such narrative exchange. My analysis in the preceding chapters shows how the genealogical affinities in individuals' life stories, across distances of time and space, sometimes yield discourses and practices that counter hegemonic power formations of biopolitics and discipline. The concrete organizational forms and protocols of social interaction among immigrant workers in the Salinas and Willamette Valleys look like precisely the kinds of innovations that would make it possible for the drawing of such genealogical ties, as a joint project of workers, allies, and intellectuals, to become an explicit and regular practice. They appear to offer routine contexts, for instance, for coaxing forth and layering together the genealogical filaments that link stories about self-care in Mexico, in the hazardous zone of illegality on the border, and in workplaces staffed by immigrants to narratives of political education in the midst of a union campaign—stories about the potencies and vulnerabilities of contemporary biopolitics alike.

Such practices of political narration by immigrant workers could nurture the more radical impulses within the labor movement today. More specifically, they could steer it away from a narrow preoccupation with marginal wage increases, health copayment ceilings, and other money-based terms of labor that leave power relations on the shop floor intact. Given the secular trends in labor policy and law, this oppositional force to the now-entrenched conservatism in this political domain, which as of this writing shows few signs of weakening in the Obama era, would be welcome indeed.

In turn, by developing a language of collective struggle out of the commonsense links that bind micropolitical exercises of freedom in immigrant workers' countries of origin, on the border, and in the factory to organized revolt and the building of alternative institutions, immigrant justice advocates can fortify their own resolve to reject concessions on labor-related issues and border-control measures alike. In their eagerness to secure at least some kind of new legalization path or guest-worker program, in a legislative bargaining context whose main contestants are hard-right Republican nativists, GOP and Democratic business conservatives, and an Obama-led center aiming at a politics of the middle ground, immigrants' rights pragmatists sometimes too readily affirm these leaders' efforts to redouble police capacities on the U.S.–Mexico border, endorse immigration reform devoid of workers' rights protections, and ventriloquize the mainstream truism that reform is needed so that immigrants can do the dangerous and menial jobs that Americans spurn. Composing a narrative of justice for immigrant workers that exposes the biopolitical pairing of two key processes of racial differentiation—the militarization of the border and the exercise of hegemonic despotism at immigrant worksites—would furnish a counterforce to the inertial momentum that constrains the audacity of advocates' vision and strategy.

Thinking Biopolitics, Hegemony, and Struggle in the Neoliberal Age

In order for such couplings of labor and immigrants' rights activism to achieve their emancipatory potential, however, they require a well-thought-out connection to a—continually and politically evolving—theory of how the complexes of power in these various domains of immigrant life relate to one another. My final notes in this book thus concern how what we have learned here assists political and social theorists' current efforts to rethink what biopolitics means in the neoliberal era. Part of my point in this regard is methodological: an exhortation that analysts study not only the institutional discourses that generate the policies, procedures, and public rhetorics by which the neoliberal state and corporations manage mass populations but also the processes of hegemony by which popular groups actively help shape or deform these discourses. In an age of mass immigration and immigrant-based production, theorists cannot adequately explain what biopolitics is or how it works without listening to immigrant workers. The path of critique supported here thus would serve as a critical complement in relation to the work of a scholar like Mae M. Ngai (2004), whose magisterial history of "illegal" subjectivities focuses on state discourses but also makes room, at least episodically, for considering how immigrants' own activist efforts sometimes have reinforced or opposed the racializing implications of immigration policies. More generally, theorists need to push the critical response to Foucault's inspiring but limited model of *how* to analyze biopolitics, and the subjects wrought by biopolitics, to its limits. Beyond acknowledging that microtechniques of the self always occur within determinate social contexts structured by power, and analyzing such practices of self-care *in addition to* the discourses of biopolitics embedded in administrative rules, organizational operating procedures, and legislative debates, the task remains of contemplating how biopolitical formations depend on contingent waves of popular commitment.

Those who study biopolitics should view even more skeptically the recent flurry of writing set off by Giorgio Agamben's (1998) provocative but deeply unsatisfying renegotiation of this concept in relation to his notions of sovereignty, "bare life," and the "state of exception." Agamben's conception of a sphere of authoritative action that lies on the unstable threshold of the law, rather than either inside or outside its purview, resonates with the circumstances faced by immigrants in multiple locations. These range from the legal limbo of immigrant detention centers to unforeseen encounters with border security personnel to the conditions of labor in the informal agricultural and food-processing industries. Thus, it might seem that critically considering such predicaments of immigrants would provide a valuable opportunity for honing a theory of biopolitics based centrally on Agamben's work. A brief consideration of Agamben's theory, however, suggests that it diverts attention far more resolutely than Foucault's from the hegemonic constitution of biopolitical power.

Agamben argues that sovereignty creates itself by generating spaces of exception to the law that it also promulgates. It fashions itself as "self-presuppositional power" rather than as an effect of law or a force dependent on any temporal or geospatial circumscription through designating certain "exceptional" bodies as existing in a "threshold" location where law both does and does not apply. In such a space, law actively "abandons" the individual, rather than simply excluding (or including) him, in the sense that legal authority is invoked to subject the individual to certain kinds of treatment but does not operate according to any characteristic, comprehensible logic (Agamben 1998, 28). Instead of either life that is governed by law or nonlife that is excluded from the law's domain, there is the paradoxical figure of "bare life." Certainly, the liminal positions of immigrants with respect to the law governing the American nation-state or the rules regulating production in the factory, as we saw in the preceding chapters, evoke just such a sense of immigrants' reduction to bare life.

Conclusion

Agamben contends that modern biopolitics extends this state of exception over an ever-broadening ambit of social life and incorporates ever-larger populations within its rubric. Biopolitics manages the threshold existence of bare life as its definitive task; bare life becomes the new political subject of modern democracy. Agamben elaborates: "The sovereignty of the living man over his own life has its immediate counterpart in the determination of a threshold beyond which life ceases to have any juridical value and can, therefore, be killed without the commission of a homicide" (139). Following this line of thought, Agamben identifies the Nazi concentration camp, where biopolitics and "thanatopolitics" (the administration of death as the primary concern of the state) merge, as the central and distinctive figure of modern political life (122). But today, one might just as easily view any of the diverse locations where the law places immigrants in states of exception as paradigmatic of modern democratic sovereignty and hence as illustrative of Agamben's theory of sovereignty's signature traits in the biopolitical age. From Agamben's perspective, that is, one might argue that the systematic rendering of immigrants as bare life only emblematizes in the most extreme form the increasingly universal subjection of the population at large to this same dynamic of power.

Agamben's strangely ontological orientation toward understanding sovereignty, however, limits the persuasiveness of his account even as he offers this provocative reading of history. Ardently committed, philosophically, to reinvigorating the study of sovereignty as the fundament of power after Foucault had inaugurated the turn toward examining the techniques of power, Agamben draws the analysis of biopolitics even further away from any analysis of how popular political formations or movements both define and unsettle the determinate social contexts that resemble spaces of exception. At best, Agamben's predilection for attributing a transhistorical, disembodied agency to sovereignty arrests the critical investigation of these processes. At worst, it recapitulates the racial logic by which immigrants are continually rendered the passive objects of power rather than active subjects who help make power what it is today and can unmake it as well. Nor is it any surprise that Agamben's dehistoricizing effort to unveil the original and perpetual logic of sovereignty, and thus to show that "the modern State therefore does nothing other than bring to light the secret tie uniting power and bare life" that has been sovereignty's hidden essence since ancient times, eschews any consideration of how the political involvement of theory might be crucial to theory's self-innovation, in the Gramscian sense I elaborated in chapter 1 (6). The preeminent problem, for Agamben, is "to think beyond" the paradoxical "relation between potentiality and actuality" that sovereignty sets in motion as it creates itself *via* establishing states of exception and to devise "a new and coherent ontology of potentiality" (44). This philosophical preoccupation, however, withdraws itself from the critically invigorating energies of popular political narrative even more intractably than, say, the discourse analyses of anti-immigrant nationalism considered in the introduction.

From an alternative perspective that approaches biopolitics as the contested product of hegemony rather than the self-expression of sovereignty, then, and that learns from the theory-in-the-flesh proffered by the people whose accounts of power are discussed in the foregoing chapters, a number of key discursive features and operational modes of contemporary biopolitics can be discerned. Above all, the biopolitical formation that implicates immigrant workers eschews explicitly racial-biological classification, quarantining, and regulation in favor of implicitly biopolitical discourses to justify and affectively animate its activities. The neoliberal conjuncture in the history of capitalism supplies some of the key enabling discourses for such biopolitics-by-implication. (And biopolitics, in turn, mobilizes populations to perform the tasks and inhabit the subjectivities that neoliberal capitalism requires.) These facilitating discourses include an aggressive assertion of *property rights,* for example, by private companies that demand deference to the bottom line when they downscale health and retirement benefits or when they claim the prerogative to manage health and safety risks in their own facilities free of state interference. The neoliberal discourses that help make biopolitics possible also involve a belief in *labor market individualism.* In Mexico, this view constructs migration as the natural response to declining employment prospects. In the United States, it legitimates and depoliticizes the racial segmentation of the labor market such that the most dangerous jobs become the lot of immigrants and appear to result from the choices of individual working persons. *Antistatist* discourses that undermine social spending and business regulation also belong to the array of neoliberal rhetorics on which contemporary biopolitics relies. These, too, operate transnationally. They undercut previously established social rights and egalitarian conventions, laying the groundwork for emigration from Mexico and the racialization of a culturally heterogeneous "Mexican" immigrant population; and they undergird the policy processes in the United States that carry the racializing process forward, in the name of responsible public budgeting and capital's liberation from government restraints, through social services cuts and regulation rollbacks.

At the same time, the discursive repertoire of the current biopolitical formation incorporates elements that complement neoliberal accumulation and governance strategies without being identifiably neoliberal in substantive terms. These public discourses are also more firmly anchored in a strident and defensive U.S. nationalism than are their neoliberal counterparts. As noted in the preceding chapters, among the former is the cultural-nationalist vision of U.S.-American identity that elevates *meat consumption,* especially eating steak and hamburgers, to the status of a prime signifier of the allied traditional values of family, Christian faith, self-reliance, hardy masculinity, and prosperity. These discursive energies, no less than the profit motives of transnational corporations like Tyson, drive the relentless pace of the chain in the slaughterhouse, draw laboring populations north from Latin America, and generate political obstacles for workers who accuse the companies of inhumane practices. Dovetailing with this discourse is the *neoconservative global imaginary* that views "our" traditional culture as under siege by foreign invaders and terrorists who need to be repelled by securitizing and militarizing the nation's "broken borders." These discourses about eating like a real American and repairing our national boundaries sound more recognizably biopolitical than the neoliberal themes discussed in the preceding paragraph. They announce themselves as efforts to protect the lives and promote the physical and psychological well-being of the "American" population by regulating the flow of external entities into the interiors of "our" imagined national corpus and individual fleshly bodies. Yet these discourses, too, work hard to obscure the full extent of their own biopolitical character. They indirectly symbolize the whiteness of the population whose biological vitality is being promoted rather than claiming it outright. And they gloss over the exposure to "killing," in Foucault's capacious sense, that ensues to immigrant workers from these practices, sanitizing the discussion with warm and homey images of the family burger cookout complemented by cool, abstract moralizing about refusing to tolerate immigrant "lawbreakers."

But as we have seen throughout the pages of this book, all these discourses, and the state and industrial practices they make possible, do indeed produce the biopolitical segregation and hierarchical ordering of racial populations. They also differentially gauge, and calibrate to one another, the life chances and risks of death, debilitation, and trauma for immigrant workers and more racially privileged groups. The implicitly biopolitical strategies of our time, it is true, do not openly strive to enhance the reproductive capacities of the white population or to suppress those of immigrant workers. Neither jeremiads about race suicide through racial miscegeny nor programs to boost white fertility belong to this current power formation.[6] Nevertheless, the biopolitical operations in force along the U.S.–Mexico border, in the illegal zones of the U.S. interior, and in industrial worksites systematically depress the chances for healthy family and reproductive lives among immigrant workers while also raising their likelihood of suffering bodily damage or death. And they improve the outlook for the racially privileged population in equal measure.

What we have learned here, additionally, is that the biopolitical administration of the immigrant worker population depends not only on an array of implicitly biopolitical public discourses but also on the consent of immigrant workers, themselves. Hopefully, readers also have come to appreciate the active, generative presence of these dynamics of hegemony *within* the biopolitical apparatus as partially constitutive—but also sometimes interfering—elements. Immigrant workers lubricate the gears of the biopolitical machine when they reflect on their experiences and picture themselves as being driven to hide, deprived of physical orientation, stripped of their dignity, abused at the whim of superiors, and compelled to work in constant pain by an arbitrary, despotic power. Yet, ironically, these workers also reinforce and constitute biopolitical power even when they depart from this narrative of abject helplessness. They do this when they tell stories that evince pride in their individual capacities to take care of themselves and their own through immigration or that claim satisfaction from having developed microtechniques to protect themselves and others in the hazardous zones of the border, the fields, and the slaughterhouse. They even add further momentum to the biopolitical project when they wage open struggle against it, when such struggle is narrowly keyed to the disciplines of the law and the resentful disposition they foster. It is a sobering thought, indeed, how deftly the biopolitical formation can adapt immigrant workers' narratives of resistance to serve its own ends. Nevertheless, immigrant workers' stories of power have other effects of narrativity that constitute contemporary biopolitics as internally inconsistent. Given an organizational context for political education, immigrant workers have shown that they can take every one of those enabling narratives—about individuality actualized through migration, about micrological prophylaxes of the body and mind, and about claiming legal rights—and connect them genealogically to a storyline about asserting militant, radical democratic power.

These popularly generated narrative affiliations not only link the struggle at Tyson/IBP in spirit to more far-reaching and long-lasting endeavors to organize immigrant workers today, such as those being carried out by PCUN and Teamsters Local 890, they also open up space for wider counterhegemonic coalitions. To pursue this concluding thought, and in the spirit of provoking further analysis in response to this book, I want to consider briefly from a skeptical outlook the argument I have consistently advanced in previous chapters: that the biopolitical schema creates a link on the metabolic level between distinct mass populations that depends on systematically rendering them *vastly different* and *strikingly unequal.* As I have contended, the subaltern mass of immigrant workers finds its hazards of dying or being traumatized on the border and of getting injured or developing health problems at work to be increasing, while its ability to find sustainable employment in Latin America and its access to health and reproductive services in the United States decline. These deprivations are enforced *so that* the racially dominant population in the north can enjoy more job security, less physically dangerous employment, better health care, a wider array of public social services, and ubiquitous opportunities to purchase high-protein and vitamin-rich foods at low prices. The stories told to us by the Tyson/IBP workers detail the sordid characteristics of this relation of biopolitical segregation and domination.

But now let's pause and reconsider what I have just written: *are* the benefits of this arrangement for the dominant group really so unqualified? Certainly, relative to the circumstances of immigrant workers, especially the undocumented who abide in the zone of illegality, the majority white, native-born U.S. population receives these advantages. In addition, and of no little importance politically, they receive ideological reassurance from their continual, systematic distinction from immigrant workers that their own lives are of fundamentally greater value to society. Yet even as biopolitical mechanisms effect this *dissimilarity*, the logic of neoliberalism incessantly draws the two groups *together* in other ways, making the conditions of immigrant workers and the racially privileged nonimmigrant population startlingly interdependent and disconcertingly isomorphic.

This practical context, where the fortunes of native-born whites and their nonwhite immigrant Others veer scandalously close to one another in terms of what I have been calling their exposure to risks of killing in the variegated sense meant by Foucault, has multiple dimensions. Paramount among the latter are certain aspects of economic production, reproduction, and consumption. Such experiences include the dwindling value of employment-based health benefits for the white working and middle classes despite their continuing privileged access to jobs with benefits, which they preserve only by bowing to the same structure of private economic power that denies such benefits entirely to large swaths of the immigrant workforce. Another parallel between practical experiences for U.S.-born white workers and low-wage immigrant workers can be found in the shrinking resources of the welfare state. White citizens retain the diminishing leftovers of a more generous era at the cost of endorsing the overall trend toward ever more privatization, of which the outright denial of educational, social, and public health services to immigrants is a phenomenon that differs in degree but not in kind from what white birthright citizens are experiencing.

Then there are the related health hazards that production practices in the food industries generate for white native-born and immigrant populations alike. Like the welfare state and the racially striated labor market, the food-production system is geared, on the one hand, toward institutionalizing distinctions between racial populations. It does so by providing a mechanism by which immigrant racial minorities subsidize the health of white society by producing nutritious foods at very low costs and at high risk to their own health. On the other hand, the same industrial processes and deregulation policies that endanger the health and safety of immigrant workers also heighten the susceptibility of fresh meat, fruit, and vegetable products to contamination by pathogens that sicken consumers. Meanwhile, the American food economy makes high-protein foods like red meat not just plentiful but hyperabundant to the point of causing manifold health problems that range from obesity to high blood pressure, diabetes, and heart disease and that cut across all sectors of the population.

Finally, the burgeoning growth of immigrant detention facilities and the proliferation of surveillance operations on and near the U.S.–Mexico border, from one perspective, seem to absolutize the boundaries between "Americans" and "foreigners." Nevertheless, they also herald a more general and all-encompassing deprivation of liberty. These prisons and military deployments immobilize, incapacitate, and isolate immigrant bodies, apparently enabling U.S. citizens to enjoy their freedom by extirpating any potential threat that alien terrorists might pose. Yet here again, the plight of incarcerated and deported immigrants can also be seen as bearing a family resemblance to the situation of ordinary Americans, albeit taken to an extreme, inasmuch as the latter, too, are being subjected to an unprecedented rollback of civil liberties in the name of homeland security. The double-edged rhetoric of being a "patriot" not only summons those who love their country to join volunteer armies to *expel* immigrants but also calls upon loyal Americans to become more *like* immigrants by conceding to heightened surveillance over their lives and to more circumscribed legal rights, as provided by the USA-PATRIOT Act.

The forward march of neoliberalism and national securitism alike thus effects not only a differentiation but also an approximation of the racially dominant and subordinate populations' social, political, and economic destinies. The specific challenge for counterhegemonic politics, then, is to make these internal reversals of the racial logic of contemporary biopolitics explicit. It is to take these shared but culturally denied experiences of nearness between groups that are supposed to stay separate and to articulate them as a new vernacular of shared, multiracial, cross-class, transnational struggle against neoliberal hegemony and its biopolitical methods. It is to train the gazes of activists and ordinary workers on the irrepressible *excess* of this late modern power formation: for instance, the way it cannot seem to help producing *too much meat*. (Recall, once more, Alejandro Méndez's humorous, and deadly serious, words about how there was "meat here, meat there, meat everywhere" when he and his line-mates suddenly started work-ing at a more human pace, and think of what those piles of beef sym-bolize about the meat production process and its political buttresses.) Or the way it demands that meatpackers swallow "fistfuls of ibuprofen" to be able to work while in pain. Or the way it ends up making not just immigrant workers but also the general population suffer by aggres-sively shifting costs for health premiums onto consumers of care, dras-tically slicing school and social service budgets, and subjecting people under no suspicion of wrongdoing to endless security checks.

Political coalitions that want to challenge this incubator of excess can and must expand their scope beyond the existing organizational network of immigrant workers and their immediate allies. And one cru-cial step toward realizing such broader possibilities is for more people among the native U.S.-born to recognize that in neoliberal America, immigrants speak as self- and world-constituting subjects. Through their narratives that alternately construe power sometimes as invulner-able to contestation but other times as mutable through personal or group practices, immigrant workers in effect make bids for new polit-ical alliances with any who would listen attentively. They invite others who do not share their specific experiences of immigration, labor, and activism to reformulate their own conceptions of power and opposi-tion in critical partnership with them. They offer a political education in the radically democratic alternatives to late modern strategies of domination and hegemony that all Americans—north and south, Anglo and Latin(o), white and brown—emphatically need.

Appendix:
Interview Methods

Interview Protocol

As noted in chapter 1, the conversations that my assistant and I conducted with our interviewees were designed to be (and in fact were) loosely structured discussions rather than tightly controlled question-and-answer sessions. We asked open-ended questions that left ample room for the interviewee to describe the features of power and conceptions of the self in terms of his or her own choice, and that gave us significant flexibility to follow up with subordinate questions of our own. I composed a formal protocol of questions to impart a general orientation to the interviews and to ensure their comparability, but the point of each individual question was to draw forth individual stories and speculations from our interlocutors. Our interview technique was intentionally geared toward permitting us to pursue the flow of the discussion into themes and experiences that emerged while the conversation was underway and that reflected previously unsuspected concerns of the particular individual with whom we were speaking (and therefore had been impossible to predict in advance).

Because we were attempting to inspire an interaction with a rhythm of its own, a sense of spontaneity, and a feeling of friendly rapport, we rarely posed these questions exactly as written here, but we made sure to cover these key themes:

Questions about Early Life and Immigration

- Please tell us about the place where you were born and about what your life as a child was like, and also about your parents and other family members.
- Please tell us about how you decided to come to the United States. How did you arrange your journey across the border? What was your experience coming into the United States like?

- How frequently are you now in contact with your friends and family in Mexico and with people you know from Mexico who now live in other cities in the United States?
- Can you give us an example of an occasion when you felt welcomed here in the United States?
- Can you give us an example of an occasion when you did *not* feel welcome here in the United States?
- In terms of your national identity, do you feel like you are "Mexican"? Or "American" *(estadounidiense)*? Both? Neither? For you, what does it mean to say that you're "Mexican" (or "American," or "Mexican American," or none of these things)?

Questions about Working Life at Tyson/IBP

- What kinds of work did you do in Mexico before you came to the United States, and in the United States before you started working at IBP?
- Please tell us about the work you do right now. What is your job like?
- What kinds of problems have you had in your work at IBP? Do you feel that the company treats you fairly *(con justicia)*? Please tell us, especially, about any health problems you've had because of your work and how the company handled those problems, and also about how the supervisors have treated you and how you feel about the wages and benefits you receive.

Questions about Union Activism

- How do you see your role in the union? What did you do during the strike? In what ways have you participated in the union's meetings and other activities?
- Please tell us what you think about the leaders in the Local. Do you consider yourself to be a leader? (Why, or why not?) What do you think are the qualities of a good leader? How strong are the connections between the leaders and the workers in the union?
- What would you say the union has achieved or failed to achieve? What kind of support from the community does the union need?

• What are your plans for the future? How long do you think you will keep working at Tyson? Are you thinking about going back to live in Mexico, or are you planning to stay in the United States?

Interview Log

The names of most individuals (marked with an asterisk) were changed to protect them against any adverse consequences from the publication of their remarks in the interviews; we offered the option of remaining anonymous. Some people were identifiable public figures.

Tyson/IBP Workers Interviewed by Author and Paola Vizcaíno Suárez

*Juanita Castillo, June 8, 2002, Pasco, Washington
*Ramona Díaz, June 20, 2002, Pasco, Washington
*Héctor Fernández, September 28, 2002, Pasco, Washington
*Guadalupe Flores, November 9, 2002, Pasco, Washington
*Nina Garza, November 9, 2002, Pasco, Washington
*Isidro Gómez, July 21, 2002, Pasco, Washington
*Francisco González, July 17, 2002, Walla Walla, Washington
*Manuel Guzmán, July 19, 2002, Pasco, Washington
*Jorge Hernández, November 2, 2002, Pasco, Washington
  Maria Martinez, December 19, 2002, Walla Walla, Washington
*Alejandro Méndez, July 2, 2002, Pasco, Washington
*Elvira Méndez, July 19, 2002, Pasco, Washington
*Rafael Mendoza, July 8, 2002, Walla Walla, Washington
*Esteban Múñoz, June 9, 2002, Pasco, Washington
*Diego Ortega, September 28, 2002, Pasco, Washington
*Felipe Ortiz, September 28, 2002, Pasco, Washington
  Melquíades Pereyra, May 28, 2002, Walla Walla, Washington
*Ignacio Ramos, July 23, 2002, Walla Walla, Washington
*Gilberto Rivera, November 9, 2002, Pasco, Washington
*Gloria Ruiz, October 6, 2002, Pasco, Washington
*Pedro Ruiz, October 6, 2002, Pasco, Washington
*Rogelio Salazar, June 16, 2002, Pasco, Washington
*Esperanza Soto, November 2, 2002, Pasco, Washington
*Rosa Vásquez, October 6, 2002, Pasco, Washington

Supplementary Interviews of Tyson/IBP Workers by
Whitman College Students

These follow-up interviews to complement the 2001 survey were conducted by Mark Brenner, Political Economy Research Institute, University of Massachusetts, and completed the research for my joint study with Brenner (2005). All interviews were conducted on October 8, 2002, in Pasco, Washington. Here I list only those interviews cited in the manuscript; the students conducted thirteen additional interviews on that day, including interviews with *Esteban Múñoz, *Isidro Gómez, *Rogelio Salazar, *Gilberto Rivera, and *Nina Garza. These additional interviews supplied further context for the discussion of workers' injuries and health problems in chapter 4.

*Juanita Castillo, interviewed by Anna Markee and Meredith
  Richardson
*Felicia Domínguez, interviewed by Sarah Sitts
*Alejandro Méndez, interviewed by Paola Vizcaíno Suárez
*Elvira Méndez, interviewed by Eric Dottarar and Carrie Gage
*Geraldo Morales, interviewed by Meghan Bowen and Meredith
  Johnson
*Agustín Peña, interviewed by Benjamin Braus and Samantha
  Howell
*Federico Reyes, interviewed by Donan Everett and Dustin
  Lambro
*Esperanza Soto, interviewed by Paola Vizcaíno Suárez

Notes

Introduction

1. I am grateful to Lee Keene at Whitman College for supporting this claim through his systematic search of major newspaper databases covering 1984 to 2009.

2. Another estimate of the number of immigrants held put the figure above 32,000 by 2007 (Wilder 2007).

3. See Bernstein 2007; Lutheran Immigration and Refugee Service 2007; Maruskin 1995; Phillips, Hagan, and Rodriguez 2006; Welch 1996. The emerging practice of private deportation by hospitals in the United States that run short of resources to care for uninsured immigrants, legal and illegal alike, offers another example of institutional processes that jeopardize the health and lives of immigrants in ways that seem to depend minimally on these individuals' consent (Sontag 2008a, 2008b).

4. For detailed accounts of these events, see CBS/Associated Press 2007; Craig 2007; Downes 2007; Ibbitson 2008; Janovich 2007; Roberts 1996; Turnbull 2008.

5. See chapter 5 for a more detailed discussion of these historical tendencies.

6. On a more general level but in a similar vein, Roxanne Doty contends that the "neo-racist" ideological strategy of targeting immigrants as culturally inassimilable to the native community seeks "to obliterate the ambiguity surrounding national identity" that results from "the decoding and deterritorialisation that is inherent in globalisation" (1999, 597).

7. Rachel Rubin and Jeffrey Melnick (2007) offer a different counterpoint to Honig by examining not only the production of immigrant identities in Hollywood films and other pop-cultural venues but also immigrant communities' receptions and interpretations of these representational patterns.

8. Elsewhere, for instance, I argue that some work by political theorists Wendy Brown and Linda Zerilli exemplifies this problem (Apostolidis 2008a).

9. Readers familiar with subaltern studies will notice an affinity between this literature and my effort to gain critical distance on Foucault with the aid of Gramsci and more generally to promote theory's vitality by situating it politically. With Gayatri Chakravorty Spivak, for instance, I trouble "the opposition between authoritative theoretical production and the unguarded practice of conversation" (1988, 272) in ways that Foucault avoided, methodologically

speaking. And as she proposes, I probe certain "subject formations that micro-logically and often erratically operate the interests that congeal the macrolo-gies" (297), thereby exposing the concepts used to identify macrological power systems (e.g., biopolitics, discipline, and neoliberalism) to critical reconsider-ation. In contrast to Spivak's Derridean move of detecting the absent presence of subaltern experience in the aporias between semiotic systems, I experiment with conceptual resources that Gramsci suggests for bringing new, positive articulations to subaltern experience, in dialogue with theory, through the politics of narrative. Yet this latter approach bears similarities to other im-portant work in subaltern studies, notably Dipesh Chakrabarty's research on Bengali jute workers' everyday language for conceiving of their managers' and trade union leaders' authority and in turn for orienting their practical strug-gles (1989).

10. William E. Connolly has largely inspired this recent trend in political theory through his influential texts that elaborate an ethos for cultivating identity's contingency and that ground radical democratic politics on such an ethical practice. For my own critique of Connolly's theory in light of racial power, see Apostolidis (2008b); for a critical exploration of Connolly's rela-tion to Foucault and their common, inadequate theorization of collective responses to the depoliticizing effects of discipline and biopolitics, see Myers (2008).

11. This tendency was evident, for example, when conservative anchors and talk show hosts on FOX News fulminated over John Edwards's wholly vague calls to do something about the poor during the 2008 Democratic pres-idential primary season.

12. This soft-pedaling of the Mexican-ethnic character of the struggle reflected not only the dwindling of the workers' cross-border ties but also strategic practicalities in a unionized workforce at Tyson/IBP where Mexican immigrants and U.S.-born Mexican Americans comprised a great majority of about 85 percent (and essentially provided all the leadership for the move-ment) but where activists also eagerly desired support from the minority groups of Bosnian, Laotian, Vietnamese, and African American workers.

13. I was initially interested in gathering supplementary discursive material from company officials, since this would have clarified certain power dynam-ics in the workers' stories as well as illuminated management's perspective on the conflict. On several occasions I contacted the company to tell them that my students and I were researching health and safety problems at the plant and to ask if I could speak to managers about the situations workers were describing to us. I was told that the managers of the local plant were not avail-able to speak to me, and I was referred to corporate headquarters in Arkansas. From Arkansas, a public communications official for Tyson responded to my questions by assuring me, in the formulaic language commonly used in the company's public statements, that Tyson had a high level of concern about its employees' health and safety, had programs in place to deal with workplace hazards, and was taking innovative steps to enhance the effectiveness of these

programs. On another occasion, an opportunity arose for local company officials to respond in person to public testimony I gave about the deplorable conditions at Tyson during a meeting in Walla Walla of the Washington State
Commission on Hispanic Affairs. The management representative at the meeting stood up after I finished and simply denied there was any real problem
with job-related injuries or health hazards at the plant and again recited Tyson's
stock lines about the company's concern for the well-being of its "Team Members" (official Tyson lingo for "employees").

14. Leo R. Chavez finds further evidence of the biopolitical governance of
immigrant bodies in the racial economy that determines the donor and recip-
ient populations for organ transplants (2008, 113–31).

1. Political Narratives, Common Sense, and Theories of Hegemony

1. The town hall meeting was convened to produce an edition of *KCTS
Connects,* a public affairs program offered by the Seattle-based public televi-
sion station. The taping occurred on November 14, 2006, at a community hall
called The Seasons of Yakima, and the program was subsequently aired on
November 16, 2006, with the title "The Immigration Debate: A Yakima Valley
Town Hall," *KCTS Connects Special Report.*

2. The video footage of Mexican immigrants as well as the comments
from the undocumented immigrant Blanca discussed in this paragraph and
the next, along with several follow-up remarks, were all included in the edited
version of this program that was broadcast and made available for purchase
as a DVD.

3. For several major contributions to this debate about how best to interpret Gramsci, see Femia (1993), Fontana (1993), Martin (1998), and Sassoon
(1987).

4. As I noted in the introduction, this critical angle on Gramsci's thought
regarding intellectuals closely resembles Gayatri Chakravorty Spivak's influential critique of European and postcolonial intellectuals. Training her gaze on
Foucault and Deleuze, Spivak famously criticizes "the unrecognized contradiction within a position that valorizes the concrete experience of the oppressed,
while being so uncritical about the historical role of the intellectual" (1988,
275). This makes critical theory complicit in ideological misrepresentations
of the subaltern, such as those performed by British imperialist and patriarchal anti-imperialist discourses about the suttee practice and the historical situation of "the woman-in-imperialism" (306).

5. Brown's comments about genealogy bear an affinity to William E. Connolly's more detailed reflections on identity reconstitution through genealogy.
Connolly focuses on what he calls the "visceral" or "affective" register of experience that crucially shapes identity and desire along with conceptual thought
(1999, 27; 2006). In these terms, narrative can be said to function genealogically when it makes audible desires that do not conform to established
dualisms of normality and abnormality, thereby implicitly—but still materially

and practically—calling those dichotomies into question and detracting from their quasi-natural feel on the level of bodily and emotional sensibilities.

6. This lack of clarity may stem from a related problem I see in Brown's work: her questionable privileging of "relatively noninstitutionalized" forms of political action and her reluctance to consider how collective action aimed at changing "policies, laws, procedures, or organization of political orders" could be conducive to the radical democratic values she advocates (8–9, 50). As I have argued elsewhere, this problem reflects the need for more space in Brown's method for encounters with the common sense of subaltern activists, for reasons I have explicated in this chapter (Apostolidis 2008a).

7. For example, Stephen introduces a recent book by noting that for the Oaxacan migrants she has studied, "living in multiple localities and discontinuous social, economic, and cultural spaces is the norm," and then defines her methodological aim as follows: "What is a challenge for the ethnographer is to try to capture their understandings and experiences" (2007, 9).

2. Hegemony in Hindsight

1. Maria Martinez, interview by author and Paola Vizcaíno Suárez, Walla Walla, Washington, December 19, 2002.

2. Jorge Hernández, interview by author and Paola Vizcaíno Suárez, Pasco, Washington, November 2, 2002. All further references to Jorge Hernández in this chapter derive from this interview.

3. See the introduction for a discussion of my reasons for designating our interviewees in this book mainly as "immigrants" rather than "migrants," noting in particular the relative lack of transnational mobility and cultural participation that characterized most of these individuals' lives by the time we spoke with them in 2002. In this chapter, nevertheless, I sometimes refer to an informant's decision to "migrate" in the cases of certain individuals who made it plain that they initially left Mexico with no intention of staying in the United States but rather planned to go and return and often ended up making multiple crossings. In addition, I use variations of the term *migration* as tools of compositional convenience to refer in a generic sense to departure(s) from Mexico for the United States when it would be cumbersome to distinguish between individuals who intended to stay and others who hoped to return.

4. I am grateful to Mark Anderson for encouraging me to address this interesting paradox.

5. While just over 40 percent of Mexico's population resided in urban areas in 1960, by 1970, this proportion was nearly 50 percent and had topped 55 percent by 1980 (Graizbord and Ruiz 1996, 379). Poverty in the countryside meanwhile remained at the highest levels in the nation throughout this period, especially in the southern states with the largest indigenous populations (Lustig 1996; Philip 1999). Additionally, as Alan Gilbert and Anne Varley remark, "If the poor's share in the fruits of [the postwar economic] miracle was rather limited, they still gained in terms of rising real incomes and

access to infrastructure and public services," particularly when they were able to move to the cities (1989, 28).

6. Rising standards of living and a slight trend toward the equalization of economic prospects continued into the 1990s in terms of aggregate statistics: between 1963 and 1992, the share of national income taken by the wealthiest 10 percent of the population dropped from 42 percent to 38 percent, while the portion going to the poorest 40 percent rose a bit from 10 percent to 13 percent (Lustig 1996, 158).

7. Esperanza Soto, interview by author and Paola Vizcaíno Suárez, Pasco, Washington, November 2, 2002. All further references to Esperanza Soto in this chapter derive from this interview.

8. Nina Garza, interview by author and Paola Vizcaíno Suárez, Pasco, Washington, November 9, 2002. All further references to Nina Garza in this chapter derive from this interview.

9. Felipe Ortiz, interview by author and Paola Vizcaíno Suárez, Pasco, Washington, September 28, 2002.

10. Gilberto Rivera, interview by author and Paola Vizcaíno Suárez, Pasco, Washington, November 9, 2002. All further references to Gilberto Rivera in this chapter derive from this interview.

11. Isidro Gómez, interview by author and Paola Vizcaíno Suárez, Pasco, Washington, July 21, 2002. All further references to Isidro Gómez in this chapter derive from this interview.

12. The one exception was Gloria Ruiz, who told us how her father had owned land and paid people to work on it, as well as a local business (a *paletería*, or sweet factory) that he had acquired to assure that his children would have future employment (as managers). None of the other individuals we spoke with had come from a family that employed farmworkers; only two had fathers who owned their own land for cultivation, and they both had lost it eventually. Among all the people we interviewed, only Ruiz had not had to work as a child. (Gloria Ruiz, interview by author and Paola Vizcaíno Suárez, Pasco, Washington, October 6, 2002. All further references to Gloria Ruiz in this chapter derive from this interview.)

13. Juanita Castillo, for example, did domestic work outside the home to earn money, serving as a babysitter for her cousins from an early age. (Juanita Castillo, interview by author and Paola Vizcaíno Suárez, Pasco, Washington, June 8, 2002. All further references to Juanita Castillo in this chapter derive from this interview.) We did not probe in detail the question of whether boys and girls were responsible for different kinds of work or the extent to which girls took on domestic duties of care for other family members and the home in addition to their income-generating activities. Only one individual, Rosa Vásquez, told us that she had worked exclusively in her home, taking care of housework and younger siblings, rather than working for money or in-kind payments like food outside the home. Even though Vásquez's family was so poor that they "didn't even have potable water," she told us, her work had consisted entirely of helping her mother with domestic work while her brothers

worked outside the home starting at the age of seven or eight. (Rosa Vásquez, interview by author and Paola Vizcaíno Suárez, Pasco, Washington, October 6, 2002. All further references to Rosa Vásquez in this chapter derive from this interview.)

14. Ramona Díaz, interview by author and Paola Vizcaíno Suárez, Pasco, Washington, June 20, 2002. All further references to Ramona Díaz in this chapter derive from this interview.

15. The latter were also less likely to obtain much education: during the 1980s, fewer students in Mexico moved on from junior high school to high school, while a lower proportion of the primary school–aged population entered school at all (Lustig 1996, 160). According to Nora Lustig, "Both phenomena clearly could be explained by the need of the children to join the work force at an earlier age or the postponement of school entry because of the high cost of the complementary expenses such as transportation and school materials" (160).

16. The 1980s saw real wages decline rapidly—a 42 percent decrease between 1982 and 1987. As real wage income fell through the floor, "the middle sectors were hurt disproportionately—even in comparison to the poor—because of their reliance on wage income" (Lustig 1996, 159). Nonwage income fell by only 1.2 percent during this period, and "nonwage income is an important share of the total income of the poor," including the "income of the small peasant or shop owner" (Lustig 1998, 71). Still, per capita consumption rates dropped substantially throughout the mid-1980s, indicating that even when low-income Mexicans had nonwage income sources (i.e., "nonmonetary income . . . and nonwage monetary income"), as almost all the families of the immigrant workers we interviewed did, mostly through their small, informal entrepreneurial activities and subsistence farming, they also felt acutely the heightened pressures of this difficult time (1996, 159; 1998, 73).

17. Lustig notes: "As a percentage of the minimum wage, the cost of the basic food basket rose from 30 percent in 1982 to over 50 percent in 1986. Moreover, this increase occurred as minimum wages declined. . . . The majority of families with incomes lower than twice the minimum wage experienced a decrease in consumption of all food products except tortillas. In addition, there was clearly a substitution away from animal proteins" (1998, 87).

18. To be sure, "self-help housing" had expanded rapidly through the 1970s, enabling many working-class Mexicans to become owner-occupiers as "the state, usually covertly . . . permitted the semi-legal, and sometimes totally illegal, occupation of rural land contiguous to urban areas." Yet these new plots often became overcrowded as the owners/builders turned to renting living quarters as additional sources of income under conditions of continuing economic deprivation (Gilbert 1989, 2, 5). In the *vecindades*, meanwhile, the conventional form of rental housing for working- and middle-class Mexican urbanites alike for most of the twentieth century, "densities [were] high, services usually deficient, and the physical state of the building often in poor condition," according to urban analysts at the close of the 1980s (Gilbert and Varley 1989, 15).

19. Alejandro Méndez, interview by author and Paola Vizcaíno Suárez, Pasco, Washington, July 2, 2002. All further references to Alejandro Méndez in this chapter derive from this interview.

20. Melquíades Pereyra, interview by author and Paola Vizcaíno Suárez, Walla Walla, Washington, May 28, 2002. All further references to Melquíades Pereyra in this chapter derive from this interview.

21. The Mexican Constitution of 1917 created a system of land redistribution with two main types of land holdings, as Horacio Mackinlay explains: "The *ejido*, a collective form of land ownership that was the principal vehicle for the distribution of land during Mexico's postrevolutionary agrarian reform, was constituted from latifundia [plantations] or private properties that exceeded the size limits established by agrarian law. Farm collectives, officially designated as '*comunidades agrarias*,' were the product of the restitution or confirmation of indigenous communities' rights to lands they had held since time immemorial" (Mackinlay 2004, 287). The history of land redistribution in Mexico has been characterized by episodic, incomplete, and highly contested initiatives to enforce these constitutional rights. In the late 1970s when Gómez became active in these issues, major new mobilizations of peasants demanding land rights had begun to emerge outside traditional corporatist organizations (Mackinlay 2004, 288). Given that the movement described by Gómez encountered stiff resistance from local governing authorities, whom he also accused of corruption in the time-honored mode of the PRI, it seems quite possible that these activists had formed such an independent organization.

22. He also emphasized the independent Christian sensibility that informed these actions and also gave him a critical view of the Catholic Church. He chastised the Church for hoarding its wealth while so many people in Mexico went hungry, saying: "We are all children of God. Logically, the one who has should give to the others. There is nothing more beautiful than when one gives."

23. Elvira Méndez, interview by author and Paola Vizcaíno Suárez, Pasco, Washington, July 19, 2002. All further references to Elvira Méndez in this chapter derive from this interview.

24. Mexican American and Mexican immigrant women who have participated in these networks of *commadrazgo* (shared mothering) historically have provided food for one another in times of illness, cared for one another's children, and generated additional customs of reciprocal assistance in the wider community (Ruiz 1998, 116).

25. Guadalupe Flores, like Elvira Méndez, stressed her ability to decide about these matters independently of her husband. She told us that when her husband decided that he wanted to go to the United States and asked her if she would come, she responded: "If I like it, I'm staying. If not, I won't." (Guadalupe Flores, interview by author and Paola Vizcaíno Suárez, Pasco, Washington, November 9, 2002.)

26. In her analysis of Mexican immigrant families in which husbands have preceded wives and children in making the move to the United States,

Hondagneu-Sotelo notes that the husband's departure typically was not a collective decision: "In those families where men migrated before their wives and children, women were not included as active participants in the decision to migrate. Rather, the husbands unilaterally decided to migrate north with little regard for their wives' concerns and opinions; migration was not the outcome of conjugal or household decision-making processes" (Hondagneu-Sotelo 1994, 57).

27. Castillo's account about being coerced into doing domestic labor for family members in Mexico has a parallel on the other side of the border in Ramona Díaz's story of how relatives in the United States let her stay with them only on condition that she do all the housework and never go out except to work in the fields; see chapter 3.

28. Pedro Ruiz, interview by author and Paola Vizcaíno Suárez, Pasco, Washington, October 6, 2002. All further references to Pedro Ruiz in this chapter derive from this interview.

29. Rafael Mendoza, interview by author and Paola Vizcaíno Suárez, Walla Walla, Washington, July 8, 2002. All further references to Rafael Mendoza in this chapter derive from this interview.

30. Diego Ortega, interview by author and Paola Vizcaíno Suárez, Pasco, Washington, September 28, 2002. All further references to Diego Ortega in this chapter derive from this interview.

31. Likewise, even though she had been shamed by her father for having a baby out of wedlock, Rosa Vásquez explained, she had found other relatives willing to help her gather funds to move north and also to arrange a job for her in the United States. Similarly, a brother helped Diego Ortega acquire the necessary money to cross the border, and Flaco Pereyra went over free of charge because one of his soccer mates' brothers worked as a *coyote*.

32. Felipe Ortiz, in parallel fashion, remembered having been impressed by the stylish clothes his cousins who worked in the United States wore; and Ortiz's father had been born in Arizona, where his own father had migrated to escape violence during the Mexican Revolution, thus setting another familial precedent for Ortiz's emigration. Juanita Castillo, Pedro Ruiz, Alejandro Méndez, Héctor Fernández, and Flaco Pereyra all noted that they had come across the border at the instigation of friends who had already resolved to make the crossing and invited them to join them. (Héctor Fernández, interview by author and Paola Vizcaíno Suárez, Pasco, Washington, September 28, 2002. All further references to Héctor Fernández in this chapter derive from this interview.)

33. Ignacio Ramos, interview by author and Paola Vizcaíno Suárez, Walla Walla, Washington, July 23, 2002. All further references to Ignacio Ramos in this chapter derive from this interview.

34. Francisco González, interview by author and Paola Vizcaíno Suárez, Walla Walla, Washington, July 17, 2002.

35. It should be noted, however, that the increasing penetration of the Mexican economy by foreign capital comprised an important link between the

ISI period and the subsequent neoliberal phase: Mexico's industrial growth occurred through increasing dependence on U.S. capital and markets, as U.S. direct foreign investment rose from $286 million in 1943 to nearly $2 billion by 1972 while foreign exchange with the United States ranged between 60 and 70 percent during the postwar period (La France 1986, 216).

36. De Genova 2005; Glick Schiller 2001; Rouse 1992; Stephen 2007. As the authors cited here point out in various ways, not taking this into account both neglects certain circumstances of immigrants' everyday lives and tends to occlude the substantial capacities that communities of immigrants possess to challenge traditional conceptions of American identity and the melting pot, and to subvert the constitution of racial, class, and gender domination by discourses that differentiate exclusive nationalities.

3. Stories of Fate and Agency in the Zone of Illegality

1. I thank Lisa Disch for suggesting this evocative way of phrasing the psychophysiological linkage between racial population groups that this account of biopolitics enacts.

2. This point is analogous to one that Peter Andreas (1998) makes about the mutually reinforcing institutional relation between U.S. immigrant control strategies and the growth of the illegal human (and drug) smuggling operations, as border militarization advanced during the 1980s and 1990s.

3. Readers familiar with Foucault's later writings on ethics and/or the recent "ethical turn" in political theory, inspired largely by Foucault and led by scholars such as William E. Connolly and Stephen K. White, should take note that I do not employ the notion of "microtechniques of the self" in a way that strictly reflects the sorts of specifically ethical endeavors that concern these theorists. That is, I do not claim that these immigrant workers' small-scale bodily and intrapsychic practices necessarily constitute practices of freedom in the form of attempts to cultivate a coherent *askesis* of self-fashioning within the context of social power discourses, much less deliberate and systematic efforts to experiment with novel self-identities in relation to interdependent formations of identity and difference. (For a helpful critical discussion of political theory's ethical turn and its problematic origins in Foucault's thought, see Myers [2008].) Rather, I use the term *microtechniques* to designate regular processes of conduct on the level of individual bodies and minds that contributed in small but significant ways to the organization and flows of power in these immigrant workers' lives, patterns of external behavior and internal emotional comportment that also were not prescribed by the institutions governing the migratory travels and working conditions these people faced.

4. Because I focus on the political ambivalence of both these micropractices and the workers' narratives about them, and furthermore, because I emphasize the efficacies of these practices with respect to biopolitics rather than discipline, this interpretation of the interviews steers away from directly

employing Foucault's germinal concept of illegalities as a tool for analyzing the narrators' actions in the illegal zone. Foucault argues that the modern state's differential management of class-specific patterns of illegal behavior, above all through isolating a social group defined as "delinquents" and subjecting it to particularly intense and publicly thematized forms of discipline, contributes vitally to the growth of state capacities as well as to *class* domination (1979). Here, by contrast, I pursue further Mae M. Ngai's conceptualization of illegality as a *racializing* condition of immigrant subjects that biopolitical strategies of the nation-state produce (2004). And while both Ngai and Foucault emphasize the subject-constituting power of the law, the state, and hegemonic public discourses about the nation, I shift the discussion toward the ways that immigrant subjects who traverse illegal spaces and perform illicit social actions help to compose this political terrain of illegality. This analysis shares Susan Bibler Coutin's interest in consulting immigrants' "situated knowledge" about the processes by which "law produces its own alterities," as she puts it, while illegal practices in turn help "produce" the law. Coutin uses extensive interviews with Salvadoran immigrants who strove to obtain legal U.S. residence after the 1986 Immigration Reform and Control Act to chart this tangled relation between "official law" and "unofficial, alternative legalities" (2000, 49, 55, 75).

5. Nina Garza, interview by author and Paola Vizcaíno Suárez, Pasco, Washington, November 9, 2002. All further references to Nina Garza in this chapter derive from this interview.

6. For a nuanced analysis of the power dynamics of prayer among religious women in relation to gendered forms of oppression, see R. Marie Griffith's (1997) study of evangelical women faced with domestic violence and other problems.

7. Esperanza Soto, interview by author and Paola Vizcaíno Suárez, Pasco, Washington, November 2, 2002. All further references to Esperanza Soto in this chapter derive from this interview.

8. Soto's story in this regard resembled those of the Salvadoran and South American migrants studied by Mahler, who found that many of these other migrants, too, were held for long stretches of time in miserable, stressful conditions in safe houses operated by *coyotes*. As Mahler explains, "Safe houses are used to sequester immigrants and hold them until their sponsors send the second portion of the trip's price to the coyote" (1995, 65).

9. Elvira Méndez, interview by author and Paola Vizcaíno Suárez, Pasco, Washington, July 19, 2002. All further references to Elvira Méndez in this chapter derive from this interview.

10. Gloria Ruiz, interview by author and Paola Vizcaíno Suárez, Pasco, Washington, October 6, 2002. All further references to Gloria Ruiz in this chapter derive from this interview.

11. Diego Ortega, interview by author and Paola Vizcaíno Suárez, Pasco, Washington, September 28, 2002. All further references to Diego Ortega in this chapter derive from this interview.

12. Only Nina Garza consistently depicted herself as wholly without some power resources of her own in the face of the eventualities she encountered during her border crossing. Looking at the other interviews suggests that in this respect our conversation with Garza was the exception that proves the rule.

13. Mahler likewise discusses the story of a Salvadoran woman separated from her six-year-old son for a period of weeks while she waited for him to make it safely across the border between Mexico and Guatemala (1995, 65).

14. Recent ethnographic research has shown the complexity and diversity among Mexicans' and Mexican Americans' gender identities, as expressed in their daily living activities and sometimes in contrast to the stories they tell about themselves. For ethnographic studies of masculinity for Mexican and other Latin American men, see Gutmann (1996, 2003). González de la Rocha (1994) provides an urban ethnography of Mexican women in working-class households. Complementary work on the complexities of masculinity in Mexican American men has been done by Mirandé (1997), while Pesquera (1997) and Mirandé and Enríquez (1979) offer ethnographically sensitive analyses of Mexican American women. De Genova (2005) devotes some attention to issues of gender identity among Mexican immigrant men and women alike.

15. Isidro Gómez, interview by author and Paola Vizcaíno Suárez, Pasco, Washington, July 21, 2002. All further references to Isidro Gómez in this chapter derive from this interview.

16. Gilberto Rivera, interview by author and Paola Vizcaíno Suárez, Pasco, Washington, November 9, 2002. All further references to Gilberto Rivera in this chapter derive from this interview. Mahler (1995) describes the similar story of a Peruvian undocumented immigrant who also risked near-suffocation to cross the border, in his case riding with nearly two hundred people in an unventilated tractor-trailer. Mahler notes that this man's "story of near suffocation is not unusual" and that two other people she interviewed had undergone parallel experiences (1995, 71).

17. Felipe Ortiz, interview by author and Paola Vizcaíno Suárez, Pasco, Washington, September 28, 2002. All further references to Felipe Ortiz in this chapter derive from this interview.

18. Pedro Ruiz, interview by author and Paola Vizcaíno Suárez, Pasco, Washington, October 6, 2002. All further references to Pedro Ruiz in this chapter derive from this interview.

19. Melquíades Pereyra, interview by author and Paola Vizcaíno Suárez, Walla Walla, Washington, May 28, 2002. All further references to Melquíades Pereyra in this chapter derive from this interview.

20. Pereyra's experience of having to hide in the garbage dump is a good example of what Coutin calls "the sullying nature of border crossings" that her informants, too, described in their accounts. One woman interviewed by Coutin, for instance, reported that "when the border patrol chased her, she hid in some trash barrels, only to find herself covered with feces and thorns"

(2000, 57). Similarly, during one of her clandestine crossings, Esperanza Soto and her husband had spent twenty-four hours hiding in a landfill, huddling together amid the garbage and chasing off skunks by lighting matches.

21. Alejandro Méndez, interview by author and Paola Vizcaíno Suárez, Pasco, Washington, July 2, 2002. All further references to Alejandro Méndez in this chapter derive from this interview.

22. Rogelio Salazar, interview by author and Paola Vizcaíno Suárez, Pasco, Washington, June 16, 2002. All further references to Rogelio Salazar in this chapter derive from this interview.

23. Rosa Vásquez, interview by author and Paola Vizcaíno Suárez, Pasco, Washington, October 6, 2002. All further references to Rosa Vásquez in this chapter derive from this interview.

24. In addition, it should be noted that there were two immigrant workers, Juanita Castillo and Guadalupe Flores, who had crossed over with valid passports and visas and hence had not even run the risks of detection and deportation. Gloria Ruiz also ran less risk than others because she could afford to purchase false documents and cross the border in the official line.

25. Ramona Díaz, interview by author and Paola Vizcaíno Suárez, Pasco, Washington, June 20, 2002. All further references to Ramona Díaz in this chapter derive from this interview.

26. Héctor Fernández, interview by author and Paola Vizcaíno Suárez, Pasco, Washington, September 28, 2002.

27. Díaz's husband here referred to bitter personal experience, saying that when they arrived they found that the police "stopped a person for any reason and asked to see their license, or if they were carrying papers. If they weren't carrying papers that person was arrested immediately. And then, after being arrested, they were turned over to immigration. . . . One time one of her brothers and one of my brothers were coming and . . . they had a problem with the car they were driving, and they pulled over to the side. Since they weren't carrying papers, much less a license, the police stopped there to help them and they arrested them; and that's what [Ramona] means, that normally we spend more time shut inside than going out, or we spent more time shut up inside because we were afraid of the police. Because the police have done the work of immigration [authorities]."

28. Francisco González, interview by author and Paola Vizcaíno Suárez, Walla Walla, Washington, July 17, 2002. All further references to Francisco González in this chapter derive from this interview.

29. Mahler argues, in addition, that immigrants often find to their surprise that in the new country after immigration, their relatives no longer fulfill traditional kinship obligations but instead seek ways of "using them to their own advantage" (1995, 94–104).

30. Coutin also notes that those who have immigrated illegally are made to disappear into this domain of legal nonexistence insofar as they lack documentation of their "physical presence" in a certain place, so that they are precluded from taking any social actions that require documents such as applying

for asylum (2000, 30). Public "policies that make their kin ties legally inert for immigration purposes" further generate the disappearance of immigrants without documents (32).

31. However, Ruiz also confirmed Alejandro Méndez's observation that wages began to drop significantly as the 1990s—and new masses of immigrants—arrived. In addition, the notion that farmwork had been a lucrative occupation even before that time was by no means universal among our interviewees. Both Francisco González and Jorge Hernández, for example, spoke vividly of the poverty they had endured during their years as farm laborers. (Jorge Hernández, interview by author and Paola Vizcaíno Suárez, Pasco, Washington, November 2, 2002. All further references to Jorge Hernández in this chapter derive from this interview.)

32. Hernández seemed to have stumbled into the trap that, as Diego Ortega told us, would befall some farmworkers when owners exploited them by having them live in dwellings with no cooking facilities on the outskirts of the fields and then deducting food, transportation, and housing expenses from their pay, to the point where workers ended up earning less than three dollars an hour.

33. Juanita Castillo, interview by author and Paola Vizcaíno Suárez, Pasco, Washington, June 8, 2002.

34. It should be noted, moreover, that the state's investments in border security have multiplied dramatically since the 1980s. The Reagan administration secured funding increases for the Immigration and Naturalization Service (INS) totaling 130 percent through the end of Reagan's second term and also boosted INS staffing by 41 percent (Nevins 2003, 68). Border Patrol apprehensions of undocumented immigrants accordingly went up during the mid-1980s, rising by nearly 50 percent in just fiscal year 1986, and although they declined steadily for several years thereafter, they did not return to pre-1977 levels (Nevins 2003, 77; González-Baker et al. 1998, 92). The Clinton years witnessed an even more spectacular expansion of the INS: between 1993 and 2001, INS funding shot up by over 230 percent, while the number of full-time, permanent staff rose by 79 percent (Welch 2002, 47).

35. Behdad also emphasizes that these disciplinary practices not only "impinge on the bodies and minds of immigrants" but also normalize "an exclusive and exclusionary form of national identity" for all citizens (2005, 145, 161).

36. For Dunn, "low-intensity conflict" strategy includes deploying new technologies and equipment to carry out surveillance and to enable the use of coercive military force, as well as conducting innovative training in special "strategy and tactics" for Border Patrol personnel (1996, 59). Border policing powers have also been spread out among other government bodies, such as the National Guard and elements of the armed forces as well as private voluntary agencies (99). In addition, the ambit for legitimately applying military techniques has expanded to take in wider segments of civilian populations (58–60, 98–99). Dunn also confirms that while the militarization of the border

accelerated in the 1990s and then even more after 2001, this process had
already begun in earnest during the 1980s when most of the people we interviewed came across.

37. "Prior to the 1980s," Welch notes, "the INS enforced a policy of detaining only those individuals deemed likely to abscond or who posed a security
risk" (2002, 107). During the 1980s, however, the INS's budget for detaining
migrants increased from just $15.7 million to nearly $150 million as a new
policy era dawned of requiring the detention of unlawful immigrants who had
been apprehended. Over the 1980s, the average length of stay in INS detention centers also increased from less than four to twenty-three days, and the
overall holding capacity in these facilities increased to over six thousand
(Welch 1996, 170). More recent expansions of immigrant detention capabilities make these numbers look small by comparison. In spring 2007, the
NACLA Report on the Americas noted: "The number of beds reserved by ICE for
noncitizens has exploded, from fewer than 7,500 in 1994 to 26,500 today.
Sometime this year the number is expected to reach 32,000." While the report
characterized "the average stay in ICE detention" as "short (about 40 days and
falling)," this figure is nearly double what it was in 1990. Meanwhile, as the
report observes, "the number of people moving through the detention system
is vast—230,000 each year and growing" (Wilder 2007).

38. One limitation of the interviews with regard to this issue is that we did
not ask our informants to tell us in any detail about their experiences seeking
legalization. Examining this transitional phase out of the condition of illegality would have led us to consider a sustained interaction that immigrant workers had with a bureaucratic apparatus of government and its instrumentalities
for exercising disciplinary power as well as immigrants' informal networks
of power developed in the context of formal legal processes of the sort that
Coutin (2000) discusses. Other accounts of the IRCA's legalization program
in the late 1980s suggest what some of these disciplinary mechanisms were
and how they may have functioned to normalize immigrant subjects. Like
other large human services and criminal justice bureaucracies, the INS maintained a massive volume of individual case files, some 40 million as of 2000
with 19 million of these being active files (Welch 2002, 50). The legalization
provisions of the IRCA precipitated an unprecedented mobilization of agency
personnel and resources to perform naturalization services, especially after it
became clear that other "qualified designated entities" empowered to conduct
legalization processes (e.g., "churches, unions, and other immigrant advocacy
groups") were experiencing serious technical difficulties (Magaña 2003, 43).
The specific attention paid to individual cases during the legalization process,
along with the normalization of immigrants in line with criteria about prior
employment experience as well as the agency's concern that immigrants view
the INS with reduced suspicion, made this brief episode in the recent history
of immigration resemble an application of disciplinary power much more than
the prevailing trends surrounding it have done. Additional research on our
informants' stories about these processes, although beyond our capabilities for

this study, thus would illuminate further the role that notions of disciplinary power played in their political conceptions.

39. A similarly explicit preoccupation with promoting the health and hygiene of the population, in part by protecting the privileged white majority from infestations thought to be borne by new immigrants, informed the public discourses of the food industry in these years, as Aaron Bobrow-Strain argues in his study of biopolitics in the bread-baking industry (2008).

40. The evidence of this consensus is plain to see when one considers multiple parallel statements by Barack Obama, Hillary Clinton, and John McCain during the 2008 presidential campaign to the effect that "securing our borders" would have to be a top priority of the person elected president.

41. Along these lines, Roberts quotes the following statement by Patrick Buchanan in 1995, proposing "a timeout from illegal immigration so that we can become one nation and one culture. So we can all learn the same customs and traditions" (1996, 211). Precisely this emphasis on cultural distinction and stability comprises the main theme in Samuel P. Huntington's more recent, influential analysis of the dangers posed by undocumented immigrants from Latin America, especially Mexico (2004).

42. This conception of undocumented immigrants as individuals who are defined by their violations of the law, along with a narrow focus on stabilizing the rule of law as the preeminent public interest in immigration matters, is a particularly strong theme in religious-conservative anti-immigrant discourse. Comments from prominent evangelical leaders at a 2006 conference held shortly before the immigrants' rights marches of that year illustrate this tendency (Land 2006; Rodriguez 2006).

43. In terms that resonate clearly with Foucault's conception of biopolitics and underscore the current power formation's turn away from modes of discipline when it comes to the imprisonment of immigrants, Michael Welch describes the "new penology" that governs the growing immigrant detention system as follows: "Whereas traditional penology stems from criminal law and criminology and emphasizes punishing and correcting individual offenders, the new penology . . . adopts an actuarial approach in which specialists assess risks of specific criminal subpopulations (e.g., drug offenders) and recommend strategies designed to control those aggregates" (2002, 152). Welch finds evidence of the spread of new penological thinking in U.S. immigration policy not only in the massive increases in immigrant detention capabilities but also in the increasingly frequent employment since the 1980s of statisticians and other technical experts to conduct population assessments by U.S. immigration authorities (152–54).

44. For all his self-reliant talk, for example, Alejandro Méndez benefited from just such unofficial, family-based channels for transferring practical knowledge; likewise, it was information from an uncle that finally led Isidro Gómez to his longer-term position with the tire company. For more in-depth analyses of immigrants' informal networks in areas including housing, employment, health services access, child care, labor activism, and migration, see

Swider (2002), Menjívar (2000), Rodriguez and Hagan (1997), Hondagneu-Sotelo (1994), Lamphere et al. (1993), and Ruiz (1987). In addition, Coutin shows how legalization through the IRCA depended on an efflorescence of illicit or quasi-legal immigrant service organizations along with accompanying informal networks for routing information to clients (2000, 63–70). Our interviewees thus may have acquired additional microtechniques of self-determination through their own processes of legalization, as our conversation with Esperanza Soto, in particular, suggested.

4. Labor, Injury, and Self-Preservation in the Slaughterhouse

1. Here, Pereyra used the verb *aguantar*, which means to stand or to bear with a difficult or onerous situation, or to "hang on" under such circumstances. Just as the saying "I was lucky, thank God" resounded through our informants' narratives about illegally crossing the U.S.–Mexico border, signaling the frightful contingencies and the sense of helplessness that passages through the zones of illegality entailed, this term, *aguantar*, turned up repeatedly throughout the interview segments dealing with working conditions at the slaughterhouse and suggested a similar sense of resignation in the face of insuperable forces of fate.

2. Melquíades Pereyra, interview by author and Paola Vizcaíno Suárez, Walla Walla, Washington, May 28, 2002. All further references to Melquíades Pereyra in this chapter derive from this interview.

3. For a more detailed discussion of these changes in meatpacking, see Broadway 1995, 18–19, 25–30; Brueggemann and Brown 2003, 333–35; Craypo 1994, 66; Fink 1998, 51–59; and Stull and Broadway 1995, 67–68.

4. For example, wages dropped from $9.50 to $5.80 an hour when IBP bought an Iowa pork plant from Oscar Mayer in 1988 and reopened it (as a nonunionized plant) in 1989, after Oscar Mayer had already been cutting wages for several years (Fink 1998, 60–66). Overall, meatpackers' wages dropped from 44 percent to 28 percent of the value added in manufacturing between 1963 and 1992 (Fink 1998, 65; see also Broadway 1995, 24–25). Higher profit rates for the industry materialized not only through its savings in labor costs but also because IBP revolutionized the product lines of the large packing companies, in particular by expanding to include the preparation of consumer-ready meat products for supermarket display cases (Broadway 1995, 19; Brueggemann and Brown 2003, 333–44; Schlosser 2002, 154).

5. Rogelio Salazar, interview by author and Paola Vizcaíno Suárez, Pasco, Washington, June 16, 2002. All further references to Rogelio Salazar in this chapter derive from this interview.

6. Elvira Méndez, interview by author and Paola Vizcaíno Suárez, Pasco, Washington, July 19, 2002.

7. Ibid.

8. Pedro Ruiz, interview by author and Paola Vizcaíno Suárez, Pasco, Washington, October 6, 2002. All further references to Pedro Ruiz in this

chapter derive from this interview. Deborah Fink speaks to a similar situation at the Iowa IBP plant where she worked and conducted her research. Initially assigned to trim fat off pork bellies, Fink was abruptly transferred to janitorial duties, then ordered to split her time between cleaning and work with a mechanical knife, then put on duty making boxes, then finally told to work full time as a janitor (1998, 15–31).

9. Exact figures about turnover at Tyson/IBP in Pasco and other meatpacking facilities are not publicly available, and the companies have generally stymied researchers' efforts to ascertain these numbers (Compa 2005, 108n). Federal population statistics, however, have shown the meat industry as a whole to have higher turnover rates than any other industry (Stull and Broadway 1995, 69). Studies of specific plants in the late 1980s showed turnover figures consistent with or surpassing Pereyra's estimate for the Tyson/IBP facility, documenting a monthly turnover rate of 6 to 8 percent at five Kansas beef plants and an annual turnover rate of "between 200 and 400 percent at the John Morrell plant in Sioux Falls, South Dakota" (Stull and Broadway 1995, 69). The extremely high injury rates in the industry, which the Pasco plant vastly exceeded, along with supporting observations by the workers we interviewed, strongly suggest that turnover at the slaughterhouse in Pasco was massive.

10. Ramona Díaz, interview by author and Paola Vizcaíno Suárez, Pasco, Washington, June 20, 2002. All further references to Ramona Díaz in this chapter derive from this interview.

11. Diego Ortega, interview by author and Paola Vizcaíno Suárez, Pasco, Washington, September 28, 2002. All further references to Diego Ortega in this chapter derive from this interview. Other workers stressed that this problem of dull blades and the need for workers to use "pure force," thereby endangering their health, was magnified by the meat often being completely or partially frozen (E. Méndez, July 19, 2002; Francisco González, interview by author and Paola Vizcaíno Suárez, Walla Walla, Washington, July 17, 2002. All further references to Francisco González in this chapter derive from this interview.)

12. Rafael Mendoza, interview by author and Paola Vizcaíno Suárez, Walla Walla, Washington, July 8, 2002; Ignacio Ramos, interview by author and Paola Vizcaíno Suárez, Walla Walla, Washington, July 23, 2002.

13. Felipe Ortiz, interview by author and Paola Vizcaíno Suárez, Pasco, Washington, September 28, 2002. All further references to Felipe Ortiz in this chapter derive from this interview.

14. Alejandro Méndez, interview by author and Paola Vizcaíno Suárez, Pasco, Washington, July 2, 2002. Here Méndez's words closely track Deborah Fink's disturbing account of how, after beginning work with a mechanical knife, her hand alternated between hurting "fiercely" and going numb: "I repeatedly awakened in the night with my hand clenched in a tight, painful knot and had to use my left hand to straighten the fingers one by one" (1998, 25).

15. A. Méndez, July 2, 2002. Méndez's narrative, again, echoes Fink's story of being overwhelmed by pain and fatigue at IBP and of being unable to read or take notes at the day's end because sleep would overcome her (1998, 37).

16. Juanita Castillo, interview by author and Paola Vizcaíno Suárez, Pasco, Washington, June 8, 2002.

17. Similarly, Fink describes how her supervisors routinely shouted at her at the IBP plant in Iowa. In a typical incident, she was told to trim pork bellies closer but was unable to do so without slowing down, at which point her manager "blew up": "He stood over me throwing meat and yelling, 'Speed! Speed! You can't stand here all day!'" (1998, 28). She also recalls feeling "the uncomfortable pounding in my chest and stomach" when two supervisors berated a coworker for working too slowly, shouting in the man's face with a "vicious" fury (22).

18. Several workers mentioned that the problem of supervisor abuse had diminished somewhat since the union's mobilization. (Esteban Múñoz, interview by author and Paola Vizcaíno Suárez, Pasco, Washington, June 9, 2002; Díaz, June 20, 2002; Isidro Gómez, interview by author and Paola Vizcaíno Suárez, Pasco, Washington, July 21, 2002. All further references to Esteban Múñoz and Isidro Gómez in this chapter derive from these interviews.) Overall, however, the interviews indicated that the issue had hardly been fully resolved.

19. Besides being shockingly degrading, these comments about workers being "disposable" also indicate how the increased automation of meatpacking through the "IBP revolution" might have led to the waning of discipline rather than its intensification. The deskilling of job descriptions that these transformations accomplished meant that workers became more replaceable (Schlosser 2002, 151). There was thus less of a material basis in the labor process for individual workers to remain attached to particular jobs or for the company to care about whether a worker developed specialized attachments, attitudes, and abilities.

20. Castillo, June 8, 2002.

21. Ibid.

22. Esperanza Soto, interview by author and Paola Vizcaíno Suárez, Pasco, Washington, November 2, 2002. Men, too, suffered from this form of abusive supervision. Francisco González explained how managers would give out disciplinary tickets (demerits) to workers who left the line to go to the bathroom without asking permission, even if a supervisor was nowhere in sight.

23. Soto, November 2, 2002.

24. Fink likewise notes that IBP systematically broke the extensive list of rules that it drummed into workers at their orientations. Ironically, many of the rules codified the company's right to exercise arbitrary power over workers, for example, by searching workers' bodies or lockers or demanding that employees submit to drug tests (Fink 1998, 12–16).

25. Another reporter who interviewed a worker at the Tyson/IBP beef plant in Amarillo, Texas, was told that over eight years, chain speed had risen

from 380 to 400 animals per hour, while staffing had decreased (Olsson 2002, 14).

26. In 2001, Mark Brenner, a political economist with the Political Economy Research Institute (PERI) of the University of Massachusetts, conducted a rigorous survey of the workers at the Tyson/IBP plant in Pasco. The survey dealt with health and safety, food safety, and humane slaughter conditions in the plant. Four hundred seventy-nine survey interviews were completed over an eight-month period, and the results are representative of the conditions facing the entire workforce of roughly fifteen hundred individuals. To complement the survey data, in October 2002, a group of Whitman College students under my supervision conducted follow-up interviews with twenty-two workers to enhance the qualitative aspect of this research. The questions were open-ended and geared toward obtaining workers' personal stories about any injuries they had suffered, any medical treatment they had received for such injuries, and their experiences on light duty. Most interviews were conducted in Spanish with the help of trained interpreters. Subsequently, Brenner and I issued a combined report through the PERI Web site, and the analysis in that report informs this chapter.

27. Human Rights Watch also reports that injury problems stemming from dull blades, high line speeds, and inadequate training are features of the meatpacking industry in general (Compa 2005, 36, 43–44).

28. Héctor Fernández, interview by author and Paola Vizcaíno Suárez, Pasco, Washington, September 28, 2002. All further references to Héctor Fernández in this chapter derive from this interview.

29. E. Méndez, July 19, 2002.

30. Ibid.

31. Jorge Hernández, interview by author and Paola Vizcaíno Suárez, Pasco, Washington, November 2, 2002. All further references to Jorge Hernández in this chapter derive from this interview. Esperanza Soto elaborated on this problem when she recounted how her own health problems had developed because she was perpetually called on to substitute for injured colleagues: "A little while ago, I would work in whatever job they put me in. So I knew how to do a lot of jobs. If someone were missing, I would go do that job. So one day I couldn't do it anymore: my hands were really swollen. And then blisters on my fingers broke open and fluid was coming out, because my hands were so swollen. So I told my supervisor. He told me: 'I'm going to take you to the infirmary.' He took me. Then, the nurse said that what I had was the flu! Can you believe it? I knew very well what it was that I had: an injury from doing jobs . . . that weren't my jobs, and I wasn't accustomed to doing them." (Esperanza Soto, interview by Paola Vizcaíno Suárez, Pasco, Washington, October 8, 2002.)

32. Gloria Ruiz, interview by author and Paola Vizcaíno Suárez, Pasco, Washington, October 6, 2002. All further references to Gloria Ruiz in this chapter derive from this interview.

33. Again, the resonances with Fink's account of IBP's Perry, Iowa, pork plant are palpable. "'You don't go to lunch until this place gets cleaned up!'"

Fink's supervisor yelled at her toward the end of her first morning doing janitorial work at the plant (1998, 16).

34. Soto, November 2, 2002.

35. See Gramsci's discussion of this issue in the *Prison Notebooks* (1971, 277–318).

36. Noted Francisco González, in parallel fashion: "Supposedly they pay you by the hour, but when you're on the job, you do the work as if you were on a contract."

37. Castillo, June 8, 2002; Díaz, June 20, 2002; Gómez, July 21, 2002.

38. Federal statistics have long shown meatpacking to be the most dangerous job in the country in the era that dawned with IBP's revolutionizing of the industry. Occupational injury and illness rates for meatpacking workers, as measured by official OSHA data, increased by about 33 percent (from 31.2 to 42.4 per 100 workers) between 1975 and 1990 (Broadway 1995, 21). These figures appear far higher than the more recent numbers because the definitions of the injuries and illnesses reported and counted by OSHA have changed. What the Bureau of Labor Statistics now calls the "incidence rate of nonfatal occupational injuries and illnesses" registered, in 2006, at 12.5 per 100 workers for animal slaughtering, 9.8 for meat processed from carcasses, and 9.9 for rendering and meat by-product processing; yet these figures were still markedly higher than those for virtually all other industrial occupations (U.S. Department of Labor 2006). Tyson, IBP, and other major meat producers typically have claimed that they take occupational safety and health very seriously, that they have developed innovative plans for decreasing worker injury rates, and that they have reduced job-related health and safety problems in the industry. Nevertheless, IBP garnered national attention in 1987 for health and safety record-keeping violations at its Dakota City, Nebraska, plant, when congressional hearings were held on the problem in the industry. Subsequently, OSHA imposed a multimillion dollar fine on IBP, but then reduced it to under $1 million after IBP agreed to reengineer the Dakota City plant and to institute an ergonomics education program for workers and managers at all its facilities (Stull and Broadway 1995, 66). The revenues from the fine then funded a study of the meat industry by the National Institute of Occupational Safety and Health (NIOSH), and IBP also funded another study of ergonomics that was conducted jointly with the United Food and Commercial Workers (UFCW) union. IBP officials later claimed to have "significantly reduced the frequency and severity of various injuries and illnesses" by technically redesigning difficult jobs and by implementing its "employee ergonomics training and medical management program" (Smith 1993, 34). The business magazine *Occupational Hazards* (1996, 103) also celebrated what it termed the "decline in on-the-job injuries and illnesses" and the "dramatic reduction in cumulative trauma disorder (CTD) rates" in the meatpacking industry between 1991 and 1996. Yet federal statistics still show that no other occupation in the country is more dangerous than meatpacking (U.S. Department of Labor 2006). At Tyson/IBP in Pasco, from 1996 to 2003, the general injury rates, the rates of

serious worker injury requiring missed workdays, and the proportion of the former made up by the latter all increased significantly (Apostolidis and Brenner 2005). Moreover, these official figures do not reflect the myriad barriers to reporting such as those described by the workers we interviewed. In addition, according to union officials at the Pasco plant, IBP had neglected to follow the core recommendation in the NIOSH study: institutionalizing the regular participation of workers in identifying and evaluating problems and in determining programs to address them (U.S. Department of Health and Human Services 1995). The company had nullified genuine worker participation, union organizers told me, by adding management-appointed worker representatives to the plant health and safety committee to match the number of representatives sent by the union, thus ensuring that the managers on the committee would retain control over its recommendations.

39. The large discrepancy between the OSHA data and the survey figures may be due to several factors. The survey question was phrased in a way that included a broader range of ailments than those counted by OSHA; and injured workers may have been more motivated than other workers to fill out the survey. Still, the researcher retrieved completed surveys from about 35 percent of the workforce, well above the standard threshold for survey validity, and used random sampling techniques, thus ensuring the representative nature of the results (Apostolidis and Brenner 2005). A much more likely factor behind the disparity in figures was that by 2002, the Bush administration had implemented new OSHA rules that no longer required reporting of the most common serious injuries among meatpacking workers: musculoskeletal disorders (MSDs) related to ergonomic issues such as repetitive motions, excessively heavy lifting, and awkward body positions (Compa 2005, 55–56). The workers we interviewed frequently mentioned such injuries, but they would not have been included in the 2002 OSHA data. Finally, given supervisors' frequent resistance to sending workers to the infirmary, the poor quality of care the workers reported receiving, and the problems with light duty—issues I explore in detail later in this chapter—it is no surprise that official OSHA figures widely diverge from the survey results regarding the frequency of worker injuries.

40. Donald D. Stull and Michael J. Broadway report: "The incidence of repeated trauma disorder among meatpacking workers increased by nearly 300 percent between 1979 and 1986. By 1986, the rate of repeated trauma disorder for meatpacking workers was 479/10,000 full-time workers, while the comparable rate for manufacturing workers was just 22/10,000" (1995, 64).

41. Castillo, June 8, 2002.

42. Human Rights Watch confirms that "slipping and falling in meat and poultry plants' wet conditions are another commonplace hazard and source of injury" (Compa 2005, 41). Still other precipitants of health and safety problems, apparently less routine but still troublesome and adding to the general picture of a workplace rife with health and safety hazards, emerged in our

interviews. Pedro Ruiz spoke of injuring himself from being forced to use faulty, broken equipment for a period of several weeks. Manuel Guzmán described how, as Felipe Ortiz had also noted, the heat in the rendering department not infrequently rose above 125 degrees. (Manuel Guzmán, interview by author and Paola Vizcaíno Suárez, Pasco, Washington, July 19, 2002. All further references to Manuel Guzmán in this chapter derive from this interview.) Rogelio Salazar did not say why he was kicked twice in the face by cows in the slaughter area, but a special probe of humane slaughter violations in the meatpacking industry by the *Washington Post* documented that high production speeds sometimes cause animals to make it past the killing zone alive. The story led off with excerpts from an interview with Salazar that the author framed as follows: "The cattle were supposed to be dead before they got to Salazar. But too often they weren't. 'They blink. They make noises,' he said softly. 'The head moves, the eyes are wide and looking around.' Still Salazar would cut. On bad days, he says, dozens of animals reached his station clearly alive and conscious. Some would survive as far as the tail cutter, the belly ripper, the hide puller. 'They die,' said Salazar, 'piece by piece'" (Warrick 2001, A1).

43. On the differences in cost and effectiveness between PPDs and engineering changes to the workplace, see my discussion of Charles Noble's (1986) analysis of the political economy of occupational safety and health policy in the last section of this chapter.

44. I discuss the significance of this major lawsuit, *IBP, Inc. v. Alvarez, 543 U.S. 1144* (2005), which went all the way to the U.S. Supreme Court, in greater detail in chapter 5.

45. A petition submitted to the U.S. Secretary of Labor in 2003 by a coalition of labor unions and the Congressional Hispanic Caucus charged that meat companies also routinely force workers to pay for their own PPDs, with the consequence that workers often rely on their equipment "beyond its useful life, putting themselves at risk of serious injury" (Nash 2003, 65). The American Meat Institute (AMI), the main trade association for the industry, simply denied these assertions and refused to testify at OSHA's public hearings on the issue. The Tyson/IBP workers we interviewed did not mention this as a problem, but the trend in the industry and the other health and safety issues at the Pasco facility suggest that further investigation of this matter at the Pasco plant would be advisable.

46. Over 20 percent of the workers surveyed did not even report their injuries, often because they rightly anticipated that they would be scolded and blamed for hurting themselves (Apostolidis and Brenner 2005).

47. Esperanza Soto, interview by Paola Vizcaíno Suárez, Pasco, Washington, October 8, 2002.

48. Rosa Vásquez, interview by author and Paola Vizcaíno Suárez, Pasco, Washington, October 6, 2002. All further references to Rosa Vásquez in this chapter derive from this interview.

49. Alejandro Méndez, interview by Paola Vizcaíno Suárez, Pasco, Washington, October 8, 2002. Francisco González likewise confirmed the company's

policy of giving the workers a steak, pizza, or hamburger dinner "if in the line, during two months, you don't have any accident."

50. This deficit of tracking and studying the health and safety problem at the plant had another, complementary aspect. Not only did supervisors on the shop floor impede the referral of workers to the infirmary and the collection of data there, but in addition, specialists who might have evaluated the problems at the workstations either were kept out of these areas, as Juanita Castillo (June 8, 2002) told us, or were misled as to what was happening there. Rogelio Salazar described an instance of the latter type: "Sometimes when outside government inspectors, or other people from outside, were going to come check the jobs, they told lies to the doctor: 'No, well, we're going to have them do this kind of job that is really easy.' And since the doctor wasn't familiar with the jobs, he'd say: 'Well, that's fine, go ahead and have them do that.'"

51. Juanita Castillo, interview by Meredith Richardson and Anna Markee, Pasco, Washington, October 8, 2002.

52. Castillo, June 8, 2002.

53. Soto, October 8, 2002. On the general prevalence of infections and other maladies related to "sullied work conditions" workers encounter as they "come into contact with blood, grease, animal feces, ingesta (food from the animal's digestive system), and other detritus from the animals they slaughter," see Compa (2005, 40–41).

54. E. Méndez, July 19, 2002. The following workers all made similar comments: Guadalupe Flores ("They just gave me some ibuprofen pills; they told me 'take them and go back to your job'"); Rosa Vásquez ("They said, 'there's not much we can do.' [They gave me] the pills they give you for inflammation, that ibuprofen—what they give everyone"); Gloria Ruiz (who said the nurse had given her "a big pile of ibuprofen"); and, most bluntly, Francisco González ("When we get hurt, they just give us fucking pills"). (Guadalupe Flores, interview by author and Paola Vizcaíno Suárez, Pasco, Washington, November 9, 2002. All further references to Guadalupe Flores in this chapter derive from this interview).

55. Geraldo Morales, interview by Meredith Johnson and Meghan Bowen, Pasco, Washington, October 8, 2002.

56. E. Méndez, July 19, 2002.

57. Federico Reyes, interview by Donan Everett and Dustin Lambro, Pasco, Washington, October 8, 2002; Agustín Peña, interview by Benjamin Braus and Samantha Howell, Pasco, Washington, October 8, 2002. All further references to Agustín Peña in this chapter derive from this interview.

58. A. Méndez, October 8, 2002.

59. A. Méndez, July 2, 2002.

60. Manuel Guzmán also confirmed that the company refused to provide workers with time off, travel expenses, or fee coverage for their visits to see this other doctor regarding job-related injuries and health problems.

61. E. Méndez, July 19, 2002; Soto, October 8, 2002.

62. E. Méndez, July 19, 2002.

63. Castillo, June 8, 2002.

64. E. Méndez, July 19, 2002; Elvira Méndez, interview by Eric Dottarar and Carrie Gage, Pasco, Washington, October 8, 2002; Felicia Domínguez, interview by Sarah Sitts, Pasco, Washington, October 8, 2002. All further references to Felicia Domínguez in this chapter derive from this interview.

65. E. Méndez, July 19, 2002.

66. Castillo, June 8, 2002; G. Ruiz, October 6, 2002; R. Vásquez, October 6, 2002; A. Méndez, October 8, 2002.

67. Castillo, June 8, 2002; E. Méndez, July 19, 2002.

68. E. Méndez, July 19, 2002.

69. A. Méndez, October 8, 2002.

70. A. Méndez, July 2, 2002.

71. Agustín Peña confirmed that he had seen fellow workers quit, in particular, when their light-duty assignments exacerbated the injuries and elevated the pain that had led to the temporary work reassignment in the first place.

72. Supervisors treat you badly when you're injured and on light duty, Gloria Ruiz echoed, because "really you're just a bother to them—like you're of no use to them anymore for what they want you to do—the work."

73. See Schlosser (2002, 217–18, 221) for a discussion of the meat industry's reliance on antibiotics and its experimentation with irradiation to counter risks of disease and contamination in the meat supply. The conjunction between production and consumption in the slaughterhouse enacted the biopolitical, hierarchical subdivision of the species in still another tangible way insofar as these workers produced meat products that were graded according to quality and destined to be eaten by different constituencies. It was the workers themselves who ended up most regularly patronizing McDonald's and the other fast-food chains where the hamburger went or buying the cheap cuts at Walmart (these corporations being among Tyson's largest customers [Schlosser 2002, 2004]), thus reinforcing their exposure to ill health and earlier death.

74. A. Méndez, July 2, 2002; Soto, November 2, 2002.

75. Nina Garza, similarly, took exception with her supervisor's attempt to blame her for getting injured by not paying attention when a coworker knocked her unconscious by mistakenly hitting her in the face with a large piece of meat he was throwing onto a conveyor belt. (Nina Garza, interview by author and Paola Vizcaíno Suárez, Pasco, Washington, November 9, 2002. All further references to Nina Garza in this chapter derive from this interview.)

76. Gilberto Rivera, interview by author and Paola Vizcaíno Suárez, Pasco, Washington, November 9, 2002. All further references to Gilberto Rivera in this chapter derive from this interview.

77. One could argue that the kinds of self-regulating behavior exhibited by Rivera were the result of institutional disciplines rather than workers' informally developed microtechniques, because according to Francisco González, the company conducted drug tests on newly hired workers and had security guards routinely check workers' lunch boxes and perform random body (even

strip) searches when workers arrived for their shifts. However, it is also quite possible that here again we see the theme of company procedures that only superficially appear to perform intensive normalization while in effect merely serving to intimidate workers into compliance. González emphasized that many workers used alcohol on the job, and this reaffirms my general point, with respect to Rivera's comments, about how workers used self-medication as a micropractice of bodily regulation. Moreover, it was clear from what Rivera said that despite the company's antidrug efforts, some workers obviously found ways to medicate themselves with illegal substances.

78. One interesting variation on such confrontations that occurred specifically in the work environment was the unmasking of supervisors' power as repressive when the company tried to dissimulate itself as a "team" on which all workers were in some sense equally valued players. Francisco González told us how he had done this when managers called him into their office one day to present him with a "diploma" recognizing his having completed ten years as an IBP employee. Said González: "You know what I did with the certificate that they gave me? [Very proudly.] I threw it in the trash. And one of those fuckers from the company saw me; he told me: 'Take that out of the trash.' 'No, that fucking thing is worthless to me,' I told him."

79. At the same time, however, Elvira Méndez's (July 19, 2002) fight with the Asian coworker she encountered after her bid job transfer, when the two literally came to blows, illustrated how the lateral conflicts among workers could also take on an explicitly racial cast.

80. Fink's account of worker relations at IBP in Iowa similarly indicates a variety of routines that workers had evolved to spread knowledge about techniques for diminishing the likelihood of supervisor abuse and avoiding injuries (1998, 31–36).

5. ¡Nosotros Somos la Unión!

1. See also Karen Olsson's story in *The Nation* (2002) on health and safety problems and worker protest in the meatpacking industry, which includes interviews with Tyson/IBP workers and union activists in Pasco, including Maria Martinez and Melquíades Pereyra.

2. For a detailed history of the origins and evolution of TDU, which is the longest-running movement within a major U.S. union advocating rank-and-file democracy, see La Botz (1990).

3. Diego Ortega, interview by author and Paola Vizcaíno Suárez, Pasco, Washington, September 28, 2002. All further references to Diego Ortega in this chapter derive from this interview.

4. Ortega further underscored this pretentious sense that he singlehandedly roused the workers to start fighting the old guard and the company when he told us how "They used to call me *el loco* [the crazy guy]. . . . They called me César Chávez the second, 'Junior.' Because they said that I was crazy, that there would never be any changes there or anything like that."

5. Along with a coworker, she had tried to organize the workers to demand a fair contract in 1992, operating outside normal union channels, which were dominated by the Anglo old guard. After this collaborator betrayed Martinez by telling her to urge the workers to support the contract that union officers had negotiated, and then disparaging the contract behind her back (thus making her look like a "sellout"), Martinez vowed she "would never get involved again." (Maria Martinez, interview by author and Paola Vizcaíno Suárez, Walla Walla, Washington, December 19, 2002. All further quotations from Maria Martinez in this chapter derive from this interview.)

6. My remarks about the campaign to change the bylaws of Local 556 also derive from my interview with David Mark, an attorney for the Local in the case *IBP, Inc. v. Alvarez,* Detroit, Michigan, October 26, 2003, as well as from Maria Martinez's presentations on several panels at the TDU Rank & File Convention, October 24–26, Detroit, Michigan.

7. Ortega's repeated use of the term *patrón* here and elsewhere to describe the company is worth contemplating. In an influential study of the conditions for successful union organizing among undocumented workers, Héctor L. Delgado notes the importance of overcoming workers' attachments to a "boss" *[patrón]* who serves as a "father figure," a "benefactor," and even a "source of inspiration" to them (1993, 24–25, 91–96). Such sentiments, Delgado argues, tend to run especially strong in small companies (17); and indeed, Ortega stressed how his previous employers on family-owned ranches and farms had given him this sort of benevolently paternalistic treatment. Moreover, it would be understandable to hear a Mexican immigrant from a rural location speaking in this way about even a larger employer like IBP, since small businesses are more common sources of employment for wage workers in rural Mexico than in the cities. Coming from a Mexico City urbanite like Ortega, however, and used in reference to a mammoth corporation such as IBP, the term sounded off-key. By using it, Ortega may have been suggesting his hope that the company would come to behave in the manner of the responsible *patrón* and that the workers, correspondingly, should approach the company with appropriate deference.

8. The document "Organizing to Win Strong Contracts" distributed at the TDU Annual Convention in Detroit explains: "A traditional view of bargaining puts almost all of the focus on what happens at the bargaining table. . . . This approach stresses the negotiating skill of union leaders and specialists. . . . Contract campaigns win better contracts by getting the whole workforce involved in the fight for a good contract. . . . Members take advantage of the expertise of different specialists—but the contract campaign is run by rank-and-file coordinators and campaign volunteers" (Teamsters for a Democratic Union 2003, 2–3).

9. Alejandro Méndez, interview by author and Paola Vizcaíno Suárez, Pasco, Washington, July 2, 2002. All further references to Alejandro Méndez in this chapter derive from this interview.

10. Rogelio Salazar, interview by author and Paola Vizcaíno Suárez, Pasco, Washington, June 16, 2002. All further references to Rogelio Salazar in this chapter derive from this interview.

11. Esperanza Soto, interview by author and Paola Vizcaíno Suárez, Pasco, Washington, November 2, 2002. All further references to Esperanza Soto in this chapter derive from this interview.

12. This history of the chain grinding on even when a worker got injured repeated itself in a particularly gruesome way just a few months after Martinez and I held this interview, when a young man from Mexico working in the slaughter section had most of his arm cut off by a giant mechanical scissors apparatus—and the chain kept going.

13. Esteban Múñoz, interview by author and Paola Vizcaíno Suárez, Pasco, Washington, June 9, 2002. All further references to Esteban Múñoz in this chapter derive from this interview.

14. Martinez essentially told the story of the walkout in the same way that Alejandro Méndez did, except that the language he used was somewhat more evocative and specific. Interestingly, though, when Martinez spoke about the moment when "the chain stopped" and the ensuing several hours, she added that at first it was not clear to her and others who had left the production line whether more workers would follow suit. "It was scary," she said candidly, until word traveled to other areas of the factory and it became evident that a massive protest was occurring.

15. Ramona Díaz, interview by author and Paola Vizcaíno Suárez, Pasco, Washington, June 20, 2002. All further references to Ramona Díaz in this chapter derive from this interview. Juanita Castillo, in turn, told us how she had been one of the others who had taken care of distributing the donations of food the strikers received from local businesses. (Interview by author and Paola Vizcaíno Suárez, Pasco, Washington, June 8, 2002. All further references to Juanita Castillo in this chapter derive from this interview.)

16. Héctor Fernández, interview by author and Paola Vizcaíno Suárez, Pasco, Washington, September 28, 2002. All further references to Héctor Fernández in this chapter derive from this interview.

17. Rosa Vásquez, interview by author and Paola Vizcaíno Suárez, Pasco, Washington, October 6, 2002. All further references to Rosa Vásquez in this chapter derive from this interview.

18. David Levin, Teamsters for a Democratic Union, personal communication with author, November 20, 2005.

19. Pedro Ruiz, interview by author and Paola Vizcaíno Suárez, Pasco, Washington, October 6, 2002. All further references to Pedro Ruiz in this chapter derive from this interview.

20. Gloria Ruiz, interview with author and Paola Vizcaíno Suárez, Pasco, Washington, October 6, 2002.

21. P. Ruiz, October 6, 2002; Soto, November 2, 2002; Martinez, December 19, 2002.

22. Manuel Guzmán, interview by author and Paola Vizcaíno Suárez, Pasco, Washington, July 19, 2002. All further references to Manuel Guzmán

in this chapter derive from this interview. Given Guzmán's subsequent leadership in the counterreform contingent, as the candidate for Maria Martinez's principal officer position in the 2002 elections and as a key organizer in the 2004 union decertification petition drive (see conclusion), it is significant that unlike the great majority of workers whose stories we heard—but like Martinez—Guzmán was a U.S.-born Mexican American. This parallel between Guzmán and Martinez suggests the desirability of analyzing the particular role of Mexican American leaders in Mexican immigrant labor organizing today, as did leadership difficulties that plagued another recent TDU-inspired rank-and-file movement among immigrant meatpackers at a Cargill/Excel plant in Fort Morgan, Colorado, who lacked any notable, bilingual Mexican American leadership. The experience of Local 556 does not permit useful generalizations in this regard, however, because Guzmán and Martinez shared little else beyond an ability to speak English; and the distinctive characteristics of Martinez's rare form of leadership went far beyond bilingualism (or cultural capital), including oratorical skill, tactical sense, and prodigious abilities for motivating people interpersonally.

23. Ignacio Ramos, interview by author and Paola Vizcaíno Suárez, Walla Walla, Washington, July 23, 2002. All further references to Ignacio Ramos in this chapter derive from this interview. Ramos and Rafael Mendoza, both of whom felt alienated from the rank-and-file movement, seemed not to fully appreciate the multiethnic dimensions of the strike force, characterizing it mainly as a movement among Mexicans. (Rafael Mendoza, interview by author and Paola Vizcaíno Suárez, Walla Walla, Washington, July 8, 2002. All further references to Rafael Mendoza in this chapter derive from this interview.) At the same time, other workers' comments suggested that despite the interethnic aspects of the undertaking, it had a distinctly Mexican cultural feeling. Juanita Castillo evoked an atmosphere on the picket line that was occasionally festive in a way that was nourished both by the thrill of seeing so many workers hanging together as well as the food donated by local Mexican businesses: "Now that we were outside, we had some fun, too, you know. Because we saw, looking at all the people, that we were united. . . . Were we hungry? No, because we ate and got really fat [laughing as she speaks]. They brought us food, sodas, tortillas, menudo."

24. In particular, Juanita Castillo told us, the publisher of a free weekly Spanish newspaper widely distributed in eastern Washington started spreading rumors that Martinez was simply out to line her own pockets by attempting to gain leadership of the union.

25. P. Ruiz, comment during interview with G. Ruiz, October 6, 2002.

26. Interview with David Mark, October 26, 2003.

27. David Levin, Teamsters for a Democratic Union, personal communication with author, November 20, 2005.

28. In the Mexican and Mexican American vernacular common among people in this region of the northwest, I have found that the Anglicized term *unión* is vastly preferred to the word *sindicato* to refer to a labor union.

29. At Teamsters Local 556, the secretary-treasurer was the principal officer, with a higher rank than the president, who after the takeover was Melquíades Pereyra.

30. Elvira Méndez, interview by author and Paola Vizcaíno Suárez, Pasco, Washington, July 19, 2002. All further references to Elvira Méndez in this chapter derive from this interview.

31. Méndez contrasted her willingness to fight for herself with the lack of initiative displayed by a coworker who faced similar problems with the company. Seeing that Martinez had been assisting Méndez, this fellow worker had asked the former for help fighting the company's decision to lay her off. But when Martinez advised her to write several letters and forward them to her so she could translate them, file an appeal, and find her an attorney, the coworker "never did anything" because she thought "the union" should do all the work for her.

32. Aside from Martinez and Guzmán, Múñoz was the one other important activist in the conflict who was a U.S.-born Mexican American.

33. Nina Garza, interview by author and Paola Vizcaíno Suárez, Pasco, Washington, November 9, 2002.

34. Jorge Hernández, interview by author and Paola Vizcaíno Suárez, Pasco, Washington, November 2, 2002.

35. A similar rhetorical tendency appeared in our interview with Ignacio Ramos, who sympathized with Ortega's faction even though he was not an active participant and who disparaged the activists allied with Maria Martinez for behaving like politicians—that is, for stirring up controversy out of an opportunistic desire to reap personal gain by securing union posts. Like Ortega, Ramos favored a brand of unionism cleansed of messy ideological conflict. He opined that when union reformers criticized workers who had refused to participate in the protest, following the end of the strike, the former were unjustified in doing so because it had been the latter's "right" to stay on the job if they wished.

36. Rafael Mendoza, who had not participated in the strike but also was not a partisan of Ortega's group, evinced a similar disregard for ordinary workers' capacities to act on their own behalf. He contemptuously told us that "70 to 80 percent of the people" at the plant had "no education at all" and were "fine for working" but lacked the ability to engage in organized political endeavors.

37. Guzmán similarly made a point of telling us that he personally had submitted multiple grievances for himself and for others but that union representatives had never processed the forms.

38. Guadalupe Flores, interview by author and Paola Vizcaíno Suárez, Pasco, Washington, November 9, 2002. All further references to Guadalupe Flores in this chapter derive from this interview.

39. Cynthia L. Estlund points out that the federal judiciary also consistently has preempted state and local efforts to expand union rights. Federal courts have prevented the states both from regulating activities that are clearly unregulated by the Wagner Act, such as the hiring of permanent striker

replacements, and from furnishing extra remedies in relation to conduct prohibited by the act so as to give the deterrent aspect of the act more bite (Estlund 2002, 1569–79).

40. As Schiller points out, following this logic, the courts have even gone so far as to allow prohibitions on spending union dues to build new union halls or to establish union savings and loan associations (1999, 68–69).

41. Francisco González, interview by author and Paola Vizcaíno Suárez, Walla Walla, Washington, July 17, 2002.

42. Local 556 organizers and their community allies spearheaded a rally in a public park in Pasco, Washington, for the bus riders from Portland and Seattle on their way to the East Coast, in conjunction with a local chapter of the Service Employees International Union (SEIU), as well as an overnight stay in supporters' homes and a free community breakfast at a Catholic church in Walla Walla, Washington. See the introduction for a more detailed discussion of the IWFR.

43. One such step was Local 556's activists' and supporters' collaboration in the IWFR with the Piñeros y Campesinos Unidos del Noroeste (PCUN; United Northwest Tree Planters and Farm Workers, the main farmworkers' union in Oregon). See conclusion for further discussion of this organization and the immigrants' justice network it spearheads.

44. The event took place at the Laborers' Union Hall in Pasco, Washington, on January 20, 2002.

45. On the allegations of inhumane treatment of animals at Tyson/IBP, confirmed by Tyson/IBP employee and Local 556 activist Rogelio Salazar, see Warrick (2001).

46. Hence the McCain-Kennedy immigration reform bill, which imposed fines on undocumented immigrants but provided a legalization process, failed to muster a majority in Congress. Nor, at this writing, has sufficient support materialized for the DREAM Act, which would address the problem of undocumented students achieving highly in school but then being blocked from pursuing a career in the United States by the lack of any opportunity to legalize. Meanwhile, prior to the 2008 elections, a bevy of restrictionist bills were introduced in Congress by Republicans and Democrats alike calling for reforms ranging from imposing large fines on employers who do not join electronic employee immigration status verification networks to declaring English the official language of the United States (Mexican American Legal Defense and Education Fund 2008).

Conclusion

1. This led Martinez to sue for libel in a case that the publisher eventually settled out of court.

2. Ultimately, the Local accused Tyson of twenty-two separate violations of federal labor law in the decertification process, and the NLRB launched an investigation of the company's actions in this regard (Lilley 2005).

3. A potentially influential report existed, which I had coauthored with a University of Massachusetts economist and which I partly discuss in chapter 4, that originally linked occupational health and safety problems to food safety issues and the treatment of animals at the plant, based on worker surveys and interviews. Union organizers ultimately decided it would be most prudent just to release the portion on occupational safety and health hazards.

4. In complementary terms supplied by feminist theorist Linda Zerilli (2005, 94), one might also argue that the more deeply enmeshed the union's activism became in normative, legal processes, the more they lost their original connection to the "politically significant relationships" that had animated the workers' extralegal mobilization in the wildcat protest. During the strike, Zerilli's distinctive conception of such relations would suggest, the workers had forged "practices of political freedom" (98) for themselves in a sphere of action not governed by preexisting, institutionally sanctioned routines of engagement.

5. According to Johnston, Local 890 and the Citizenship Project had completed over ten thousand new citizenship applications and recruited over one thousand community volunteers by 2004 (2004b, 89). In addition, the union successfully waged a twenty-seven-month strike against Basic Vegetable Products, a midsized company that ConAgra bought during this labor conflict. Johnston's account of the strike suggests that despite interesting parallels to the Tyson/IBP campaigns, such as the use of legalist strategies to contest an NLRB decertification process in the aftermath of a major business acquisition, key differences contributed to the California workers' victory. The latter especially included their much deeper support in the local community, relative to Local 556, which in turn reflected the Citizenship Project's efforts (Johnston 2004a).

6. I am grateful to Anna Marie Smith for noting that the system of implicit biopolitics I conceptualize here does not involve a strong connection to specifically reproductive processes. In this sense, the procedures at issue contrast instructively with the "neoeugenic" effects that Smith finds result from public welfare and child support enforcement programs in the United States, which she argues function "in tandem with the already harsh labor market, to discourage childbirth and childrearing among poor women" (2007, 80). Of course, to the extent that Hispanics are overrepresented among the impoverished population, the neoeugenic processes that Smith highlights can be seen as yet another aspect of the biopolitical formation that implicates the communities to which Latin American immigrants belong, although research suggests that among Latinos, the U.S.-born are more likely than immigrants to depend on public supports (Engstrom 2002).

Bibliography

Agamben, Giorgio. 1998. *Homo Sacer: Sovereign Power and Bare Life.* Trans. Daniel Heller-Roazen. Stanford, Calif.: Stanford University Press.

Andreas, Peter. 1998. "The U.S. Immigration Control Offensive: Constructing an Image of Order on the Southwest Border." In *Crossings: Mexican Immigration in Interdisciplinary Perspectives,* ed. Marcel M. Suárez-Orozco, 341–56. Cambridge, Mass.: Harvard University Press & David Rockefeller Center for Latin American Studies.

———. 2000. *Border Games: Policing the U.S.–Mexico Divide.* Ithaca, N.Y.: Cornell University Press.

Apostolidis, Paul. 2008a. "Feminist Theory, Immigrant Workers' Stories, and Counterhegemony in the United States Today." *Signs: Journal of Women in Culture and Society* 33, no. 3: 545–68.

———. 2008b. "Politics and Connolly's Ethics: Immigrant Narratives, Racism, and Identity's Contingency." *Theory & Event* 11, no. 3.

Apostolidis, Paul, and Mark Brenner. 2005. "An Evaluation of Worker Health and Safety at the Tyson Fresh Meats Plant in Pasco, Washington." Political Economy Research Institute, University of Massachusetts. http://www.people.umass.edu/brenner/pdfs/pasco.report.pdf.

Associated Press. 2008. "Rural Iowa Community Struggles after Immigration Raid." *Walla Walla Union-Bulletin,* August 21, A9.

Bartra, Armando. 2004. "Rebellious Cornfields: Towards Food and Labour Self-Sufficiency." In *Mexico in Transition: Neoliberal Globalism, the State and Civil Society,* ed. Gerardo Otero, 18–36. London: Zed Books.

Behdad, Ali. 2005. *A Forgetful Nation: On Immigration and Cultural Identity in the United States.* Durham, N.C.: Duke University Press.

Bernstein, Nina. 2007. "New Scrutiny as Immigrants Die in Custody." *New York Times,* June 26, A1.

Bjerklie, Steve. 1995. "On the Horns of a Dilemma: The U.S. Meat and Poultry Industry." In *Any Way You Cut It: Meat Processing and Small-Town America,* ed. Donald D. Stull, Michael J. Broadway, and David Griffith, 41–60. Lawrence: University Press of Kansas.

Bobrow-Strain, Aaron. 2008. "White Bread Bio-Politics: Purity, Health, and the Triumph of Industrial Baking." *Cultural Geographies* 15: 19–40.

Broadway, Michael J. 1995. "From City to Countryside: Recent Changes in the Structure and Location of the Meat- and Fish-Processing Industries." In *Any Way You Cut It: Meat Processing and Small-Town America,* ed. Donald D. Stull,

Michael J. Broadway, and David Griffith, 17–40. Lawrence: University Press of Kansas.

Brown, Wendy. 1995. *States of Injury: Power and Freedom in Late Modernity.* Princeton, N.J.: Princeton University Press.

———. 2005. *Edgework: Critical Essays on Power and Knowledge.* Princeton, N.J.: Princeton University Press.

Brown, Wendy, and Janet Halley, eds. 2002. *Left Legalism/Left Critique.* Durham, N.C.: Duke University Press.

Brueggemann, John, and Cliff Brown. 2003. "The Decline of Industrial Unionism in the Meatpacking Industry: Event-Structure Analyses of Labor Unrest, 1946–1987." *Work and Occupations* 30, no. 3: 327–60.

Burawoy, Michael. 1979. *Manufacturing Consent: Changes in the Labor Process under Monopoly Capitalism.* Chicago: University of Chicago Press.

———. 1990. *The Politics of Production.* New York: Verso.

Carl, Traci. 2008. "Life with the Fence." *Walla Walla Union-Bulletin,* September 21, 2008, D1, D4.

CBS/Associated Press. 2007. "Texas Anti-Immigrant Rule Goes to Voters." January 9.

Chakrabarty, Dipesh. 1989. *Rethinking Working-Class History: Bengal 1890–1940.* Princeton, N.J.: Princeton University Press.

Chavez, Leo R. 2008. *The Latino Threat: Constructing Immigrants, Citizens, and the Nation.* Stanford, Calif.: Stanford University Press.

CNN. 2007. "CNN: Klan Growing, Fed by Anti-Immigrant Feelings, Report Says." February 6. http://www.cnn.com.

———. 2009. "New Reality Show Exposes Broken Borders." January 7. http://loudobbs.tv.cnn.com.

Compa, Lance A. 2000. *Unfair Advantage: Workers' Freedom of Association in the United States under International Human Rights Standards.* New York: Human Rights Watch.

———. 2005. *Blood, Sweat, and Fear: Workers' Rights in U.S. Meat and Poultry Plants.* New York: Human Rights Watch.

Congressional Digest. 2001. "OSHA Rulemaking: Avoiding and Addressing Work-Related Illness." *Congressional Digest,* May, 131–33.

Connolly, William E. 1999. *Why I Am Not a Secularist.* Minneapolis: University of Minnesota Press.

———. 2002. *Identity\Difference: Democratic Negotiations of Political Paradox.* 2nd ed. Minneapolis: University of Minnesota Press.

———. 2006. "Experience & Experiment." *Daedalus* 135, no. 3: 67–75.

Cook, Maria Lorena. 1996. *Organizing Dissent: Unions, the State, and the Democratic Teachers' Movement in Mexico.* University Park: Pennsylvania State University Press.

Coutin, Susan Bibler. 2000. *Legalizing Moves: Salvadoran Immigrants' Struggle for U.S. Residency.* Ann Arbor: University of Michigan Press.

Craig, Tim. 2007. "Va. Republican Bill Would Bar Illegal Immigrants from College." *Washington Post,* August 30, A1.

Craypo, Charles. 1994. "Meatpacking Industry: Restructuring and Union Decline." In *Contemporary Collective Bargaining in the Private Sector*, ed. P. Voos, 63–96. Madison, Wis.: Industrial Relations Research Association.

De Genova, Nicholas. 2005. *Working the Boundaries: Race, Space, and "Illegality" in Mexican Chicago.* Durham, N.C.: Duke University Press.

Delgado, Héctor L. 1993. *New Immigrants, Old Unions: Organizing Undocumented Workers in Los Angeles.* Philadelphia: Temple University Press.

Delgado, Richard. 1998. "Storytelling for Oppositionists and Others." In *The Latino/a Condition: A Critical Reader*, ed. Richard Delgado and Jean Stefancic, 259–70. New York: New York University Press.

Disch, Lisa. 2003. "Impartiality, Storytelling, and the Seductions of Narrative: An Essay at an Impasse." *Alternatives: Global, Local, Political* 28, no. 2: 253–66.

Doty, Roxanne. 1999. "Racism, Desire, and the Politics of Immigration." *Millennium–Journal of International Studies* 28, no. 3: 585–606.

Downes, Lawrence. 2007. "After an Anti-Immigrant Flare-Up, Texas Gets Back to Business." *New York Times*, April 2, A22.

Dunn, Timothy J. 1996. *The Militarization of the U.S.–Mexico Border, 1978–1992: Low-Intensity Conflict Doctrine Comes Home.* Austin: University of Texas Press.

Engstrom, David W. 2002. "Hispanic Immigration at the New Millennium." In *Hispanics in the United States: An Agenda for the Twenty-First Century*, ed. Pastora San Juan Cafferty and David W. Engstrom, 31–68. New Brunswick, N.J.: Transaction Publishers.

Estlund, Cynthia L. 2002. "The Ossification of American Labor Law." *Columbia Law Review* 102: 1527–1612.

Fears, Darryl. 2008. "Threats Worry Hispanic Activists." *Walla Walla Union-Bulletin*, November 9, A1, A4.

Feher, Michel. 2008. "Self-Appreciation; or, The Aspirations of Human Capital." Trans. Ivan Ascher. *Public Culture* 21, no. 1: 21–41.

Femia, Joseph V. 1993. *Marxism and Democracy.* New York: Oxford University Press.

Fink, Deborah. 1998. *Cutting into the Meatpacking Line: Workers and Change in the Rural Midwest.* Chapel Hill: University of North Carolina Press.

Fink, Leon. 2003. *The Maya of Morgenton: Work and Community in the Nuevo New South.* Chapel Hill: University of North Carolina Press.

Fontana, Benedetto. 1993. *Hegemony and Power: On the Relation between Gramsci and Machiavelli.* Minneapolis: University of Minnesota Press.

Foucault, Michel. 1979. *Discipline and Punish: The Birth of the Prison.* Trans. Alan Sheridan. New York: Vintage.

———. 1990. *The History of Sexuality, Volume I: An Introduction.* Trans. Robert Hurley. New York: Vintage.

———. 2003. *"Society Must Be Defended": Lectures at the Collége de France, 1975–76.* Ed. Mauro Bertani and Alessandro Fontana. Trans. David Macey. New York: Picador.

Fox, Jonathan. 1994. "Political Change in Mexico's New Peasant Economy." In *The Politics of Economic Restructuring: State-Society Relations and Regime Change in Mexico,* ed. Maria Lorena Cook, Kevin J. Middlebrook, and Juan Molinar Horcasitas, 243–76. San Diego: Center for U.S.–Mexican Studies, University of California.

Garcia, Sean. 2003. "Immigration Reform Key to Border Security." Americas Program. Silver City, N.M.: Interhemispheric Resource Center, Aug. 19. http://americas.irc-online.org/.

García y Griego, Manuel. 1996. "The Importation of Mexican Contract Laborers to the United States, 1942–1964." In *Between Two Worlds: Mexican Immigrants in the United States,* ed. David G. Gutiérrez, 45–85. Wilmington, Del.: Scholarly Resources.

Gaouette, Nicole. 2007. "U.S. Working to Let in More Immigrants." *Los Angeles Times,* October 7, A1.

Gilbert, Alan. 1989. Introduction to *Housing and Land in Urban Mexico,* ed. Alan Gilbert, 1–11. San Diego: Center for U.S.–Mexico Studies, University of California.

Gilbert, Alan, and Ann Varley. 1989. "From Renting to Self-Help Ownership? Residential Tenure in Urban Mexico since 1940." In *Housing and Land in Urban Mexico,* ed. Alan Gilbert, 13–37. San Diego: Center for U.S.–Mexico Studies, University of California.

Glick Schiller, Nina. 2001. *Georges Woke Up Laughing: Long-Distance Nationalism and the Search for Home.* Durham, N.C.: Duke University Press.

Goldsborough, Robert H. 2006. "Senate Vote Score: Mexicans 1, Americans 0." *Immigration Watch,* August/September, 6.

González-Baker, Susan, Frank D. Bean, Augustin Escobar Latapi, and Sidney Weintraub. 1998. "U.S. Immigration Policies and Trends: The Growing Importance of Migration from Mexico." In *Crossings: Mexican Immigration in Interdisciplinary Perspectives,* ed. Marcel M. Suárez-Orozco, 79–105. Cambridge, Mass.: Harvard University Press & David Rockefeller Center for Latin American Studies.

González de la Rocha, Mercedes. 1994. *The Resources of Poverty: Women and Survival in a Mexican City.* Oxford: Blackwell Publishers.

Gottesman, Michael H. 1996. "Union Summer: A Reawakened Interest in the Law of Labor?" *Supreme Court Review,* 285–329.

Gouveia, Lourdes, and Donald D. Stull. 1995. "Dances with Cows: Beefpacking's Impact on Garden City, Kansas, and Lexington, Nebraska." In *Any Way You Cut It: Meat Processing and Small-Town America,* ed. Donald D. Stull, Michael J. Broadway, and David Griffith, 85–107. Lawrence: University Press of Kansas.

Graizbord, Boris, and Crescencio Ruiz. 1996. "Recent Changes in the Economic and Social Structure of Mexico's Regions." In *Changing Structure of Mexico: Political, Social, and Economic Prospects,* ed. Laura Randall, 365–90. Armonk, N.Y.: M. E. Sharpe.

Gramsci, Antonio. 1971. *Selections from the Prison Notebooks.* Ed. and trans. Quintin Hoare and Geoffrey Nowell Smith. New York: International Publishers.

Grassroots On Fire. 2006. "Statement of Grassrootsonfire.org." Unpublished leaflet.

Griffith, David, and Edward Kissam, with Jeronimo Camposeco et al. 1995. *Working Poor: Farm Workers in the United States.* Philadelphia: Temple University Press.

Griffith, R. Marie. 1997. *God's Daughters: Evangelical Women and the Power of Submission.* Berkeley: University of California Press.

Gutiérrez, David G. 1996. "*Sin Fronteras?* Chicanos, Mexican Americans, and the Emergence of the Contemporary Immigration Debate, 1968–1978." In *Between Two Worlds: Mexican Immigrants in the United States,* ed. David G. Gutiérrez, 175–209. Wilmington, Del.: Scholarly Resources.

Gutmann, Matthew C. 1996. *The Meanings of Macho: Being a Man in Mexico City.* Berkeley: University of California Press.

———, ed. 2003. *Changing Men and Masculinities in Latin America.* Durham, N.C.: Duke University Press.

Haber, Paul. 1994. "The Art and Implications of Political Restructuring in Mexico: The Case of Urban Popular Movements." In *The Politics of Economic Restructuring: State-Society Relations and Regime Change in Mexico,* ed. Maria Lorena Cook, Kevin J. Middlebrook, and Juan Molinar Horcasitas, 277–303. San Diego: Center for U.S.–Mexican Studies, University of California.

Harvey, David. 2005. *The New Imperialism.* Oxford: Oxford University Press.

———. 2007. *A Brief History of Neoliberalism.* Oxford: Oxford University Press.

Hecker, Steven. 2001. "OSHA Regulation of Workplace Ergonomics in the U.S.: Political and Scientific Challenges." Proceedings of the VII National Congress: Ergonomics in the Information Society, Italian Ergonomics Society, Florence (September 26–28), 746–52.

Hill, Sarah. 2006. "Purity and Danger on the U.S.–Mexico Border, 1991–1994." In *The Last Frontier: The Contemporary Configuration of the U.S.–Mexico Border,* ed. Jane Juffer. Special issue of *South Atlantic Quarterly* 105, no. 4: 777–99.

Hondagneu-Sotelo, Pierrette. 1994. *Gendered Transitions: Mexican Experiences of Immigration.* Berkeley: University of California Press.

Honig, Bonnie. 2001. *Democracy and the Foreigner.* Princeton, N.J.: Princeton University Press.

Hsu, Spencer S. 2008. "Immigration Prosecutions Hit New High." *Washington Post,* June 2, A1.

Huntington, Samuel P. 2004. "One Nation, Out of Many." *American Enterprise* 15, no. 6: 20–26.

Ibbitson, John. 2008. "Latinos' Mass Exodus from Manassas Puts City at Forefront of Immigrant Shift." *Globe and Mail* (Vancouver), A1, A9.

Immigrant Workers Freedom Ride. 2003. "Key Messages." Internal document.

Institute for Agriculture and Trade Policy. 2005. "Tyson Workers Vote to De-Certify Union." *Agribusiness Center.* http://www.agobservatory.org.

Janovich, Adriana. 2007. "Initiative Focuses on Benefits Eligibility." *Yakima Herald-Republic,* April 10, B1.

Johnston, Paul. 2004a. "Organising Citizenship at Local 890's Citizenship Project: Unleashing Innovation through an Affiliate Organisation." *Development in Practice* 14, nos. 1–2: 85–99.

———. 2004b. "Outflanking Power, Reframing Unionism: The Basic Strike of 1999–2001." *Labor Studies Journal* 28, no. 4: 1–24.

Juffer, Jane. 2006. Introduction to "The Last Frontier: The Contemporary Configuration of the U.S.–Mexico Border." Special issue, *South Atlantic Quarterly* 105, no. 4: 663–80.

KCTS Television. 2006. "The Immigration Debate: A Yakima Valley Town Hall." *KCTS Connects* Special Report. Taped November 14, Yakima, Washington. Broadcast November 16.

La Botz, Dan. 1990. *Rank-and-File Rebellion: Teamsters for a Democratic Union.* New York: Verso.

La France, David G. 1986. "Mexico since Cárdenas." In *Twentieth-Century Mexico,* ed. W. Dirk Raat and William H. Beezley, 206–22. Lincoln: University of Nebraska Press.

Lamphere, Louise, Patricia Zavella, and Felipe Gonzales, with Peter B. Evans. 1993. *Sunbelt Working Mothers: Reconciling Family and Factory.* Ithaca, N.Y.: Cornell University Press.

Land, Richard. 2006. Speech at the Family Research Council Immigration Forum, April 28. http://www.frc.org.

Latina Feminist Group. 2001. *Telling to Live: Latina Feminist Testimonios.* Durham, N.C.: Duke University Press.

Leonhardt, David. 2007. "Truth, Fiction and Lou Dobbs." *New York Times,* May 30, C1.

Levin, David. 2004. "Tyson Decert Try Foiled by Teamster Reformers." *Labor Notes,* April 30. http://labornotes.org.

———. 2005. "World's Largest Meatpacker Busts Teamsters Reform Local." *Labor Notes,* March 1. http://labornotes.org.

Lilley, Sasha. 2005. "Meat Packer's Union on the Chopping Block." *CorpWatch,* April 18. http://www.corpwatch.org.

Louie, Miriam Ching Yoon. 2001. *Sweatshop Warriors: Immigrant Women Workers Take On the Global Factory.* Boston: South End Press.

Lustig, Nora. 1996. "The 1982 Debt Crisis, Chiapas, NAFTA, and Mexico's Poor." In *Changing Structure of Mexico: Political, Social, and Economic Prospects,* ed. Laura Randall, 157–65. Armonk, N.Y.: M. E. Sharpe.

———. 1998. *Mexico: The Remaking of an Economy.* 2d ed. Washington, D.C.: Brookings Institution.

Lutheran Immigration and Refugee Service, and Women's Commission for Refugee Women and Children. 2007. *Locking Up Family Values: The Detention of Immigrant Families.* Baltimore, Md.: Lutheran Immigration and Refugee Service.

Mackinlay, Horacio. 2004. "Rural Producers' Organizations and the State in Mexico: The Political Consequences of Economic Restructuring." In *Dilemmas of Political Change in Mexico,* ed. Kevin J. Middlebrook, 286–331. San Diego: Center for U.S.–Mexican Studies, University of California.

Magaña, Lisa. 2003. *Straddling the Border: Immigration Policy and the INS*. Austin: University of Texas Press.

Mahler, Sarah J. 1995. *American Dreaming: Immigrant Life on the Margins*. Princeton, N.J.: Princeton University Press.

Martin, James. 1998. *Gramsci's Political Analysis: A Critical Introduction*. New York: St. Martin's Press.

Martin, Philip L. 2003. *Promise Unfulfilled: Unions, Immigration, and the Farm Workers*. Ithaca, N.Y.: Cornell University Press.

Maruskin, Joan M. 1995. "Voices around the Country Call for INS Detention Reform." *Migration World Magazine* 23, no. 4: 32.

Marx, Karl. 1976. *Wage-Labour and Capital/Value, Price and Profit*. New York: International Publishers.

McCombs, Brady. 2007. "Huge Hikes Ahead in Immigrant Processing." *Arizona Daily Star*, February 1, A1.

Menjívar, Cecilia. 2000. *Fragmented Ties: Salvadoran Immigrant Networks in America*. Berkeley: University of California Press.

Mexican American Legal Defense and Education Fund. 2008. "Now Is the Time to Act against Anti-Immigrant Bills in Congress." *MALDEFian*. Listserv newsletter. March 12.

Middlebrook, Kevin J. 1995. *The Paradox of Revolution: Labor, the State, and Authoritarianism in Mexico*. Baltimore, Md.: Johns Hopkins University Press.

Milkman, Ruth, ed. 2000. *Organizing Immigrants: The Challenge for Unions in Contemporary California*. Ithaca, N.Y.: Cornell University Press.

Mirandé, Alfredo. 1997. *Hombres y Machos: Masculinity and Latino Culture*. Boulder, Colo.: Westview Press.

Mirandé, Alfredo, and Evangelina Enríquez. 1979. *La Chicana: The Mexican American Woman*. Chicago: University of Chicago Press.

Moraga, Cherríe L., and Gloria E. Anzaldúa, ed. 2002. *This Bridge Called My Back: Writings by Radical Women of Color*. Berkeley, Calif.: Third Woman Press.

Myers, Ella. 2008. "Resisting Foucauldian Ethics: Associative Politics and the Limits of the Care of the Self." *Contemporary Political Theory* 7, no. 2: 125–46.

Nash, James L. 2003. "Union, Hispanic Caucus Demand OSHA Issue PPE Rule." *Occupational Hazards* 65, no. 6: 12.

Nevins, Joseph. 2002. *Operation Gatekeeper: The Rise of the "Illegal Alien" and the Making of the U.S.–Mexico Boundary*. New York: Routledge.

New York Times. 2008. "A Death in Patchogue." *New York Times*, November 11.

Ngai, Mae M. 2004. *Impossible Subjects: Illegal Aliens and the Making of Modern America*. Princeton, N.J.: Princeton University Press.

Noble, Charles. 1986. *Liberalism at Work: The Rise and Fall of OSHA*. Philadelphia: Temple University Press.

Occupational Hazards. 1996. "Meatpacking Industry Cuts Comp Claims." *Occupational Hazards* 58, no. 5: 103.

Olsson, Karen. 2002. "The Shame of Meatpacking." *The Nation*, September 16: 11–16.

Ong, Aihwa. 2006. *Neoliberalism as Exception: Mutations in Citizenship and Sovereignty.* Durham, N.C.: Duke University Press.

Otero, Gerardo. 1996. "Neoliberal Reform and Politics in Mexico: An Overview." In *Neoliberalism Revisited: Economic Restructuring and Mexico's Political Future,* ed. Gerardo Otero, 1–25. Boulder, Colo.: Westview Press.

Pesquera, Beatríz M. 1997. "'In the Beginning He Wouldn't Even Lift a Spoon': The Division of Household Labor." In *Situated Lives: Gender and Culture in Everyday Life,* ed. Louise Lamphere, Helena Ragoné, and Patricia Zavella, 208–22. New York: Routledge.

Philip, George. 1999. "Democratisation and Social Conflict in Mexico." *Conflict Studies* 318 (May). Warwickshire, U.K.: Research Institute for the Study of Conflict and Terrorism.

Phillips, Scott, Jacqueline Maria Hagan, and Nestor Rodriguez. 2006. "Brutal Borders? Examining the Treatment of Deportees during Arrest and Detention." *Social Forces* 85, no. 1: 93–109.

Preston, Julia. 2007a. "Government Set for a Crackdown on Illegal Hiring." *New York Times,* August 8, A1.

———. 2007b. "Revised Rule for Employers That Hire Immigrants." *New York Times,* November 25, 1, 34.

———. 2007c. "7-Year Immigration Rate Is Highest in U.S. History." *New York Times,* November 29, A20.

———. 2008a. "270 Immigrants Sent to Prison in Federal Push." *New York Times,* May 24, A1, A15.

———. 2008b. "Meatpacker Is Fined Nearly $10 Million." *New York Times,* October 30, A22.

———. 2008c. "Large Iowa Meatpacker in Illegal Immigrant Raid Files for Bankruptcy." *New York Times,* November 6, A19.

Rachleff, Peter. 2008. "Immigrant Rights Are Labor Rights." *Monthly Review,* August 19. http://mrzine.monthlyreview.org/.

Reed, Alfred C. 1913. "Immigration and the Public Health." *Popular Science Monthly* 83 (October): 313–38.

Reisler, Mark. 1996. "Always the Laborer, Never the Citizen: Anglo Perceptions of the Mexican Immigrant during the 1920s." In *Between Two Worlds: Mexican Immigrants in the United States,* ed. David G. Gutiérrez, 23–43. Wilmington, Del.: Scholarly Resources.

Riccardi, Nicholas. 2007. "The Nation: Going behind Bars for Laborers." *Los Angeles Times,* March 7: A1.

Roberts, Dorothy E. 1996. "Who May Give Birth to Citizens? Reproduction, Eugenics, and Immigration." In *Immigrants Out! The New Nativism and the Anti-Immigrant Impulse in the United States,* ed. Juan F. Perea, 205–19. New York: New York University Press.

Rodriguez, Nestor P., and Jacqueline Maria Hagan. 1997. "Apartment Restructuring and Latino Immigrant Tenant Struggles: A Case Study of Human Agency." In *Challenging Fronteras: Structuring Latina and Latino Lives in the U.S.,* ed. Mary Romero, Pierrette Hondagneu-Sotelo, and Vilma Ortiz, 297–309. New York: Routledge.

Rodriguez, Samuel. 2006. Speech at the Family Research Council Immigration Forum, April 28. http://www.frc.org.

Rogin, Michael. 1987. *Ronald Reagan, the Movie and Other Episodes in Political Demonology.* Berkeley: University of California Press.

Rouse, Roger. 1992. "Making Sense of Settlement: Class Transformation, Cultural Struggle, and Transnationalism among Mexican Migrants in the United States." *Annals of the New York Academy of Sciences* 645 (July): 25–52.

Rubin, Jeffrey W. 1997. *Decentering the Regime: Ethnicity, Radicalism, and Democracy in Juchitán, Mexico.* Durham, N.C.: Duke University Press.

Rubin, Rachel, and Jeffrey Melnick. 2007. *Immigration and American Popular Culture: An Introduction.* New York: New York University Press.

Rubio-Goldsmith, Raquel, M. Melissa McCormick, Daniel Martinez, and Inez Magdalena Duarte. 2007. *A Humanitarian Crisis at the Border: New Estimates of Deaths Among Unauthorized Immigrants.* Washington, D.C.: Immigration Policy Center.

Ruiz, Vicki L. 1987. *Cannery Women, Cannery Lives: Mexican Women, Unionization, and the California Food Processing Industry, 1930–1950.* Albuquerque: University of New Mexico Press.

———. 1998. *From Out of the Shadows: Mexican Women in Twentieth-Century America.* New York: Oxford University Press.

Sanders, Thomas G. 1986. "Mexico's Food Problem." In *Twentieth-Century Mexico,* ed. W. Dirk Raat and William H. Beezley, 267–85. Lincoln: University of Nebraska Press.

Sassoon, Anne Showstack. 1987. *Gramsci's Politics.* Minneapolis: University of Minnesota Press.

Schiller, Reuel E. 1999. "From Group Rights to Individual Liberties: Post-War Labor Law, Liberalism, and the Waning of Union Strength." *Berkeley Journal of Employment and Labor Law* 20, no. 1: 2–73.

Schlosser, Eric. 2001. "The Chain Never Stops." *Mother Jones,* July/August, 38–47, 86–87.

———. 2002. *Fast Food Nation: The Dark Side of the All-American Meal.* New York: HarperCollins.

———. 2004. "Tyson's Moral Anchor." *The Nation* 279, no. 2: 5–6.

Scott, James C. 1990. *Domination and the Arts of Resistance: Hidden Transcripts.* New Haven, Conn.: Yale University Press.

Sinclair, Upton. 1926 [1906]. *The Jungle.* New York: Vanguard Press.

Smith, Anna Marie. 2007. *Welfare Reform and Sexual Regulation.* New York: Cambridge University Press.

Smith, R. Blake. 1993. "Food Processing: Ergonomic Controls Cut the Shackles of Meatpacking's Cumulative Traumas." *Occupational Health & Safety* 62, no. 8: 32–35.

Snyder, Richard. 2001. *Politics after Neoliberalism: Reregulation in Mexico.* Cambridge: Cambridge University Press.

Sontag, Deborah. 2008a. "Deported, by U.S. Hospitals: Immigrants, Spurned on Rehabilitation, Are Forced Out." *New York Times,* August 3, A1, A12–A14.

————. 2008b. "Deported in a Coma, Saved Back in U.S." *New York Times,* November 9, A1.

Spivak, Gayatri Chakravorty. 1988. "Can the Subaltern Speak?" In *Marxism and the Interpretation of Culture,* ed. Cary Nelson and Lawrence Grossberg, 271–313. Urbana: University of Illinois Press.

Stephen, Lynn. 1996. "Democracy for Whom? Women's Grassroots Political Activism in the 1990s, Mexico City and Chiapas." In *Neoliberalism Revisited: Economic Restructuring and Mexico's Political Future,* ed. Gerardo Otero, 167–85. Boulder, Colo.: Westview Press.

————. 2007. *Transborder Lives: Indigenous Oaxacans in Mexico, California, and Oregon.* Durham, N.C.: Duke University Press.

Stull, Donald D., and Michael J. Broadway. 1995. "Killing Them Softly: Work in Meatpacking Plants and What It Does to Workers." In *Any Way You Cut It: Meat Processing and Small-Town America,* ed. Donald D. Stull, Michael J. Broadway, and David Griffith, 61–83. Lawrence: University Press of Kansas.

Swider, Susan M. 2002. "Outcome Effectiveness of Community Health Workers: An Integrative Literature Review." *Public Health Nursing* 19, no. 1: 11–20.

Teamsters for a Democratic Union. 2003. "Organizing to Win Strong Contracts." Document distributed at TDU Annual Convention. Detroit: October 26.

————. 2005. "Teamsters Lose Battle at Tyson Foods." February 17. http://tdu.org.

Turnbull, Lornet. 2008. "Immigration Initiative Seeks State Crackdown." *Seattle Times,* August 26, B1.

U.S. Department of Labor, Bureau of Labor Statistics. 2006. "Incidence Rates of Nonfatal Occupational Injuries and Illnesses by Industry and Case Types, 2006." http://www.bls.gov.

U.S. Department of Health and Human Services, National Institute of Occupational Safety and Health. 1995. "NIOSH Finds Effective Interventions to Reduce Ergonomic Injuries in Meatpacking and Other Industries." DHHS (NIOSH) Publication No. 95–102, January 6.

Urrea, Luis Alberto. 2004. *The Devil's Highway: A True Story.* New York: Little Brown.

Verhovek, Sam Howe. 1999. "Meat-Plant Workers Are the Latest Example of Immigrants Packing the Picket Lines." *New York Times,* June 26, A8.

Warrick, Joby. 2001. "'They Die Piece by Piece.' In Overtaxed Plants, Humane Treatment of Cattle Is Often a Battle Lost." *Washington Post,* April 10, A1, A10–11.

Welch, Michael. 1996. "The Immigration Crisis: Detention as an Emerging Mechanism of Social Control." *Social Justice: A Journal of Crime, Conflict & World Order* 23, no. 3: 169–84.

————. 2002. *Detained: Immigration Laws and the Expanding I.N.S. Jail Complex.* Philadelphia: Temple University Press.

White, Hayden. 1987. *The Content of the Form: Narrative Discourse and Historical Representation.* Baltimore: Johns Hopkins University Press.

Wilder, Forrest. 2007. "Detention Archipelago: Jailing Immigrants for Profit."
    NACLA Report on the Americas 40, no. 3: 19–26.
Young, Iris Marion. 2000. *Inclusion and Democracy.* Oxford: Oxford University
    Press.
Zavella, Patricia. 1987. *Women's Work and Chicano Families: Cannery Workers of
    the Santa Clara Valley.* Ithaca, N.Y.: Cornell University Press.
Zerilli, Linda. 2005. *Feminism and the Abyss of Freedom.* Chicago: University of
    Chicago Press.

Index

Agamben, Giorgio, xlvi, 225–27
agricultural labor. *See* farm labor
American Meat Institute, 260n45
Andreas, Peter, xxvii, 247n2
animal rights and welfare, 162, 175–
  76, 209, 260n42, 269n3
anti-immigrant activities. *See*
  immigration

Behdad, Ali, xxiv–xxvi, xxix, 95–96,
  99, 251n35
biopolitics: and discipline, xli, xliv,
  xlvi, 97–98, 199–200, 201, 204–5,
  210, 223, 253n43; and food
  production, 68–69, 101–2, 115–
  16, 149–50, 158, 253n39;
  Foucault's concept of, xxxi, 68,
  97–98, 148–49; and illegal
  immigration, xli–xliii, 66–70, 99–
  109, 148, 199–200, 223, 253n43;
  and immigrant narratives, xxxii,
  xxxvii, xli–xlv, xlvii, 7–8, 32, 66–
  70, 102–9, 115–18, 148–52, 156,
  157–60, 166, 199–200, 204–5,
  207, 208, 212, 219, 223, 229–30;
  and immigrant worker organizing,
  xlv, xlvi, 166, 204–5, 207, 208,
  223; and meat consumption,
  xlii, 115–16, 149–50, 158, 200,
  228, 262n73; and meatpacking
  work, xli–xliii, 115–18, 148–52,
  156, 157–60, 199–200, 227,
  262n73; and neoliberalism, xlvi,
  66, 201, 208, 212, 224, 227–28,
  231–32; and reproduction,
  229, 269n6

Bjerklie, Steve, 129
Bobrow-Strain, Aaron, 253n39
border. *See* immigration
Bracero program, xxiii, 112
Brenner, Mark, 238, 257n26
Broadway, Michael J., 259n40
Brown, Wendy: on genealogy and
  desire, 7, 17–20; on neoliberal
  subjectivity, 35–36, 38, 59; on
  the politics of *ressentiment*, xliv,
  17–18, 165–66, 186, 201, 204,
  217–18; on radical democracy,
  242n6
Buchanan, Patrick, 253n41
Burawoy, Michael: on hegemonic
  despotism, 116–17, 204; on
  hegemony in the workplace, 118–
  20, 122
Bureau of Labor and Industries
  (Washington State), 167, 171,
  194–95, 198
Bush, George H. W., 151
Bush (George W.) administration,
  xiii, xvii, xxiii, 210, 214,
  259n39

Carey, Ron, 168, 169
Cargill, Inc., 161
Chakrabarty, Dipesh, 240n9
Chavez, Leo R., 241n14
citizenship. *See* immigration
Clinton administration, 151,
  251n34
ConAgra, Inc., 269n5
Connolly, William E.: on identity
  and genealogy, 241n5; on

288   Index

1–4, 65, 99; about Mexico,
xxxviii, 36–64, 166, 199, 205–6,
223, 243n12, 243–44n13,
245n22; and neoliberalism,
xxxviii–xxxix, 7–8, 32, 35–41,
57–64, 201, 204, 207–8; and
political power, xviii; relation to
abstract discourses, 1–4, 13–16,
27–28; and self-reflective theory,
xxxvi–xxxvii, 4–8, 13–21,
224–25
National Institute of Occupational
Safety and Health (NIOSH), 258–
59n38
nationalism. *See* immigration
National Labor Relations Board
(NLRB), xvii, xxiii, xlv, 185, 192,
195, 202–3, 204, 210, 213, 214–
15, 217, 268n2
neoliberalism: and biopolitics, xlvi,
66, 201, 208, 212, 224, 227–28,
231–32; and immigrant narratives, xxxviii–xxxix, 7–8, 32, 35–
41, 57–64, 201, 204, 207–8; and
immigration, xxv–xxvii, xxviii, xix;
and meatpacking, 113; in Mexico,
34–35, 36–41, 46, 227, 243n6,
244nn15–18, 246–47n35; political opposition to, 212, 224–33;
and reproduction, 229, 269n6;
and subjectivity, xxxviii, xxxix,
35–38, 59–64; theories of, 35–36,
38–39, 116; and workers' rights,
204, 207
Ngai, Mae M., 95–96, 224, 248n4
Noble, Charles, 150

Obama, Barack, xxviii, 223, 253n40
occupational safety and health:
ergonomics standards and
programs, 151, 209, 258n38;
Occupational Safety and Health
Act, 116, 150, 158; personal
protective devices (PPDs), 134,
136, 150, 151, 260n45. *See also*

meatpacking; Tyson Foods,
Inc./IBP; U.S. Occupational
Safety and Health Administration
Ong, Aihwa, xxix
OSHA. *See* U.S. Occupational Safety
and Health Administration

Partido Revolucionario Institucional
(PRI), 39, 59
Piñeros y Campesinos Unidos del
Noroeste (PCUN), 63, 220, 221–
23, 230, 268n43
Proposition 187 (California), xxv,
100, 268

race: and biopolitics, xxxi, xxxii,
xli–xliii, xlv, xlvii, 66, 68–70, 99–
109, 115–18, 148–52, 158–59,
199–200, 227–33, 241n14,
248n4; and conflict among
workers, 121–22, 155, 156, 157,
263n79; and counterhegemonic
coalitions, xlvii, 108, 224, 230–
33; and cultural differences
among Mexicans, xxxix, xlii, 40,
64, 228; in Foucault's theory,
xxxi, xli, 68, 98, 148–49; and illegal immigration, xli–xliii, 65, 66,
68–70, 99–109, 148, 199–200,
248n4; and immigrant narratives,
xxxii, xxxv, xxxix, xli–xlv, xlvii,
69–70, 102–9, 115–18, 148–52,
158–59; and immigrant worker
organizing, xlv, xlvi, 108, 218;
and interview method, 21, 27–
28; and meat consumption, xlii,
115–16, 149–50, 158; and
meatpacking work, xviii, xli–xliii,
115–18, 148–52, 156, 157–59,
199–200, 227; and narrative,
14; and neoliberalism, 38, 227–
28, 231–32; and social activism,
xv; and transnationalism, xxix,
xxxiii, 62, 247n36; and workers'
rights, 203. *See also* biopolitics

Paul Apostolidis holds the Judge and Mrs. Timothy A. Paul Chair of Political Science at Whitman College. He is the author of *Stations of the Cross: Adorno and Christian Right Radio* and coeditor of *Public Affairs: Politics in the Age of Sex Scandals.*